EX LIBRIS
STEPHEN CHAPMAN

John Osman

LIFE LOVE LAUGHTER LIBERTY

REFLECTIONS ON A LONG AND FULL EXISTENCE

authorHOUSE®

AuthorHouse™ UK Ltd.
1663 Liberty Drive
Bloomington, IN 47403 USA
www.authorhouse.co.uk
Phone: 0800.197.4150

Published by AuthorHouse 1/20/2015

ISBN: 978-1-4969-9713-5 (sc)
ISBN: 978-1-4969-9714-2 (hc)
ISBN: 978-1-4969-9715-9 (e)

"We all start off as young, unknown reporters,
and we all end up as old, unknown reporters."
—Homer Bigart of the *New York Times*,
twice winner of the Pulitzer Prize for Journalism.
(He was speaking to the author on the island of Martha's Vineyard,
Massachusetts, when both were reporting the 1970 inquest into the
death of Mary Jo Kopechne at Chappaquiddick, an event that put paid
to any presidential hopes held by the late Senator Edward Kennedy.)

"Golden lads and girls all must,
As chimney-sweepers, come to dust."
—Guiderius, in *Cymbeline*, by William Shakespeare

"And one man in his time plays many parts, His acts being seven ages."
—Jacques, a lord attending on the banished duke,
in *As You Like It*, by William Shakespeare

To my beloved wife and travelling companion, Virginia;
to my three beloved children and my son-in-law;
to my two beloved granddaughters and my grandson-in-law;
to my three beloved great-grandchildren;
and to journalists and broadcasters everywhere.

CONTENTS

PERSONAL RESURRECTION

In August 2012, while holidaying on the island of Vis, in Croatia, I received a telephone call from *The Guardian* newspaper in London, informing me that I had been reported by the BBC World Service as having passed away. This was not only news *about* me but also news *to* me. I was pleased to confirm to *The Guardian*'s columnist that in fact I was still alive. The newspaper had a lot of fun with the BBC's mistake and described it under an online heading as "a cock-up by the BBC".

Well, given the far greater BBC cock-up that erupted a month or two later over the scandalous past of Jimmy Savile and so on (leading to the resignation of the newly appointed director general of the corporation), my prematurely reported demise was a minor matter. It was, of course, inevitable that I received a joking note or two from old chums, on the lines of me "keeping good company" with the great American writer Mark Twain, who, when he too was wrongly said to have perished, quipped that reports of his death were "greatly exaggerated". The corporation's slip-up did not overly upset me, for the context in which it occurred was essentially flattering. Important also was that, as usual, the BBC Pensions Department continued to pay my pension, undisturbed by what another part of the organisation apparently thought about my mortality.

To explain the context of the incorrect report, I cannot do better than to quote briefly from what *Guardian* columnist Hugh Muir actually wrote:

> *Sadness at the BBC and beyond as editors and former colleagues noted the passing of a news titan. In his time on the road, on TV, and on radio, John Osman was regarded as one of the elite.*

East Africa Correspondent in the era of Idi Amin, interrogator of Mountbatten over the partition of India, Washington Correspondent at the time of Nixon, Royal and Diplomatic Correspondent. There were many such trail-blazers, wrote John Williams, World News Editor, highlighting the exploits of Anthony Lawrence, now one hundred years old. "Lawrence was one of the BBC's 'greatest generation' of foreign correspondents – a foreign legion that included legendary names such as Charles Wheeler, Erik de Mauny, and John Osman. They built the BBC's reputation around the world, on crackly telephone lines and film flown back from distant shores. All have now passed. All but Tony Lawrence." Which was fine and certainly respectful. But it came as a shock indeed to close friends of Osman. Hang on a minute, they said, we're pretty sure he isn't dead. And so we did a few checks on their behalf.

Muir then explained how he had checked with "neighbours of Osman's home in West Sussex" and how they "attested that, barring hitherto undisclosed calamity, the legend lives on, confounding the BBC's account of his demise". Amusingly, Muir added, "Indeed, Osman, eighty-three, and his wife, Virginia, appear to be having the sort of retirement one reads about in the Saga ads."

One of our neighbours was quoted as saying, "They're hardly ever here"– because we went skiing in the winter; sailing in Cyprus in the summer; had a house in the south of France; and at that moment, we were "thought to be" driving through Europe in our camping-car.

All of this was correct.

Muir then added the following:

A week after first being told of the error, the BBC on Tuesday acknowledged its mistake. "We are glad that he is still with us and sad that he is not still at the BBC," a spokesman said. But Osman couldn't go back. He wouldn't. Too busy.

Five days after these first comments were published, the *Guardian* returned in triumph to the subject:

Rejoicing among the BBC old guard that the corporation, three days after being told by the Diary *and a full ten days after being warned by former colleagues, has retracted its assertion that legendary correspondent John Osman is dead ... He is merely camping in Europe. That is not the same thing.*

Spurred into laughter, thought, and (more importantly) action by this publicity about my continuing existence, I began writing about aspects of my life -- if only to prove to myself that I am indeed still extant. Tony Lawrence, alas, died at the impressive age of 101, just a year after the BBC World Service publicity about him; but at 85, I am still here, and some of the lessons I've learned along the way, and that I feel still have some contemporary significance, are recorded herein.

INTRODUCTION

When I retired from a lifetime of reporting, writing, broadcasting, and travelling in 1987, I swore that I would never write another word. First, on purely financial grounds, the need to earn money was less urgent for me than when I was young. Second, I was in any case a convinced Johnsonian, believing, with the great Dr Samuel Johnson (1709-1784) that "no man but a blockhead ever wrote, except for money." What's more, I did not -- and do not -- want to be a literary bore, any more than I want to be a bore at the bar in the pub or the club, wittering on about events long ago. I was in agreement, too, with the views of a regular book reviewer, Anthony Daniels, when (in criticising a work produced by a much younger BBC practitioner than myself, Fergal Keane) he pronounced scathingly, "All autobiographers have a sense of self-importance; otherwise, they would hardly set pen to paper, but when combined with the self-regard of the modern media, it is not surprising that the genre is not without its defects." Quite brutally, he launched an onslaught upon poor Fergal and the "memoirs of modern war correspondents", saying he felt that "once you've read one, you've read them all".

Apart from my personal sympathy for Keane as a victim of Daniels's dismissal of his work, the criticism itself administered a warning to any journalist of the perils of book writing. This was reinforced for me when I came across another example of Daniels's apparent antipathy towards his fellow journalists (for as a regular book reviewer for newspapers and magazines, Daniels himself could fairly be described as a journalist) when, assessing a work by the columnist Nick Cohen, Daniels condescendingly described Cohen as "a journalist whose work has an unusual aroma – that of thought". So if any reviewer like Daniels is ever unleashed upon this book, I can only hope that the "aroma" of my thought processes, personal or journalistic, does not overpower him or her.

In any case, I have decided to risk criticism because some of my friends, as well as my family, after hearing me talk about something or other, have urged me to "get it down on paper". Succumbing to their suggestions, stimulated by the genuine intellectual challenge of trying to produce a readable and marketable book – and combined, I suppose, with a touch of personal vanity – I began work. I have not dealt with events consecutively, preferring to address myself to themes arising from them. However, to assist the reader with my own history, I append a brief biography giving dates of the main events in my own life, both professional and personal; and to maintain some sort of chronological framework around the themes with which I deal, I have chosen to tell what I term my "unfinished stories" within the broad drama of "one man's" existence in the "seven ages" defined by William Shakespeare. At eighty-five, I regard myself as having certainly reached his fifth "age" (that of the "justice"), although in reality I have long ago passed it, because (I am told) in England these days, anyone who is more than seventy is not actually permitted to be either a juror or a JP (justice of the peace). Yet I have not yet reached the bard's sixth "age" of the "lean and slippered pantaloon", if for no other reason than that I still possess that attribute of the "justice", the "fair round belly with good capon lined". Like the "justice", I am not averse to uttering what might pass as "wise saws and modern instances", although the reader's personal judgement will decide on the actual wisdom or modernity.

My views might please or displease. Whatever the case, a satisfying motivation in writing the book has been the chance offered to get many things off my chest. I do not see why I should not express my thoughts simply because I am an old man and therefore regarded possibly as being either senile or incapable of fresh thought – dismissible in the manner in which the young (but maddened) Hamlet, after just killing Ophelia's father, poor old Polonius, so unkindly and contemptuously dismissed his victim as "a foolish prating knave".

In fact, I like to think that at a time when there seems to be some sort of general mild contempt among elderly persons about the youth, inexperience, and apparent superficiality of our politicians (as well as a mild vogue for condemnation of "age-ist" behaviour, or "age discrimination"), then people might even feel it worth their while to read the impressions of an old reporter about the many stories he covered and to wonder, with him, why they have deteriorated into such endless ghastly serials.

The canvas I exhibit for view is large, simply because my experience of work and life itself has been broad, full, exciting, and varied. For example, I believe I remain the only BBC staff correspondent ever to have been appointed by that remarkable organisation to cover, for some years at each point, the White House (as Washington correspondent); the Kremlin (as Moscow correspondent); and Buckingham Palace (as court correspondent, these days known as "royal" correspondent). That is an unusual trio of assignments, and, of course, in the last-mentioned role, I enjoyed visiting palaces and the fun of covering events such as Royal Ascot, just as I had earlier endured many less pleasurable assignments, in over one hundred countries, that had entailed physical hardship; prison detention; being shot at, tear-gassed, shelled, rocketed, or bombed; being chased by rioters; and deportation from (or being forbidden entry to) a number of countries.

The book has been written with five hopes. First: the reader will enjoy it and not regret paying for it. Second: it will provide my three children, my two grandchildren, and my three great-grandchildren with some understanding of why I have been absent for so much of their lives and thus have been less than a good father, grandfather, or great-grandfather. Third: I hope that younger journalists and broadcasters might find my experiences and mistakes instructive and therefore pick up a few tips on how to pursue the news and how not to do so. It is a topical subject in these days of illegal telephone hacking; controversial "tweeting"; the Leveson Inquiry; the "hacked-off" lobby group; parliamentary and public argument over a royal charter to oversee the newspaper and magazine industry; and, indeed, an entirely new set of problems. These involve publication on the Internet of officially secret material from an individual like the fugitive United States intelligence contractor Edward Snowden or an organisation such as WikiLeaks.

Fourth: I hope that constructive thought might be prompted among policymakers (as well as among readers) on serious subjects over which I ponder: the role and the future of the monarchy (it looks pretty secure after the Queen's diamond jubilee and the birth of Prince George); the survival of the United Kingdom as a union, (even though the referendum in Scotland in September calling for Scottish independence was defeated); the dubious future of the European Union ("It's the economy, stupid!"); the questionable permanence and nature of my old employer, the BBC (dear old "Auntie"); and the credibility of the United Nations, the Geneva rules of war, and the very concept itself of international law (especially in its world-wide application against terrorism, subjugation of women, slavery, and piracy).

Fifth and finally: I hope that the book will earn some money for the work that has been put into it.

John Osman
January 2015

ARTHUR JOHN OSMAN

(always known personally and professionally as John Osman)

July 3, 1929: Born, Durrington, Worthing, West Sussex.

1934–39: Durrington Primary (Infant) School.

1939–45: Worthing High School for Boys, a grammar school that has now evolved into Worthing College. Evacuated, with school, to Nottinghamshire during war.

1945: Cambridge School Certificate with Matriculation.

1945–49: Apprentice junior reporter with the *Brighton Evening Argus* (now the *Argus*); its now-defunct sister morning newspaper, the *Sussex Daily News*; and their sister weekly newspapers (also now defunct), the *Southern Weekly News* and the *Brighton and Hove Gazette*.

1946: Winner, age seventeen, of the Ford Madox Ford triennial national essay competition for junior journalists, organised by the world's oldest association of journalists, the Chartered Institute of Journalists.

1949–51: Sports editor and general reporter, the *Worthing Herald*.

1951–54: General reporter and feature writer, the *Bristol Evening Post*. One of the first batch of journalists after the war to qualify with the still-recognised General Certificate of Proficiency in Journalism, covering acquisition of Royal Society of Arts Certificates in Public Administration and in English (with particular knowledge of the laws of copyright and libel), as well as old-fashioned but still useful skills such as shorthand.

1954–56: In Fleet Street as a general reporter with the Press Association News Agency.

1956–65: Staff reporter and, from 1958, foreign correspondent with the *Daily Telegraph*, plus, from its foundation, its sister newspaper, the *Sunday Telegraph*. Covered Cyprus pre-independence emergency through 1958 and the flight of the Dalai Lama from Tibet to India in 1959, travelling in Assam, Nepal, Sikkim, Pakistan, and so forth.

1959–62: *Telegraph* Middle East correspondent, the first British correspondent to establish himself with his family in Cairo after Suez, eventually declared a prohibited immigrant by Nasser but allowed back years later as BBC diplomatic correspondent. During this stint as Middle East correspondent, produced for the *Sunday Telegraph* an acclaimed series on slavery (described by one major commentator as "compelling journalism") after a year's travel across Africa, from Timbuktu to Saudi Arabia, on an investigation into the subject, culminating in the discovery of three hundred slaves sheltering in an embassy in Jeddah and passing the evidence to the Saudi government (who soon afterwards outlawed slavery) and to the United Nations. Made member of the Anti-Slavery Society, which used the photograph of one of the slaves on its Christmas card.

1965–87: Staff correspondent for BBC Radio, TV, and World Service, travelling, working, and reporting from one hundred or so countries. Hanging on the wall in his study today are eighteen of the British passports used over the years – all but one of the nineteen issued to him in his lifetime.

1965: First BBC job: Commonwealth and colonial correspondent. Reported 1965 Rann of Kutch War between India and Pakistan and the 1971 war between the two countries that led to the birth of Bangladesh and the end of East Pakistan. Reported Rhodesian illegal declaration of independence and sanctions against Ian Smith regime; arrested and deported by the regime. Reported Nigerian-Biafran War, the guerrilla wars against the Portuguese in Angola and Mozambique, the troubles in Aden, and the British withdrawal from East of Suez.

1969–72: BBC United Nations Correspondent and, from 1970, as well as continuing to cover the UN, performed a happy "double act" with the late Charles Wheeler as BBC Washington correspondent. Major news he covered included Communist China's admission to the UN Security Council and Nationalist China's exit from it; Kissinger's diplomatic breakthrough visit to Communist China (opening that country up to the world); the end of the 1944 "Bretton Woods" international financial system and of the fixed convertibility of the US dollar at thirty-five dollars to an ounce of gold (remembered today as the "devaluation of the dollar"). Last report from the United States before being posted elsewhere was from the Democratic National Convention in Miami, which selected George McGovern as their presidential candidate. However, Osman's final Miami dispatch was not about that but about a mysterious break-in at a place in Washington, DC, known as Watergate, an episode that brought down President Nixon. Osman also enjoyed lighter US assignments such as the opening of Disney World in Florida (where he appeared on BBC TV with his "friends" Mickey Mouse, Minnie Mouse, Donald Duck, and Goofy); the reopening of the old London Bridge, near Lake Havasu City, Arizona, after its dismantlement, sale, Atlantic trans-shipment, and American reconstruction; and the MGM auction of Hollywood garments such as dance shoes worn by Judy Garland in *The Wizard of Oz* and a trilby hat and macintosh worn by Humphrey Bogart.

1972–75: BBC Southern Africa correspondent. While on the way to South Africa, in Uganda, en route to new posting, reported on Idi Amin's expulsion of Asians and was arrested, detained, and deported. Covered independence and post-independence struggles in Zimbabwe, Angola, Mozambique, the Congo, Namibia, and Somalia as well as the overthrow and later murder of Emperor Haile Selassie of Ethiopia.

1975–80: BBC Africa Correspondent, continuing to cover upheavals all over the continent and on one occasion being asked by the late dictator of Uganda, Idi Amin, if he (Osman) thought he (Amin) was mad, the only time in a lifetime of journalism that Osman was ever asked such a question by a head of state. Osman scooped the news of Amin's flight later from Uganda.

1980–83: BBC Moscow correspondent. In an extraordinary period of transition, covered a series of Kremlin deaths, starting with Alexei Kosygin in 1980, when Kosygin was succeeded onto the ruling politburo of septuagenarians and octogenarians by a then-unknown fifty-year-old Mikhail Gorbachev. There followed coverage over the next five years of the deaths of Soviet leaders Leonid Brezhnev, Yuri Andropov, and Konstatin Chernenko before Gorbachev finally came to power (Osman's last assignment in Moscow, by which time he was BBC diplomatic correspondent).

In 1982, Osman and the BBC first alerted the world to the possibility that Brezhnev *might* be dead a day before the official announcement. It was a long night before confirmation came! Osman predicted Andropov's succession after Brezhnev's death and was again correct. During the Moscow posting, Osman travelled widely within the old Soviet Union, from Murmansk in the north to places farther south – such as Tajikistan, Uzbekistan, Georgia and Armenia – and to Siberia and Lake Baikal.

He was also the first BBC correspondent to travel to the Republic of Outer Mongolia and to broadcast from there. The worst moment of his Moscow stint was when he annoyed the Soviet authorities after disclosing to the world the collusion between the Soviet Union and white-ruled apartheid South Africa on gold, platinum, and diamond prices, an arrangement which ended up as the subject of a full *Panorama* programme. At one uncomfortable stage, he was almost classed as a spy when Soviet propaganda suggested he was "an imperialist agent".

1983–87: BBC diplomatic and court (Buckingham Palace) correspondent, travelling the world with the Queen, the prime minister, and the foreign secretary. Resigned from full-time journalism and broadcasting after reporting the Queen's tour of China and feeling that he wanted to do something other than often going to places that he did not really want to go to and often meeting people he did not really want to meet – a personal "opt-out" that the constitutionally duty-bound and dedicated monarch herself would find almost impossible to be able to emulate. Thus he exercised his fortunate freedom to be able to stop work and abandoned his reporting of world events to enjoy himself – skiing (until he was eighty-three), climbing and walking mountains, sailing (in the sunshine), and spending more time with the family.

1987–2013: Freelancing: usually writing or contributing as requested to obituaries!

Worked in over one hundred countries in fifty years. Twice married; once divorced. Three children, two grandchildren, three great-grandchildren. Continues to travel widely with his second wife, Virginia Waite – journalist, author, broadcaster, and his partner of forty-six years – in their small Romahome camper-car.

CHAPTER 1

===

Age One:
"At First the Infant, Mewling and Puking"

When born, I was unable to mewl. My lungs were congested, so the doctor grasped my ankles with one hand and suspended me out of the first-floor bedroom window, my head dangling down. With his other hand, he beat me on the back. I then puked, mewled, and survived. So began my life, the first of my unfinished stories.

Although I cannot remember my birth, I have no doubt that I am telling the truth, for the story was related to me with some gusto by my beloved and robust mother, who died in 1998, a month short of her ninety-fifth birthday.

Now, a good deal later on in life from the first of Shakespeare's "seven ages", I am reverting to mewling. The reason is that I simply cannot understand much of what is going on around me.

It is worrying because my job for most of my life has been reporting on what was happening, and trying to explain it, for television viewers, radio listeners, and newspaper readers. Not only am I disturbed by the mighty sweep of national and international events and annoyed by the largely unattractive output of the Internet, television, radio, the stage and film industry, and of many publishers, but even more disconcerting to a Sussex wanderer through more than a hundred countries who has come home finally to rest, I find myself unable to comprehend things happening on my own doorstep.

For instance, I found myself baffled in November 1999 when I came across a barely disguised call for Sussex to break away from the United

Kingdom. It struck me as bizarre yet somehow typical of the disintegration of familiar habits of existence in England. What made it even more incredible to my possibly atrophying mind is that the call came from, of all people, the then-chairman of the West Sussex County Council, who, later, after thirty years of elected public service, was appointed deputy lieutenant of Sussex.

Although when I was a boy, Scottish, Welsh, and Irish nationalist independence aspirations would have generally been held unlikely as short-term political objectives, such aspirations have nevertheless been achieved, if somewhat incompletely, over recent years. However, even in these unpredictably transitional days, who on earth, I ask myself, would dream of thinking, even semi-seriously, of a potential unilateral declaration of independence by Sussex?

Well, the answer was Mr Ian Elliott. At the time, he was the county council chairman. Surely, I thought when I read his suggestion, he must be joking – perhaps on the lines of that funny old post-war film *Passport to Pimlico* (the main theme of which was a declaration of independence by the Pimlico area of London).

But no, the call for Sussex to "go it alone" did not appear to have been made in jest. Buttressed with solemn economic arguments, there, for all to see, was the summons in the *West Sussex Gazette*, the respected two-hundred-year-old weekly newspaper. Expressing a personal, apparently reluctant, secessionist view, Mr Elliott complained about governmental plans to build more houses in Sussex and asked under a six-column headline, "Do we really need the rest of the UK if it treats us like this?"

Sympathetic though I am to the traditional county philosophy that "Sussex folk wunt be druv", ("Sussex folk won't be driven") Mr Elliott's call for severance from the UK made me sharply sit up.

Even after I had added a generous pinch of salt to the unexpected dish he was cooking, I felt nervous. This was exacerbated because of the source from which the proposition came, for the county council over which Mr Elliott presided was not a revolutionary red-rose–garlanded Labour-run council with the red flag flying over county hall as it used to flutter over the town hall in St. Pancras. On the contrary, it was a deeply dyed staunch Conservative-controlled council in the ancient cathedral city of Chichester.

Others might possibly express perplexities similar to my own at the idea of an English county declaring its independence. They too might share the mixed emotions that Mr Elliott's call aroused in me: wanting to laugh in disbelief or simply to mewl in misery. Whatever the reaction, though, to his musings, I hope that in some form or other, both Sussex and England will survive with rather more certainty than I survived my own first moments.

Since that critical initiation into this world, the life I have led has enabled me to nurse real warmth towards the county of my childhood, and even towards the house out of the window of which I was suspended when born. I am pleased to see that the place is not only still there but remains a home. Much else has changed. The stony and chalky "un-adopted" or "un-made-up" rough lane in which the house stood in 1929 retains its name, Stone Lane, but is now a proper road. Opposite the house, what was a grocer's shop where I once worked as an errand boy had become (when I last saw it) an Alzheimer Society centre.

The village itself, Durrington – with surrounding fields, woods, farms, nurseries, and ponds where we children used to roam, catching newts and frogs and collecting eggs from birds' nests (now forbidden) – has been subsumed as a part of the south coast resort town of Worthing and at one stage was reported to have a serious vandalism and hooliganism problem. Worthing itself is now a sprawling home for thousands who want seaside bungalows or apartments for their retirement, plus supermarkets for their motorised shopping. Vanished now is the village bakery where we went to buy hot bread direct from the oven; vanished is the dairy where we went to get milk fresh from the cows in the barn; and vanished too is a building that stood next to the dairy, an ancient thatched cottage that was occupied by an old woman called Mrs Elliott, who gave us sweets during my childhood. I wonder if she was one of the ancestors of the secessionist county council chairman? I wonder what she would have thought of his ideas?

The cottage had been the sixteenth-century home of the lawyer, MP, and essayist John Selden (1584–1654), who, at the age of ten, had carved an inscription in Latin over the door. The translation:

Walk in and welcome; honest friend, repose.
Thief, get thee gone! To thee I'll not unclose.

Selden played an important part in the Commons impeachment of the archbishop of Canterbury, William Laud, who was sent to the Tower and beheaded, and in the later trial of Charles I, who lost his head as well. Despite this not inconsiderable role in English history, John Selden's name is not a household one, and it will probably remain generally forgotten unless and until some TV historian like Simon Schama, David Starkey, or Lucy Worsley comes along and resuscitates Selden's memory.

"Selden's Cottage", as his home was known, was (apart from churches) Worthing's oldest building, and it was pulled down in 1954 by what the local newspaper described as a "tragic town council decision". Certainly, the council of the time was influenced by developmental and financial considerations rather than by any concern for protecting a little bit of the local patrimony, but Worthing Council was probably no more philistine than many other British municipal authorities of the day.

Three hundred or so years after Selden's death, the author E. V. Lucas was probably correct when he commented in a book, "Nowadays, when we choose our glories among classes of men other than jurists or wits, it is more than possible for even cultured persons who are interested in books to go through life very happily without knowledge at all of the great John Selden, the friend of great men and the writer best endowed with common sense of any of his day."

I especially like Lucas's wry reference to the ignorance of "even cultured persons who are interested in books". What would Lucas have made of today's Internet or television-orientated version of "culture" (let alone the so-called celebrity cult)?

Selden's common-sense writing preceded by a century or more (and has therefore been overshadowed by) the works of Britain's greatest essayist, William Hazlitt, so beloved by the late Michael Foot, the Labour Party leader. Some of Selden's aphorisms, however, still find their way into the quotation books, and one of my favourites, more apposite as the years roll by and friends pass on, is this: "Old friends are best. King James used to call for his old shoes; they were easiest for his feet."

Selden's cottage may have disappeared, but the road in which it stood still bears his name, Selden's Way, and so does a nearby local pub. This, though, is much smarter than it was when my father and his friends drank there in the 1930s. Born in 1893, my father was a regular soldier and then an agricultural labourer.

He came from a large Oxfordshire family (fourteen brothers and sisters) of rural workers, and he died at the age of fifty-four from tuberculosis. His shortish life had been hard. A gunner first class in the Royal Artillery, the Royal Horse Artillery, the Royal Field Artillery, and the Royal Garrison Artillery, he had served in India before the first world war, the Great War, and a rare photograph of him that survived from his moustache-wearing youth was taken of him, in uniform, in a photographic studio on the north-west frontier of the Raj.

During the Great War, he fought against the Ottoman Empire and the Turks in what he always used to refer to as the "Messpot", meaning Mesopotamia, today called Iraq and perhaps as messy a pot now as it was then. He survived fighting in the relief of Kut-el-Amara, and I remember seeing desert pictures taken of his battery in action. He had the greatest respect for the Turks as soldiers.

At the end of the war, he had another difficult posting, to Ireland, before completing his service. After spending a quarter of his life with the army, he left it with three medals, including the 1914 Star, of which he was very proud. It was known as the "Old Contemptibles" award, the "Contemptibles" deriving their nickname from the Kaiser's dismissive remark about Britain's "contemptible" little army. The other two medals were the standard 1914–1918 awards; the three of them together were collectively known to my father's generation as "Pip, Squeak and Wilfred", after popular cartoon characters of the time.

He also had an army discharge certificate, which he cherished, I think, more than the medals. This was because his conduct as a soldier was described in one word: "exemplary".

His name was inscribed on the rear of the Star Medal and on the circular edges of the round medals. Sadly, the old War Office practice of inscribing individual names on campaign medals and other awards for service or courage was ended years ago, simply to save the government – and, I suppose, the taxpayer – some money. However, as a taxpayer, I for one would be happy to cough up for the continuation of such recognition on medals, and I imagine that many others might feel the same way, if one is to judge by the annual turnout every November at Remembrance Day ceremonies at the Cenotaph and elsewhere.

My father would not have regarded himself in any way as being a hero, but I know he did not think much of the politicians' failure to bring about their stated aim of making Great Britain, after the Great War of 1914–18, a "land fit for heroes to live in". When he got back to "Civvy Street" and Oxfordshire in the 1920s, he could find no work, so he tramped, sleeping in haystacks, hedgerows, and outhouses, to Sussex, where he had an old army chum. According to my mother, he was in an exhausted state when he arrived in Sussex and she met him. They married in 1928, and a year later, I came along, beginning a rather long and quite full existence that started on July 3, 1929. That was the year of the Great Wall Street Crash, and crashing about the world ever since has formed a large part of my own personal performance in Shakespeare's "strange eventful history".

First as a newspaperman and then as a BBC man, it was my routine task to cover wars, disturbances, revolutions, and crises wherever my employers sent me. Sometimes I witnessed events from far too uncomfortably close a position, but I managed over half a century or more to preserve life and limb in times of strife, even though my liberty was restricted now and again. As a prisoner, I became familiar with the grimy walls of a prison or two. I was also deported from more than one country because of my journalistic endeavours and declared a prohibited immigrant to such states before returning to them later after changes of regime. As a pleasant change from such vicissitudes, I was also often welcomed as a guest in royal and presidential palaces, especially in the last five years of my career, when travelling the world with the Queen, the prime minister, and the foreign secretary as BBC diplomatic and court correspondent.

Eventually, though, after the Queen's exotic tour of China, I felt I had experienced enough full-time reporting to last me for the rest of my life. I took myself off to France to enjoy existence there with my wife. These days we divide our time between a barn converted into a house in the French Pyrenees; an apartment and – until recently – a sailing boat in Paphos in Cyprus; and a cottage in my native part of the world, tucked away in a fold of the Sussex Downs, in Steyning. My pleasant Sussex life today contrasts greatly with my memories of a childhood that now would be regarded as one of outright hardship.

My father, debilitated by his war service and struggling with poverty, got himself a job in a West Tarring nursery growing tomatoes, cucumbers, and chrysanthemums. He was chummy with another nursery owner and former fellow soldier from India and the "Messpot", Fred Boxall. He became my Uncle Fred when the two men married sisters.

Dad's wage in the 1930s was two pounds per week. On that, he and my mother managed to rent a house and bring up my two younger sisters and myself. He died in 1947. Survival was a struggle, and we three children calculated carefully how we should spend our weekly pocket money, our "Saturday penny".

The first thing we did was to change each penny into four farthings (long since abolished), the farthing being a copper coin roughly the size of today's copper penny. But the farthing was enough then to buy more than a penny does today.

Its value to us was most familiar. We could get a "Golliwog" bar (so-called because it had a golliwog on its paper wrapper) of toffee, or liquorice strips, for one farthing. In those days, before race became an issue, nobody seemed to mind about the name of cheap confectionery. Two farthings made up a halfpenny (another abolished coin), which we knew as the "ha'penny". With that, we could buy an ice cream, a ha'penny's worth of monkey nuts, or a ha'penny's worth of broken biscuits. In those days, biscuits arrived at the grocer's in large biscuit tins, out of which we could buy broken biscuits in paper bags.

Another abolished coin that was a favourite with us was the three-penny piece, better known as the "thru'penny bit" or the "thru'penny joey". Granny always put this coin into Christmas puddings, where we bit on it with great happiness. When the joey also disappeared, it was replaced in the Christmas pudding by the somewhat bigger sixpence, or "tanner". Gone too is the silvery tanner, its nearest equivalent in new pence being the five-pence silvery coin.

The five-penny piece now is one-twentieth of the pound, but in my childhood, one-twentieth of a pound was not five pence but twelve pence. Twelve pennies made up the shilling, or "bob", and twenty bob made one pound. The bob equalled two tanners, and there were 240 pence in the pound!

It sounds pretty complicated today, but all of us children had a good idea of the value of each coin, so hard were they to come by. We could work out in our heads – quickly, accurately, and without calculators – the sums needed to check the price and any change. These coins are seen now only in museums or numismatic collections; but to millions of old men and women like me, they remain real – certainly as real as today's pound sterling, itself threatened with extinction by the euro – assuming, that is, that the euro itself survives.

Nearly half of my father's weekly wage of two pounds, earned over a five-and-a-half-day working week, went to pay the rent of seventeen shillings a week. The rent was paid to our landlady, who happened to be my mother's aunt.

She was an ex-nurse called Ruth, and her husband was called Arthur. My younger sister was given the name of Ruth, and I myself was given Arthur as a first forename, even though I have always been called by my second forename, John. My great-uncle was a retired London policeman from the days when London policemen had to be at least six feet tall; when they were respected; and when they were neither dodging fire extinguishers hurled down in their direction from a roof by rioters, nor being pilloried for incompetence and corruption, nor being accused of "institutionalised racism".

I liked Great-Uncle Arthur, but I was none too fond of Great-Aunt Ruth. This resulted, I think, from my father's fury when the rent went up one Saturday from seventeen shillings to one pound, half of my father's weekly wage. My father and great-aunt Ruth had never really got on well, and I suspect that the reason was that she felt that my mother had "married down". After the rent was raised, I cannot recall my father ever speaking to Great-Aunt Ruth again, and he rarely mentioned her name unaccompanied by insults. The upshot was that when she died, the house in which we lived and which my mother had hoped she would inherit (especially after she had given the names of her aunt and uncle to two of her children) was bequeathed instead to a more favoured sister of my mother, who had named her child after neither her aunt nor her uncle. My mother never really accepted what she saw as the injustice of that.

One could never describe my father as romantic. An aunt described to me once how disconcerted she had been when my father and mother became engaged. Congratulating him, my aunt mentioned in a sisterly way my mother's shapely beauty. To that, my father replied in his Oxfordshire rural manner, "Aarr, she's got some good timbers on 'er!"

My father was essentially a loving man, but he could be a good hater. He was on uneasy terms with the neighbours on each side of us. Great-Aunt Ruth was on one side, and on the other side lived the Jones family. Mr Jones was a mild but stubborn man who, in the Great War, had been what my father always referred to contemptuously as a "conchie": a conscientious objector to war. As far as my father was concerned, it was just an excuse to be a coward and to avoid military service. He let everyone know his views, especially Mr Jones.

Dad was always polite, though, to Mrs Jones. After the Second World War, she became one of the first Labour councillors (if not the first) to be elected to the overwhelmingly conservative Worthing Town Council. She founded in Durrington a branch of the Young Socialist League, which many of us, including myself, joined as teenagers. This was largely because we were able to meet teenagers of the opposite sex in her "front room", a room not in daily use but employed only for entertaining visitors (as was the general habit in those days for working-class households such as ours). In that front room, we youngsters explored together, in Mrs Jones's absence, subjects of a nature other than the purely political.

It was often said in rural England in the days of my youth that the Young Conservatives (later to be transformed into a body called "Conservative Future") were not so much a political organisation as they were an unofficial matrimonial agency. If that was broadly true, it was just as true (in Durrington anyway) that the Young Socialists were an unofficial sex education course. As far as I can remember, none of us had any strong political commitment; but the teenage girls seemed keen to meet the boys, and we boys were interested in the girls. The weekly meetings at Mrs Jones's house were popular among us, but not for the ideological reasons which she might have wished. Its major attraction was simply that in an age when teenage boys and girls lived separate existences, with girls going to girls' schools and boys to boys' schools, the regular get-together provided a chance for us to learn about each other a bit more. We were mysteries to each other, and discovering differences was exciting.

Politics and sex just after the war may have been more favoured activities for young lovers than politics and sex appear to be nowadays. I was distressed, for instance, to read in 2001 that politics is a "killer for the love life". The authority for this was Hannah Parker, then the "chair" (how I hate the term!) of Conservative Future. She was speaking at the age of twenty-seven, which, admittedly, was ten years or more further on in life than the ages at which we teenage Young Socialists had arrived when we were busily exploring each other. Even so, despite that age gap, I was staggered to learn that young politicos were finding it difficult to get married because their boyfriends or girlfriends could not face the thought of being an MP's wife or husband. The series of well-publicised marital scandals in recent years involving politicians and ex-politicians might be one cause for lovers' doubts.

However, apart from the threat posed by the fact that intimate areas of private life might all too easily become prey to public examination, it appears that women especially are "turned off" by the idea of marrying an MP because of the expectation that they should be on public show, when necessary, with their husbands. No wonder there is such hesitation!

There were few such hesitations among us when we indulged in our esoteric teenage pleasures in Councillor Mrs Jones's front room. Such teenage high jinks followed earlier infantile pleasures. One of these arrived every Sunday morning to brighten up for my two sisters and myself our somewhat spartan childhood. Before we got up to go to Sunday school, we were allowed to snuggle in my parents' double bed, with my mother and father, where he would produce a memorable luxury which we shared between the five of us.

This was a packet of nuts and raisins, bought the night before on his weekly Saturday evening visit to the "John Selden". There, with villagers and workmates, he would drink beer, smoke his pipe, and play darts. The men used the Public Bar, where the beer was slightly cheaper than the posher Saloon Bar. On summer evenings, my mother and the wives of other men in the pub would sit outside at wooden tables with the children, including myself. A popular drink with the women was a "port and lemon", and we children had lemonade.

The pub was, for most of the customers, a wonderful oasis of relaxation in an endless desert of hard labouring work. I developed affection for it that has stayed with me throughout my life. I refer not only to the institution of the pub in general but to the John Selden in particular, even though it felt unfamiliar to me when I recently visited it. It was not so much that the bar and the rooms are now more attractive than they were seventy years ago, nor that the meals served there are a marked improvement on the rudimentary fare of old, nor was it that the exterior veranda and benches at which the women and we children used to sit and drink have all disappeared; no, it was simply that the customers are so utterly different!

None of them resembled even remotely the old clientele, the rural working class of my youth. Not a soul wore trousers tied with string at the bottom of the legs. Not a cloth cap was in sight, nor was a pair of heavy boots or mucky "wellies". The old gear had been replaced by tracksuits, real suits, comfortable sports jackets and cardigans, shoes, trainers, and baseball caps. This is all the better, I suppose, insofar as it reflects greater prosperity.

The inn sign has changed as well. Instead of the former unadorned name "John Selden", there is on display a "cod" olde worlde sign reading, "Ye John Selden". I make a point of this because I have a vested journalistic interest in that sign.

Soon after the Second World War ended, sixty or more years ago, I became a junior reporter on the *Worthing Herald*, and while bicycling past the inn one day, I noticed that the brewers had put up a new sign. Instead of the former plain "John Selden", it read, "Sir John Selden".

This intrigued me, because given the part which a prominent parliamentarian such as Selden had played in presenting the case against Charles I, it would seem unlikely that he would have been knighted. Off to the history books I went, as well as to the brewers. They admitted they had made a mistake and that they had over-promoted Selden.

Selden was duly un-knighted; the sign was changed, and the *Herald* printed my report with pictures showing the right sign and the wrong sign.

The old landlord was delighted by the publicity, which had caused trade to pick up and beer sales to increase. He offered me a pint or two on the house, which provided welcome assistance to my tight weekly budget.

I am glad that the John Selden is still there. It is still a pleasant pub, and I hope that if this reminiscence ever sees the light of day, there might be a bit of local publicity spin-off for the new landlord as there was for the old. I might even get another free pint!

In any case, despite the changes, the John Selden remains a just recognisable part of my childhood and youth in the world of today, in which such recognisable features have largely ceased to be visible. If, as I approach my second childhood, the strain of trying to understand what is happening around me just gets too baffling, I shall return to the Selden to sit discreetly in the corner, tippling away like the old curmudgeon I appear to be; and there I shall mewl quietly to myself.

My father as a soldier pictured in a photographic studio on the
north-west frontier of India before the Great War of 1914-18.

Victorian attitudes! A curtain was placed over the outside lavatory ("privy")
door to half-conceal it when this picture was taken at my grand-parents'
home in Worthing, West Sussex, in 1903. My mother is the baby on my
grandmother's knee and her elder sister is on my grandfather's lap.

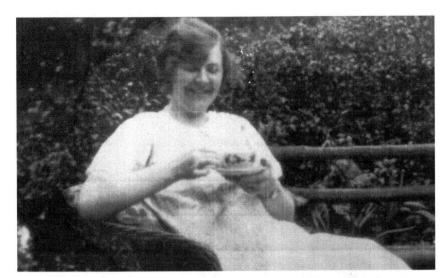

My mother, with tea-cup, pictured in the 1920s in Worthing. When her sister congratulated my father on his engagement and remarked on my mother's attractiveness as a young woman, my father replied in his Oxfordshire rural manner to my aunt (as she told me): "Arr, she's got some good timbers on 'er!"

My mother on her 90th birthday in 1993.

My parents at their 1928 wedding, a year before my birth.

My maternal grand-parents with me as a baby. My grandfather
holds me and my grandmother holds the dog.

My paternal grandparents at their home in Ipsden in Oxfordshire.
There are several "Osmans" in the Ipsden churchyard and there is
no known family connection with Islam, despite the name, which
led to me being nicknamed by journalistic colleagues as "Osman
Pasha", "Osman Bey", "Osman Effendi", or simply as "Ali bin Osman."
Greek colleagues Hellenicised me and called me "Osmanides."

My mother holds me as a baby.

CHAPTER 2

===

Why the Mewling?

Nearly everyone I meet these days complains about existence, although as one joker has put it, "Despite the high cost of living, it remains popular." Sitting in my corner in the pub, mewling away to myself, the question presents itself: why am I so glum? I find myself endorsing more and more some of the words of the hymn "Abide with Me", which (before football hooliganism became computer organised) used to be sung at F.A. Cup Finals and I believe still is: "Change and decay all around I see." Change does not necessarily equate with decay, but neither does it always equate with progress. So does gloom come with age? No, not automatically.

It may be encouraged by natural and inevitable physical and mental decay, but it arises also from events themselves, ranging from terrorism and war at the alarming end of the scale to "state nannying" at the comic end. In an effort to distance myself from despair about politicians in particular and my fellow men and women in general; and when trying to forget about the follies of the human race (including my own); I usually turn to the pub, a book, a theatre visit, a film, radio, television, or just go for a walk. Then I sometimes find myself feeling even gloomier than before!

Plunged disconcertingly further into misanthropy, I identify myself utterly with the grumpy "Wishes of an Elderly Man":

I wish I loved the human race;
I wish I loved its silly face;

I wish I liked the way it walks;
I wish I liked the way it talks;
And when I'm introduced to one,
I wish I thought "What jolly fun!"

In my view, the composer of those lines, lecturer and critic Sir Walter Raleigh (1861–1922), got it about right. However, neither he, I, nor most of us would want to be cured of any of our miseries by the treatment meted out to Sir Walter's earlier namesake, the other Sir Walter Raleigh (1552–1618), the explorer and courtier who, on one famous occasion, spread out his cloak for Queen Elizabeth I to tread on so that she did not muddy her feet. Following the Queen's death, when he had fallen fatally out of subsequent royal favour, that earlier Raleigh felt the edge of the axe just prior to his execution and commented: "'Tis a sharp remedy, but a sure one for all ills."

I am not so far gone in my depression as to welcome the removal of my head, but I have often contemplated the removal of the TV or radio from my home. I find myself increasingly reluctant to watch television or new films because I am so often disappointed with what I see. Much of the output lacks substance. I am, of course, not alone in my poor opinion. For example, as long ago as 2004, broadcaster John Humphrys attacked TV for what he termed its "populist pap" and for being vulgar, obsessed with sex, bad, socially corrosive, and for coarsening and brutalising viewers. As an old friend and colleague of John, I know that he has never been short of apposite phrases; but on that occasion in 2004, when he was addressing an audience of broadcasting chiefs in Edinburgh, he was on especially good form and his pungent views must have left at least some of those chiefs feeling uncomfortable. Not that it seems to have done any good!

My old employer (and, importantly, dispenser of my pension), the BBC, is just as guilty of populist pap output as other broadcasters. I have therefore become a regular switcher-off. Many acquaintances, including several younger ones, tell me that they feel the same way. Since there are several million of us elderly fellows and women about who would prefer to be regular viewers rather than switchers-off, and since younger perceptive viewers and listeners can also presumably be counted in their millions, I cannot help feeling that the broadcasting authorities are missing an opportunity for potential audience growth.

Long before the chairman of the Conservative Party and Minister without Portfolio, Gregg Shapps, in October 2013, threatened the BBC with the loss of its exclusive right to the licence fee if it did not tackle what was suggested to be its "culture" of secrecy, waste, and unbalanced reporting; long before the Jimmy Savile scandal and the swift departure of George Entwistle as director general; long before the BBC was criticised by Lord Hutton, with consequent departures of big-wigs like the chairman of the Board of Governors and an earlier BBC director general, Greg Dyke; many of us older hacks had already concluded sadly that even with its news and current affairs outlets, the BBC was simply not what it used to be.

First open signs of major differences of opinion between BBC management and BBC journalists about BBC journalism emerged as long ago as 1987 (mercifully the year of my retirement from the BBC staff). Then, at a famous meeting in the old Lime Grove TV studios, the newly appointed deputy director general, John Birt (now Lord Birt), addressed journalists and – according to a *Panorama* reporter, Peter Taylor – declared "year zero" on much of the BBC's journalism. Taylor reported that Birt was "challenged from the floor by a bold and outspoken Charles Wheeler". Taylor wrote, "Charles, with his enormous authority, spoke for all of us bruised journalists."

Alas, in 2008 we lost that superb reporter, another colleague – and friend of mine – for half a century. He had an impressive 60 years of work for the BBC and his 1987 run-in with BBC management did not seem to affect him adversely. He was (somewhat belatedly, in my view) eventually knighted for his services to broadcasting and journalism. Alastair Cooke, another super veteran, also survived a run-in with management in an utterly dissimilar way, knowing nothing at all about the hatchet job planned against him at the time.

What happened was this: the BBC management, for unclear reasons, was seeking to kill off his weekly Radio 4 *Letter from America*, incredible though that might have seemed to Cooke's enormous following of listeners. Fortunately, that same management chose exactly the wrong man to go to New York to fire Cooke: the fine producer Alastair Osborne, who died in 2009.

Osborne told me the story of how he arrived in New York with the letter of dismissal in his pocket; how he lunched happily with Cooke and simply could not bring himself to fire him; and how he returned to London with the letter still in his pocket!

Many people in authority, especially those just appointed to it, seem to like changing things, even if those things are working well. I suppose they feel compelled to "do something". This applies particularly so, in my experience, to broadcasting executives and government ministers.

While accepting that change cannot be avoided when technical and other advances more or less impose it, I suppose I have never accepted any argument for change just for change's sake. I prefer to be convinced that change will be for the better. In that sense I can, I suppose, be regarded as conservative with a little *c*. As far as the BBC is concerned, my doubts about changes there go back almost to the moment when I joined the corporation in 1965 from the *Daily Telegraph*.

The first thing that happened to mystify me was when the stirring signature tune to the old *Radio Newsreel* programme, which listeners around the world had come to recognise when they tuned in, suddenly disappeared. What was the need for the abolition of an immediately recognisable programme marker? I do not know and probably never will, but I have always suspected that it was because it was called "Imperial Echoes", with its unfashionable link with Empire. I still hold that suspicion.

Soon after that, *Radio Newsreel* itself disappeared from the domestic airwaves, although the programme continued on the World Service. Then I was mildly surprised when, after being with the BBC for a year or so, I was called in for a chat by the late John Crawley, who, as foreign news editor, had invited me to apply for a job with the corporation and later went on to become special assistant to the director general.

A civilised man, John asked me on my return from covering the 1965 war between Pakistan and India if I was happy with the BBC. Did I have any doubts about having switched from Fleet Street and the written word to the BBC and the spoken word? The question puzzled me a bit because I was quite happy and had received praise for my coverage of the war (especially important for me then because the war was my first major assignment for the corporation, when I was making the transition from print to radio and television journalism). However, I remember replying that while, on the whole, I was glad I had made the move (more money and a solid pension, for starters), I sometimes felt like a journalist who had gone to work for *The Times* and found himself instead working for the *Daily Mirror*.

The reason for this response was because Crawley's question came at a time when the corporation was cutting down the time allowed for news dispatches to much shorter pieces. From the old recognised voice piece for *Radio Newsreel* of anything up to four and a half minutes (then used in testing job applicants), the "reeler" was reduced to a couple of minutes; and for television and radio news bulletin outlets, the new required voice piece lasted from thirty seconds up to one minute. In essence, it was a cut in airtime on news outlets which left a journalist with less time to be reflective and hardly enough time to sketch in anything more than the barest of facts.

Crawley's reaction was sympathetic. He pointed out, justly, that the BBC was in the business of communicating with "the masses" (he employed those words) and we had to communicate with *Daily Mirror* readers as well as those of the *Times*. His BBC equivalent today would doubtless select the *Sun* to illustrate his argument; but in those days, the *Sun* had not erupted upon the face of British journalism. The point, though, was valid and remains so; but as the years have gone by, my doubts have grown.

I wonder, for instance, if the BBC is managing to retain its communication not just with "the masses" but with, say, the readers of the *Times*, even of today's workaday *Times*, far removed from the quite unique *Times* I remember as a youngster. Then, it really was the newspaper read by "the Establishment", with a front page of small advertisements.

On the inside pages were columns of material written by anonymous journalists whose only byline was "Our Political Correspondent", or "Our Rugby Football Correspondent", or whatever the relevant speciality might have been. In a curious way, the anonymity added to the authority of what was being published, especially since everybody in those far-off days used to say that something "was in the *Times*", meaning that it was the truth. To the reader, the name of the author of the piece was irrelevant; and so far as the author himself or herself was concerned, no consideration was involved in polishing a public image. The focus of concentration was on getting things right.

Inevitably, the impact of broadcasting (not to mention a change in the ownership of the *Times*) changed all that, for it is unreasonable to suggest that any radio or television journalist who actually goes onto the air or the screen should not be identified to listeners and viewers, who quite rightly expect to know who is addressing them. Journalism is of course an eternally changing craft, and the *Times* eventually followed the broadcasters' example and began identifying its writers. Meanwhile, other newspapers, less hidebound than the *Times* of old, had for years already been publishing plenty of named reports and columns, and they have continued to do so, as we see today, with much robust and varied journalism to delight or anger the public. After all, any lively journalist agrees with the ancient maxim of the craft: "Love me or hate me, but for God's sake don't ignore me!" The trouble is that many contemporary practitioners these days seem to have forgotten basic principles about how to go about properly (and legally) gathering facts; how to ensure responsible editorial control is maintained if any resort is made to seek facts by methods that are, shall I say, arguable; and how to differentiate between news and comment.

The line between these two aspects of journalism seems to me to be crossed far too frequently these days, with the two being blurred both in newspaper reports and on TV and radio news bulletins, especially in the process of interviewing. Often the personal feeling (or bias?) of the reporter or interviewer seems to emerge as more important than any facts sought from the person interviewed. A news interview is supposed to elicit facts, not simply to provoke a slanging match from which few facts are garnered except for the obvious mutual antipathy of the participants.

The ultimate effect of too much of this kind of interviewing would be that the process of newsgathering could be overtaken by showbiz punch-ups. I am not arguing for dull or tame interviewers, interviewees, or interviews; I am simply reminding the news interviewers among them of the enduring ground rule for journalists defined in 1921 by C. P. Scott, that great editor of the *Guardian's* predecessor, the *Manchester Guardian*: "Comment is free, but facts are sacred."

As for BBC communication with readers of newspapers other than the *Times*, well, although readers of the *Guardian* might broadly be sympathetic, like their newspaper, towards the BBC, I wonder if readers of, say, the *Daily Telegraph* feel the same after that newspaper's long campaign against the perceived failings and bias of the BBC (the "Blatantly Biased Corporation", as the *Telegraph* dubbed it in 2000). The same goes for readers of the *Daily Mail*, another unrelenting BBC critic.

It is not the alleged liberal or left-wing political prejudice in the corporation's output that concerns me, because there is no doubt that in trying to fulfil one at least of its three major obligations (to inform, to entertain, and to educate), I think that most people would agree that, over its seventy years or so of existence, the BBC has on the whole succeeded on the information front.

Also bearing in mind the BBC involvement with The Open University as well as its own schools' programmes and programmes for the young, I would guess that most fair-minded people would regard the BBC record as creditable on the education front as well.

No! The real problem is the third front: entertainment. It is the sheer amount of rubbish that is broadcast which infuriates me. Sometimes in "Auntie's" efforts to "entertain" the Great British Public she seems to have been adopting a deliberate policy of "dumbing down", with intelligent content of BBC output relentlessly diminishing.

Away from all this, but as an example of a slipping of BBC editorial standards that affected my personal attitude towards my employers, I am saddened to recall an incident on the television, journalistic, information side. I was only peripherally involved in what was an unpleasant episode for the BBC, but it helped me to make up my mind that it was perhaps time to leave a corporation that was possibly going in a direction that I did not much like – and while I could leave gracefully and on good terms with my editors and producers.

It involved Princess Michael of Kent, and it illustrated what could – and did – happen when uninhibited and gung-ho editors or producers failed to treat a sensational tabloid story with caution. Like most members of the royal family, Princess Michael has become, to some extent, inured over the years to hurtful and sometimes malicious attacks. On the occasion in question, an unusually nasty smear job, with no new information in it at all to justify its publication on news grounds, was perpetrated by the *Daily Mirror*, then owned by the late Robert Maxwell.

For some unknown reason, the newspaper had chosen to make a great song and dance about her late father having been a Nazi, even though the background of both her family and herself (born as Baroness Marie-Christine von Reibnitz) was well known. However, the *Mirror* (perhaps Maxwell himself) had decided to rake up her father's dubious past again and to plaster it all over the front page as if it were something scandalously fresh.

My editors asked me to try to obtain an interview with Princess Michael for radio and TV. I made a direct approach to staff at Kensington Palace and an indirect approach through Buckingham Palace because in those days, members of "The Firm" (a royal nickname for members of the royal family) were supposed, under a family arrangement, to seek the Queen's informal approval before giving interviews.

The idea of this arrangement was to head off any potentially embarrassing encounters or at least to give the head of "The Firm" some warning over any row about royalty that might be about to blow up. Essentially and understandably a defensive move by Buckingham Palace, it never really succeeded against elements in the media hostile to the monarchy, and by now, for all I know, it may well have disappeared. In any event, I was assured from the palace that the BBC would be at the top of the list for any interviews given, but in fact the list was simply bypassed.

What happened was that the BBC, me, and all other media organisations requesting an interview were "scooped" by a commercial morning television company. Prince Michael, husband of the besieged princess, happened to occupy a seat on the company's board. He was naturally sympathetic to his wife, so the TV company got the interview. As one of my BBC colleagues put it, Prince Michael "earned his director's fee".

Now things began to become bad – for the BBC. When the commercial channel interview was screened, it was monitored and recorded by breakfast time BBC TV, which then promptly broadcast it to BBC viewers. Things worsened when in the process, the commercial company's screen credit was overlaid with the BBC logo.

Despite irritation as BBC court correspondent at having been scooped (no journalist worth his salt is complacent about that), I remember being pretty disgusted as a working journalist over the BBC shoddy behaviour. The opposition had beaten us, and BBC TV had swiped the opposition scoop and presented it as its own material. Quite simply, it was journalistic theft.

It was at about this stage, when I had already begun to have doubts about what some quarters of the BBC were up to, that I felt that I really did not want to work for the corporation much longer. It was no longer the outfit I had joined nearly a quarter of a century earlier. A demand for pictures and sensation had overwhelmed proper journalistic practice, something inconceivable in my earlier BBC days.

I did not disguise my thoughts about this when asked by colleagues within the BBC and in Fleet Street about the affair. The final blow came when the commercial company brought the BBC to court and the judge decided firmly in favour of the company. He gave the BBC a severe wigging; money had to be coughed up by the corporation in damages and costs; and a notable dent in the BBC's reputation was suffered.

At one stage during the court proceedings, I found myself in the un-desirable position of acting for the BBC as a go-between with Kensington Palace. I sat at my desk with two telephones, one at each ear, with two lines open: one to the high court, the other to Kensington Palace. From the high court, a senior BBC editorial executive accompanying the unfor-tunate director general of the day asked me to appeal to Prince Michael to get the case called off. So I talked to the prince's private secretary at the time, Colonel Michael Farmer. Trying to be a loyal BBC man, although personally convinced of the impossibility of any BBC defence succeeding, I explained to Colonel Farmer that I was acting upon top-level BBC instructions in transmitting the BBC appeal to the prince.

Colonel Farmer left the telephone to confer with his employers, and after doing so, he returned to respond. In his turn, he pointed out that he too was acting as a mere secretary passing on the decision of His Royal Highness and his wife. The answer was no. The case was not called off.

Even at that awkward moment, however, I was amused by the way in which we two messengers, royal private secretary and BBC court correspondent, preserved the proper courtesies while their principals engaged in legal dispute.

It is an unfortunate fact that the mistakes made by people and organ-isations are remembered as much as their accomplishments, sometimes more so.

No wonder I find myself mewling so much, for although I've had some successes in my life, I have also made more than enough mistakes.

CHAPTER 3

Mistakes, Errors,
Plain Criminality, and
More Mewling

Never in British history, I imagine, have the mistakes and errors of the newspaper and broadcasting industries been as heavily publicised as in the last year or two. What's more, rarely, if ever, has any criminality involving people who have worked in those industries been so publicised.

The industries themselves, it should be noted, have been largely responsible for reporting upon their own omissions and misdeeds and other people's views of them, as well as being responsible in some ways for actually originating the troubles about which there is such criticism. Coverage by newspapers and broadcasters about their own problems has been immense: headlines about BBC soul-searching and internal inquiries after the Savile scandal; headlines about public inquiries by Hutton and Leveson into journalistic practices; headlines about Wikileaks and the media damaging foreign relations by circulating stolen American diplomatic exchanges; and headlines about the *Guardian* damaging not only diplomatic relations but national and international security as well, by publishing more stolen American secrets on the Internet and telephone monitoring, including the private conversations of foreign heads of state, among them Angela Merkel.

The list is formidable, and ferocious debate on issues arising from it looks as if it will last for a long time and perhaps become even fiercer. On one side are the uncompromising champions of the freedom of information, who seem to think that everyone is entitled to know everything about anything at any time, and on the other side are those who argue that this is dangerous and unrealistic and who uphold legal and governmental rights to control information in certain necessary circumstances, as in times of war or of the modern curse of terrorism.

The debate has already produced what appears to be an unprecedented attempt by British politicians in the modern era to control the newspaper industry by statute law. This attempt to implement state oversight of the press came when, in 2013, the Queen consented (whether she privately wanted to or not – we shall probably never know) to a Privy Council proposal emanating from a cross-party deal. This was between the Conservatives, Labour, and Liberal-Democrats, involving the engagement also of a group called "Hacked-Off", campaigners against telephone hacking and for greater press responsibility.

Under the proposal, according to the Privy Council website in a ten-word sentence, the monarch made an order approving a royal charter of "Incorporation to the Recognition Panel". The deployment by politicians of the Privy Council for potential state meddling with the press immediately triggered journalistic opposition, with one perceptive columnist, Matthew Norman, declaring, "There is something a touch Soviet about this styling of the forthcoming press watchdog."

Eloquently, if possibly hyperbolically, he argued, "The Recognition Panel might have been a presidium of the Supreme Soviet, instituted under Stalin to recognise those comrades in urgent need of a refreshing break in a Gulag." He added, "One need not be a George Orwell fanatic to appreciate that the choice of language is significant."

The Recognition Panel (according to information in November 2013) is planned to be a watchdog over a new regulating body for the press to replace the old Press Complaints Commission.

The panel would "check that the regulator remains independent". That regulator would be set up by the press but with no editors on its board. Nor would the Recognition Panel have any editors among its four to eight members; in addition, there would be no journalists, civil servants, or MPs. At the time of this writing, all the signs were that the press would continue to oppose the whole idea, while continuing with its own ideas for self-regulation.

The executive director of the Society of Editors, Bob Satchwell, commented that royal charters "are usually granted to those who ask for them – not forced upon an industry or group that doesn't want it". He described the decision of the Privy Council and politicians as "disappointing" and said, "It was a pity the Queen has been brought into controversy."

One of the arguments by newspapers against the statutory involvement of the government is the fact that the industry itself had put forward a plan for its own regulatory body, with tough penalties for offenders in any cases brought by complainants. The publishers also point out that laws already exist anyway to deal with newspapers where actual crimes have been committed, as distinct from mistakes and errors of judgement. The industry points to the closure of The News of the World as an example of the sort of suicidal price that a newspaper has to pay when it misbehaves. It also reminds people that trials that have taken place already, (such as those involving Andrew Coulson, Rebekah Brookes, and others), provide ample evidence that journalists are not, and never have been, immune from prosecution and are in some way above the law.

There is also a suspicion within the industry that some MPs, savaged by the exposures not so long ago of their expense claims by the *Daily Telegraph*, want to ensure that no such painful experience should be inflicted upon them again. The underlying suggestion is that politicians are deviously trying to get their own back on the media.

Within days of the Privy Council's approval of the royal charter, one of the ministers in attendance, the culture secretary at the time, Maria Miller, indicated that the new rules drawn up by politicians to regulate the Press could become "redundant", provided that newspapers successfully established their own watchdog. She said she was willing to give the industry time to make its own proposed regulatory system work. She still, however, hoped that newspapers would sign up to the royal charter, which, she suggested, would offer them some protection from high damages in libel claims and a new system for resolving complaints against the media.

Newspaper groups, however, remained opposed to the royal charter because, they say, it risks granting politicians control over the press for the first time in three hundred years. Instead, they drew up proposals for an Independent Press Standards Organisation (IPSO), fully independent of any state-backed body.

Well, the saga will doubtless continue, as will the wider general debate about standards in the media. More cynical publishers and broadcasters have for a long time argued that nobody in their line of business has ever lost readers, listeners, or viewers by under-estimating the intelligence of the "masses", but such an ethos is directly opposed to the original BBC concept of "public service broadcasting" or "public value broadcasting" (a later BBC-ism).

Whether or not the masses are as moronic as the cynics seem to think, a feeling has built up over the years in many quarters that the bulk of much TV and radio output these days has perhaps become over-aimed at attracting the more stupid among those masses (what communist dogmatists used to describe as the "lumpen proletariat").

If my hypothesis is right, it implies that not enough broadcasting output, by the BBC among others, is directed towards what Red thinkers used to describe as the "bourgeoisie" or, more particularly, "intelligentsia". BBC Radio Four has traditionally been regarded as the last stronghold of the white middle-class listener, but I note that fears have even been expressed about the future of that channel.

Broadcasting output in general is obviously produced with something never far away from the thoughts of the bosses: the so-called "ratings", meaning the claimed figures for viewing and listening. Post-Hutton BBC chairman Michael Grade was reported to have said that the corporation would not be "chasing the ratings" under his regime, but that regime did not last long anyway because he absconded late in 2006 to be the boss of ITV, before departing from there too.

However, during his short tenure as BBC "supremo", it was hard (for me anyway) to discern any marked improvement in programme quality. Whether or not any dumbing down process actually attracts more viewers and listeners, I do not know. I doubt if anybody else really does, including the "ratings agencies", although as full-time opinion-sounders and number crunchers, they might have a better idea than most.

The question of who views or listens to what, on television or radio, remains one of the great imponderables for broadcasting organisations, just as, for newspaper executives, the question of who exactly reads their newspaper, and why, is equally inexplicable. An amusing answer to that was offered by a scriptwriter for (I seem to remember) the excellent *Yes, Minister* TV series. This amusing Press Readership Analysis was produced when then, as now, the *Daily Mail* was noted for its large feminine readership (claimed in 2010 to be over 50 per cent) and when the commitment of the *Morning Star* to communism was when Russia was still the Soviet Union.

The analysis went something like this, complete with the long-standing but unproven boast of the *Times*:

The *Times* is read by the people who run the country.

The *Daily Mirror* is read by the people who think they run the country.

The *Guardian* is read by the people who think they ought to run the country.

The *Morning Star* is read by the people who think the country ought to be run by another country.

The *Independent* is read by the people who don't know who runs the country but are sure they're doing it wrong.

The *Daily Mail* is read by the wives of the people who run the country.

The *Financial Times* is read by the people who own the country.

The *Daily Express* is read by the people who think the country ought to be run as it used to be run.

The *Daily Telegraph* is read by the people who still think it is their country.

The *Sun's* readers don't care who runs the country as long as she's got big tits.

It took near revolutionary political upheaval – Gorbachev, Perestroika, an abortive coup d'état, Yeltsin, and crowds of Muscovites defying troops and tanks – to turn around the drifting Russian ship of state; and it takes nearly as much disturbance to produce major change in a vast organisation like the BBC (despite the persistent urge by executives to "do something").

It will be interesting in the next few years to see what effects the Hutton and Savile fallouts will have on a BBC surviving from such judicial and scandalous blasts. With constant debate about the continuation or abolition of the BBC licence fee; on the renewal of the terms of the BBC royal charter; and on the standards of the BBC's current performance, doubts about the future of the corporation – and indeed its very survival – are strong.

Even though my own direct interest in the BBC today concerns principally the health of its pension fund, as a BBC servant for a quarter of a century or so and as an admirer and consumer of much of its work for my entire life, my sympathies are with those struggling to preserve and develop the corporation. It is, after all, a truly unique national and international broadcasting institution.

I maintain as much interest in and awareness of what "Auntie" is getting up to, especially on the news and current affairs side, as does anyone who appreciates what a great force for truth the organisation has been. Controversial and dubious though many of its programmes and productions may seem to be today (judging by endless publicised criticisms), it is fair to point out that many of those criticisms come from quarters with vested commercial or political interest in the dismantlement or weakening of the BBC.

Even more dubious than the activities of the BBC are many of the organisations and people who attack it and whose actions provide raw material for news and current affairs. As a reporter, my life has been largely spent in dealing with figures and forces like politicians (in power or in opposition), lobbyists (and lobby groups), demonstrators, protesters, and self-styled freedom fighters and guerrillas, many guilty of all kinds of thuggery while waging what they euphemistically call "armed struggle". This protracted reporting has induced in me a strong personal scepticism about many such figures and forces. Several will stop at little to further their cause.

They range from animal rights activists to barbarians who seek to justify their terrorism by what they see as the sacred nature of their aim, whether they are motivated by ISIL or Al Quaeda-style Islamic fundamentalism, extreme Zionism, Irish republicanism, or ETA-style Basque nationalism (to name just a few of the plagues of the twentieth and twenty-first centuries). Publicity by such groups has been sophisticated and much media coverage of their criminality so gullible or sympathetic that a political and moral climate has developed during my lifetime to a degree where tolerance, acceptance, and even encouragement of such extremism has become somewhat common.

For a while, governments seemed incapable, unwilling, or simply afraid to challenge such forces, although signs that American attitudes were changing emerged after the United States was directly attacked in September 2001. For instance, on St. Patrick's Day in 2005, the leader of Sinn Fein, Gerry Adams, was conspicuously not invited to the White House in Washington; but five women members of the family of a man murdered by the IRA, Robert McCartney, were guests instead. It was an indication from a superpower displaying acceptance by responsible governments that real international effort had to be made to counter all forms of terrorism, with argument continuing over the most effective way of doing this.

This, of course, has further developed with the so-called "Arab Spring" of 2011, and it has led to suggestions that countering international group terrorism also involves combating forms of governmental terrorism, as displayed in places like Libya and Syria. Progress against terrorism, difficult though it is, can nevertheless apparently be made, as has been shown in countries like Ireland and Spain. In Spain, the Basque secessionist ETA movement seems to have quietened down; and in Ireland, although the "peace process" is still in its early years, it has at least been making headway, as was illustrated by the success of the Queen's 2011 state visit. Apart from the problems posed by severe economic difficulties (which always tend to heighten political tensions anywhere), there remains in Ireland and Northern Ireland a rump of extremists employing terrorism, a group threatening enough to compel strong security measures for the Queen's visit.

In offering my thoughts on what is a deeply serious and indeed depressing subject, I make no apologies because it really is a universal problem. (I am, of course, now at the "alarming" end of the causes of my perennial gloom, as distinct from the "state nannying" comic end).

So here is my personal perspective on terrorism. It began by being at the receiving end of German bombs and rockets like the doodlebug as a child in the Second World War: a form of governmental terrorism that became known as unlimited or total warfare. Then as a reporter, I first encountered non-governmental terrorism fifty years or more ago in the Middle East. At that time, worldwide terrorism of the sort experienced these days did not exist, even though there had been plenty of terror before, not least of which was the assassin's shot in Sarajevo in 1914 that precipitated the 1914–18 Great War.

During the course of that conflict, there emerged the Balfour Declaration of November 1917. From that date, seeds were sown for the present-day instability and terror in the Middle East. In a letter (the "Balfour Declaration") that British Foreign Secretary Arthur Balfour sent to a leading representative of British Jewry, Lord Rothschild, support was promised for the establishment in Palestine of a national home for the Jewish people, on the understanding that "nothing shall be done which may prejudice the civil and religious rights of existing non-Jewish communities in Palestine".

How remote and empty that sounds today!

After Arabs rejected the declaration, blood began to flow as early as 1920, with Arabs killing five Jews and injuring another two hundred in Palestine. However, contemporary Islamic terrorism of the ISIL or al-Qaeda kind developed fairly slowly compared with the calculated and organised terrorism of pioneer twentieth-century terrorist practitioners of the skills of slaughter. Those experts included Irish republicans and nationalists with the IRA as well as Zionists with the Stern Gang and Irgun Zvai Leumi. Such groups received, from quite early on, considerable and special support from Irish American and Jewish American voters in the United States. Their support was indirect. It came in the shape of sympathetic propaganda for the cause of the terrorists and as hard cash for those campaigning for the terrorist cause, raised in America through such organisations as, for example, in the Irish case, Noraid.

With such international backing and sympathy from influential groups, well-organised terrorists had no hesitation in putting to practical use Lenin's maxim: "The object of terrorism is to terrorise."

The influence of Catholic nationalist Ireland in America has been emphasised by Sir Christopher Meyer, British ambassador in Washington from 1997 to 2003 in the run-up to 9/11 and the Iraq War. He is a man I dealt with on a daily basis for some time, and I have great respect for his intelligence and professionalism as a diplomatist. I first met him in Moscow, when he was with the British Embassy, and then later, when he was head of the news department at the Foreign Office.

In his controversial and compellingly candid book, *DC Confidential*, he stresses the clout of the Irish lobby in America: "Only Jewish America had a tighter grip on American politics."

It is depressing to recall that both Irish and Zionist terrorism against Britain continued to be conducted during the Second World War. Zionist killers assassinated Lord Moyne, British minister of state, in Cairo in 1944, their murderousness at least being explicable, to some extent, because of their desperation for a homeland for Jews amidst growing realisation that Jews were being systematically exterminated in Germany.

No such mitigatory considerations, however, applied to the IRA in Ireland, where nobody (so far as anyone was aware) was systematically exterminating the Irish. The IRA, though, was so fanatical that significant members did not hesitate to ally themselves with Nazi Germany. Thus in one particular way, Irish terrorists were worse than the Zionist variety. They actually chose to cosy up to the Nazis, so fierce was their detestation of England. Old Englishmen like me recall how shocked we were when, at the end of the Second World War, a man born in New York who thrice became prime minister of the Irish Republic, Eamon de Valera, signed an official German condolences book upon the death of Hitler.

That was bad enough, but much worse was what one Irish writer, Kevin Myers, has called "the IRA's formal alliance with the Nazis". Specifically detailing an example, Myers, in January 2005, told the story of an IRA man, Sean Russell, "a collaborator who died on board a U-boat as he travelled to Ireland to foment a pro-Nazi rising in 1941". In the 1950s, the IRA put up a statue to his memory in Dublin, a work that was destroyed over the Christmas holiday of 2004 by people described by Myers as "leftist vandals". Eighteen months earlier, in 2003, the IRA's political front organisation, Sinn Fein, had held a rally at the statue to "pay homage to a Quisling who would be reviled anywhere else in Europe".

So much for IRA terrorism as seen by an Irishman whose bluntness reportedly led in December 2004 to his regular column in the *Irish Times* being dropped because he had made the suggestion, apparently unwelcome to his appeasement-minded editors, that the biggest bank robbery ever staged in Ireland had been the work of the IRA. The editors looked a bit silly when the Irish police chief and others soon confirmed the unpalatable suggestion as the truth. It is difficult to resist the conclusion that, until recently anyway, Irish republican terrorism appeared to have paid off over the years.

The IRA's wartime links with Nazi Germany have always contrasted strikingly with the reluctant wartime involvement, on Nazi Germany's side, of an unlucky Scandinavian country from where I sometimes found myself filing or broadcasting dispatches: Finland. The post-war gains of the Irish, compared with the post-war losses of the Finns, must be somewhat galling for the Finns.

They earned nothing from their resistance to Soviet invaders of their country in the bitter "Winter War" of the late 1930s and early 1940s, when I remember as a boy seeing newsreel pictures of ghostly, white-clad Finnish ski troops gliding through dark forests to bring the Red Army to a juddering halt. Admired though the Finns were for standing up to Stalin's bullying, defending themselves successfully and alone, they nevertheless found themselves compelled, willy-nilly, to be an ally of Hitler when he later invaded Russia.

The result was that the Finns were deprived by the Soviets of large parts of Finnish territory at the end of the Second World War, brutally punished for an alliance imposed upon them by events. To Finns, whose countrymen resisted totalitarian Russia and who lost out by being on the wrong side, allied with Germany through no choice of their own, it must seem unjust that Irish republicans who not only embraced terrorism but also allied themselves with Nazism have profited so much. The phrase about the "luck of the Irish" must have a somewhat sour meaning in Finland.

Far away from Finland, Israel, or Ireland, across the Atlantic, Americans committed in various ways to the Irish republican or Zionist causes have included many prominent people. They have included the Kennedy family (sympathetic to Irish republicans) and Jewish newspaper owners, television bosses, and Hollywood magnates who have never concealed their Israeli sympathies. Although the terrorist groups were never openly backed, occasionally sympathy was publicly expressed for them, and I recall one occasion that attracted headlines during the last days of the old British-administered League of Nations mandate in Palestine.

This was after British soldiers were killed following a Zionist attack. A well-known American Jewish playwright and film producer chose the moment to pronounce that he had experienced a "holiday in his heart". Zionist terrorists not only blew up the King David Hotel in Jerusalem in 1946, viewing it as a military target, but also they assassinated, in 1948, the United Nations mediator on Palestine, the Swedish diplomatist and nephew of King Gustav V, Count Bernadotte.

Well, having experienced themselves what happens when terrorism is unleashed, perhaps Americans (and in particular Irish and Jewish New Yorkers) might be less enthusiastic in future about backing terrorist groups describing themselves as "freedom fighters'.

Of course, Irish terrorists perpetrated a series of publicity-motivated atrocities, ranging from the Brighton attempt on the life of Mrs Thatcher to coldly targeted high-profile murders such as the assassination in Ireland of Lord Mountbatten, in a spectacular display of Irish republican inhospitality. This deeply affected his kinsman, the Prince of Wales, just as indiscriminate mass murder in Omagh affected the friends and relatives of the dead. As for the Hyde Park explosion, where terrorists blew up not only military bandsmen but their horses as well, that has always seemed to me to have been a particularly unnatural sort of thing for Irishmen to have done, given their renowned love for the beasts.

All of these excursions into horror, though, were but a prelude to what the world has since witnessed in the way of international multiple murder in a growing number of countries all over the world. The list will probably grow and there will almost certainly continue to be sympathisers with the terrorist cause, if not for the terrorists.

In addition, there is often criticism of countermeasures taken by the authorities, especially when suggestions emerge of such countermeasures getting out of hand. In short, if terrorism is adopted as a method of furthering a cause and people who support that cause condone the terrorism, then it is no great surprise if internationally agreed rules of war as defined by the Geneva Conventions are themselves eroded.

So the American and British armed forces and governments in particular have come under fire because of alleged brutality. Such behaviour is, of course, inexcusable in a civilised society, but critics attacking governments who as a general rule at least try to observe the Geneva Conventions seem frequently to overlook that these selfsame Geneva rules are routinely ignored by the habitual practitioners of terrorism as a weapon; in other words, terrorists. The BBC has come under heavy fire because of its apparent reluctance to employ that word "terrorist" in news bulletins, preferring in a mealy-mouthed manner to describe the terrorists as, say, "militants", "dissidents", "activists", or some other euphemism. I find it hard to understand the reasoning behind the corporation's reluctance to speak plain English when terrorists with the objective of terrorising have carried out an act of terrorism.

Still, even if prisoners accused or suspected of terrorism are contemptuous of other people's lives and rights and disregard any of their own legal responsibilities, it is a fair bet that they will know about their own rights. If they do not, their lawyers will – not to mention the campaigners whose vocation it is to ensure that such rights are respected even though corresponding responsibilities are brushed aside.

What does a concept such as "international law" actually mean to men and women who are willing to commit suicide while murdering many others and to butchers prepared to hack off the heads of their hostages on camera? Rules of war? Geneva Conventions? United Nations? Such things are academic to the genuine terrorist.

Although as a fairly worldly old journalist, I am habituated to remaining as cool and objective as correspondents of my day were expected to be (and, broadly speaking, still are expected to be), I have nevertheless been unable to acquire the air of relaxed, almost insouciant, detachment from hideous events which I have sometimes observed in professional diplomatists and senior civil servants. Many must be raised on a Foreign Office textbook exemplar whose behaviour I heard Edward Heath describe once when he was prime minister.

According to him, the long-departed diplomatic paragon was a British consul in the Sudan (but not General Gordon in Khartoum) during the Mahdist uprising in Queen Victoria's reign. As his end in the shape of a murderous rabble swiftly approached him, the consul busied himself by sending his last message, signing himself off with due but slightly amended formal courtesies to the Secretary of State: "The mob is now breaking down my door and I remain, sir, your (about-to-be late) humble, obedient servant."

Such coolness is admirable, and I have been impressed upon occasion by the iron nerve displayed by Her Majesty's representatives overseas. For example, I remember in particular the British consul in what was then the Portuguese colony of Macao, Norman Ions, in 1967, during the so-called "Cultural Revolution" in China.

He refused to bow or kneel down to images of Mao Tse Tung when his consulate was besieged by a mob of Chinese intent upon humiliating him. He was lucky to get away unhurt to Hong Kong, as were my cameraman and I when we too were more or less chased out of Macao back to the British colony (as it then still was).

I have also sometimes been amused by the dry, sometimes black, humour on display from officials, no matter what the prevailing crisis or situation. An instance that leaps to mind came after the 1973 coup in Lisbon that swiftly resulted in the collapse of the Portuguese Empire in Africa. There I had become closely acquainted with the struggle for independence (complete, of course, with the deployment of terrorism) in countries such as Angola and Mozambique. The collapse in Lisbon and inevitable independence for the Portuguese territories in Africa neighbouring the white-controlled Republic of South Africa and what was then the illegal Republic of Rhodesia (now Zimbabwe) undermined the governments of both of those states.

Rhodesian leader Ian Smith flew to Pretoria to confer with South African leader John Vorster. As the BBC Africa correspondent, I covered the encounter. While the two leaders had a private talk in one room, I had a chat in the next room with Jack Gaylard, who for years was Rhodesia's cabinet secretary. I have never forgotten his succinct and entirely accurate summing-up of a major political development that was to affect the lives of millions: "The Portuguese really have uncorked the bottle!"

And so they had.

CHAPTER 4

Age Two: "The Whining Schoolboy"

Today's headlines display much controversy about higher education's quality or lack of quality and the cost – for example, university charges, loans, and differences within the United Kingdom between what is to be paid by English, Scottish, Welsh, and Northern Irish students.

On a much lower educational level (with which I am more familiar, never myself having been to university), one continuing and typical row could be described in both journalistic and botanical terms as a "hardy annual", namely should naughty (or "whining") children be smacked?

Another endless argument is about the best (often devious) way to get a child into a good school and avoid a sink school. Yet another is about the allegedly weak teaching of basic subjects like reading, writing, arithmetic, history, geography, physics, chemistry, and languages. More issues on the educational agenda include the desirability of familiarity with computers and information technology and the importance of equality between the sexes and races. In addition, occasionally a news item is published disapproving the use of a word describing a toy familiar to the children of my generation, the golliwog.

Such controversies are all included on my list of unfinished stories, though not all date back – thank God! – as far as my childhood. My formal education has been limited, but I have mostly pleasant memories of it. My first school, to which I was taken by my mother at the age of five, was what was then known as the village infant school. I cannot recall whether I crept there "like snail, unwillingly", but I think not, because I enjoyed it. For instance, I remember with pleasure how, on cold winter days, all of us children would take a potato to school and, during the morning break from lessons, place it, wrapped in greaseproof paper or sometimes just in its jacket of skin, onto or actually into the coal-burning stove in our classroom. We would gather round the stove and eat our hot potatoes as we each drank our one-third pint of school milk. It was wonderful then; now it seems like a Winter's Dream.

We were from hard-up working-class families, but none of us realised we were living in the depressed 1930s until we were told this much later. I remember with fondness my first schoolteacher, a spinster lady long since dead, like the description itself of "spinster lady". "Spinster" is a word rarely seen anywhere these days, and "lady", I read in 2000, had been outlawed as "offensive" in a policy document produced by academics for Stockport College, Greater Manchester.

Anyhow, my spinster lady teacher was called Miss Griffiths. When she whacked us five-year-olds and six-year-olds across the knuckles with a wooden ruler for misbehaviour, we were not at that moment overly fond of her, but generally we knew we had deserved it. We hesitated before we misbehaved again. None of us dreamed of complaining to our parents about the whack, for fear of getting another one at home just to reinforce the teacher's treatment. In those far-off days, it would have been unthinkable that any parent would take action of any kind, whether legal or thuggish, against a school or teacher for the sort of discipline that was administered.

By the time we were seven or eight, most of us could read, write, do our sums and recognise authority when we came up against it. What did not happen then but is reported to be quite common now is the deliberate practice of violence against and victimisation of teachers by unruly pupils and their parents. A survey published in February 2007 by a charity, the Teacher Support Network, claimed that pupils had attacked no fewer than half of the teachers questioned. Covering 450 teachers, the survey revealed that as concerns grew over thuggery levels in schools, 92 per cent of the teachers had been verbally abused and that 49 per cent had been the victims of physical attack. More than one-third said personal property had been defaced or stolen and more than one-third said they had been forced to take time off work due to injuries, including stabbings with scissors and nails. One quarter of those saying that they were victims of physical violence had been attacked by pupils brandishing weapons. Four teachers had been threatened with a gun.

What a picture! It followed complaints earlier by the Association of Teachers and Lecturers, and the National Union of Teachers, about malicious attacks on teachers' property, especially their cars. Several cases were reported in which teachers had found, waiting outside their homes, aggressive pupils, accompanied by mother or father, with the specific purpose of intimidation. According to the general secretary of the National Association of Head Teachers, Mr David Hart, in 2001, some of the "more appalling pupils" of one headmistress had defied a ban on mobile telephones being brought into their school and had then proceeded to employ the mobiles to telephone their parents from the classroom to complain about the conduct of a teacher before the teacher concerned was even aware that a complaint was being made.

It was estimated in 2001 that 350,000 pupils under sixteen possessed mobile phone and schools were finding it hard to enforce bans on them. In 2005, with children receiving them at the reported average age of eight, it must have become even harder! Sadly, Mr Hart observed the following: "The simple, basic fact is that there are too many 'parents from hell' that delight in making the lives of heads and their staffs as difficult as possible. Too many parents are steeped in the 'blame culture' and blame schools for their own inadequacies."

This conjures up an unappetising spectacle of at least some aspects of state education in the twenty-first century. Many reasons are adduced for it apart from the "blame culture". These include an alleged deterioration in teaching standards, an alleged decline in parental responsibility, a rise in truancy, the influence of low-grade television programmes, and the easy availability of curious material on the Internet. The charge is also made of excessive interference in education both by the state and by people known as "educationists". Many of those are reported to be "ideologically motivated" (although by what, such reports rarely say). Highly publicised rows are common about examination standards, university admissions, graduate loans, and so on. The alleged deterioration of educational standards, like the alleged shortcomings of the National Health Service, compose the daily content of newspaper columns and radio and TV news bulletins.

Less often mentioned as a possible reason for bad behaviour in schools (as well, I suppose, as in the home) is the widespread abolition of, and disapproval of, corporal punishment. However, a government-backed study showed in 2007 that some parents were calling for the return of the cane to restore order in the classroom. Families expressed the view that discipline had deteriorated since corporal punishment was abolished some twenty years earlier, head teachers in state schools having been allowed to cane unruly pupils until 1986.

Such signs of rethinking about corporal punishment emerged in a study undertaken by Mori, commissioned by the Department for Education and Skills to conduct eight discussion groups with members of the public in London and Manchester to investigate understanding of school reforms. It emerged that the key issue for the majority of parents was discipline, something of course which my first teacher, Miss Griffiths, knew and understood without the involvement of discussion groups or an educational department.

Yet Miss Griffiths might have been sacked these days, and possibly prosecuted, for alleged brutality or cruelty. Despite the findings of the Mori inquiry, many, if not most, modern parents, together with teachers, reject outright the well-known injunction by Samuel "Hudibras" Butler: "Then spare the rod, and spoil the child." Even more do they dislike the ancient warning in the Proverbs of Solomon: "He that spareth his rod hateth his son."

Well, in my childhood, both the teachers and the parents were more inclined towards Old Testament discipline than they are today. When the straightforward methods of Miss Griffiths failed to achieve their aim, which was rare, we were dispatched to the headmaster to be caned (or, later in senior school, to taste either the cane or the rope's end).

I do not recall either my school chums or myself ever really resenting this; it was accepted as normality. However, the very idea of punishment has been under attack from some quarters for a long time. Gone are the days when it would be taken for granted that crime would be followed by punishment. Arguments over the best way to deal with criminals and confusion over the law itself are baffling for most "normal people" (to use an "unacceptable" Stockport College phrase). Clarity of the law is important for continuance of a law-abiding society because most civilised men and women support a just law when they understand it. Not much can be clearer than the magisterial simplicity of the judicial advice inscribed over the entrance to the Old Bailey: "Defend the Children of the Poor and Punish the Wrongdoer."

As a sometimes naughty boy, I learned early in my life that wrong-doing would be followed by retribution. In later years, as an apprentice junior reporter on the local newspaper doing the news-seeking rounds, I became quite close to Miss Griffiths; I began to realise how the old girl, by then an ancient spinster lady indeed, had genuinely devoted her life to attempting to educate and thus to better the prospects of scruffy urchins like myself. Teaching in those days was an honoured profession, and it had not become what these days it sometimes appears to be: an unloved, difficult job in which theories of education and multiculturalism are endlessly argued over, set against a background of hooliganism, crime, trade union moans, and class war.

Real war was declared in 1939, when I was still at that village school. However, my memories of the word "war" dated back to even earlier years, far preceding the time when war, in all its varying forms, especially terrorism, became such an established feature of the twentieth and, so far, twenty-first centuries.

The first war I remember being talked about at home was, of course, the First World War, the Great War (in which my father fought).

Then into our consciousness came a new war, outside Europe, in what was then called Abyssinia and is now Ethiopia. For we children at Durrington Infants' School, it was an excuse for a game that we played, "Italians and Abyssinians". There was no television, but we knew from the wireless (as we then called the radio), the newspapers, and above all from our parents that an Italian dictator had invaded this African kingdom. His name was Benito Mussolini, and he had a funny title, "Il Duce", which sounded something like "The Duchy" and which meant "The Leader".

Well, Ethiopia was a country I got to know first-hand later in life, but even in my childhood, it had a particular connotation in sunny Sussex because Emperor Haile Selassie lived there for a time in exile during those desperate days when he was trying to save his country. He was installed in an impressive Worthing Hotel, Warnes, which for a long time afterwards displayed over its front door the imperial Ethiopian coat of arms.

The hotel has since been knocked down, and I have often wondered what became of the coat of arms. The failure of the old League of Nations to halt Mussolini's African empire building passed beyond the knowledge or understanding of the Durrington infants, but we could all sense the tension as our parents became ever more obviously worried while the Second World War loomed threateningly into prospect. Meanwhile, our games continued.

If we were "Italian" during playtime, we ran around the school playground with our arms stretched out, being aeroplanes dropping bombs. If we were "Abyssinian", we pranced about as fierce tribesmen, or "Fuzzy-Wuzzies", as we called them in Kiplingesque style. Later, when the Italians became our wartime enemies, they became known as "Eyeteyes", or "Wops", both of which appellations had deliberately contemptuous tones about them. This, though, was certainly not applicable to Rudyard Kipling's "Fuzzy-Wuzzy":

> So 'ere's to you, Fuzzy-Wuzzy, at your 'ome in the Soudan;
> You're a pore benighted 'eathen but a first-class fightin' man ...
> An' 'ere's to you, Fuzzy-Wuzzy, with your 'ayrick 'ead of 'air—
> You big black boundin' beggar – for you broke a British square!

We had no inhibitions about racism; we did not know what racism was. Many of us possessed and cherished not only teddy bears but also toys which to my grandchildren and great-grandchildren are quite unknown because their production has long since ended as they are generally viewed these days as offensive and definitely as incorrect in political and racial terms. These toys were called golliwogs.

One character, Gilbert the Golliwog, created by bestselling children's story writer Enid Blyton, had to be dropped following accusations of racism. So was Ms Rap, who, like Miss Griffiths in my own early years, was a teacher who used to dish out raps as corporal punishment.

New Blyton characters were created while originals disappeared and others were reportedly "refashioned". This apparently was supposed to maintain political and moral acceptability, not to mention the commercial sales, of Blyton's works.

Other favourite books among children in my young days have vanished altogether.

Because of such changes, my own racially unaware and possibly naive generation began to wonder, as we grew older, if we ourselves should feel guilty about having possessed golliwogs. However, I for one have no regrets for cuddling my sister's golliwog in precisely the same way I cuddled my teddy bear.

The point is, we loved our gollies. We did not use the word "golliwog" as a term of abuse. Despite the more or less general thumbs down on golliwogs these days, it is nevertheless interesting to note that memories of them are still alive. Toy collectors or connoisseurs still find them desirable, whether for commercial or other reasons. I have read advertisements in local newspapers seeking the purchase of golliwog badges that were produced for the Robertson jam and marmalade manufacturers who, as a sales gimmick during my childhood, offered them for acquisition by children. Given the inflated price which a teddy bear can now attract, I should not be surprised if one day the unpleasant racial connotations now attached to the unfortunate toy called a golliwog might become less objectionable as popular sensitivities decrease about skin colour. The actual colourful aspect of such toys, plus financial considerations, might come to play a part in any toy collector's calculation, so it conceivably could be only a matter of time before rare old golliwogs are offered, like teddy bears, at auction for thousands of pounds.

At what stage the word "golliwog" became employed as an insult I do not know; but it undoubtedly happened. Whereas I have affectionate memories of my sister's happy black and cuddly toy golliwog, others have anything but kindly remembrances for either the word "golliwog" or for golliwog badges. One is Tessa Sanderson, Olympic champion javelin thrower. In 2001, the *Observer* reported that she was subject to racial abuse throughout her school life, and she complained that guys would call her things like "coon" and "golliwog". She added, "In those days, golliwogs were on the jam jars, and we black kids hated them."

A similar complaint, from model Naomi Campbell, was reported in the *Daily Telegraph* in 2004. A newspaper fashion team had asked her if she minded if she was "painted darker" for a picture, and she replied that she was a model, "not some golly on a jam jar".

I sympathise with both women because they obviously felt they were at the receiving end of deliberate denigration. Both Tessa Sanderson and

Naomi Campbell are a good deal younger than I am, though, and I was rather surprised when I read their references to golliwog badges. This was because I would have thought that the two of them were too young to remember when the marmalade makers still produced such badges (although I have no idea exactly when that ended).

If I am correct and the two cannot actually remember the badges, it would mean that a folk memory about them lives on in the minds of people at the receiving end of racist insults. It is all very depressing for an old golliwog lover like me.

The fact that as a boy I loved my sister's golly as an individual toy does not mean that as a man I have any sympathy for racists. However, I resent the way that anti-racist campaigners have succeeded in virtually outlawing golliwogs in the same way they drove into oblivion *The Black and White Minstrel Show*, which gave millions of people so much musical enjoyment. These days, legendary singers like Al Jolson, dressed as a black minstrel while he sang "Swanee", simply could not exist.

I also resent the way some campaigners have condemned the innocent pleasure of reading books that children of my generation enjoyed, as a pursuit inducing attitudes verging upon the criminal towards people of another race.

I feel the same resentment towards feminists who make hostile assumptions about male attitudes towards females. I don't want to be told that the adventure stories that I read with such passion and excitement in my tender years, by writers like John Buchan and "Sapper", with heroes like Bulldog Drummond, are racist and corrupting. Because I have read and enjoyed such books, I am left with the feeling that perhaps I really have contracted some sort of mysterious non-medical disease called "racism".

Worse, I wonder if I need some sort of treatment for something that I feel I don't actually have. No wonder I am confused! Judging by comments from old friends who long ago also absorbed such "infra dig" books, I am not alone in my discomfort. I reject assumptions that people are racist without wanting to be racist or without knowing that they are racist. Most of the racists I have met over many years in many countries are obviously so and make no bones about where they stand. They include white haters of blacks; black haters of whites; Zionists who hate Arabs and Muslims; and Islamic fundamentalists who hate Jews, Christians, the West in general and emancipated women in particular. The list is endless.

Fears that people are being pressured to become linguistically or racially hypersensitive with the development of what the venerable feudalist columnist Peter Simple long ago described as the race relations industry may all too easily have some substance. For instance, that was exemplified by an ominous reported threat from Stockport College as to the sort of people it might or might not employ, depending upon the political correctitude of their language.

Apart from the unwelcome word "lady", the academic censors of Stockport reportedly disliked "gentleman" (like "lady", it has class implications); "queer" (not unless approved of and employed by homosexuals, apparently regarded as etymological authorities on the word); "postman" and "chairman" (sexist); "mad", "crazy", and "manic" (offensive to anyone with mental health problems); and perhaps the most ludicrous proposed censorship example of the lot, the word "history".

Some writers and philosophers have advanced a dubious proposition that there is either no such thing as history or even that history itself has ended, but apparently some view the very word as sexist. With what word would it be replaced? Herstory? Humanstory? Huwomanstory?

Also reportedly disapproved of by the would-be censors as inappropriate were phrases like "man in the street" (what about "woman in the street"?); "slaving over a hot stove" (minimises the horror of the slave trade); "normal couple" (what is normal?); and "taking the mickey" (anti-Irish). The whole reported rigmarole was quite comic, except that it had a sinister undertone.

To ensure that language rules were followed, the college, with fifteen thousand students from sixteen and up, indicated that it proposed to "make it a condition of service and admission" that employees and students adhered to its policy of not risking offence. The ensuing publicity and controversy over what was described as "unacceptable language" followed an earlier row a few days beforehand, when a job centre in Walsall had refused to accept an advertisement in which an employer sought a "hard-working" recruit. The manager of the job centre had apparently felt that this could offend the disabled. Eventually, the manager was overruled and the advertisement was accepted after the intervention of the man who was then the education and employment secretary, David Blunkett.

Amazingly, a similar case cropped up again four years later in Hampshire, where, in 2004, a job centre reportedly refused an advertisement also seeking a "hard worker".

The explanation given this time was that such an advertisement "discriminated against people who were not industrious". It would appear that any employer wanting a hard worker must not say so at a job centre.

Perhaps the employer should first consult the Oxford *Dictionary of Euphemisms*, a publication for our times which tells people "how not to say what you mean".

Attitudes towards race, like attitudes towards words, are sometimes truly weird.

Clifford Longley, a veteran commentator on church affairs, brought a worrying instance to light not so long ago. Analysing a publication by the Institute of Economic Affairs entitled "Political Correctness and Social Work", he cited a case from the IEA report. "A mixed-race couple were turned down for the adoption of a mixed-race child by social workers, because the couple said they had not experienced racism themselves. The dogmas of political correctness, or to give it its technical name, 'anti-oppressive practice', said that the whole of society was racist, but this fact was invisible to, or denied by, racists. Ergo someone who did not think the whole of society was racist must themselves be racist. Adoption request refused."

I suppose I am one of those who find "invisible" the alleged "fact" that "the whole of society" is racist. To that extent, I suppose further that I "deny" what is presented as a "fact". I certainly doubt it.

What I do not understand in my increasingly wide field of incomprehension about contemporary existence is why should such a questioning attitude result in the questioner being labelled as racist? Andrew Alexander, another commentator, suggested a few years ago that a National Paranoia Board should be set up to replace existing race relations bodies. Such a body would inevitably open up fresh opportunities for those seeking lucrative quango appointments.

Although we have yet to see the establishment of a Paranoia Board (and this would not surprise me) government plans were announced in

2004 to replace the racial equality commission. Together with two other commissions, those for disability rights and for equal opportunities, it was to be subsumed into a single commission, the "Equality and Human Rights Commission", to fight "all forms of discrimination". There were immediate squawks from civil service unions about how it was to be funded. Possibly job losses were feared. However, the Equality and Human Rights Commission duly emerged.

The seemingly endless expansion of ill-defined, but highly paid, public posts advertised in the *Guardian* and elsewhere might indeed have been one of the reasons the government was trying to save some money and to streamline, so to speak, the bureaucratic infrastructure of not only Peter Simple's well-entrenched "Race Relations Industry" but also the growth of two other burgeoning industries, the "Grievance Industry" and the "Indignation Industry." Apart from those successfully claiming to be the victims of unfair discrimination, the principal beneficiaries of such developing modern phenomena appear to be lawyers and civil servants.

The fact is that a lot of money could be saved for the government – and therefore, in theory, for the taxpayer – if discrimination commissions were abolished and laws already existing against boorish behaviour and hooliganism were more rigorously applied. This is plain from the size of the salaries advertised for the jobs on offer. As long ago as 1999, the job of chair to the Commission for Racial Equality was advertised as "£82,000 pa (or pro rata)". In addition, the deputy chair pulled in £51,115 pa at that time.

Mere commissioners willing to commit themselves "to a minimum of twenty days per annum, including attendance at regular meetings during normal office hours" would be offered "a daily fee of £142 plus expenses". What did their twenty-days-a-year job entail? "Commissioners are responsible for ensuring that the Commission is effectively discharging its statutory duties. They will consider a range of strategic and policy issues, making choices as to the areas of discrimination on which the Commission should concentrate and the methods used to achieve the agreed objective." That objective, set out at the head of the advertisement, was defined by the home secretary of the time, Jack Straw. It said the following: "Racial equality has to become a reality. We must strive to create a society where every individual, regardless of colour, creed, or race, has the same opportunities and respect as his or her neighbour."

Few reasonable people would dispute those sentiments. But many would, and do, challenge some of the controversial "methods" employed. The defined objective is to achieve "racial equality", equality being a concept much beloved by mankind but something that in itself is not easily defined and which remains an elusive attribute. The *Concise Oxford Dictionary*, rather unhelpfully, states merely that equality is "the state of being equal". Referring then to the word "equal", I read the following: "Being the same in quantity, size, degree, value, or status; evenly or fairly balanced".

Evenly or fairly balanced, eh? Thus (say, perhaps in the eyes of a keen equality commissioner) I should have referred above (in the interests of being evenly or fairly balanced) not only to mankind but to womankind as well – or possibly to humankind. This, I venture to suggest at the risk of outraging any ultra-feminists, would be verbose, semantic nonsense.

Apart from the sheer clumsiness of adding extra words (or using cumbersome words such as "humankind") to the definition of desirable but somewhat amorphous objectives, I would argue anyway that such extra words are often redundant. Despite years of politically motivated public indoctrination about the use of language, most people still take it for granted (I suppose) that when anybody refers to mankind, this includes womankind too.

Personal thoughts about the use of a plain, universal word like "mankind" have been triggered off in my own admittedly somewhat limited mind as the predictable result of publicity about the sustained endeavours of equality commissions and commissioners. Somehow the whole expensive and bureaucratic exercise seems comically remote from 1776 and the fervent words of the American Declaration of Independence, still echoing around the world and down the years: "We hold these truths to be self-evident, that all men are created equal."

Equally far removed from the administrative complications of a commission are the rousing words of the French national slogan: "Liberty! Equality! Fraternity!"

At least two of the concepts enshrined in that revolutionary war cry – liberty and equality – are uneasy companions. Long ago, Sir Isaiah Berlin summed up the incompatibility: "Liberty is liberty; not equality or fairness or justice or human happiness or a quiet conscience."

One of the contemporary methods of trying to bring about equality is what Andrew Alexander (the prophet of the National Paranoia Board) has described as "brainwashing and censorship". He reported in 1999 that in a BBC books programme, the political correspondent of the corporation at the time, John Sergeant, had said he was "repelled" by the language in Evelyn Waugh's novel *Scoop* (another of my favourite books).

According to Alexander, among words which Sergeant found "completely, utterly unacceptable" were "Negro" and "native". A fellow contributor to the programme, Hunter Davies, agreed. Alexander commented, "One really wonders how such people manage to read anything more than five years old without a bottle of smelling salts at hand. Can they tackle Shakespeare or Dickens without swooning away out of shock?" He stated, "Negro is a perfectly proper word to describe a race"; and as for "native", well, "it means native, for heaven's sake." Alexander concluded, "When people whose trade is language do not evidently know the meaning of common words, one can only despair." I could not agree more.

Writing apparently more in sorrow than in anger, Alexander noted that he regarded John Sergeant as "normally a sensible sort of chap", another comment with which I would agree from my own memories of John as a BBC colleague, before he went on to work elsewhere – to write an amusing book titled *Give Me Ten Seconds* and to become a television dancer!

Alexander's essential point was right: what is wrong with the employment of words like "Negro" and "native"? Are they also doomed to be classed in the dictionary, like the word "nigger", as offensive? Addiction to political correctness has the effect of encouraging what Alexander called the "grievance industry" among ethnic minorities; or what another commentator, Minette Marrin, has dubbed the "indignation industry". Whatever the labels, there is little doubt of the existence of the industries. They are not confined to racial issues but extend to other areas of existence.

Feminist attitudes, for example, are sometimes extreme. Like many men, I am alarmed and affected by this, to the extent that when I learned that even the *William* books (written by female author Richmal Crompton) were being sanitised, I almost collapsed into hysterical laughter. My immediate reaction was that the detestable but fictional girl character, Violet Elizabeth Bott ("I'll thcweam and thcweam until I'm thick!"), must by now be grown up and doubtless presiding bossily over some organisation dealing with discrimination. That would undoubtedly enable her to "get her own back" on the outlaw William. It would be the sort of thing that he and his sympathisers, like myself, would expect.

The very word "discrimination" has taken on a disapproving shade, and it is hard to recall that when I was young, being described as a discriminating kind of person was regarded as a compliment. The meaning of the word seems to have changed.

So has the context in which it is usually used. The truth is that a lot of the contemporary argument over race, homosexuality, smoking, drinking, women, animals, fur farming, and fox hunting is, for old reporters, simply old hat. Some of the news reports I read today, or listen to on radio, or hear on TV cause me to turn to my wife and say something like, "What's new in that? I covered that in nineteen forty-nine." She will reply with something like, "Yes, dear." If, though, I hazard an unfashionable opinion on a subject about which she feels strongly, and on which she disagrees with me, she will say something like, "We can't all be Genghis Khan, dear."

I interpret this as a put-down, but she knows that as I grumble on, like Alf Garnett, quite often I have a point.

Woolly thinking about race well preceded the establishment of commissions on equality. As a young man, I was always puzzled by the aversion that some of my otherwise quite intelligent friends displayed towards Rudyard Kipling, wrongly accusing him of being a racist. In support of their race theme, they always quoted at me his unforgettable lines from "The Ballad of East and West":

> *Oh, East is East, and West is West, and never the twain shall meet,*
> *Till Earth and Sky stand presently at God's great Judgement Seat.*

What they never quoted, though, were Kipling's next two lines, illustrating that Kipling was the antithesis of a racist:

> *But there is neither East nor West, Border, nor Breed, nor Birth,*
> *When two strong men stand face to face, tho' they come from*
> *the ends of the earth!*

What could be geographically, racially, educationally, or even theologically more equal than that? The truth is that they detested Kipling because he was a proud and unregenerate imperialist and they simply could not bring themselves to accept that an imperialist was not necessarily a racist, even though some imperialists might be so.

Racial sensitivities can surface in unexpected ways. Once I was unintentionally caught up in such a case. It involved the late Major Ronald Ferguson, father of the Duchess of York, always these days referred to in newspaper headlines as "Fergie". I felt personally guilty, and sorry for him as well, after he came under attack following an interview that he gave to me when his daughter became engaged in 1986 to Prince Andrew. It came just a few days before the actual announcement of the engagement, after which, as the BBC court correspondent of the time, I conducted an interview with the young couple themselves.

The engagement interview went off pleasantly enough, as did the earlier interview with Major Ferguson. I had driven to Windsor to meet him in the Guards Polo Club, which he was then more or less running. He had agreed to talk to me largely as the result of an old acquaintanceship dating back to the troubles of the 1950s and 1960s in Cyprus (troubles which remain with us today in the shape of a still-divided island).

His regiment, the Life Guards, had on one night during those disturbances extracted from difficulty a news photographer called Anthony Marshall and myself, both of us then working for the Daily Telegraph. We had come under crossfire between Greek Cypriots and Turkish Cypriots while driving through a military no man's land just outside Nicosia. We stopped the car, jumped out, and took refuge in a roadside ditch, trying every now and again to get back into the vehicle and drive off. But each time we tried to get into the car, the second we opened the door, the interior light went on and Cypriot weaponry went off. Bullets whistled above us and beside us, but we were unhurt. However, we were trapped until the crew of a Life Guards armoured personnel carrier of the United Nations peacekeeping force, having spotted our abandoned vehicle, materialised out of the dark.

A beam shone down onto us in the ditch, and a voice shouted, "What are you doing down there, John?" I offered a somewhat acerbic reply. The voice, appreciating both our predicament and my response to the question, laughingly invited us to sprint from the ditch and to hop into to the APC.

This we did, and the Life Guards gave us a personal and well-protected taxi trip back to safety in the Ledra Palace Hotel in Nicosia. From that moment of rescue, I became, and remain, a fan of the Household Cavalry, among whose young officers with whom I became friendly figured Ronald Ferguson.

Nearly half a century after that incident on the Isle of Aphrodite, where love has not always been the most distinguishing feature of existence, Major Ferguson and I met once more for the BBC interview. He talked well and honestly about his spirited daughter, showing himself proud of her various achievements, from her flying abilities to her horse-womanship. Among other things, he recalled her much-loved little black pony. The interview went well; it was broadcast by the BBC and was widely picked up and re-quoted all over the world.

Alas, Major Ferguson and I discovered quickly that we had unwittingly stirred up a hornet's nest of resentment and hatred. This was because he had mentioned, quite casually and factually, the name of the little black pony. This happened to have been "Nigger".

Not long afterwards, Major Ferguson rebuked me at a dinner party for my having undammed a flood of abuse and hate mail which had flowed in his direction. I was mortified. I apologised for not having thought of censoring the pony's name. I further elaborated upon my apology, explaining that it had not occurred to me that such a passing reference would offend people to such an extent that they felt they had to shower him with insults. I further explained that even if I had in fact thought of trying to edit out the pony's name, any censoring might not have been easy to implement because on getting back to the BBC, I had immediately handed the recording to the programme producer. Any suggestion of mucking about with its content would have had to be argued through, possibly against the opposition of the producer.

Perhaps, though, the producer would have edited "Nigger" out, just as some years later (in 2001) ITV did when it re-screened a 1954 film called *The Dam Busters*, based on the 1943 raid on the Ruhr dams. Anti-censorship campaigners criticised ITV for expunging from the film all mention of the name of another animal called "Nigger", this time the famous black Labrador dog owned by the leader of the raid, Wing Commander Guy Gibson. The actor who played Gibson reacted strongly about the censorship in an interview reported in January 2005 in the *Sunday Telegraph*:

> *Given that the F-word and C-word were used respectively 2,000 and 297 times in* Jerry Springer – the Opera *when it was broadcast on BBC 2 last weekend, the actor Richard Todd now wants just one word – used in all innocence – in his 1954 film* The Dam Busters *to be reinstated forthwith. That word is Nigger.*
>
> *"It is a historical fact that it was the name of the black Labrador that was owned by Guy Gibson," says Todd. "Since 2001, when the film has been shown in this country, the name of the dog is almost always overdubbed. This was done without reference to me or to the director of the film, Michael Anderson. The film is rightly regarded as a classic, and I don't see why people should be allowed to meddle with it. It is a typical example of applying the politically correct values of today on another time. No sensible person who sees the film could possibly take exception to the word in that context."*

ITV and Granada, responsible for ensuring that the film complied with broadcasting standards, have argued that they wanted to avoid offending viewers.

They cited recent research by broadcasting regulators suggesting that modern viewers regarded "nigger" as one of the most offensive words in the English language, which is probably true. Is that a strong enough reason, though, to airbrush out of history or of literature a word, a name or, say, a character such as Shakespeare's "Shylock"? Would the seeker of the payment of his debt of a "pound of flesh" be censored out of existence in *The Merchant of Venice* because Jewish sensitivities might be hurt?

Offensive it might be, but the word "nigger" still crops up every now and again, and some unfortunate person employing the word gets it in the neck. Union officials in particular tend to worry about the reaction to the use of the word among what one official described as "ethnic minorities in the profession we represent".

Not all people in ethnic minorities, however, are hypersensitive about tasteless, casual speech about their ethnic origin. Indeed, many of my chums who happen to be black (most of them journalists and TV or radio producers) are quite robust about peoples' attitudes towards their colour. I have congenial memories, for instance, of a black American top TV reporter who worked for the CBS network when I was in Washington for the BBC.

He and I were having a beer together one night when I complained to him that I felt sometimes that perhaps I was not quite left wing or liberal enough for BBC taste. I recounted to him what one producer had said when we were having an argument about something.

The producer had told me, only half jokingly, that he sometimes felt I was kept on the staff because whenever the BBC was accused of being too far to the left, the corporation could point at me and say, "What about Osman?" It was comparable to another quip made about me when I left the *Daily Telegraph* and a colleague (one of a number of left-wingers who worked on the *Telegraph* in those days) described me as "the only man who left the *Telegraph* because he thought it was getting dangerously liberal!"

The BBC producer about whom I was telling my CBS chum was somewhat given to leftist hyperbole, and I ended my story by recalling the producer's parting shot at me: "You're the house fascist!" My black colleague nodded sympathetically and then joked, "Well, what about me? I'm regarded in CBS as the house nigger!" We both choked with laughter on our beers.

Not many professional writers or broadcasters are fond of people or organisations wanting to be thought-controllers, speech-controllers, or news manipulators. I believe that millions of other people share our doubts. I was encouraged in this belief after the ITV Dam Busters act of censorship, when I read that there had been a string of complaints in the London Weekend Television duty log of viewers' calls, including one from a thirty-eight-year-old black man. He said he was more offended by the overdubbing of the dog's name than if it had been included. "This film is based on fact; you can't go changing history just to make white do-gooders feel better. Political correctness is a disease, and for a television company to succumb is pathetic."

My bet is that he was a black journalist concerned with facts and even more concerned about censorship of them. In a lifetime of journalism, I have known many courageous and effective black journalists, and my sympathy and support goes to those in places like Zimbabwe, Uganda, and elsewhere who try to soldier on doing whatever they can despite the appalling odds against them.

At the time of my embarrassment over the Ferguson interview, what I did not tell him, but what he probably knew anyway from long experience, was simply this: many if not most TV and radio producers, like many if not most newspaper editors, are more interested in controversy, rows, and scandals than they are in realising the exemplary spirit of the BBC motto: "Nation shall speak peace unto nation."

Emphasis is often placed on the sensational rather than the thoughtful. The nature of news itself involves coverage of controversial issues, of course; and much of the daily grist in the journalistic and broadcasting mills is legitimately a matter of genuine public interest. It is undeniable, however, that much published material, largely involving gossip of a personal nature, is sheer garbage and is relevant not to public interest but only to public titillation, sales figures, and broadcasting ratings.

This is not only the fault of the publishers, broadcasters, editors, and journalists who produce the material; it is also because of the strong complicity from consumers who appear to like it. If readers did not buy newspapers specialising in scandals, and if viewers and listeners did not switch on programmes broadcasting about scandals, the supply would quickly dry up. There is little sign of any slackening of appetite among consumers and precious little sign of scandals themselves drying up.

The struggle to preserve hard-won rights like the freedom of speech and of publishing, against authoritarian government as well as against the (generally commercial) abuse of those rights, seems set to be eternal.

There is, though, a relatively new restraint on the unscrupulous exploitation of the freedom of the press or of broadcasting: growing public awareness about meretricious political or commercial news manipulation. There has been a proliferation in recent years of newspaper coverage and analysis of what other publications are up to, plus daily criticisms of radio and television output. It all at least points to a growing awareness within the media of the reality and scale of the problem facing the media in dealing with the abuse of freedom by the media.

Christmas Greetings

Durrington School
1939

John Osman at Durrington Village Infants' School in 1939,
soon after the outbreak of the Second World War.

John Osman as a wartime evacuee: a photograph sent to my mother by the woman with whom I was billeted in Nottinghamshire during the evacuation of Worthing High School for Boys from the south coast of England, after the fall of France in 1940. I found this picture lovingly preserved among my mother's belongings after my mother's death in 1998 at the age of 94.

Even before the Second World War, we children at the village infants' school knew about the war in Africa between Italy and Abyssinia, as Ethiopia was then known. The Italians were expelled in 1941 by troops commanded by General Sir Alan Cunningham, here being received that year in Fiche by Emperor Haile Selassie when he was restored to his throne.

CHAPTER 5

Newspaper Boy and Press Appreciation

My bleak appreciation of the communications industry has been acquired the hard way, after a lifetime in it, dating back to when I was a newspaper delivery boy. Looking back to those far-off days at Durrington infant school, something happened then which directly changed my life and led me into my trade as a wordsmith.

At the age of eleven, I managed to pass what later became known as the Eleven Plus examination. My mother always talked with excessive maternal pride of my "winning the scholarship". This meant that instead of proceeding from the infant school to one of the local secondary modern schools, I could go to the local grammar school, Worthing High School for Boys (now transformed into Worthing College), which took fee-paying pupils as well as "scholarship boys". Some pupils from the high school, with its higher academic standards than the others, went on to university, whereas fewer pupils did so from the "secondary moderns". There was a snag, though, in my childhood scholastic success. If my parents accepted a place for me at the high school, they had to commit themselves to keeping me there until I was at least sixteen years old.

At that stage, I would be expected to take the old Cambridge School Certificate examination. However, if I went to the secondary modern school, I would be able to leave school and start work at the age of fourteen, then the official minimum school leaving age. My scholastic future became the cause of the only major dispute I can remember between my father and mother. She was determined that I would go to the high school;

he thought that I ought to get out to work as soon as possible at fourteen and earn some money. Overall, I was on my father's side.

Like my two sisters, I already knew the importance of money by the age of eleven. Like them, I not only did a newspaper round every morning before going to school; but on Saturday mornings, I also earned a "bob or two" by doing delivery rounds for the butcher or the grocer. What's more, I suppose I was no fonder of serious study than many boys are, although I much enjoyed reading. I was also perhaps a bit scared of being sent off to what I regarded as a "posh" school when my playmates were going on to other schools with the prospect of getting a job two years earlier than I would be able to do.

My mother won the argument. In 1939, she clinched it by managing to extract from the local authorities a grant for the enormous sum of five pounds. With this, she was enabled to buy me the high school uniform. If the grant had been refused, I would not have gone to the high school. This maternal feat impressed my father. He accepted defeat but continued to inquire about the alleged benefits of education "for the likes of us".

Looking back, in fact, the only specific item of educational advice that I can recall receiving from my father (apart from basic knowledge on vegetable gardening) emerged from experiences he had undergone while he was in the army.

His counsel came in the form of a terse geography lesson, offered while we were talking about India and his experiences there in the army in the days of the Raj before the Great War of 1914–18, when he sailed from India to fight in the Middle East against the Turks.

"The River Hooghly," said my father, "is the arsehole of the Orient, and Calcutta is eighty miles up it." Years later, when I found myself in that extraordinary city of enormous riches and hideous poverty, I understood more fully what he must have had in mind. A similar form of tactless education, this time on the political level, was at one point in his career reportedly experienced by Labour Party politician Mr Alan Johnson, who was the shadow chancellor in 2010. According to a newspaper report in September 2006, when Mr Johnson was offered the safe Labour seat of Hull West to enable him first to become an MP, he "nervously" inquired of a local official what the Yorkshire constituency was like. The newspaper reported: "He was told, 'The Humber is the a***hole of Britain, and Hull is eight miles up it.'"

Notwithstanding the newspaper's asterisks, the meaning and message was clear and much the same as my father's was. I cannot help wondering what Mr Johnson's own views are of the constituency. Obviously my Oxfordshire father's blunt way of speaking was still alive and well in Yorkshire over sixty years after his death.

Only once do I remember my father conceding that, as he put it, "There might be something after all in this education nonsense." The occasion came not long before his death, when he was already an extremely ill man, and a year or so after I had duly passed, at sixteen, the requisite "Cambridge School Certificate" examination "with Matriculation". That was in 1945, when, the day after leaving school, I started work as an apprenticed junior reporter for four newspapers produced by what was then the Southern Publishing Company: the now-defunct morning daily newspaper the *Sussex Daily News*; the now-defunct weekly the *Brighton and Hove Gazette*; another now-defunct weekly, the *Southern Weekly News*; and (hurrah!) the still-publishing Brighton *Argus*.

After a year or so of beginning to learn the job and (more immediately important in family eyes) of contributing what my father regarded as a "man's wage" of two pounds per week to the family budget, I suddenly found myself the winner of a journalistic national essay competition for junior journalists.

I was seventeen. I shall never forget the astonishment and delight in my father's eyes when he read the letter from the Chartered Institute of Journalists, dated 27 September 27 1946, from the general secretary. The letter was headed "Oliver Madox Hueffer Essay Competition for Junior Members" (Oliver Madox Hueffer, the journalist, is better remembered these days as novelist Ford Madox Ford).

I was awarded the first prize of "five guineas" for my essay on the set subject: "My favourite newspaper, and why?" I was invited to London, with travelling expenses paid, to the annual meeting of the institute to receive the prize from its president, Sir Linton Andrews, editor of the *Yorkshire Post*. A guinea was one pound one shilling, or, in today's currency, £1-05P. My father exclaimed, "Five guineas! That's more than I get for two whole weeks' work at the nursery – and you're getting it just for scribbling some words!" He added: "If you keep on like this, you'll soon be a ten-pound-a-week man!"

A ten-pound-a-week man in my childhood was, for my father and many of his workmates, the apotheosis of material success. My mother was also proud of me because I was, so to speak, her product.

She was also pleased for another reason: she knew that my "pigheaded" father (her favourite adjective for him) was "beginning to see sense".

Despite himself, he was impressed, although belatedly, by the economic benefits possibly to be derived from some sort of education. Altogether, it was a big day in my mother's life as well as in my own.

It gave a useful fillip to my own barely started career, and it caused my father from that day onwards to treat me as a man and not as a boy. This was just as well because death took him away six months later. He did not utter any memorable last words to me but simply grunted with what appeared to be approval when, in an attempt to show him I was being a dutiful son and had carried out his instructions, I spoke my own banal and final words to him: "I've planted the beans, Dad." He died that night in my mother's arms.

With more than three years to go before reaching official adulthood (twenty-one in those days) and with three months to pass before my eighteenth birthday, I found that, willy-nilly, I really had become the man of the family, with a widowed mother of forty-four and two younger sisters.

My mother continued to hold us together, as she always had. She was, until the time of her death in 1998, a living example of working-class matriarchy at its finest. Her progeny at my most recent count consisted of three children; ten grandchildren; fifteen great-grandchildren; and, so far, eight great-great-grandchildren.

As her firstborn child and her only son, I was a prime recipient of the personal sacrifices she made to ensure that her family should have a better material existence than she herself ever enjoyed. In spiritual terms, though, all in the family who remember her know that she was wealthier than any of us were. She possessed a truly Christian self-abnegation and warmth which none of the rest of us has ever come close to equalling.

After winning her personal battle with my father in 1939 to get me to the high school, much wider battles erupted, in the shape of the Second World War. Adolf Hitler, "Der Fuhrer", had overtaken Benito Mussolini,

"Il Duce". There were now two leaders, but Adolf was obviously Europe's number one top dictator, if one were to exclude Stalin in the Soviet Union, just as much Asian as European. Whatever Adolf might or might not do worried everyone, especially the British governments of Neville Chamberlain, with his umbrella and the spurious "peace in our time" of the 1938 Munich Agreement; followed by Winston Churchill, with his cigar and his accurate 1940 offering to us of "blood, sweat, toil and tears".

My high school arrival coincided with the outbreak of war. The teachers were reduced to working in shifts; air raid shelters were built on the playing fields; and a searchlight was set up on the middle of the cricket pitch. We had to trek to Worthing Rugby Club for our game periods. The last fortnight of the official school holidays was actually occupied with lessons.

The fall of France in 1940 was undoubtedly the school's strangest year ever. Staff and pupils stuck strips of paper on the school windows to try to make them splinter proof; we dug allotments ("Dig for Victory"); we went potato picking to help the Women's Land Army get in crops; we prepared splints; and we helped construct defence works. The war had already taken its toll on friends and "Old Boys", but we were proud to record the first decoration among them, a DFC, the forerunner of a long list of such honours.

Fearing a Nazi blitz (which soon arrived in London and other cities) and a south coast invasion, the authorities decided that Battersea Grammar School evacuees from London who were already sharing our school premises should be sent "somewhere safer" than the south coast, and we ourselves were evacuated.

With hundreds of mothers, mine came to Worthing railway station to see us off, our gas masks hanging in brown boxes round our necks. Many parents cried but most of the children were far too excited for that sort of thing.

It was a great adventure until we found ourselves billeted somewhere and began to understand that perhaps we were not always welcome arrivals. For most of the children of my age, it was the first time away from home without the accompaniment of a member of the family.

We seemed to travel by train forever, although it was probably only a day or so. We overnighted in a hall somewhere near Newark, in Nottinghamshire. The junior school, including me, were moved to nearby Southwell, where we were subsumed into Southwell Grammar School, next to the cathedral. Two classmates and myself were at first billeted in a stately country home where we were warmly received by a staff of servants and were looked after in the servants' hall. It was in this manor house that the first disaster of the evacuation struck me, although I was not aware of the catastrophe until after it had actually happened. Indeed, the cause of the trouble was an enjoyably exciting experience, a fire escape exercise.

It involved the three of us being lowered by ropes down the outside of a tall tower from our bedroom window. Swinging in the air above upturned faces far below, with ropes snugged tightly beneath each armpit, I imagined to myself, with pleasure, that I had parachuted out of a damaged fighter plane. Like one of my heroes, Biggles, I had been flying it when the enemy, probably the Red Baron, Von Richthoven himself, had outgunned me.

Having reached Earth safely, my wonderful dreams dissolved brutally when it was discovered that my brand-new school blazer, just purchased with the grant obtained by my mother, had been badly torn under the armpits by the ropes. Like my dreams, I too dissolved, but into tears. What would my mother say? What would everybody say?

The servants at the big house said: "Never mind!" One of them performed a miraculous feat of invisible mending, and I wore the blazer for another year or two until it got too small for me.

After a week or more, I was found a permanent billet for the remaining period of evacuation. This too was in a big country house, but not so big as to need a staff of servants. The middle-aged couple who accepted another boy and myself into their home were Mr and Mrs Walton. He was a bank manager, and she was a disciplinarian but essentially a warmhearted woman of ample proportions. I had a miserable time to begin with, falling ill with either chicken pox or measles; feeling homesick; and being compelled to adjust myself to unfamiliar ways of existence.

Odd little things stick in the memory. I remember that Mrs Walton ordered me to throw away my face flannel because it was such a "dirty rag". Face flannels were not necessary, decreed Mrs Walton, to wash the face or any other portion of the body. So to this day, I've never since bothered with a flannel, although I have recently acquired one from my granddaughter because the family thought it was just right for me. It is a flannel with a picture on it of A. A. Milne's character the misanthropic ass Eeyore. Round the edge of the flannel it reads, "E is for Eeyore, who often feels gloomy." I think I'm being got at.

Once Mr Walton, Mrs Walton, and the evacuee guests became used to each other, we got along well enough. Later I realised that many of the upheavals experienced by evacuees and the persons upon whom they were billeted might ultimately have been good for us.

However, some of the experiences were troubling, and anything comparable these days would probably lead to demands for counselling for suffering trauma of one kind or another.

It was certainly a shock for me when I came face-to-face for the first time with slums in the Midlands. It was an initiation into the meaning of Disraeli's phrase about the existence of "two Britains". I discovered it when I bicycled one weekend from Southwell to Mansfield Woodhouse, where some of my evacuated chums from secondary modern schools had been billeted, including my cousin. They were lodged in rows of miners' terraced houses. I know that many of the evacuees did not relish their stay there, because they told me so.

Even if the families with whom they were billeted were kind (not always the case) and even though many of us were not unacquainted with poverty, the reality was that being poor in rural Sussex was not so stark as poverty in the industrial Midlands.

The occupants of the terraced houses also spoke an entirely different language from Sussex English. It took my companions and me some time to work out what a miner's wife meant when she told one of her family, "Ee, lad! Get off to petty; tha's thrumped!" In southern English, it would have been, "Hey, lad! Get off to the lav; you've farted!"

Apart from such crudities, I found the linguistic differences fascinating. The richness and variety of different accents and local dialects left an impression upon my young mind, already attracted to reading, poetry, and drama. I was just beginning to realise what a treasury English literature and the English language had to offer to anyone who cared to look into that treasury. I began to enjoy the act of writing when composing the weekly letter that evacuees were required to send home.

Mrs Walton, while overseeing the weekly dispatch, also kept an eye on incoming letters. Beneath her forbidding exterior was a sympathetic quality, as I appreciated when she organised a photograph to be taken of me, in my new school blazer, to be sent home to my mother. I found it lovingly preserved when, fifty-eight years later, I had the melancholy task with my sisters of sifting through my mother's few belongings after her death.

Eventually, the government decided that we south coast evacuees should be sent home, and we returned to Sussex in time to witness much of the Battle of Britain.

What a war it was! We enjoyed a lot of it. Some of the time we spent in the underground shelters on the playing fields, with our enemies doing their worst to upset the even tenor of the school curriculum. We spent so many hours in the shelters that we missed some lessons, and eventually we were compelled to continue them below ground. Those shelters have long gone, replaced with prefabricated classrooms on the old playing fields.

Below ground, we joyously sang ribald songs, such as this one to a tune popularised worldwide in the film *The Bridge on the River Kwai*, namely "Colonel Bogey":

> *Hitler has only got one ball; Goering has two – but very small;*
> *Himmler has got some similar; but poor old Goebbels has no*
> *balls at all!*

In the construction of a new Europe, and indeed of a new world, people are rightly encouraged not to perpetuate old hatreds; and I do not wish to do so. However, I do want to convey with as much accuracy as my memory permits something of the flavour of those times.

German and Japanese national sensitivities are understandable among the couple of generations or so who are too young to remember the war, yet sometimes they appear to be overdone. One such instance came in 2001, when the German Embassy in London was upset by an advertisement describing the Germans as "krauts". A spokesperson commented, "It is not a very nice name, and it is certainly not nice to be called a name related to cabbage. I think over time the word has attracted negative connotations, so most people would be offended by it."

The company employing the word defended itself by saying it had regarded "kraut" as a "humorous reference to the Germans' high consumption of sauerkraut". The company said it would not use the word again even though the Advertising Standards Authority, the industrial watchdog, rejected the original complaint against the company. The watchdog said that although "krauts" did carry negative connotations, it would be "generally understood as a light-hearted reference to a national stereotype, and was unlikely to cause serious or widespread offence".

Another oblique reference to national eating habits was regarded as offensive by yet another media watchdog. Before the row over the cabbage word, the Independent Television Commission had ruled that "frog" was offensive when applied to the French, who for years have produced frog legs on restaurant menus. In 2000, the ITC condemned former England rugby captain Steve Smith for racism, for referring to a French player as a "stroppy little frog".

I cannot help wondering what one of the most famous sons of France, Voltaire, would have thought of all this official anguish over pejorative words or phrases. To Voltaire is attributed the saying "I disapprove of what you say, but I will defend to the death your right to say it." He was often in conflict with the French establishment, to the extent of living in exile in England for three years. Whether or not he would rush to seek sanctuary here nowadays, I do not know. If he did, and if he did not measure every word he uttered very carefully, he would almost certainly find himself in trouble quite quickly with today's British establishment.

As we teenage boys uninhibitedly bellowed out our songs of insult to the Nazi leadership, we looked forward to going out on night patrols and exercises with, first, the Local Defence Volunteers, the LDV, later known as the Home Guard and now more widely called "Dad's Army". We wore khaki uniforms as members of the Army Cadet Force but were not permitted to carry rifles until we were eighteen, when every male was subject anyway to National Service.

We made friends with the crews of anti-aircraft gun batteries at their emplacements on the Sussex Downs and with troops stationed locally in the build-up to D-Day. We all desperately wanted the war to go on so that we could get into it, though now I thank the Lord that it did not. We were adventurous to the point of stupidity, even managing occasionally to get a swim in the sea after finding our way into the water from the Worthing promenade through beach fortifications such as barbed wire and tank traps. We were not so foolish, however, as to risk negotiating minefields.

Like other south coast towns, Worthing got bombed occasionally, and the first body I ever saw was that of a German airman dragged from his Heinkel 111 bomber after it had been shot down. I had jumped onto my bicycle and pedalled hard with my friends up the hill from Durrington and onto the South Downs at High Salvington to a field just off a track called Honeysuckle Lane. We were in time to see the corpse being dragged from the wreckage. A couple of boys began to cheer, but the local bobby (police constable) was having none of that and quickly shut them up.

As the body in its flying suit was borne off on a stretcher, we gazed at it in silence. The airman had been young.

As soon as the police officer and the ambulance men had their backs turned, we raided the plane, tearing off chunks of its wings and fuselage, covered in an evil-smelling camouflage paint. I am not the only one to have remembered the smell of that paint, as I learned sixty-four years later from Mrs Barbara Chipper. In a letter to the *Worthing Herald* at the time of the sixtieth anniversary of D-Day, she recalls that she too was one of the many schoolchildren who had "rushed with great excitement" to view the plane and if possible to "obtain a souvenir".

She added, "I remember taking home my 'booty', a small strip of metal from a wing, I think, and placing it upon the mantelpiece" (shelf above the fireplace). "It gave off a peculiar pungent smell, and to my disgust, my mother made me remove it to the garden shed. I was aged thirteen at the time."

Mrs Chipper's letter provoked a stream of letters to the newspaper, including one from Bill Baldwin, my friend of seventy years. He had lived next door to me in Durrington, and he had watched from an upstairs window in his home as the Heinkel passed quite low overhead, with two Spitfires and a Hurricane in hot pursuit. Bill still possesses a cutting from the next week's newspaper, showing a picture of him at the scene as he collected his souvenir from the enemy plane with an apparently unconcerned police constable standing guard in the background.

In the garden shed at home, I ran into trouble with my own souvenirs. I had not only ripped off a piece of the plane itself, but between us boys we had also managed to pocket belts of machine gun ammunition. I had just clamped a bullet into my father's bench vice and was about to begin striking the cartridge end of the bullet with a hammer and a nail, simply to see what would happen, when my father caught me as I was about to make the first swing of the hammer.

He acted swiftly and boxed my ears. It hurt, and I was momentarily stunned – but not so stunned as I would have been had the bullet exploded. I dropped the hammer, and the bullet remained unstruck. My father's crisp order never to play around with live ammunition had the required effect, and it was another little piece of educational advice from him which I have remembered, apart from his views on Calcutta.

Although some aspects of war were exciting, I learned also for the first time the meaning of fear. The authorities had furnished millions of families with bomb shelters. Two principal models were issued, each of them named after government ministers. The "Anderson" was a shelter sited in the garden, and the "Morrison" went indoors. We acquired the "Morrison table shelter", as it was known, and it replaced the table we usually sat round at mealtimes.

It was so big in our living room that there was scarcely room to put chairs round it, and it was far too wide for passing things back and forth. When the air-raid sirens sounded, the entire family would take refuge beneath the steel plate that was the top of the table shelter. One night, as my mother, my sisters, my father, and I shared a mattress beneath the steel, a loud and close explosion shook the house. My father, against whose body I was huddled, began to shake also.

He trembled and shivered in a way that reflected some of his Great War experiences of being shelled and bombed. To my amazement, I realised that he was afraid, and this made me afraid too. In the morning, though, we were up as usual by six o'clock, my mother getting us tea, porridge, and bread and margarine, in the absence of strictly rationed butter.

To this day, I decline to eat margarine because for me it is indelibly associated with wartime shortages, whereas butter has long been associated in my mind with unimaginable luxury. So butter makers can be said to profit from my childish prejudices.

None of us got fat on our wartime diet of rations, and there was none of the contemporary obsession with obesity among both children and adults. It comes as no surprise to people of my vintage to learn that our survival diet was better for us than the food and drink which children consume today.

With whatever she had available, my mother got my father off to work and my sisters and me off to our newspaper rounds before going on to school. Newspapers were lean. They were published within the confines not only of wartime censorship but of newsprint rationing. There were four pages to a broadsheet – perhaps six sometimes – and about eight to a tabloid. Despite the limitations, the tightness and terseness of wartime journalism in Britain was superb. It compares favourably with much of today's surfeit of wordage, often on subjects of no intrinsic importance. Each morning on my newspaper round, I managed to get a free read of each newspaper. This helped to stimulate my appetite not only for information but also for the pleasures of reading and writing.

In the middle of the war I was, like many youngsters, more concerned with getting into uniform as soon as possible rather than worrying about what I would do when I finished school. In addition to being an army cadet, I was also a Sea Scout. Living by the sea as we did, a number of my relatives had connections with it. A handsome elder cousin whom I much admired, Max, was a sailor in the Royal Navy; an uncle was a chief petty officer in the Royal Navy; and my maternal grandfather had at one time been in the Worthing lifeboat crew.

My grandfather and uncle died a long time ago, but my cousin Max survived the war and kept his own fishing boat on Worthing beach for most of the rest of his life, until he died at the age of eighty in 1999.

With an interest in things maritime and my adolescent desire to join the war effort, it is hardly surprising that I managed to pass an examination during the war to join the Royal Navy on a cadetship. It is all so long ago now, and so dim in my memory, that I cannot remember the precise details. But I do remember that I was delighted and so was my father.

Alas, on going to Portsmouth for the medical examination, it was discovered that I was short-sighted. The navy, with high standards for eyesight, turned me down. I was disappointed and so was my father. Instead of putting on an attractive uniform with a smart peaked cap, which is what I wanted, I found myself back at school with a lot of studying to do if I was to acquire the dreaded "school cert".

Somehow or other my schoolmasters managed to steer awkward teenagers such as myself to examination success. I remember three teachers in particular: one taught English, one history, and the other Latin and rugby. Between them, they planted in me a love of all four subjects.

The history master especially was a flamboyant figure with a reputation for being a communist. However, his lessons did not seem to be contaminated with indoctrination and they stuck in the mind. One of his teaching methods was to write down a lesson and put it to music. We would learn the words and sing it together. From the next-door classroom would then emerge a boy sent from the maths class by the maths master. The boy would politely hand over to the history master a coin, accompanied by the compliments of the maths master.

We loved this regular pantomime, and our singing of history lessons became lustier. One of those lessons, about prehistoric man, I still sometimes sing to my grandchildren and my great-grandchildren. It goes to the tune of "Polly Wolly Doodle", a song made familiar in my childhood by the late Shirley Temple, the Hollywood child film star who subsequently became the United States ambassador to Ghana. Two of the verses of the history lesson went like this:

Verse: Oh, the Megalithic men of the Megalithic Age of the Mediterranean race, Average five feet six in height and fairly dark in the face.

Chorus: Listen well, listen well, to what your history master says; Books may deceive but you must believe what your history master says.

Verse: Now Cissbury was a village of theirs where they dug for flints in the mine, Down in the forest there were wolves and bears and 'Honk!' went the Megalithic swine.

Cissbury is now a National Trust property on the Sussex Downs, above Worthing and Findon. As for the honks, we all revelled in making our individual noises. We liked our history master, but when I come to examine more closely the words of the chorus, and observe that authoritarian note (urging us to believe him but to doubt what books say), then I suspect a hint of authentic Stalinist mind-control. Never mind! We learned his lessons without any apparent ill effect.

My English master was also effective. He illustrated vividly the importance of grammar: "There is a great difference between an 'active verb' and a 'passive verb': between 'I raped' and 'I am raped'!"

If I was lucky with my teachers, I was perhaps even luckier with my headmaster and with my first employer. Having failed to get into the navy, I went round while I was still in my last few months at school, knocking on local newspaper doors and writing letters asking for a chance to get into journalism.

My headmaster recommended my enthusiasm as well as my reading and writing abilities to the Worthing district reporter for the Southern Publishing Company, and so I was offered, at the age of sixteen, a trial period of one month with the chance at the end of that month to become an apprentice junior reporter for a period of five years.

That led to a rather full life.

CHAPTER 6

Age Three: "The Lover, Sighing Like Furnace"

Since adolescence, seventy years or so ago, I have loved quite a few women, and I am fortunate enough to have been loved by some of them. I have been married twice and divorced once. I was twenty-three when I first married, and that union produced three children and lasted for seventeen years. The second marriage followed the divorce and has lasted until the moment of this writing, for forty-four years now. I hope that with Virginia's apparent affection for me and her continued toleration of my bad habits, plus a bit of luck, that our liaison will endure for another twenty years or so, although by then I shall be over one hundred, so the odds in favour of it are fairly long.

My ex-wife, who was a beautiful woman, remarried a kind and civilised man whose existence was more settled than mine, and occasionally, after our divorce, she and I would meet at family weddings, christenings, and so on. In 2010, she died at the age of eighty. I attended her funeral with our three children.

I am reluctant to write about my own love life, which, like everyone else's, can never be anything other than an unfinished story until either separation or death ends a partnership. One reason for my reluctance is that any individual woman with whom I was at one time emotionally entangled might still be alive, even though this becomes less likely as time passes. If any still exist and retain memories of me as I retain memories of them, the mere mention of my name, let alone publication of a book, could be enough to trigger some sort of discomfort, pain, or anger, as well as to recall ephemeral happiness. The last thing I want to do is to reignite any old flame; it might burn.

I like to think that enough years have rolled away to enable any woman once close to me to feel now rather as I do, perhaps best summed up in words from the song "Time Goes By". The memories linger: "A kiss is still a kiss, a sigh is just a sigh."

Of course, my thinking might be wrong. I doubt if a man ever truly knows what a woman feels after a parting of the ways. He may know how badly he himself feels and thus assume from his own misery that she, too, must be feeling none too good. Such an assumption, however, could be incorrect. She might feel thoroughly pleased to be rid of him, while still, perhaps, retaining a fondness as expressed by a poet who, although he was a man (Robert Browning), might have got somewhere near the truth:

> We loved, sir – used to meet:
> How sad and bad and mad it was –
> But then, how it was sweet!

Perhaps, though, she might feel betrayed and bitter, as defined by yet another man (William Congreve):

> Heaven has no rage like love to hatred turned,
> Nor hell a fury like a woman scorned.

When recriminations are bluntly expressed after a split, a man does, of course, get to know what a woman feels. If, though, a mutual effort is made to separate as painlessly as possible and to minimise damage, then more volcanic feelings tend to be disguised by cold, relatively polite expressions of regret, plus possibly an acceptance of guilt. The circumstances of any separation or divorce are inevitably personal, and all differ. In any case, I am loath to enlarge upon my romantic existence simply because I come from a generation that did not (and in the main probably still does not) like the practice of "kiss and tell". We believed, and many still do believe, that an individual's private life should remain just that.

However, publishers, in their not unnatural search for sales, encourage writers to unveil their sex lives, especially if somebody famous or notorious is involved, a person now called a "celebrity". That problem happily does not concern me because I have never slept with a celebrity. I have met a lot of them in the course of my work and have become close to a few. Most have been men and some women, but never has any of them become part of my love life.

There was, though, an occasion when I was youngish and still pretty impressionable, when my employers seemed to fear that I might get too tied up with one of the most beautiful celebrities I have ever encountered. She was an ex-queen of royal descent. This was the only occasion upon which such a remarkable thing happened to me, so I shall tell the story.

It happened when I was the Middle East correspondent for the *Daily Telegraph*. At the age of thirty-two, I obtained a scoop involving a king and the ex-queen. The newspaper's managing editor of the day was clearly worried about my potential susceptibility to feminine charm because he warned me against becoming overcommitted.

I was reminded of this when, years later, Andrew Morton broke a much more sensational royal story than my own, in his book about Princess Diana. Somewhere or other I read that the princess might have "got the hots" (as it was so inelegantly put) for Morton while he was compiling her side of the sad tale of a disintegrating marriage. This caused me to wonder if the *Sunday Times* (which serialised extracts from Morton's book) or his publishers were ever concerned about his becoming overcommitted, in the way that the *Daily Telegraph* had been about me when I too was involved in helping a royal woman to present her case publicly after more discreet methods of furthering her cause had failed.

At the time I knew him in the 1980s, Andrew Morton was covering the royal beat for the *Daily Star* when I was the BBC court correspondent. I remember him as a pleasant young fellow, clearly keen and hard-working, while I was well into my fifties in my last full-time job. While I was still trying to give my best, I was already looking forward to the pleasures of a quieter life than that provided by covering the news.

I know that Andrew burrowed away assiduously, digging up facts before publishing, and I recalled that this was a feature of my own royal story in the Middle East. In other respects, however, our stories differed, and the outcomes of them both, so far as the two women were concerned, were dramatically different.

Princess Diana died suddenly in that Paris car accident after a divorce from her husband, while the ex-queen was remarried after her royal divorce, lived on after it, and above all achieved what she was seeking: namely a reunion with her princess daughter, from whom she had been unwillingly separated.

As I look back over my lifetime of reporting, it is with real satisfaction that I can claim that I helped bring about this positive conclusion by my journalistic efforts.

The woman involved in my story was Dina, first wife and first queen of the late King Hussein of Jordan. Part of her education had been at Girton after she had been born and brought up in Egypt. She was married in April 1955 to King Hussein, when she was twenty-six and he was nineteen. In 1956, their daughter, Princess Alia, was born, but the couple divorced in 1957. At that time, Dina saw her daughter in Istanbul, and then the child was returned to the Jordanian capital, Amman, while Dina went back to her parents' home in Cairo. It was in that city that I met her.

Cultured, lovely, and charming, Dina introduced me to the marvels of Islamic art and history. She became my personal guide around old Cairo and helped me to understand more fully than I could from just reading alone, something of the wonders of Arab and Ottoman civilisation. My enjoyment of this was interrupted when one day she mentioned that she was unhappy because she was unable to obtain access to her daughter, living with her father at the court in Amman.

Obviously and immediately, I sensed news. Dina's position as a royal woman and mother was by itself enough to ensure that it possessed the ingredients necessary to ensure wide interest. Equally immediately, however, I recognised that handling such news would be delicate because over and beyond the human element, there were political undertones with possible danger to the Hashemite ruling dynasty in Jordan. By extension, there would be risks to Western and particularly British foreign policy interests.

In the months following, well before the *Daily Telegraph* was able to publish its scoop, I learned much about the vulnerability of anybody who is born royal or who has royal connections. Dina qualified on both counts. She was not only connected to royalty by being the ex-queen of Jordan and mother of the king's first child, but she was also royal in her own right by being a descendant of the last sultan of Turkey, Abdul Hamid. Like King Hussein, she also claimed family descent from the Hashemites, the original direct or collateral descendants of the prophet Mohammed.

After the *Daily Telegraph* had published, there was considerable political fallout and diplomatic activity, starting, so far as I was concerned, with the British ambassador in Egypt, Sir Harold Beeley. He summoned me to a talk during which he expressed Foreign Office concern at the news and offered me information which I was later able to use constructively to help bring the whole saga to a more or less happy conclusion. In the process, I gained a deeper understanding of the internecine nature of Arab and Middle Eastern politics.

When Dina first mentioned her plight to me, I responded to what was essentially a request for guidance as to how she might go about pursuing her aim of reunion with her daughter, by employing, if all else failed, the notoriously double-edged weapon of publicity.

The upshot of subsequent months of discussion between us was a front-page splash for the *Telegraph* on 15 January 15 1962. The headline: "Ex-Queen Dina Begs to See Her Child. Appeal to King Hussein after Five-Year Silence." A delightful picture which I wired to London of the attractive appellant was prominently displayed alongside the report.

This said that, in a statement signed by her, she was asking for "every normal woman's right of free access to her child" after not being allowed to see the princess since the divorce.

Pictures of the king and of Princess Alia (whose name was used for years by the main Jordanian airline) were also published alongside the full statement. Queen Dina had carefully framed this over the months, with my help, to allow His Majesty an escape route from any suggestion that he himself had been responsible for the imbroglio.

Dina specifically stated that she doubted whether her private appeals to the king had reached him. So she had reluctantly decided on a public appeal "after long and painful consideration". The plea was her last resort to get access to her child. The decision to issue the statement had been taken only after she "had weighed carefully" her "duties, obligations, and feelings as a mother" against the equally heavy responsibilities and requirements of restraint placed upon a woman in her position. "As a former wife and queen to His Majesty, I have always been aware of my duties both towards His Majesty and towards the people of Jordan." She had "exhausted every private method" of trying to see her daughter. She felt justified in taking public action after a patient but fruitless wait. "For five years, my appeals to His Majesty for the removal of harsh barriers erected inexplicably against me have gone unheard. I have received occasional assurances that I would be allowed to see my daughter, but in reality no contact has been permitted. I am in doubt as to whether or not His Majesty has received all of my appeals. I have refrained hitherto from drawing public attention to the position in the hope that a settlement would be reached. But there are, unfortunately, no signs of this."

The ex-queen complained that she had suffered "considerable personal distress" from reports that she was complacent about the situation and was happy to be separated from Princess Alia. "Part of my purpose in issuing this statement is to refute such allegations. Nothing could be further from the truth. On the contrary, my energy and thought over the past five years have been directed towards gaining access to my daughter and subsequently fulfilling my responsibilities towards her."

The statement ended: "In the circumstances, having failed to make any progress in the matter by private approaches, I now address myself openly to His Majesty, in full hope and expectation that once he is in full possession of the facts of the situation he will respond to my plea."

Well, in the end it worked, but not without a lot more publicity and a good deal more effort, including a trip by myself from Egypt to Jordan when I carried a private note from the ex-queen to the king. This I handed over to him personally. I then passed back to Dina, from the king, his verbal, private, but hopeful reply along the lines of "The door is not closed."

The dignified and well-measured tone of her public statement had impressed most of the diplomatists and politicians, and they found themselves trying to help to resolve the royal family problem. Most important of all, it impressed the king himself.

Inevitably, though, there was political and propaganda point scoring. Dina was trapped uncomfortably between the ruler of Egypt, President Gamal Abdel Nasser, and the ruler of Jordan, the king, who were then at daggers drawn. Nasser had been doing all he could to overthrow Hussein, portrayed in the Egyptian state-controlled media as "the poisoned dwarf". The Jordanians, on their part, were understandably worried about Nasser.

King Hussein was under virulent attack from Egypt for his close contacts with Britain and for being what the Nasserists and their allies called a "bridgehead for imperialism". Responding in somewhat calmer tones, the king told me in an interview when I handed over Dina's note to him that Jordanians wanted Arab unity as much as anybody but felt it had to come "from the people" and not be centred "on one man or one particular concept of government".

Between these hostile leaders, the ex-queen was compelled to watch her step. In many ways, she was a prisoner. For example, she did not find it easy to travel. She had no Jordanian passport after the divorce. It had expired, and if she had applied for a renewal, the odds were that those at the court in Amman who did not like her would have blocked her application.

Possibly even worse, given that she was then living with her parents in the family home in Egypt, the Egyptians would have disapproved of any application for a Jordanian passport and could even have expelled her as the citizen of a country with which Egypt had no diplomatic relations. If, on the other hand, the ex-queen had applied for an Egyptian passport, this would have played into the hands of her enemies in Jordan. They could have exploited this to portray her as subject to Nasser's power, and so suspect in her attitude towards Jordan. In effect, she was stateless.

Luckily, Britain was able to help her, as Sir Harold Beeley explained. The Foreign Office provided her with a British "laissez-passer" when she required it or helped to facilitate for her the provision of a Turkish "laissez-passer" because of her Ottoman forebears. Her position was fraught with diplomatic sensitivities.

In my original report on the ex-queen's appeal, I had tried to throw light on questions not dealt with in her statement. No reason for the royal divorce had ever been announced, but it was no secret that the king's mother, Queen Zain, had not taken too kindly to his first wife. Dina was well educated and as politically conscious as most women of her calibre, and she found that some of her ideas clashed with those of the queen mother. Zain felt that her daughter-in-law's influence over the king might become too strong, and before long, rumours were circulating that Dina was plotting with Nasser, which Dina denied. She ridiculed the idea of dabbling in politics in a way that would have affected her own family adversely.

Nevertheless, the atmosphere in Amman eventually became impossible for her, and when the marriage broke down, she returned to live with her parents in Cairo.

In 1957, when it was thought that there might be a reconciliation, King Hussein visited her, but as one British diplomatist said, "The marriage never had a chance."

While the ex-queen never mentioned Queen Zain's hostility towards her, she was fully conscious of it. Towards King Hussein himself, though, she displayed no hard feelings whatever, making a point of telling me that he was "very fond of Alia".

Indeed, during the months that I spent patiently waiting for her to decide what she was going to do, and giving her my thoughts on the matter when asked to do so, I formed the impression that she was still rather fond of the king.

I said as much to the foreign news editor of the *Daily Telegraph*, "Ricky" Marsh, in a letter of September 1961, when I first apprised my employers of what was developing. That letter was sent from the old Golden Beach Hotel in Kuwait, where I was covering a crisis sparked off in 1961 by an early threat to invade the Emirate soon after its independence.

That threat came from Iraq, the same country which, a couple of decades later, did actually move into Kuwait, only to be expelled. However, the Iraqi bully boy in 1961 was not Saddam Hussein, leader of the actual disastrous intervention in the 1980s, but another of his predecessors as a military dictator of Iraq, Abdul Karim Kassem, who, like Saddam Hussein, also came to a sticky end.

British forces had been sent to the Gulf to warn Kassem off, after Kuwait had just become independent and had signed a defence treaty with Britain. The British move worked then, at less cost of lives and effort than was required later.

All of these disturbances started after upheaval in Bagdad, the Iraqi capital, three years earlier, and the murder of King Feisal of Iraq. His assassination was just the first of a series of violent deaths for Iraqi leaders over the past half-century.

Dina's name had earlier been much linked with that of King Feisal, and it was widely suggested, and even expected, that they might have married. This was especially so since the two of them were thought to have more intellectual empathy than any she might have shared with Hussein. Fortunately for Dina, however, she did not marry the murdered king, as she might well have died with him.

These historical details underline two things: (1) the regularly murderous nature of Iraqi political activity during most of my lifetime; and (2) the unusual pressures placed at the time upon a busy Middle East correspondent of a big London newspaper who had to continue to chase run-of-the-mill news like political crises and potential wars and to keep that news flowing, even while engaged in careful, delicate, patient, long-term pursuit of a sizeable scoop quite outside the usual run of the news.

Reading my letter from Kuwait fifty years after it was written, I can discern why my bosses might have been worried about possible overcommitment on my part. I began by informing them that I had been working on the Dina story "for four or five months" and that it was "an extraordinary reflection on the state of court affairs in Amman". I went on to add: "I have known Dina for some time now, and she is that old-fashioned thing, a lady." I told them that she had written final letters to both King Hussein and his prime minister in trying to achieve some sort of settlement before resorting to publicity. "Because of my personal friendship with her, Dina has told me that she would like the *Daily Telegraph* to break the news first."

In a further letter, of November 1961, I informed "Ricky" Marsh that Dina had received no response from her final letters and had decided it would be necessary to publish. I explained that the ex-queen wanted the timing of her statement to be right. She wanted to avoid issuing a statement at a moment when it might clash with the expected birth of a baby to King Hussein's second wife, Englishwoman Toni Gardiner. Dina thought that such a coincidence "would be unnecessarily cruel".

I wrote, "I must add, on personal grounds, I sympathise with her entirely."

Well, when what I had described to "Ricky" Marsh as a "delicate-to-handle" news story was eventually published as an exclusive, every single news agency, newspaper, or broadcasting station with an office or correspondent in the Middle East was on my neck, not to mention the ex-queen's. The story developed quickly, with Dina conducting herself impeccably as befitted a Girton girl.

She talked to correspondents the day after issuing her statement. She was asked if the king's marriage to Toni Gardiner might soften him, and she replied, "Yes. It might make him think more of family affairs, not in a sense that Alia would come to mean less, but that he would see things from a woman's point of view. In Islamic law, a mother has the custody of a child in infant years, divorced or otherwise."

Asked if she might approach King Hussein's new wife as "woman to woman", the ex-queen replied, "Anything devious should not be done. Anything other than through the king personally is wrong, and I have not considered approaching her personally."

The following day, Dina was "at it again", rather like Alice in Noel Coward's naughty song. However, unlike Alice, whose activities were libidinous and mercenary, the ex-queen was fighting her maternal good fight with distinction and bravery, winning the admiration of reporters and diplomatists following her every word. She successfully countered attempts to politicise her struggle.

She reacted to a statement issued by "palace sources" in Amman, saying that the king would "refuse to permit anyone to use Princess Alia as a political instrument of slander and blackmail". To that salvo, Dina responded by telling correspondents, "I am a mother and not a politician." She said that in appealing to the king for access to her daughter, she was not attempting to use the child as a political instrument.

"Speaking in a low voice," [as I reported at the time], "she commented, 'It should be quite clear that a mother's first concern should be that her child should not be used as an instrument by anybody. I had hoped that this question could be solved in the family circle and through private personal contacts."

She dismissed the Amman statement as "no answer" and expressed herself as "still hopeful that His Majesty will consider my statement in its true light".

With both sides looking for a way out of the cul-de-sac in which they found themselves, a bit of a lull followed. Then King Hussein's second wife, Toni Gardiner, transformed by that stage into Princess Muna, bore a son to the king at the end of January 1962, a boy who is now King Abdullah of Jordan.

Nasser's Cairo could not wait to object. The official Egyptian newspaper *Al Akhbar* was first off the mark, the day after the birth. It pointed out that the heir to the Jordanian throne had been named after King Hussein's grandfather, described by the newspaper as "the traitor who betrayed the Arabs in the Palestine war". This was calculatedly offensive to King Hussein, who as a youngster had been present when King Abdullah was assassinated in Jerusalem and who learned early on in this dreadful way the harshness of Arab infighting.

Not content with slandering the memory of King Abdullah, the newspaper went on to declare in disgust that Jordan's next king would be "of British origin". Meanwhile, a columnist in another leading Cairo daily, Al Goumhouria, commented that while King Hussein had every right to rejoice at the birth of a son, it was also the right of every Arab to question "whether or not the baby may be appropriately proclaimed crown prince". Indirectly raising the spectre of religious and racial intolerance, the columnist argued that it was inappropriate that an Arab state "whose religion is Islam and whose language is Arabic should have a crown prince with an Arab father and a non-Arab mother".

The Egyptian columnist continued: "Miss Gardiner, who has become her Royal Highness the Princess Muna, will in due course become Her Majesty the Queen." Then, in a final blast against the young Hashemite king, the columnist predicted the following: "So the prophecy that a blow will be dealt to the Moslem nation by the misguided actions of boys claiming descent from the Prophet of Islam may be realised."

Nearly fifty years later, with King Hussein having died a natural death (to the astonishment of observers of Arabian politics), and with his son King Abdullah now on the throne, the Cairo outpourings of Nasser's day sound curiously hysterical. They reflect, however, a strand in Islamic and Arabic politics and thinking which ultimately finds its expression in terrorism of one kind or another.

While the political mud-slinging worsened and the royal family stalemate continued, I took myself off to Amman, with the reluctant blessing of both the nervous Foreign Office and the British Embassy in Cairo, and the almost equally anxious approval of my employers. All knew that Dina had given me a message to deliver to the king, and all feared that I might turn out to be less than diplomatic.

I knew that I had to be careful to retain my objectivity despite any personal sympathy with Dina or with her case. So I was not irritated when, at this sensitive stage, while en route via Cyprus from Egypt to Jordan, I received a warning cable from the managing editor against overcommitment of whatever kind.

In fact, I was amused since I respected the sender, "Pop" Pawley, who was never the most communicative of men verbally and, in his written and cabled messages, chose his words with infinite care and the utmost economy. A veteran journalist from World War II, a recipient of the OBE, and foreign news editor when, at the age of twenty-six, I joined the *Daily Telegraph*, "Pop" had subsequently been promoted to the heavyweight post of the managing editorship, which he held for years. As a heavyweight character himself, he knew well the weaknesses of younger journalists such as myself.

I received the cable on 6 February 6 1962, at the Ledra Palace Hotel in Nicosia, some three weeks after I had first reported Dina's appeal. It advised me thus:

> *YOUR AMMAN TRIP EMPHASISE SHOULD HAVE*
> *APPEARANCE VISIT PROANOTHER PURPOSE AND*
> *MERELY CARRYING LETTER AS COURTESY STOP*
> *UNWANT YOU PLEAD DINAS CASE AT ALL NOR GET*
> *PERSONALLY INVOLVED PAWLEY*

I had no difficulty in following these instructions and acted accordingly. My last report on the whole sequence of events appeared on 15 March 1962, just a couple of months after I had broken the news of the appeal.

The ex-queen told reporters that she had received a private message from King Hussein in which he stated that she would be permitted to see their daughter, Princess Alia, "at his discretion". Dina asked, "What is meant by his discretion?" She said that in a verbal message passed on to her, the king had indicated, "The door is not closed."

It was not. It was duly reopened, and she and her daughter were reunited, the first get-together for many years of mother and daughter being on Alia's seventh birthday. Dina left Cairo for a two-week visit to Amman with her uncle, Sherif Hassan, to attend the birthday party in the royal palace. As the princess blew out the candles on her birthday cake, Dina and her uncle looked on, together with King Hussein and Princess Muna.

An Arab League source said that it was the British-born second wife of the king who had interceded with him on her predecessor's behalf, after the little princess had tearfully asked if she was not going to be able to see her mother.

Years later, the ex-queen and I dined together in London and looked back on it all with a sense of relief and, on the whole, satisfaction. Thus ended an episode involving a working relationship with a "celebrity", which worried my bosses far more than it ever worried me.

The cable from "Pop" Pawley still amuses me when I look at it. Couched in the curious language of "cablese", which we always employed in those days in order to cut wordage to the minimum and to save on telegraphic costs, "Pop" employed it even when it saved the newspaper the cost of only a couple of words. What was more, since it was sent to Cyprus, it was transmitted at the cheaper Commonwealth Press Rate.

I wonder if the Commonwealth Press Rate still exists. I wonder if cabling itself, or "cablese", still exists in these days of emails, mobile telephones, and the Internet. I hope so, if only so that young foreign correspondents might rise to the challenge of trying to outdo Ernest Hemingway. Legend has it that he sent the most famous cablese service message of all time. In every newsroom in which I ever worked, it was believed that it was dispatched by the author to the news agency employing him during the Spanish Civil War.

When he decided that he had experienced enough of war reporting and resigned, he allegedly put it like this:

UPSTICK JOB ARSEWISE

I shall not be surprised if somebody tells me that the story is just a myth. True or not, its cablese meaning was clear, if coarse.

Ex-Queen Dina, 33, former wife of King Hussein making her statement yesterday at her parents' villa at Maadi, Cairo.

Ex-Queen Dina of Jordan, the first wife of the late King Hussein of Jordan, when she appealed through "The Daily Telegraph" and me as that newspaper's Middle East Correspondent, to her former husband for "every normal woman's right of free access to her daughter," Princess Alia, after five years of separation from the child. (This picture was loaned to me by the ex-Queen to cable from Cairo to London to "The Daily Telegraph," which printed it on the front page with my exclusive story in the 1960s. I returned the picture to Dina and have only a picture from the Telegraph's front page).

Two pictures of the late King Hussein of Jordan and John Osman when, as the Middle East Correspondent of "The Daily Telegraph," and as a "go-between," he journeyed from Cairo to Amman and back, taking messages between the king and his ex-wife. Her appeal succeeded and mother and child were re-united. John Osman remembers the story as being one of the most satisfying and successful "scoops" of his career. (Pictures were taken by the Jordanian Court photographer in 1962).

CHAPTER 7

"The Lover" (continued)
Hooked by Satellite

Despite my reasons for not wanting to dwell too much upon my private life, I am compelled to concede that I would be less than honest in attempting to produce a rounded account of my existence if I ignored altogether any personal participation in Shakespeare's "third stage" of "the lover". Having launched myself into an autobiographical project, I have come to understand more clearly than I did before the reservations about writing any form of personal life story that were held by my friend and colleague for fifty or more years, one of the greatest reporters I've ever known, the late Sir Charles Wheeler.

When I once asked him why he had not tried his hand at autobiography, his succinct reply was, "Too much 'I' in it." He was right. So in my role as "lover", even as an inadequate one, I shall confine myself to what I see as the essentials and mention no names, apart from that of my wife, Virginia.

In the physical sense, at least, I imagine that I was a bit of a late starter. I was nineteen before I first copulated. The principal memory I retain is that my girlfriend and I indulged ourselves on a benevolently sunny evening on the slopes of the Sussex Downs, on Cissbury Hill, where, as my history master had taught, Megalithic men dug for flints in the mine.

My girlfriend and I became engaged, and somehow or other I raked up enough money, which I had been saving to buy myself a new bicycle, to acquire a second-hand ring of a ruby and tiny diamonds, which I presented to her. Not long afterwards, she sensibly ditched me for an older man with greater appeal. She kept the ring, and I did not and do not blame her for that.

I quit Sussex to head for the *Bristol Evening Post*. I had by then become what was in those days classified by newspaper owners and the journalistic unions as a "junior reporter", but my junior position did not prevent me from falling in love at twenty-two.

Having ventured as far as the West Country, I did not return to live in my native county for sixty years, and in those six decades, I married twice. My first wife I met in Somerset one sunny weekend at a village fete. She was my junior by six months, and by the end of the year, we were wed. Each of us was twenty-three.

We did not, I am afraid, "live together happily ever after", although we were content enough for some years and between us produced three children. We always loved our offspring and tried to help them despite inevitable difficulties.

My second wife remains so: Virginia Waite, author, journalist, broadcaster, and intrepid traveller, with whom I have lived happily in many and varied parts of the world, from America to Russia and from Africa to France. If I live long enough, I propose to write a book about her.

The resilience and longevity of our union, in addition to the continuing and mutual comfort we find with each other, would easily propel her to the top of any "little list" of those I have loved, if, like *The Mikado* of Gilbert and Sullivan, I actually possessed such a "little list". I do not. What I do possess, though, like many old men and women, is a number of happy amorous memories and the odd unhappy one.

The unhappy recollections involve sometimes thoughtless or bad behaviour on my part towards a woman, shortcomings that I do not wish to publicise, although one of them has always been a fondness for wine, whisky, or beer. More rarely, such recollections involve what I regard as having been thoughtless or bad behaviour on the part of a woman towards me, and I would not want to publicise that either. The happy memories well outnumber the unhappy ones.

As denizens of the old Fleet Street, where generations of journalists had worked for years and imbibed so copiously, Virginia and I first met, appropriately enough, in the downstairs dive bar of what used to be the Falstaff pub, opposite the old office of the *Daily Telegraph*. That was in 1967.

She was then the travel writer on the "Woman's Page" of the *Daily Telegraph*. Although I had been working for that newspaper for nine years, I had never met her. I had been tempted from the *Telegraph* by more money and a good post to move over to TV and Radio as the BBC Commonwealth and Colonial Correspondent (there was still a Colonial Office in 1965). Although Virginia and I belonged to the stimulating, if rackety and now vanished Fleet Street world of journalism, we moved in distinctly different sectors of it. The crew on the "Woman's Page" usually sailed in different, calmer waters to those stormier seas patrolled by foreign correspondents.

A "Woman's Page" travel writer, while often adventurous and capable of looking after herself, normally found herself looking for winter sunshine or golden beaches while a foreign correspondent specialised in other kinds of hot spots. We viewed each other, with caution, as unknown quantities.

The "Woman's Page" team ranged from elderly women journalistic battleaxes who were formidably efficient and competent to younger, attractive and fashionable women journalists (although I have to report that my wife was viewed by most of her colleagues as the worst-dressed woman on the "Woman's Page"). Whatever their age or dress sense, however, they all contrived to appear ladylike – I can think of no more suitable description.

I had first met a glamorous member of this feminine tribe in Athens, where she had been sent by the newspaper to report a Greek royal wedding. I was driving back to England through the Balkans and had stopped off in Athens to see something of what was going on. The woman in question, Serena Sinclair, was a stunningly pretty and superbly dressed American who was then the principal fashion writer of the *Daily Telegraph*.

She was well known on television for her beauty, articulacy, and fashion expertise; but for me, wending my way northwards and home from stricken, disturbed, and unsettled countries in Africa and the Middle East, she possessed a Hollywood star quality unlike any woman reporter I had ever met.

After meeting her, I reeled off on my own into the night determined that I should seize any chance I could to establish closer acquaintance with the denizens of the "Woman's Page".

I was not so far gone in any romantic notion as to think that I would end up marrying one of them, but I did. I was thirty-seven, my first marriage was crumbling, and my affair with Virginia began when one evening I ventured all the way to Fleet Street from Broadcasting House to see an old chum. I was quite bowled over when he introduced me to one of the lissom creatures from the "Woman's Page".

Tanned and lively, a laughing blonde of thirty or so, she sparkled with an adventurous, humorous glint in her brown-green eyes.

She had just returned from writing about a ski trip and was setting off soon for the 1968 Grenoble Winter Olympics with the British Women's Ski team. It was a year when for the first time the *Daily Telegraph* was sponsoring the British women skiers team, who that year achieved the feat at Grenoble of winning an Olympic bronze medal. As a skier herself, Virginia had been assigned to accompany the team, train with them, and write about it. She was enthusiastic about the assignment but badly shocked when, under the heading of "training", she found herself at first with the team not on sunny ski slopes but at Aldershot, under the orders of a sergeant major: "Get fell in, Waite! You're a bit weedy, aren't you?"

The ski slopes came later. Virginia produced good, amusing material of the kind she has never stopped writing. She also produced the effect on me of what the French call a "coup de foudre": struck by lightning! I have never recovered.

At first, though, I found her conversation about skiing a bit of a bore. Perhaps she felt the same about my own talk, much of which was about Africa. I had just returned from an assignment in Southern Africa, where three wars were going on. I had been filming all three of them, one after the other, for BBC TV News, completing over three months or so a series of a couple of dozen reports from Angola, Mozambique, South Africa, and what was then Rhodesia, now Zimbabwe. There, because the BBC was officially banned during that country's unrecognised period of independence, I found myself imprisoned, deported, and declared a prohibited immigrant, before being permitted to return later.

I still keep my "Prisoner's property" tags as souvenirs, just as I keep my deportation order from Idi Amin's Uganda. They help to adorn the wall of my study.

At first, there might have been a degree of mutual incomprehension between Virginia and myself of whatever it was we were talking about, but we hit it off nevertheless. We subsequently "lived in sin" together for a spell until the divorce laws were altered to enable easier access to divorce, and eventually that came through, followed by our marriage.

Since then, I have learned a lot about skiing from Virginia, as well as other things. I became just as keen a skier as she, and in her turn, Virginia has accompanied me to Africa, among other places, and has come to know the continent better than she might have expected, or perhaps wished.

For example, she contracted malaria in 1979 after trekking by night through the bush in Tsavo, in Kenya, to try to get help for her travelling companions when their car ran into trouble. Flown to the London Hospital for Tropical Diseases, she was lucky to be saved.

When I was reporting on the onslaught of Asians by "Big Daddy" and she was gathering material for a book on East Africa, she was also arrested and imprisoned with me in Uganda under Amin's regime. Good trouper as always, she never complained. Such adventures all had their origin in the Falstaff bar, and despite our ups and downs, we have remained lovers ever since.

The disappearance of old Fleet Street journalism has left a gap in the hearts of many old hacks like me. The last time I saw the Falstaff premises, the pub had become a pizza house and the old *Telegraph* building housed a bank.

Occasionally, as my first marriage fell apart and I spent much time away from home, I would find myself enjoying a brief affair with a woman, each of us regarding ourselves as what we used to call in those days "ships that pass in the night". The phrase was much more romantic than today's "one-night stand".

The earlier occasion on Cissbury Hill when my first girlfriend and I made love was probably for her (although I do not actually know) the occasion when she "lost her virginity", a phrase that I note is still in popular employment when applied to women and girls. It is less commonly applied these days to men and boys, though it used to be quite routinely used for the male sex as well.

One of my favourite epitaphs mentions it. Inscribed on a tombstone in the graveyard of St. Andrew's Church, West Tarring, in West Sussex, is this:

Nineteen his age,
Virginity his state,
Learning his love,
Consumption his fate.

Poor young man! At his age, when I finally succeeded in divesting myself of my own virginity, it was not for want of trying. For three or four years before that, I had been tentatively exploring the charms of the opposite sex, with or without the assistance of the Young Socialists and well outside and beyond Councillor Mrs Jones's front room.

We talked about our adolescent love play in slang words: "petting", "necking", "canoodling", "snogging", and so on. I wonder if such words still figure in the amatory vocabulary of the young.

We did not possess, let alone use, words that later became familiar, such as "bonking". The fact that use of the word in the sexual sense was unknown to my group of teenagers does not mean that it did not exist. It probably means that we adolescents in deepest Sussex were perhaps retarded in sexual matters compared with more sophisticated teenagers elsewhere.

We also knew words like "screwing" and "shagging" but did not employ them much because actual copulation was generally practised by people a bit older than us. As for the four-letter F-word, described in the *Concise Oxford Dictionary* as "vulgar slang", well, that was a straight-forward obscenity. It had yet to become what it is today: overworked in at least three grammatical forms as an expletive, a verb, or an adjective; routinely uttered in television and film dialogue; printed in books; and heard all too often in pubs, buses and trains, and on every street corner. Its vulgarity has long ago lost its initial power to shock, and it has become f-----g boring by sheer f------g repetition.

Vocabularies, like attitudes, change all the time. Often vocabularies reflect attitudes. The attitude and behaviour in the 1940s of teenage males like me towards females was clumsy and gauche, and I wonder if that still applies to the teenage males of today. Possibly it does.

We had a preoccupation with smartness, neatness, and tidiness. That reflected teenage respect held by us for those we nicknamed the "Brylcreem Boys". These included heroic fighter pilots of "The Few" in the Battle of Britain, cricketers like Denis Compton, and army subalterns not much older than we were. Many of them slicked down their hair with Brylcreem hair cream, and we adolescents followed suit, just as youngsters today tend to ape any contemporary hero (say, the footballer David Beckham before he started to miss penalties and before he failed with Prince William and Prime Minister David Cameron to convince FIFA that England rather than Russia should play host to the World Football Cup competition).

The heroes have changed, male hairstyles have changed, and standards of sartorial correctness have changed. This seems hardly a top priority these days, when "city high-flyers" (as they're called) "dress down" (as they say). Why, even in my club, where men are usually properly attired, it has been necessary once or twice to remind members to maintain standards of dress and to ensure that their guests do the same.

Yet paradoxically, the teenage obsession with exactly how one looks seems to remain as constant as ever with today's youth. It is the sought-after image that has altered. To my jaundiced eye, the contemporary look is often one of slovenliness and downright ugliness. Most notably of all, however, the look indicates almost universal acceptance of commercial exploitation. For example, today's teenagers do the manufacturers' advertising for them, free. From top to toe, from baseball cap (wrong way round) on the head to gaudily outsized trainers on the feet, the garments worn by the young and by the not so young display prominently the name or trademark of the maker.

I gather that for many it is important that such labelling is flaunted, because this helps to ensure acceptance of the wearer by the band of fellow fashion addicts it is to which the wearer wants to belong. What a triumph of the advertising industry!

An individualist youngster would have to go to some effort now if he or she wanted to buy clothes without advertisements on them. Such effort can hardly be expected, especially since the youngster concerned would almost certainly have to possess enough money to be able actually to afford to buy anything so plainly different from those worn by the rest.

I am presuming that such clothes or shoes, with a discreet tailor's or maker's label tucked away somewhere on them, would normally be more expensive than those with advertisements on them, but even that I am not sure about, because "the brand" itself appears to have become the thing. This appears to apply particularly to sports or "leisure" goods. I suppose that to be different is regarded anyway by many in these egalitarian days as being rather "non-U", (Nancy Mitford's amusing label, which by itself probably irritates many egalitarians).

How would an old man like me know about these things? Well, I listen to my children and grandchildren, so I pick up a little. It will be a few years yet, however, before I shall benefit from listening to my great-grandchildren, although I am just beginning to do so. Then I shall really be "with it".

Given the pressures among the young to be part of a sartorial advertising herd, I am glad that I am old enough to disregard fashion without a qualm. I can just about afford to discriminate for myself by refusing regularly to buy self-advertising goods, apart from wine, whisky, or a car.

Old age consolations also include a free TV licence and the cheaper purchase of rail tickets, cinema and theatre seats, and free ski lift passes. The reductions are real, even though they are offset by restrictions or higher costs in other directions. For example, while the cost of a ski pass for "veterans" and "super-veterans" (that was me until I gave up skiing at eighty-three) was nothing, the cost of ski insurance simultaneously went up, to pay for longer hospital stays while old bones set.

Indeed, for years I skied at my own risk because no insurance company would touch a skier of my age, except at exorbitant cost. Restrictions also include attendance at theatres and cinemas for cut-rate shows at matinee performances only, as well as railway travel outside rush hour. We oldies do not mind that, because who in their right minds would actually want to travel during rush hour?

We adjust to such financial swings and roundabouts because overall we save money on the merry-go-round and we are in any case in no position to dispute the calculations behind the limitations. We still, however, resent the arbitrary nature of actuarial decisions based on age alone.

The real trouble, though, with being old is undeniable and self-evident: youth has disappeared. Thus old men and women are widely regarded, by the young in particular and the world in general, as being quite incapable of performing a lover's sexual role.

This is mistaken. My wife and I know a couple who recently got married when each of them was well into their seventies and who claim openly that (as the bride put it) "Septuagenarian sex is wonderful!"

Nor is there any shortage of evidence about famous and happy marriages between couples in which one is many years older than the other, let alone informal liaisons of the Picasso variety. Many "modern instances" of happy marriages involving old people come swiftly to mind.

One of the most shining examples was the twentieth-century union, late in his life, between the great Catalan cello virtuoso Pablo Casals and his much younger Puerto Rican wife. Another example was film comic Charlie Chaplin's marriage to Oona O'Neill, daughter of the playwright Eugene O'Neill. True, the earlier marital life of the screen's "little tramp" had been stormy, and even after Oona had become his fourth wife in 1943, the marriage was followed by a headline-making scandal that involved a paternity lawsuit. Nevertheless, Oona remained Chaplin's last wife until he died thirty-four years after their marriage, and they produced no fewer than six children.

Such fecundity, unfashionable in the West and officially discouraged in countries like India or China, was probably unlikely to be reproduced by the Chinese-born and most recent ex-wife of the media magnate Rupert Murdoch, although she lost little time in bearing a child to him. Murdoch and I, like many men, are fellow-ancients, fellow-husbands (or ex-husbands), fellow-divorcees, and fellow-members of the newspaper and broadcasting industries; but I am not, I regret, a fellow-millionaire.

Statistically, I imagine that elderly lovers remain a minority (at least in the physical sense) and young lovers a majority, but what about youngish lovers? There are plenty of those around these days, with youngish lovers outnumbering young lovers in the amount of newspaper space and airtime devoted to their romances.

These "relationships" or "partnerships", to use descriptions in vogue, do not necessarily lead to marriage, and many of those involved in them are already married.

Extramarital affairs like these, often short-lived, are viewed by those of a serious, religious, moralistic, or legalistic bent as constituting the sin of adultery. To those less inclined to worry about sin, such affairs are regarded as romps or as "having a bit of a fling". Whichever view is adopted, prominent actors in their interpretation of the role of "the lover" playing star parts have included two recent American presidents, Bill Clinton and John Kennedy, although Kennedy's performance was not widely reported until well after his death. Clinton (whose Secretary of State wife remains centre stage in the theatre of politics) avoided impeachment after critics had analysed his performance and torn it apart.

Other youngish examples, nearer to home in recent years, also abound: the Prince of Wales and his Camilla, now happily and mercifully a respectable couple; the late Princess of Wales and her British telltale officer as well as her Egyptian companion in death; Mr Blair's first foreign secretary, the late Robin Cook, and his former secretary and second wife; the former prime minister, John Major, and former MP Edwina Currie; former home secretary David Blunkett and the publisher of the *Spectator*, Mrs Quinn; former deputy prime minister John Prescott and a member of his staff; the mayor of London and former editor of the *Spectator*, Boris Johnson, and Petronella Wyatt; and not so long ago, the late politician and diarist Alan Clark and his "coven" of mother and daughters.

In short, it is obvious that men and women are capable of being "the lover" at a much later point in their existences than in the youthful third "stage" envisaged by Shakespeare. It has probably always been so, but it did not merit the attention of the poet when he was penning "As You Like It", just as the status of being a husband failed to inspire Shakespeare enough for him to create what could have been another role to add to his seven "ages", that of "the husband". It is a conspicuous omission.

Everybody agrees, though, that the bard was spot on insofar as first love comes naturally to the young simply in the course of normal human development. The sheer poignancy of fresh young love battling against the stale, ancient brutalities of the world is what gives eternal appeal to *Romeo and Juliet*. Young love, however, can itself be appallingly brutal, as I learned as a junior reporter.

While working on the *Worthing Herald*, I was a member of a youngsters' dramatic society called "The Oberon Players" (we were all keen Shakespeareans). One of our amateur actresses was a teenager called Jacqueline and one of our actors a teenager called Brian. They had a romance and then horror struck. They went to bed together, and something happened which resulted in her death by strangulation.

Our little world of stage-struck adolescents was shaken to its immature core. Brian was arrested and charged with murder. He was due to appear at Lewes Assizes when, in the pretrial period, I received a telephone call from Jacqueline's mother. She asked me to come and see her, because "Jackie" had mentioned my name when talking about what plays we were doing. I was nineteen or so, had never met Jackie's mother, and was nervous about possibly upsetting a woman suffering from losing her daughter in such a terrible way.

I bicycled off to see the bereaved mother. I need not have worried: she turned out to be a woman of about my own mother's age and was extraordinarily sympathetic and understanding. She told me immediately what she wanted from me as a reporter. She wanted me to write a story about the case that would save Brian from the rope (death by hanging was still the penalty for murder in those days).

She had viewed and loved Brian as a potential son-in-law. She achieved her objective through what she had to say, my shorthand note of it in my notebook, and my published report. Rather as ex-Queen Dina did years later in Egypt with a youngish foreign correspondent, a Worthing woman turned to an even younger cub reporter to get something put over which she wanted people in authority to know about in a way that they could not ignore.

Jackie's mother issued an appeal to the jury and the judge for a verdict and a sentence sparing Brian's life. She calculated that even if he were to be found guilty, it would have been difficult in terms of public opinion for him to be hanged if his victim's mother wanted the killer to escape the noose.

It all happened a long time ago. I have reported the true forenames of those concerned but have avoided regurgitating the surnames because, for all I know, Jackie's mother might still be alive (though she would be a very old woman indeed). Brian, around my own age, may well still be alive. My memory is that he escaped execution and received a custodial sentence of some kind or another. I hope that he managed to live a decent life after the nightmare.

The story, for such it was in journalistic terms, had a profound impact upon me at an impressionable age. It taught me quite a bit about the curious aspects of love. One aspect was sexual: what really happened between the two lovers, Jackie and Brian, to lead to her death? Another aspect was feminine and maternal: how clever Jackie's mother was! She did not hesitate to draw into the affair a young man unknown to her but who had been a friend of her daughter's and who was able, simply by reporting accurately her case, to help the mother get what she wanted: the saving of Brian's life.

Another aspect of the love she displayed was political, philosophical, and intellectual: Jackie's mother was opposed to the death penalty for murder and almost certainly lived on to see it abolished.

The tragic episode served other purposes, useful to me so early in my career. It educated me in two respects about journalism: on finance and on the public perception of journalists.

The commercial side of this part of my education came when I bicycled back to the office, typed out my report, and handed it to the news editor, an apparently cynical but in reality a humane and experienced journalist named Frank Gillis. He happened to be the Worthing stringer for the late *News of the World* (a "stringer" being a local journalist paid for specific contributions to a bigger, national newspaper). Not wanting to take advantage of my naivety in such things, he asked me if I had any objection to his passing my story on to the *News of the World* (subject to the views of the *Worthing Herald*, who contractually owned the copyright of my story in my capacity as a staff junior reporter).

I had no objections; the *Herald* was content with its own version; and the *News of the World* duly gave prominence to Gillis's report about a mother wishing to save the alleged murderer of her daughter from hanging.

I was pleased when, a week or so later, Gillis called me in to his office to give me ten pounds, which amounted to twice my weekly wage at the time. He told me it was my "fair share" of the *News of the World* proceeds. When I somewhat boastfully mentioned this windfall in the newsroom later, the chief reporter laughed and commented that it all depended upon what was meant by "fair", revealing that Gillis had received what was then the colossal sum of fifty pounds!

The other journalistic fallout was criticism aimed at me personally by acquaintances who had read my report on the appeal by Jackie's mother and who accused me of being "an intruder into private grief". It had simply never occurred to them that the journalist concerned had not made the first approach, nor that it could have been the mother herself who had first sought journalistic contact. They duly accepted my explanations, but the point is that it was a good example of how journalists can sometimes be unjustly criticised for intrusion when there has been no intrusion at all.

Unjustified intrusion does of course occur, but the effect of the experience was to warn me off, for the rest of my life, from working for any of the more aggressively intrusive tabloids, no matter how much money was on offer, and to confine myself to the more solid, if less profitable, columns of relatively sober newspapers.

Mature and deeper love than sexual attraction, such as that shown by Jackie's mother, is a blessing for everybody. As most people know, or learn as they grow older, real love is not just about sex, important though this might be as a component of love.

To assume that the old are incapable of sex is silly, surprising though that may seem to beautiful teenagers. Many of those are reported to regard a person aged twenty as old, someone aged thirty as ancient, and anybody over that as more or less dead. From the inconceivably distant viewpoint (for them) of my eighty-five years, things look quite different.

To me, anyone less than twenty is a child, thirty-year-olds are young, and those in their forties and fifties, like the last couple of British prime ministers and many cabinet ministers, are youngish. For my generation, this explains why the country seems a lot of the time to be so ill governed. What else can be expected when the youngish, if not the positively young, are put in charge?

It is all a matter of perspective and, where love and sex are concerned, of individual libido. Many men of my age, plus their wives or mistresses, would happily join me in claiming, and perhaps bragging, that they are not yet impotent, nor has all passion been spent.

We laugh off sneers about being a "dirty old man" or "dirty old woman", which are jibes that tend to come anyway from ill-mannered people. Sex, after all, remains for most people a highly personal matter, despite the hours of television time and the columns of newsprint devoted to those perhaps exhibitionistically inclined, who appear for some curious reason or other actually to want to talk about their sex lives. Could the major reason be money?

Peering back to the period in my life when, as an adolescent boy, I began to become aware of girls and women other than my mother and sisters, I recall the reality of confused emotions. I suppose that boys growing up today still gallop through a similar gamut of feelings, just as girls perhaps do. Such perplexing confusion has never been more beautifully defined than by Mozart, when, in musical terms, his page-boy character, "Cherubino", in *The Marriage of Figaro* sings about feeling icy cold and burning hot. The fact that the boy's part is habitually sung by a woman adds to a listener's appreciation of the wonders of human biology as well as opera itself.

Well, I do not think that many young men in the post-war years of the late 1940s were so "burning hot" that we were "sighing like furnace" in the direction of the girls. I could be wrong, because it is difficult to tell what other people are up to in their private lives. "Icy cold", though, we were without a doubt in the dreadful 1947 winter. The more poetic among us could quite easily have been composing "a woeful ballad", for there was much to be woeful about. It would not, however, have been a ballad made to a "mistress' eyebrow".

It would more likely have been something of a dirge on the terrible, cold grimness of everything. We continued to endure rationing and austerity, restrictions on foreign trade and exchange, and a fairly rapid loss of belief in the benefits of nationalisation and the promises of socialism. Still, the war had been won and Britain existed more strongly then as a United Kingdom than appears to be the case today.

In that same dreary year, there was one publicly glamorous occasion that, by its historic timelessness, lifted the spirit of millions of tired and war-weary people in Britain. This was the wedding between Princess Elizabeth, now the Queen, and the Duke of Edinburgh. That marriage, widely accepted as a genuine love match and not an engineered dynastic contract, has proved to be admirably enduring and apparently happy. Efforts to portray Prince Philip as a philanderer have been unsuccessful.

Literally hundreds of stories and rumours have been published over the years, largely in the foreign press, about alleged extramarital fun and games by the prince, whose staff (in my day as a BBC court correspondent) smilingly maintained an ever-expanding collection of cuttings about his supposed activities as a super-Casanova. The files illustrated two things:

(1) what the sleazier sections of the publishing industry could do to bump up readership; and (2) to what depths some republicans would go to grind an anti-monarchical axe.

If the Buckingham Palace team has continued to accumulate such material (and in the normal course of things, this would be the case), then I imagine the number of suggested princely mistresses must by now run into thousands, rather than mere hundreds. The relentless digging for dirt about the royal consort to Britain's head of state, however, has failed to turn up anything at all credible, in marked contrast to the dirt about American heads of state or British politicians.

In view of Prince Philip's age, perhaps the dirt diggers might be slackening in their efforts, but I would not bet on it.

Enduring marriages are not always happy, and in the view of many people, of whom I am one, become less admirable the more the marriages are a sham. This is what the younger members of the royal family obviously have concluded, as is testified by the fact of their divorces. Their problems are well understood by thousands of British citizens who have themselves been processed through the divorce courts.

They find objectionable much of the spurious moral indignation displayed by some of the less scrupulous tabloid newspapers, commentators, and sections of TV and radio whenever a scandal has broken. What is more, millions of undivorced British citizens tend not to condemn automatically royal personages suffering personal problems but rather to sympathise with them. This is because British people remain tolerant and kind, even in these days of harsher and cruder public behaviour than that displayed, or indeed permitted, in the days of my youth.

Old men like me may seem to be curmudgeonly, but we actually want, and would like to believe in, the survival of essential British decency despite evidence to the contrary, such as nasty incidents of road rage or the hounding of a paediatrician out of her home because ignorant people confused a paediatrician with a paedophile.

Accepting that my own first marriage had become a sham was just one aspect of life and love with which I was compelled to deal when I asked for a divorce in 1968. I write with painful personal knowledge on the issue.

The divorce was granted two years later, and I shall never forget how I learned of it. I was far away from London, reporting from Brazil on the kidnapping of the West German ambassador to that country. In Rio de Janeiro, I received a laconic cable from my mistress:

DAOK LOVE VIRGINIA

This I interpreted accurately as meaning that a divorce absolute had been granted. At the end of my next TV satellite news broadcast on latest kidnapping developments, I sent a service message asking the BBC to pass on a personal message to Virginia Waite at the *Daily Telegraph* to tell her that I loved her and ask her to marry me.

There was an audible gasp from the foreign news traffic manager at the London end of the link, for it was unusual in those days (and probably still is) for a correspondent in the field to ask the corporation to play Cupid. Still, I was in a hurry to get my proposal to Virginia. For one thing, competing males surrounded her. For another, she and I were like gypsies, continually moving about when on assignment. So we communicated by any method handily available. This, of course, was well before mobile telephony came into daily use.

Corporation Cupid Number One assumed the shape of a woman, the foreign news traffic manager recording my dispatch and service message. In those days, BBC foreign news traffic managers were required not only to speak a couple of foreign languages when dealing with the recording of dispatches and the correspondent on the other side of the world, but they had to be diplomatic enough, as their job advertisements skilfully put it, "to cope tactfully with foreign correspondents under stress". (Does the BBC still employ such talented saints?)

The traffic manager carefully read the message back to me to ensure that there was no mistake, then handed my proposal to Corporation Cupid Number Two. This was a kind, grizzled BBC administrator, Clive Lewis-Barclay, who was a justice of the peace and a good squash player. He was a member of the MCC and used to invite me to play squash with him sometimes on the MCC courts when I was in London. He, in his turn, telephoned my proposal to Virginia at the "Woman's Page" of the *Daily Telegraph*.

A few hours after my proposal, I received in Rio a second laconic cable from Virginia:

YES STOP HAMPSTEAD REGISTER OFFICE JUNE 29TH
12 NOON STOP LOVE

The lover had hooked himself into marriage via by satellite.

CHAPTER 8
=====

The Path from School to Fleet Street

The day after I left school, the results were announced of the 1945 general election that brought Clement Attlee and the Labour Party into power. The poll provided me with my first assignment as a probationary apprentice junior reporter. I was told to stand outside Worthing Town Hall while from its steps the returning officer read out the voting figures for the Worthing constituency election. My task was to get those figures correctly down into my notebook.

Twelve years later, I was in Downing Street reporting for the *Daily Telegraph* the arrival in power of Harold Macmillan. Seven years after that, I was at his country home, Birch Grove, in Sussex, when he announced his retirement from the Commons and told me that his greatest disappointment while in office was the failure of his efforts for European unity. He thought, however, that the move towards unity was only postponed. Half a century later, the political shape of Europe remains yet another of my unfinished stories.

In the election that put Attlee into number ten, Tory Worthing remained solidly right wing, despite the left-wing lurch in most of England. I noted the voting figures correctly, but I was deemed neither experienced nor responsible enough to be allowed to actually report them. My duty was simply to be a backup for the reporter who was really doing the job, an experienced and elderly journalist called Percy Mattey, for many years the Worthing District reporter for my first employers, the *Brighton Argus*, a newspaper that celebrated its 125th anniversary in 2005.

In the run-down old district office, looking at the end of the war like a lot of British property, a bit battered and sorry for itself, we had a scruffy front counter for dealing with advertisers; a rear room with a small printing press used to put any late news into the newspaper's "Stop Press" box (most importantly, of course, all the football results on a Saturday afternoon); and, squeezed between the two rooms, Mr Mattey's office, with a desk, chair and two telephones, one on the desk and the other on the wall. One was the normal telephone line, and the other was the inter-office line. The latter connected the head office in Brighton with all the West Sussex offices.

From the district offices, we would call Brighton by turning round and round a handle in a box on the wall and dictating any urgent copy. If Brighton wanted to call us, we had to count the rings, because there was one ring for Shoreham, two for Worthing, three for Littlehampton, four for Bognor Regis, five for Chichester, and so on. It sounds cumbersome, but it worked.

Soon after I began to work as Percy Mattey's apprentice, another small desk was put into our cramped little room for me to use. There was no typewriter, though! We wrote all our copy in longhand on paper, often using a pencil rather than a pen, and then we sent it by train envelope to Brighton. If it was urgent, we often dictated it over the telephone, composing our reports from our notebooks without any writing whatsoever.

It was in this "inner sanctum" of Percy's, on my very first day at work as his probationary apprentice junior, that he asked me what I wanted to do in journalism. I replied that I wanted to be a foreign correspondent. He growled back that if I wanted something like that, then I would have to work very hard.

His own career (and he was much respected in Sussex journalism) dated back to pre-telephonic days when he covered football matches, carrying with him to the soccer field a basket containing carrier pigeons. One flew back to the Argus office with the half-time score and a second with the full-time result. Percy told me that often the newspaper's pigeon handler had difficulty enticing the birds to land on the Brighton office roof in order to detach their messages from them, but that on the whole the operation worked well.

Pigeons have played a useful role in news reporting for a long time. They were used by war correspondents as recently as the 1944 D-Day landings to get back to England early dispatches from the beaches; but a hundred years before then, a man born in Germany of Jewish parentage, Israel Beer Josaphat, had employed pigeons from Paris during the Revolutions of 1848 to send news to German newspapers.

He became a Christian, moved to London, was naturalized as a British subject, and, under his new name (and later title) of Baron Paul Julius Reuter, founded and gave his name to the mighty Reuter news agency. A foundation of his success was his employment of pigeons to fly between telegraphic offices still being established on the European continent during the nineteenth century; so plugging the gaps between them and thus getting the news, especially market prices, from one place to the other more speedily than competitors. It was a long way from today's Internet instantaneity.

As a twentieth-century foreign correspondent, I myself used "pigeons" from places as far apart as Russia, India, Cuba, and Africa. My "pigeons", however, were human: people willing to act as couriers in getting television film, radio tapes, and written dispatches back to the BBC from places where communication was difficult.

"Pigeon" was – and still is – the trade word used by journalists and cameramen for such helpful men and women. It is a tribute to the bird that I think would have amused old Percy Mattey. He was a wonderful tutor. For four years, he taught me all he knew about reporting, and during the evenings when I was free from covering a meeting of some sort or other, I attended what was in those days called "night school", learning shorthand and typing.

I did the rounds of fetes, flower shows, and funerals, ensuring that I got all the names and initials right; did the daily calls on the fire station, the police station, the ambulance station, and the hospital, to report on the usual run of accidents, crimes and deaths; covered courts and councils and learned about the way the country was run; and, at the end of every week, put in my expense account.

My claims consisted mainly of bus fares around the district and, most importantly, a bicycle allowance of one shilling and sixpence a week, the equivalent now of seven and a half pence (except that there is no halfpenny these days, so the nearest approximation would be eight pence). This sum was vital to me in maintaining my bicycle as my main method of transport, covering running costs such as puncture repairs and the occasional new tyre.

The bulk of the output produced by Percy and myself for the four newspapers for which we worked was destined for the two dailies – the long since dead but lovely old county morning newspaper the *Sussex Daily News* and the still lively *Argus*, in those days a specifically evening newspaper in direct competition with no fewer than three London evening newspapers. Two of those (the *Evening News* and the *Star*) have died, while the *Standard* has survived as a Russian-owned giveaway.

Percy was impressed when I enabled him to pull off a great south coast scoop early one morning through the good offices of Mr Jones, the neighbour so despised by my father as a "conchie".

My own relations with Mr Jones were friendly enough, as a regular visitor to his front room for those sexy meetings of the Young Socialists, arranged so unwittingly by his town councillor wife.

Mr Jones was a part-time fireman, and I was awoken in the early hours of the morning by stones being thrown up from the road below, tinkling and clattering as they hit the window of the little first-floor box room that was my bedroom (we did not possess a telephone, as Mr Jones did). As quietly as possible, so that he did not wake up the rest of the street, Mr Jones called up to me, "John, there's a big fire at Hubbard's!"

This was a major department store in Worthing (it has since become Debenham's). I rose, jumped onto my bicycle, and pedalled into town to see the biggest blaze there since the days of the "blitz". Off I hurried to Percy Mattey's house, knowing that he sometimes took pictures with an old Speed Graphic camera with glass slides. With trepidation (because he was sixty or more, could be tetchy, and was very much "Mr Mattey" to me, not Percy), I woke him up at around five that morning. He got dressed and joined me, and together we covered the story.

By six that morning, I was at Worthing Railway Station, sending off by train envelope the slides with Percy's pictures on them to be picked up at Brighton Railway Station. The report itself we dictated over the office telephone to Brighton. The first edition of the *Argus* and all subsequent editions beat every other newspaper, with excellent coverage of the most dramatic south coast fire since the war.

Our main channel for sending copy, however, especially at night for the morning newspaper after evening council meetings and any late news, was by train envelope. We put our copy (often handwritten onto paper at the meetings themselves but sometimes typed later if we had more time) onto a train, handing it to a guard or porter at the station in the freight office to be put on the next train. We then rang the head office to say that the material was on the way. It was collected at the Brighton end, and into the newspaper it went.

In those days, the trains ran on time, and I cannot recall any occasion when the system broke down. Late copy and pictures got into the newspaper with extraordinary speed, and the material was printed with accuracy after having been both subedited and then scrutinised properly by proofreaders. My impression today is that despite undoubted advances brought by information technology, now obsolete methods of communication were in some ways infinitely more reliable than anything yet produced by computers. That is certainly so if judgement is made by the failures in proofreading exhibited so disgracefully in today's newspapers, even in headlines. With ubiquitous and daily printing and spelling errors, it is plain that proper proofreading as such is now more or less extinct.

From all the accounts I have heard from today's journalists, earlier copy deadlines are also required for computer consumption than were ever required in the days of hot metal printing. Is this progress?

Percy was again impressed when I won the junior journalists' essay competition, which, as I have already mentioned, gave my embryo career as a reporter a little fillip. Paragraphs about my youthful success appeared in the trade press, one of them attracting the eye of Robin Cruickshank, who in 1947 was editing the great liberal newspaper, the *News Chronicle*, long since subsumed into *Daily Mail* ownership. He was interested because I had chosen his newspaper as the subject of my essay, for which the set theme was "My favourite newspaper, and why."

So after being invited to London on an expenses-paid trip to receive my award, I enjoyed yet another such outing, this time at the invitation of an influential editor. He had been a distinguished Washington correspondent during the war, and he wrote a lively history of the News Chronicle called "Roaring Century". Then aged sixty or so, this busy man nevertheless took it upon himself to spare an hour or so of his precious time talking in his office to an unknown cub reporter from the provinces. How many editors of national newspapers, I wonder, would do that today?

He asked me to write to him once a year telling him what I was up to and what I was doing. He also urged me, whatever I did, to find time to read as much as I possibly could. For five years, I sent him a short annual note and continued to read as much as possible, as I had done always. Most of my reading was done courtesy of the public libraries, although now and again I was just about able to afford to buy a book myself. After completing my apprenticeship at the age of twenty, by which time I was earning four pounds a week, I was enticed by the *Worthing Herald*'s offer of an extra pound a week to leave the *Argus* and join the *Herald*. Eventually, after a year or more, the prospect of wider experience and even more money led me to leave Sussex for the West Country and the *Bristol Evening Post*.

By now, I was out of apprenticeship and qualified as a junior reporter. During my three or four years with the *Post* in Bristol, Cruickshank invited me to spend my annual holiday one year as a summer relief reporter on the *News Chronicle*. I had plenty of work to do and enjoyed every moment. Sadly, however, the writing was already on the wall presaging the death of the newspaper. Cruickshank was in ill health as well. Another journalist, Norman Cursley, was deputising as editor, and he did me a good turn. While encouraging me as a reporter, he discouraged me in any long-term hopes about joining the *News Chronicle*, hinting at its financial problems and indicating that I would be sensible to look elsewhere for work in Fleet Street.

I returned in a rather resigned way to *Bristol*, determined to have a crack at Fleet Street at the first opportunity. Meanwhile, I worked hard. On joining the *Post*, I began as a general reporter in Bristol, living for a month or so in the YMCA before finding a room as a lodger in a private home with a pleasant landlord and landlady. Then, given a Somerset district of my own to cover, I found new lodgings above a café in the ancient cathedral city of Wells, from where I reported local events in Wells itself and in neighbouring districts like Shepton Mallet, Glastonbury, and Street. After that came a spell in the Somerset county town of Taunton, from where, during the summer months, I would head south with a photographer for places like Torquay and Exmouth or north to places like Minehead and Ilfracombe, to produce articles and pictures aimed at boosting circulation among holiday-makers, hoping to score against our regional competitors, the *Exeter Express* and *Echo*, and the now extinct *Bristol Evening World*, long ago swallowed by the *Evening Post*.

From Taunton, I was moved to Weston-super Mare, with my young bride and the first of our children on the way. In addition to news coverage, I produced a weekly show business column with a less-than-arresting title: "Spotlight on Weston Entertainment". I wrote about anything and everything that was remotely connected with showbiz, greasepaint, and amusement, from seaside concert parties to seaside donkeys; from Christmas pantomimes to Christmas hotel entertainers like magicians, conjurers, dancers and dance bands; and from events on the pier to plays at the local repertory theatre.

The latter produced many young actors and actresses who went on to fame in films, on TV, and on the London stage, as had the repertory theatre in Worthing. Away from the stage, though, one of my favourite summer seasonal subjects was a group of young men billed as "The Water Wizards of Weston-super-Mare".

They were high divers and springboard divers performing spectacular stunt shows during the summer months at the Weston swimming pool, which in those days was one of the few municipal pools in the country with a diving board as high as ten metres. Being a bit of a water baby myself, I not only wrote about the Water Wizards but also actually joined them, at their invitation, in one or two performances. I wrote about it, naturally, and I enjoyed the larking about as a Water Wizard, but to this day, I do not know how I managed to survive my descents from the top board.

Eventually, I was recalled to Bristol, where, in addition to general news coverage and feature writing, I was told that I was also the university correspondent, covering Bristol University for a spell. Busy though I was with all of this, I somehow or other found time to join other young reporters (some of whom went on to greater things in Fleet Street and in broadcasting) who regularly attended night school. We were among the first post-war batch of journalists to acquire the officially recognised General Proficiency Certificate in Journalism, a document that required diplomas from the Royal Society of Arts on knowledge of the English language, English literature, and public administration, not to mention understanding of the Laws of Copyright and Libel (plus, of course, short-hand and typing!).

I was by now well equipped with a collection of relevant pieces of paper. They showed that I had obtained the academic and craft quali-fications vouching for my ability to read and write; another document confirmed that I had some sort of knowledge as to how the country was administered. I also possessed a collection of scrapbooks and exercise books containing published cuttings of my work from six newspapers over seven years and ranging over a wide field: general news coverage and sports reports; features writing and book reviews; theatre, art, and music criticism; and my columns on Weston-super-Mare show business. I also possessed a string of good references from news editors.

However, these were not enough to get a job in the Fleet Street of those days on most newspapers. Managements then broadly stuck to an agreement made between the proprietors and the journalists' unions that jobs should go only to senior reporters, namely those who were at least twenty-three. So I had to wait to head to Fleet Street.

As I neared the magic number of years, I sent off letters to various national newspapers, asking for a job. I also received a letter from the editor of the *Bristol Evening Post*. Wanting, I suppose, to retain any prom-ising youngsters on the staff, and knowing that I would soon be formally a senior reporter, the *Post* offered me my own district in Yeovil, complete with a car and a house.

This was a tremendous temptation for a penurious young reporter who had a wife and child to support. The offer arrived as I set off to Badminton to cover the 1954 Three-Day Olympic Horse Trials, attended by the Queen Mother and Princess Margaret. It was the first time I had seen any members of the royal family in the flesh, and I was impressed by the sheer, youthful beauty of the late Princess Margaret, then in early blossom as an attractive woman, and the poise and innate grace of the late Queen Mother, who had not long before lost her husband, King George VI.

The young queen herself was unable to be at Badminton, unlike the vast crowds who turned up both to enjoy the event and to catch glimpses of her mother, her sister, and the late Duchess of Gloucester with her two small sons, Princes William and Richard. The monarch could not get to this equine and royal occasion because she was far away on royal duty in Ceylon, in these days known as Sri Lanka. There she celebrated her twenty-eighth birthday. She was not forgotten, however. The Duke of Beaufort, host to the royal visitors, sent the Queen a telegram of greetings from "all at Badminton", some sixty-nine thousand people over three days. "We greatly miss Your Majesty's presence," he cabled, "but are pleased to report we are favoured with lovely weather and good entries."

For three or four days, I filled columns of the newspaper from Badminton, and against the background of this great West Country scene, I pondered my future.

This was because soon after the letter from the *Evening Post* arrived, so had another. It was from the major British news agency the Press Association, offering me a Fleet Street job. Much as I liked the thought of running a car and of having a house provided for me, I knew that even if I made a wild success of things in Somerset and ended up as mayor, county councillor, or chairman of the Rotary Club, I would forever afterwards have been permanently discontented because I would have been asking myself what I might have done if I had gone instead to Fleet Street.

So I opted for the PA, and off we went to London to start our new lives. We rented a rather primitive, barely adequate flat in Brixton, and I attacked a new journalistic challenge with all the vigour of an ambitious twenty-three-year-old.

I was delighted to receive a letter from Percy Mattey, who for years had been the Worthing stringer for the PA and who was by then retired. He wrote, "I was pleased to hear that you are to start with the PA. You'll do all right with them. Keep your eyes in front of you, John, and you'll be made for life with the PA."

As a young reporter on the "Worthing Herald" in the
early 1950s I tried, by smoking a pipe at my desk in the
News Room, to present a more mature image.

CHAPTER 9

<hr/>

News Encounters with Newsmakers

Slogging away with enthusiasm at whatever assignment came my way, I travelled all over England covering the run of general news for three years or so. I reported political gatherings with fiery orators in full spate like Barbara Castle or "Nye" Bevan; tragedies like the South Goodwin lightship disaster and a big train crash in the Midlands; major trials at the Old Bailey and elsewhere; hearings of Parliamentary Select Committees; and I made my first acquaintance with Russian politicians, reporting the unprecedented visit to London of two Soviet leaders, Nikolai Bulganin and Nikita Khruschev, known to all as "B and K". Curiously, the next Soviet "B and K" duo, Leonid Brezhnev and Alexei Kosygin, were never thus bracketed as a pair of initials, perhaps because they never toured London to be noticed first-hand by Londoners and the tabloid newspapers.

In 1956, I had my first major foreign news scoop, shared with another young reporter, "Ricky" Marsh from Reuters. We obtained it during the Suez Crisis when, in a last-ditch diplomatic attempt to resolve the problem created by Nasser's seizure of the Suez Canal by nationalising it, John Foster Dulles, the American secretary of state flew to London for talks with Prime Minister Anthony Eden.

Arrangements were made at the United States Embassy for Dulles to brief American correspondents afterwards. Marsh and I were refused access to the briefing because we were not working for American news organisations, so we stood outside on the embassy steps. When Dulles arrived we "doorstepped" him, asking him what had happened. To our delight and surprise, he told us.

A plan had been discussed, he said, for the formation of an international Suez Canal Users' Association to place pressure upon Nasser. It was a plan that in the end came to nothing, but at the time, it was big news. Marsh and I filed our stories, which winged their way around the world well before the American correspondents were able to produce their dispatches. They had been tucked away inside the embassy waiting for Dulles to talk to them while outside he was spilling the beans to us.

The result was predictable and gratifying. The American reporters were furious at being upstaged, and Dulles was requested to keep his mouth shut in future until he had first talked to them. When Marsh and I returned to the embassy steps the following day and asked him once again what he and Eden had talked about, he simply smiled and said, "The Suez Canal, gentlemen." Then he walked past us to brief the Americans. We had nevertheless enjoyed our brief moment of triumph.

Towards the end of 1956, I crossed Fleet Street from the PA, at Number 85, to join the staff of the *Daily Telegraph*, nearly opposite, at Number 135, years before the newspaper moved to Canary Wharf and subsequently to Victoria.

My first report to appear in its columns in November 1956 touched upon the immediate effects of the disastrous Suez Crisis that had come to a head a month or so before with the abortive intervention in Egypt of Israeli, British, and French forces. The subject of my report was a speech in the city of London by the Chancellor of the Exchequer, Harold Macmillan. With masterly understatement, he told his audience, "We live in rather difficult times. But we have done that before. For the moment we seem rather isolated. But we have been that before. Nothing matters so long as we think that what we have done is right and that what we will do will lead to something better coming out of it. That, I think, will happen."

From Macmillan's personal viewpoint, it certainly did. In a couple of months, he had taken over as prime minister from Anthony Eden. I was in Downing Street on the day the Queen invited him to be her prime minister.

At 1.40 p.m., he left his official residence of chancellor of the exchequer, at Number 11, while his wife and daughter watched him from a window with a portrait of Disraeli behind them also looking down on the scene. Macmillan got into a family-sized black Wolsely car and sat next to the chauffeur as he was driven off to Buckingham Palace.

An hour later, still sitting next to the chauffeur, he returned to Downing Street – in those days with no barred gates at the end of the road to be the scene for squabbles between bicycling politicians and uneasy police officers. By now, although Macmillan was the Queen's new chief minister, he would not say so because that was for the palace to announce.

He did not go into Number 10 but went back into his residence as Chancellor of the Exchequer. Nobody could have guessed from his relaxed demeanour that he had been just as keen to replace Anthony Eden as Gordon Brown was for years reported to be aching to take over from Tony Blair.

I described the scene on the front page of the *Daily Telegraph*:

> He stood for a minute or so on the pavement in front of the door of No. 11 genially talking to reporters and turning in every direction to oblige every photographer. Calm, smiling, immaculately dressed, he was in complete command of the situation.
>
> The first question to him as he clambered out of his car was, "Are you prime minister, sir?" He smiled and said, "You will be getting an official announcement."
>
> Another reporter put the question in a different way. "Can we congratulate you, sir?" he asked. Mr Macmillan beamed broadly and said, "You will be getting an announcement from Buckingham Palace."
>
> I then asked him, "Will you hold a general election, sir?" He looked straight at me and answered emphatically, "No. If there was, we would win it."

He was one of the most skilled politicians and one of the most polished prime ministers I have ever met. A wonderful picture taken of him that day was published by Time magazine, showing him on his return from the palace, still in black coat and striped trousers, with a gold watch chain across his waistcoat, looking for all the world like a successful, gentlemanly bookmaker who has just happily made a fortune. Beside him, wearing an overcoat and holding a notebook in a gloved left hand and a pen taking notes in an ungloved right hand was myself, looking suitably enough like the bookie's runner. The caption could well have been "Mac the bookie and his runner".

In at the start of his premiership, I was also there at the end of his long political career, when I drove to his country home in Sussex on the eve of his seventieth birthday, when he formally announced his retirement to the Commons. He was in nostalgic mood as he talked to a group of us and declared that the failure of his efforts towards European unity was his greatest disappointment.

Before inviting us inside, he posed for cameramen and pointed a blackthorn walking stick at me as I stood among the photographers. He said, "Now I know you. Where are you from?"

I told him that I worked for the *Telegraph* (once described by the late Malcolm Muggeridge as "the repository of the soul of the Tory Party"). My reply led him to become nostalgic in an unusually moving way.

He recalled the enormous loss of life among the young men of his generation in the Great War and stressed the need for a government minister to have strong physical stamina. This is how I reported the exchange:

> *I reminded him that in 1956 I was one of the first reporters to talk to him in Downing Street when he took over as prime minister. "Ah, yes." He smiled in reply, then paused and added, "That was some time ago, and I am now a sadder and wiser man."*
>
> *He said that though he felt quite all right, he got very tired. "I don't think I could undertake any great effort, not more than four or five hours a day." During his premiership, he worked [fifteen] hours a day and never got to bed before 2 [a.m.]. "I cannot feel I have got the strength to go on, nor do I think it is right. I have had [forty] years in the House, and it is quite a long time. I feel I should make way for younger people."*
>
> *He said he had spent seventeen years in office as Foreign Secretary, Chancellor of the Exchequer, and Prime Minister. "A very strong physique" was needed and "You have got to have good comrades which I was very fortunate in having."*

People of his age felt that they were lucky to be alive at all.
"Nearly all the comrades of my youth were killed. You have to
take the good and the bad together, and of course you have to
have a great sense of humour."
He said he had had many kind messages on his birthday.
Perhaps the chief characteristic of the British people was their
kindness to their neighbours, their comrades, and people in trouble.

So Macmillan bowed out. At the other end of the political spectrum, one year earlier, I had first become acquainted with the new Leader of the Opposition, Harold Wilson. To meet him, I flew to Scilly, where he had agreed to talk to me while on a three-week holiday with his wife, Mary; his sons, Robin and Giles; and his sister, Marjorie, who had chosen the name of the three-bedroomed bungalow that the Wilsons owned on the island. That name was "Lowenwa", which, Mrs Wilson informed me, was Cornish for "House of Happiness".

I interviewed Harold Wilson several times later, after he had become prime minister, and our first encounter was undoubtedly our most congenial. I quoted him in my report as telling me: "This is complete relaxation. There are to be no private meetings of politicians or party managers, no policy hatching, or anything like that. I am here for the cobwebs of Westminster to be swept away."

With a fresh-air tan and his inevitable pipe in his mouth, Mr Wilson looked every inch a carefree tourist as he wandered around in open-necked shirt and sandals.

I was touched when Mary Wilson gave me a handwritten copy of a poem she had just written. It is a work that I still keep among other less welcome souvenirs, such as documents from various prisons where I was held in detention, expulsion orders from one or two countries, and prohibited immigrant decrees forbidding me to enter them.

Such less pleasing memorabilia also include sundry items like the fragment of a Pakistan Air Force plane that attacked Indian positions near which I found myself during the 1970 Indo-Pakistani War. The plane itself was shot down by Indian gunners, the pilot surviving to be entertained in an Indian Army officers' mess where, speaking in English, he chatted away with his English-speaking enemy as if he and his opponents were not at war but discussing things as if it they were on different sides in another kind of contest, such as an India versus Pakistan cricket match!

With more pleasure than any I felt when I obtained that particular chunk of aircraft wreckage, I recall the gift of Mary Wilson's poem. This is what I reported at the time:

> Mrs Wilson, comfortably lounging about in slacks, occasionally composes poetry to suit the peaceful mood. One poem she has written, called "Isles of Scilly", ends this way:
>
> > Now, when the purple dusk comes down,
> > With what a sure tranquillity
> > The lights glow from the little town,
> > And lights flash back across the sea
> > From watchers round the coast, who keep
> > Night-long their vigil without rest,
> > That all of us may safely sleep
> > Upon the islands of the blest.
>
> "At least it rhymes and scans, though that may not be very fashionable," said Mrs Wilson.

She was charming and kind to wandering scribes like myself. The wife of the other Harold and prime minister, Lady Dorothy Macmillan was perhaps rather more aloof from journalists, probably with reason. The whole of Westminster and Fleet Street in those days was aware of a relationship between Lady Dorothy and the Conservative MP, Sir Robert Boothby (later made a Baron), but none of this got into the newspapers at the time. Such discretion simply could not be maintained now, so eager are newspaper publishers and broadcasting organisations to supply their millions of readers, listeners, and viewers with all the latest sexual news about those governing us.

When Harold Wilson became prime minister, he and I remained on amiable terms for years, even though on at least two subsequent occasions we crossed swords on TV while he made the news and I covered it.

Over the years, I met and interviewed half a dozen British prime ministers (Macmillan, Douglas-Home, Wilson, Callaghan, Heath, and Thatcher), not to mention other top British politicians, plus scores, if not hundreds, of foreign and commonwealth leaders. Whatever their politics, I felt that many could well have become actors, even if their apparently natural ability to dissemble would not, on its own, have been enough to ensure stage or screen stardom.

If they had ever needed to do so, however, they could have made a living in the theatre, in the cinema, or on television, just as President Ronald Reagan had once done. He was the only American President with whom I have actually shaken hands … and pleased I was to do so.

Apart from politicians, my work enabled me to meet and interview many other famous figures such as genuine actors and actresses, ranging from glamorous women to crusty old men. The women included Vivien Leigh, the unforgettable Scarlett O'Hara of *Gone with the Wind*. I spent a lot of time with her when she was campaigning to save the Theatre Royal, Haymarket, from destruction for so-called "property development". I am glad that it is still there.

Other memorable encounters with stars included coverage of a stimulating visit to London by a Hollywood film actress who at that time had the most famously beautiful embonpoint in the world, Jayne Mansfield. I found her irresistible and reported so from what I described as "the quietude and safety" of her seventh-floor suite at the Dorchester Hotel, after she had managed to get through the crowd that wanted to see her.

My impressions appeared the next day:

> *With large brown eyes and a Californian tan, she relaxed on a sofa in a toast-brown dress, sipped pink Champagne, and looked beautiful. "Pink," said Miss Mansfield, "is my favourite colour; my swimming pool is pink." Surrounding her were her hairdresser, her publicist, her studio officials and her more or less permanent entourage of reporters and photographers.*
>
> *Her arrival in England was Miss Mansfield's first trip abroad. She talked for over two hours with a charm and a simple friendliness which enchanted almost everyone in sight. She loved, she told us, "our sweet little cars" and thought our "accents are out of this world".*

It was funny, she said, but since arriving in the country this morning, she had begun to feel almost English. The transition, she agreed, might seem a little abrupt, but she had two English grandmothers, one who came from Cornwall.

For such a sexually charged creature whose impressive but decently clad breasts were displayed on film posters all over the world, she was surprisingly capable of appearing less provocative. For a reception later, I reported, "She had changed from her toast-brown dress to one of black that was spectacular in its modesty. It matches her manner perfectly."

Another happy encounter I had with a lovely star was with an opera singer who had sung with the New York Metropolitan Opera for many years and who had appeared at Glyndebourne. On the occasion I met her, she was making her first appearance at Covent Garden in the first English professional stage production of *The Trojans*, the opera by Berlioz. I reported:

Rehearsals were begun in London yesterday by an opera star who will never let her hair down except by appointment. She is the American mezzo-soprano Blanche Thebom, whose height is five feet, seven inches and whose hair is six feet, six inches long. Dark and attractive, she is taking the great role of Dido.

I interviewed Miss Thebom at the Royal Opera House last night after she had spent the day in rehearsals with Sir John Gielgud, the producer, and Rafael Kubelik, the musical director. Her hair was bound in three thick coils round her head. She said, "I always have to wash and rinse it in the bathtub, as a basin is too small. I used to shower it, but the tangles became a bit too difficult to sort out." The problem of avoiding tangles is to be faced by Miss Thebom when the opera is staged.

In Dido's great seven-minute-long death scene, the singer will each night have her hair trailing behind her in all its glory as she lies dying on the funeral pyre. "I shan't have any dresser for it, as I find I am the only person who can put it up and let it down without it getting into knots." Her hair has been growing uncut for thirteen years. Miss Thebom says she has always loved long hair. To go to bed, she always binds it into very tight braids.

"I never brush it, and it takes me only ten minutes in the morning to choose and set my style for the day, unless I am washing it. That takes well over an hour.'

She has a collection of 150 combs, including ivory and tortoise shell devices.

It was not only Miss Thebom, with her need to avoid onstage tangles, who faced problems. For Sir John Gielgud, it was his first attempt at opera production, and in an interview with me, he said, "I hope to goodness I can make some go of all this." I described him as being "almost as anxious as a young actor getting his first part".

An immense challenge even for Covent Garden, the opera entailed a stage and its wings being able to accommodate a huge Trojan horse, an orchestra behind the scenes, and a chorus of 120. Gielgud told me, *"The Trojans* is tremendously difficult but for that reason alone is worth trying. It is new and exciting. I have always wanted to produce a full opera but have always been too frightened to do it. Now that I am at last trying it I am glad it is in an outsize way. The work is really two operas in one: a sort of mix of Virgil and Homer. It is so huge that it's going to be like Trooping the Colour or something."

In keeping with this unrestrained theatricality, Covent Garden sought five Irish wolfhounds, said to be the tallest dogs, for the royal hunt scene where Dido appears as Diana the Huntress. Gielgud said, "But they must not bark and must be very gentle." This was a distinctly challenging requirement, because the dog's reputation was known by the ancient Irish kings, whose arms it supported, as "gentle when stroked, fierce when provoked". A good deal of stroking, then, was needed.

One of the oldest breeds, its origins were apparently unknown, although seven were reputed to have fought in the Rome Circus in AD 391 and some dogs had reached a shoulder height of thirty-seven inches, just over a yard!

I was lucky enough in 1958 also to cover the Covent Garden Centenary Gala performance of opera and ballet, enhanced by royal splendour. The opera house was decorated with rare beauty, and the Queen and Prince

Philip were present among the twenty-three hundred well-dressed people assembled for a historic celebration.

The royal party made their way up the grand staircase, passing tall mirrors flanked by pink and scarlet rhododendrons that matched the scarlet carpet.

They walked through the splendidly decorated crush bar to the royal box in the centre of the grand tier. Guardsmen in blue, scarlet, and gold livery lined the stairs.

Maria Callas was one of the singers, receiving six curtain calls and a prolonged ovation after she had performed as Elvira in the mad scene from Bellini's *I Puritani*.

I still treasure the two-foot-long programme in the form of a prettily fringed nylon-silk scroll, suitably framed and hanging on a wall. Many of the performers with their names on it have since died (Callas and Joan Sutherland to name but just two), but many remain. Just looking at the programme brings to life for me the feeling of what was a truly great occasion. It included Margot Fonteyn, Nadia Nerina, Svetlana Beriosova, Rowena Jackson, Ninette de Valois, Frederick Ashton, Sylvia Fisher, John Lanigan, Forbes Robertson, Owen Brannigan, Otakar Kraus, Joseph Rouleau, and many others. The major singers, dancers, and choreographers, not to mention conductors, would fill their biographies with considerable chunks of musical reference books.

There they all were, together, marking the first one hundred years of Covent Garden. I am quite sorry that I shall not be around to be at the bi-centenary, which I hope will be celebrated in the new Covent Garden setting as magnificently as the centenary.

Interviewing beautiful actresses was fun, as was interviewing comic actors. Among the funniest I have met during my life, the funniest offstage was without doubt the late A. E. Matthews – "Matty". He was eighty-eight when I met him (three years older than I am as I write this), but he was in tremendous form, which helped amusingly to fill the columns of the *Daily Telegraph*.

> He was demonstrating in an uninhibited way against the erection of a concrete lamp post outside his three-hundred-year-old Hertfordshire cottage in which he had lived for fifty-one years.

It was the very last lamp post out of 250 being put up under a scheme for improved street lighting, 249 having been erected until the council ran into unexpected opposition from Matty.

When I got to his home in Bushey Heath in March 1958, he was standing on his snow-covered lawn amid the daffodils, wearing fur-lined boots, a deerstalker hat, and, over his clothes, a dressing gown, two mufflers, and a rug. He announced his plans for battle against Bushey Urban Council: "I'll sit on sentry duty night and day, but they'll never put that gibbet up outside my home."

The offending object, fifteen feet long, lay on its side down the road. It should have been put up a day or two before, but when four workmen arrived to put it up, "Matty" defied them by sitting in a Chippendale chair for four hours over the hole in which they were to have entrenched the lamp post.

He explained to me, with determination, his position: "They'll see me dead before it goes up," he said.

Earlier, while returning from a walk, he slipped down the two-foot deep hole and sprained an ankle. "I am thinking of bringing an action against the council for damages."

Mr Matthews is asking for permission to address the council. 'I'll have plenty to say if I get the chance. The damned thing is just like a gallows. I am sure they're going to finish up by hanging me outside the place and I'm not ready to go yet.'"

Matty explained that while sitting in his Chippendale chair over the hole for the lamp post, he had been strengthened with necessary victuals.

He said, "My wife kept bringing me hot drinks of milk and brandy. It's the only way I can get it! My wife hides it! It was worth sitting out there to get it. I am going to start again if necessary. I don't want that gibbet outside my house. I only need a light there when I go up to the King's Head. It doesn't matter coming back!"

In a long experience of covering "demos", I never heard impromptu and hilarious lines delivered with such panache as that displayed by Matty as a solitary, aged demonstrator. He was just one of many extraordinary characters with whom, as a reporter, I had dealings. Many fell into the category of what a younger colleague and chum, John Simpson, has described in one of his books as "questionable people".

One such, for instance, was Adolf Hitler's former intimate friend and private pianist, Ernst Hanfstaengl, nicknamed "Putzi" and the subject of a biography published not all that long ago. When I met him in 1957 in a London hotel, he had been brought to Britain by the BBC and with the help of the late Randolph Churchill, who had personally intervened on Putzi's behalf with the home secretary.

Earlier, in 1950, Putzi had been refused a visa to enter Britain, and when he tried to get into the country again for the coronation, he was turned back at the port of entry. He had experienced a career that truly was chequered. Having sheltered Hitler after the 1923 Munich beer hall "putsch", he later became a leading Nazi official as foreign press chief. An accomplished pianist, he often played privately for Hitler. He fled from Germany in 1937 when he quarrelled with "Der Fuhrer", his fall being attributed at the time to a dispute with von Ribbentrop, whose influence as Hitler's foreign minister was increasing.

Putzi had been detained in Britain upon the outbreak of the Second World War, and he was detained during and immediately after the war at various times in the Isle of Man, in a house in Wimbledon, and in Canada. While in Canada, he apparently smuggled a letter to President Roosevelt, who, despite Churchill's opposition, agreed to let him work in Washington. Putzi's two sons served in the United States forces during the war.

After Roosevelt's death, Putzi returned to Canada and then to Britain as an internee. In 1947, he was returned to Germany with prisoners of war and in 1949 appeared before a denazification court at Weilheim in Bavaria, being cleared of doing anything terribly bad, even though by sheltering Hitler in 1923, he had inadvertently helped to cause the world a lot of trouble.

Putzi told the court that he had done "valuable" psychological work in Washington during the war. He was an amusing man, producing quips in an unsuccessful attempt to hide his intelligence. This was considerable, as proved by his success in being a survivor from Hitler's early set.

Another controversial German with whom I had dealings was the former head of the West German Intelligence Service. He too had led an unusual life.

In 1944, he had escaped from Germany after the failure of the German generals' plot against Hitler, and he found his way via Spain to Britain. For the remaining months of the war, he worked for the BBC's German transmission service and later for the Foreign Office and a London law firm. He married a British subject, a singing teacher, and I met him in 1959 while he was trying to enter England to join her in her flat in Hampstead while he negotiated book deals with British publishers.

On reaching Dover, however, he was refused permission to land and was detained as an undesirable alien.

The Home Office said he would be sent back to the continent the following day, and I travelled with him on board a Belgian ship to Ostend. From there, I reported his reactions to all of this:

> Dr Otto John, forty-nine, former head of West Germany's political security branch, said today: "I am hurt and surprised at Britain's refusal to allow me to land. I do not want to come to a country where I am an undesirable alien. In Germany, I am regarded as a British agent, and in Britain it seems I am regarded as a Communist."
>
> When the ship reached Ostend, Dr John was escorted by a Belgian police officer onto the Trans-European Express, the Saphir, and instructed to go straight to the German border. He went straight back to Cologne, where he lives in a two-room attic flat.
>
> His parting words to me, as the train left Ostend, were: "Thanks to the English, it looks as if the Belgians also are anxious to get rid of me quickly."

Why had this happened? There was no official explanation given at the time, but after a previous visit to England in 1953, Dr John had disappeared in July 1954, while head of the West German security service. Eventually, he was traced to East Germany and returned to the West in December 1955. He was arrested in West Germany on charges of treason and of maintaining treasonable relations. A year later, he was found guilty of "treacherous falsification" and "treasonous conspiracy". He was sentenced to four years' penal servitude although the federal prosecutor demanded only a two-year sentence, taking into account the year that John had already been in custody. In July 1958, the federal president granted a reprieve.

John claimed at his trial that he had been drugged, abducted to East Germany, and held against his will by the communists. He had, he said, deliberately given them the impression that he was working for them in order to keep open a chance of escape.

This extraordinarily murky story was typical of several with which I dealt over the years involving the careful handling of cloak-and-dagger style personal histories. Equally extraordinary, if less murky, were two encounters I had with an American character of quite a different nature. His undoubted gift was of eloquence allied to commercial enterprise.

At one stage, in 1960, he turned up in the Congo, and to the surprise of everyone, especially the American Embassy, he signed with the late Patrice Lumumba, then the Congolese leader, a deal that virtually gave him control of Congolese mineral wealth. It was the second time I had come across him and his activities, as I reported from the Congolese capital, then still Leopoldville and now Kinshasa:

> *Mr Lumumba, prime minister of the Congo, left Leopoldville today for New York in an RAF Comet. Before his departure, he announced that he had signed a financial and administrative "convention" with an American company for developing the Congo's resources.*
>
> *President and chairman of the company, La Congo International Management Corporation, CIMCO, is Mr Edgar Detwiler, sixty-two. He, too, left in the Comet.*
>
> *I first met Mr Detwiler in London three years ago. He then expounded to me his idea for building 100,000-ton liners to cater for tourists between the United States and Europe.*
>
> *The convention has to be ratified by the Congolese parliament. Mr Lumumba said there were no political strings attached to it. CIMCO was composed of "bankers, industrialists, consulting engineers, economists, lawyers and experts" from*

many countries, in particular "England, Japan, Holland, West Germany, Eire, Canada, France, and the United States". At the airport, Mr Detwiler produced the contract, which was for a term of fifty years. He said that in the initial phase it would be worth about £700 million. "We have three or four hundred companies all over the world who are working with us."

A United States Embassy spokesman described Mr Detwiler as being "a man of imagination". There was no prior consultation with the embassy. The deal is regarded in business circles as being much too wide and general in its terms. The contract makes CIMCO "adviser and operator" in every conceivable type of industrial development.

There is no hiding the fact that the United States Embassy is highly embarrassed. The thing that is feared chiefly is that the contract will fail dismally and discredit American businessmen in Africa.

Four days after its announcement, the contract was denounced by the personal assistant to the Congolese finance minister, saying that the contract was "not legally binding". The Congolese Parliament still had to ratify it, and the Congolese cabinet was split. I reported that it was clear Lumumba's signing of the contract had been done entirely off his own bat and that the reservations of the finance ministry were easily understandable. Neither the contract nor Lumumba lasted long, but I have no idea what happened later to Edgar Detwiler.

Apart from the British traitor "Kim" Philby, I would place at the top of my list of questionable people I have met (even before the names of the late Idi Amin of Uganda and of President Robert Mugabe of Zimbabwe) an unregenerate Nazi. This was a former official of the Nazi foreign office and a Nazi propagandist, Professor Johann von Leers. I met him in Cairo in 1960, after Israel's arrest of Adolf Eichmann, who was accused of supervising for Hitler the extermination of six million Jews. Eichmann was tried in court before television cameras, found guilty of crimes against humanity, and executed. The professor suggested to me that the arrest "may be part of a big Israeli plot".

Three years before I interviewed him, von Leers had embraced the

Islamic faith and used the name "Amin Omar". He disclosed to me that he had met Eichmann in Buenos Aires in 1955, before Israeli agents had tracked him down there. I reported:

> Eichmann, he said, was then living in Argentina with a false Vatican City passport. He talked to him for twenty minutes at an engineering firm called Capri, which was staffed largely by former SS officers and Nazis.
>
> I talked to von Leers and his wife in the pleasant villa of the Cairo suburb of Maadi, where they have lived with their daughter since 1956. It was the first time they had received a British journalist since they came to the United Arab Republic (as Nasser's Egypt was then known) "after Peron's fall in Argentina".
>
> The fifty-eight-year-old German professor, who showed me an anti-Semitic tract which he wrote in Germany before the war, emphasised to me, "I am of the opinion that Israel has no right to judge Eichmann. That state has no right to judge anybody."
>
> Von Leers stated that he first met Eichmann "when I went to live in Argentina, in a free country under Peron, because Germany was already enslaved by the so-called free democracy". There were, he added, "stinking lies" in the newspapers about five million Jews having been gassed, and "as [a] historian, I wanted to talk to Eichmann to know the truth".
>
> However, Eichmann refused to talk to him.

I asked him why. Then Von Leers (or "Amin Omar") went on to make claims of such extravagance that I found difficulty in believing he was actually advancing them, although I reported them faithfully:

> "It was known everywhere in Argentina that Eichmann was living under the protection of Jews whom he had helped to escape from Germany. They were the Rothschilds and the Hungarian Scheyer family. He had done this as an act of insurance when he had foreseen the end of the Third Reich. Many

people felt that Eichmann himself was a Jew who had been made an honorary Aryan. I did not like the man. He was dull and unimaginative. I told him he should tell the truth about the gassing of the Jews as so many people had been accused of it."

In Argentina, said von Leers, Eichmann had used two names. "After Peron's fall, when the Jews and clerics, vultures and ravens, took over in Argentina, I came here."

It was a bizarre and somewhat chilling interview. Chilling too was the front-page splash story that I wrote for the *Daily Telegraph* of 15 May 1964, reporting the confirmation by the Defence Ministry of the beheading of two British soldiers in what was then the South Arabian Federation and is now part of the Yemen.

During the troubles prior to the independence of Aden and its absorption by the Yemen, they had been decapitated after their capture during a skirmish with Arab dissidents. There was a huge row about the disclosure of the news by the general officer commanding the Middle East Land Forces, with Labour MPs criticising him for giving "international currency" on "scanty evidence" to the beheading reports.

The Left, envisaging the later implementation under Harold Wilson's government of a pull-out from "east of Suez", simply did not want the problems of what might follow such a pull-out publicised, because of the prospect of even greater bloodletting. Labour Party defence spokesman Denis Healey expressed "horror and revulsion" at the report. Unfortunately, it turned out to be true.

It was a forerunner to more recent, more frequent, and even more publicised decapitations. The beheading of a captive by the captors of the victim has since been performed "on camera" in places like Iraq and Pakistan for subsequent broadcast by television, to such a degree that not much surprise is now expressed at such barbarism, even though the shock remains.

Another form of twentieth-century barbarism I observed much nearer at home and at close quarters in 1964, when, in Margate of all places, rival gangs of hooligans known as "Mods" and "Rockers" fought on the seafront with each other and with the police.

Youths were stabbed, police officers injured, and forty arrests made.

This was a hitherto unknown form of hooligan blood sport, contrasting with a more ancient kind of blood sport that I reported upon from Dulverton, Somerset, in 1957, when the Devon and Somerset Staghounds met on a misty grey morning at the most publicised stag hunt the West Country had ever seen.

Fifty reporters and cameramen had been invited to the hunt, and some rode with it. Also in conspicuous attendance were campaigners from the League Against Cruel Sports and the Royal Society for the Prevention of Cruelty to Animals, who, forty-eight years later, thought they had won their struggle to outlaw traditional customs like fox and stag hunting when Parliament outlawed those pursuits. However, ten years after that, as I write, there is much talk of Parliament reversing the decision to ban hunting. For the moment anyway, anti-hunt lobbies have been more successful than anti-nuclear lobbies like CND, the Campaign for Nuclear Disarmament.

Among my most unforgettable assignments was covering the start of the first "Aldermaston March" in 1958. It began in Trafalgar Square, with about ten thousand in attendance and with an estimated four thousand or so setting off on the fifty-mile walk to the Atomic Weapons Research Establishment at Aldermaston, Berkshire. I reported the Trafalgar Square scene:

> *Mr Michael Foot, almost shouting into the five microphones before him, raised the loudest cheers, frightening away the pigeons, when he informed the rally: "This can be the greatest march in British history. It can be the start of the greatest movement in British history. This is a crusade that we are going to win."*

Doughty crusader though the old leader of the Labour Party was, his crusade has not yet been won, and it is obvious that it has been easier for Parliament to outlaw hunting than to outlaw nuclear weapons. I know which I would sooner see out of the way.

Quite apart from the threat to the world – and all of us – presented by nuclear arms, there is continuing, vigorous debate over the desirability or otherwise of the peaceful use of nuclear energy. Events such as the disasters of Chernobyl and the 2011 Japanese earthquake and tsunami have highlighted the debate.

A "nuclear option" of my own, on the domestic and emotional front, emerged in the 1960s. I had to decide to continue with an already collapsing marriage or to finish it and start again. As success at work burgeoned, my personal life and marriage deteriorated, with ill effects for the family. I was not a lover or husband of the kind that my first wife really wanted, nor was I a lover or husband of the kind I wanted to be. True marital happiness came later.

In Downing Street with the late Harold Macmillan on the day he became
Prime Minister. He had just returned from Buckingham Palace and looked,
with his watch-chain across his waist-coat, like a successful bookmaker –
while I, with my notebook, looked like a "bookie's runner." © UPI.

In Downing Street again with Jacquetta Hawkes, novelist wife of the
author J.B. Priestley, in 1959, when she handed in to Number 10 a copy
of the Nuclear Disarmament Charter from anti-H. Bomb marchers
at the end of their march from Aldermaston. © Keystone.

CHAPTER 10

Age Four: "Then a Soldier" Different types

If I have doubts about my capacity as a lover, I have no doubts at all about my capability as a soldier: nil.

Although I was an Army Cadet during the 1939–45 war, after it I failed miserably to get into the army. This was unusual during the epoch of National Service, when every eighteen year-old was called up, or drafted. While the war was still being fought, I had been consumed with adolescent enthusiasm to get into it, so it was with a feeling of shame that after hostilities had ended, and following my National Service medical examination, I found myself classed as D4 instead of A1. I was rejected as unfit.

To this day, I feel that I have missed out on an experience then undergone by all young British men: two years of compulsory military, naval, or air force duty. I console myself with the thought that at least my old soldier father, who had just died, was spared the knowledge that the army had declined the services of his son. He would have been distressed and possibly infuriated.

Unlike the Royal Navy, who had turned me down earlier because I was short-sighted, the Army said no because I was suffering from asthma. From my childhood until I was nearly thirty, I suffered severely from that malady, which compelled me for years to carry, wherever I went, an inhaler for use in the event of gasping for breath. It is an appalling affliction, and my sympathies are with those who suffer from it. The asthma simply disappeared in my early thirties, and I hope that it will never return.

Lack of military experience, however, has not stopped me from spending a good deal of time with the army, the Royal Navy, and the Royal Air Force in various parts of the world. I have also experienced close acquaintance with the forces of many other countries as well as with the armed bands of independence (or "liberation" or "freedom") movements and guerrilla groups, the relatively primitive forerunners of today's sophisticated terrorist organisations which recruit suicide bombers and hijack aircraft to crash into skyscrapers.

The development of international terrorism and governmental efforts to defeat it provide what is probably the greatest unfinished story of my lifetime, with nuclear weapons proliferation, current economic crises, and the future of the European Union and indeed of the United Kingdom itself being close runners-up. Often closely linked to terrorism are the unfinished stories of war, violence, dictatorship, and rebellion arising from political, economic, nationalist, or religious struggle in places like Afghanistan or Yemen (to mention just a couple of chronic trouble spots); the endless confrontation in the Middle East between Israel and Muslims determined to destroy that still fairly young state; and the seemingly eternal post-imperial problems of Africa, displayed in geographical, tribal, and demographic areas (such as the Congo, Somalia, or the Sudan), all recognised by the United Nations and our own government as modern states. All are notable for international lawbreaking, whether by armed forces, secret police, desperate mobs, calculating politicians, or simply by pirates, bandits, or plain criminals. It is a depressing list.

First-hand observation of mayhem of one kind or another has led me to detest war in all its forms. However, I have a high regard for professional military men. Most of those I have met dislike war even while practising it. There are exceptions, of course, as there probably always have been.

I think immediately of one particularly flamboyant historic figure, World War II American General George Patton, so superbly portrayed by George C. Scott in the film *Patton*, declaring his passionate love for combat after the particularly bloody Kasserine Pass battle in North Africa.

It has always seemed to me that soldiers tend to be not only fitter than politicians overall but also more straightforward. In that respect, they are probably better qualified than politicians to lead people, although a certain amount of wiliness, or ability to deceive an opponent, are qualities just as necessary for a successful military commander as they are for a politician. This is a general observation and not an argument for military dictatorship, even though in some countries, the conduct of affairs by soldiers has sometimes appeared more effective than when such countries have been run, or run-down by, politicians. My mind turns immediately to Turkey in the 1920s and 1930s under Mustafa Kemal, or Ataturk (a name he assumed in 1935, meaning "Father of the Turks").

Pakistan, too, tottering on the brink of instability ever since independence in 1947, seems to me to have been a much less volatile place when I first visited it, back in the 1950s and 1960s, when ruled by Field Marshal Ayub Khan, than it has been ever since his death. Alternating spasms of political or military rule have ensued in both countries, with Pakistan appearing under political rule somewhat less stable than Turkey.

Much grimmer is the list of corrupt or inadequate military, as well as political dictatorships produced by African states since their post-war creation. For much of my life, it has been my frequently unhappy lot to report upon turbulences following the British withdrawal from Empire, not to mention the departure of other powers from the imperial scene such as France, Portugal, and Belgium.

Exceptions to my broad assertion about worthy soldiers and their ability to lead people are all too obvious, however, and I tend to agree with Prime Minister David Cameron when, in June 2011, during vigorous debate on defence policy involving army, navy, and air force senior officers as well as politicians, he chided the chiefs of staff with these words: "You do the fighting and I'll do the talking."

It was suggested that although it was good that service chiefs were not just yes men but were prepared to stand up to ministers, it would be even better, and more helpful, if they did it in private rather than in public. It is, after all, over 350 years since a soldierly dictator, Oliver Cromwell, ruled – and bullied – England, Scotland, Wales, and Ireland as "Protector of the Commonwealth".

Having survived the difficulties of working in countries run by the worst kind of dictators, military or otherwise, I am able to fully appreciate the simple fact that I am still here at all to reflect upon those difficulties. As somebody who, from the age of ten, grew up in wartime, soldiers, sailors, and aviators were a ubiquitous feature of daily existence. The crews of the anti-aircraft gun batteries on the Sussex Downs sometimes gave us wonderful presents such as chewing gum or chocolate; and we watched them with interest and laughter as they tried to seduce any young woman who flirted with them and who, perhaps, was trying to obtain something glamorous like a pair of nylon stockings (a much sought-after gift). Those young women were girls older than us but known to us from our village infant school days. They included our elder sisters, cousins, and even young aunts.

Some wore the green jersey and khaki trousers of the Women's Land Army, the trilby-like hats of the Women's Voluntary Service (WVS), or the black dungaree-like kit of the Auxiliary Fire Service (AFS). I had one particularly pretty and flighty aunt who was in the AFS and whose antics always fascinated the family. We often wondered what she might be getting up to during her all-night watches, but we were perhaps a little uncharitable. Women in military uniform were a familiar sight, especially those who became known as the "Ack-Ack girls".

They worked in anti-aircraft units and performed non-combatant duties, like plotting and ranging enemy aircraft, thus releasing men for active service. These women served, like the Queen when she was Princess Elizabeth, in the army's ATS (Auxiliary Territorial Service) or were WAAFs (Women's Auxiliary Air Force) or Wrens (Women's Royal Naval Service).

The woman who was eventually to become my mother-in-law was a beautiful apparently fey but impressively competent Wren first officer, attractively photographed in her smart tricorn hat during the war while her husband was away in North Africa and Italy as a squadron leader in the RAF. My sister later became a WAAF and talks with happy nostalgia about her service years with the Women's Auxiliary Air Force. As for the Queen (who qualified as an army lorry driver and mechanic), it was while wearing her ATS uniform that she chose to slip out of Buckingham Palace on the night of victory at the end of the war to mingle, unidentified, with the crowds outside as her parents, George VI and Queen Elizabeth, went onto the balcony to respond to the cheers.

That, of course, was a happy night for millions and a culminating point that marked at least the end of one war, before others erupted.

Education about the tougher side of military service, like death, injury, or imprisonment, began for me at the age of eleven, with the sight of that German airman's body being removed from the wreck of his Luftwaffe Heinkel and a glimpse of a survivor of the aircrew being led away as a prisoner of war.

That education continued when, towards the end of the war, when I was sixteen, hundreds of Russian soldiers arrived in Worthing. They were different to the British, Canadian, and American troops, with the sight of whom we were familiar. Among the Americans were many black soldiers, the first black men my chums and I had ever seen, so unsophisticated and parochial was existence in the country fields of Durrington in those days.

We soon became friendly with the Americans and Canadians, accepting with alacrity their gifts of chewing gum. We were not at all surprised when one of the young women living in our street produced a baby by a black man, although all of us were concerned about what her absent soldier husband would have to say about it when he got back from the war. In the end, he helped bring the child up as his own, the little infant bringing a touch of exoticism to life in Mardale Road, Durrington.

The Russians in Worthing were far from exotic, however. They were not happy men. British forces advancing into Germany had freed them from German prisoner of war camps after the Germans on the eastern front seized the Russians. They rightly feared what Stalin had in store for them when they got home. No matter how hopeless their position might have been, Soviet troops were expected to die rather than surrender. Death was often the Stalinist penalty for men who had fought for their country but who had been imprisoned by the enemy.

When released from Nazi captivity, such a man's freedom sometimes did not last long. Instead of a welcoming return home, he found himself in front of a firing squad.

His unpleasant position, though, as an ordinary Russian soldier released from German captivity, was infinitely preferable to the position of a number of anti-Soviet soldiers who came from areas within the Soviet Union like the Tartar regions and the Ukraine. Such areas had suffered so great and severe Soviet oppression that thousands of men actually joined the Germans to fight against the Russians. For them, after enforced repatriation back to the Soviet Union, there was no hope whatsoever.

I do not know into which category fell the Russians who discovered themselves in Worthing, of all places. What I do remember, though, is that one night they got their hands on a supply of alcohol and went berserk. Many had been billeted in buildings overlooking the seafront promenade. They were "dossing" on the floor of a large upper-storey room opposite the Worthing Pier Pavilion, with a view over the English Channel. In a drunken fury, they wrecked the place.

They tore off the walls radiators which crashed down through the floors below, causing extensive damage. I saw it the next day, as did other people, but I recall no reports of the disturbance. My own feeling was, and is, that they knew they were doomed men; and that an outburst of anguish, fuelled by booze, was the cause of the trouble. Even then, many people in England had doubts about our ally, "Uncle Joe" Stalin, despite his status as a hero, particularly among communists.

The Russians soon disappeared from Worthing, but not before I had become chummy with one of the younger men among them who could speak a little English.

I was deep into teenage enchantment with, and discovery of, Russian writers like Tolstoy, Chekhov, Dostoevsky, and Gogol; and the Russian soldier and I somehow or other managed to conduct halting conversations about Russian literature.

He taught me my first word of Russian, a language that I tackled in a fairly determined way before being posted some thirty-five years later to the Soviet Union as the BBC Moscow correspondent. The young soldier made me repeat the word several times before he said farewell. The word was *dosvidanya*, meaning goodbye. I have often wondered if he made it home again and what happened to him when he got there.

I suppose, though, that I really started to learn something about the difficulties and problems of a soldier's life when I received my first major foreign news assignment in the 1950s. It was to cover the Cyprus troubles. The abortive Suez invasion of 1956 had ended, but its effects were being felt all over the world as post-imperial fervour was at its height and the process of colonial dismantlement was operating in overdrive.

After Indian independence in 1947 and creation of the new post-partition state of Pakistan came independence for Burma (now Myanmar). Earlier, in 1956, the Sudan became independent after the end of the

Anglo-Egyptian condominium. Independence for the Gold Coast, as Ghana, followed. A whole series of imperial departures from Africa, by Britain and other European powers, succeeded this, and it fell to my lot to cover many of these developments.

New states were born with new names: Nyasaland became Malawi; Basutoland, Lesotho; Bechuanaland, Botswana; the Belgian Congo changed to Zaire and later changed back to Congo; Upper Volta became Burkina Faso; Tanganyika and Zanzibar were joined to become Tanzania; Northern Rhodesia became Zambia; Southern Rhodesia was transformed into the unhappy Zimbabwe of today; and South-West Africa became Namibia. Much of the transition was accompanied by upheaval.

Also developing in fits and starts, headed by outsize figures such as Nasser, Nehru, and Tito, was the much publicised "Non-Aligned Movement" of countries that rejected Western colonialism but were unable to decide how genuinely anti-totalitarian they were.

Non-alignment never really recovered fully from the shock of the collapse of what became known as the "Bandung" spirit of "Afro-Asian Solidarity". This got its name from the Indonesian city of Bandung, where, in 1955, a conference of Afro-Asian states was held to establish this tenuous "solidarity". It more or less vanished in the 1960s, together with the laboriously constructed but rather spurious period of Indian and Chinese friendship, known familiarly in India at the time as "Hindi-Chini Bai-Bai".

After the flight of the Dalai Lama from Tibet to India in 1959, and the brief but nasty Indo-Chinese Himalayan frontier war in Ladakh that followed when India had granted asylum to the god-king, "Bye-bye" was waved to "Bai-bai". Cautiously, Indo-Chinese relations have since been laboriously but somewhat more realistically reconstructed.

The traditional anti-colonialist and anti-imperialist posture of the United States, derived from their anti-imperial origins, benefited the Americans for some time. Since then, however, while forgetting the generosity of the Americans in rebuilding Europe in particular after the war (with efforts such as "Marshall Aid"), many critics have come to view some United States policies as projecting America's own form of imperialism, involving the export of its own ideas of republican democracy, not to mention the power of Washington, DC.

From the other side of what was, for much of my lifetime, the superpower divide of Churchill's memorable "Iron Curtain", the Soviet Union tried to extend from Moscow its own "empire of evil", as President Ronald Reagan equally memorably labelled it.

Meanwhile, we older European empires were undergoing irresistible dismantlement. One difficult case, still unresolved despite fifty-four years of independence, was provided by the third largest island in the Mediterranean Sea, Cyprus. Occupied in 1878 by Great Britain in agreement with the sovereign power, the Ottoman Empire, the island was part of a deal by which Britain became the administrative power in Cyprus in return for assuring Turkey of British help if the Russian empire of the Tsars ever attacked Turkish eastern provinces.

However, after the First World War and the defeat of Germany and its allies, including Turkey, Cyprus formally became a British colony. Influential figures in the island and in Greece started a campaign among the majority Greek-speaking population for Cypriot union with mainland Greece ("Enosis").

Such demands were unwelcome to Turkey for its own reasons, including the welfare of the large minority of Turkish Cypriots, and to Britain for other reasons, including defence considerations.

Both sets of reasons were understandable, not only because of the objections of the Turkish Cypriots to union with Greece but also because of the danger of Greece upsetting Turkey if the "Enosis" campaign went too far (as it did) and so encouraged militant Muslim tendencies to weaken in Turkey the comparatively recent Turkish inheritance from Kamal Ataturk of democracy and secularism. The position was thus complex and needed careful handling. Unluckily, it did not get it. The problem was exacerbated when during the 1950s Enosis campaign the colonial secretary of the time committed Britain to a policy which plainly was likely to collapse. While empire was being discarded elsewhere, he declared that Cyprus would "never" be independent.

That "never" (deplored even at the time) had unfortunate results. The Enosis campaign became more violent. Repression followed terrorism. Mistrust developed between Greek Cypriots, Turkish Cypriots, Greece, Turkey, and Britain. A violent role was played by EOKA ("Ethniki Organosis Kypriakou Agonos", the "National Organisation of Cypriot Struggle"), led by a former Greek Army officer, Colonel Georgios Grivas, who became known as "Dighenis", or "The Leader" (the same unambiguous title as that employed in their heydays by Adolf Hitler ("Der Fuhrer") and Benito Mussolini ("El Duce").

Unlike them, however, Grivas did not come to a sticky end. Neither, however, did he achieve his objective of Cypriot union with Greece. His actions, though, together with the Byzantine political and religious leadership of Archbishop Makarios, did help to result in the establishment of the Republic of Cyprus in 1960, less than ten years after the colonial secretary had declared that the colony would "never" be independent.

I reached the island at the height of the troubles, with soldiers and civilians (including women) being murdered almost daily. I got to know many of the troops and their officers, as well as Greek Cypriot leaders such as Glafkos Clerides and Turkish Cypriot leaders such as Rauf Denktash, both of whom lived to become old men.

As the months went by and the blood continued to flow, the future of Cyprus became a major issue. Among the up-and-coming politicians who involved themselves in the problem was the late Dame Barbara Castle. She flew to the island and delivered some controversial remarks about the behaviour of British soldiers that infuriated them and did her no good in England, although Greek Cypriot propagandists approved of her. Mrs Castle criticised not only the troops but also the British authorities and countermeasures taken against terrorists.

It was a familiar pattern for our age, with more recent examples of it provided from Iraq, where the authorities came under fire because of natural indignation over what appeared to have happened with prisoners held there. In a civilised society, it is right that there should be such concern. So official inquiries are pursued, findings are made, and anybody found responsible should pay for it.

Sometimes, however, indignation over what might have occurred in nasty circumstances can end up with a politician or journalist committing an error by accepting as fact something that is disputable. Personal feelings are perhaps permitted to overcome professional doubts. The consequences can be painful. Falling into this category perhaps (to cite an example from not so long ago) involved the alleged bad behaviour of British forces not in Cyprus but in Iraq. The editor of the *Daily Mirror* at the time, Piers Morgan, paid the price.

Unlike Barbara Castle, who did not lose her job as an MP, Morgan was sacked after his newspaper published pictures of what was purported to be mistreatment of prisoners by British troops in Iraq. He had been convinced that the pictures were genuine; then it turned out that they had not been taken in Iraq at all.

Although Mrs Castle kept her job, she suffered financially much more than Morgan apparently did. It was reported that he was well paid off by the *Mirror* on his departure. However, the home of the Castles, I was told at the time, had to be sold by her husband, Ted, (like myself, a journalist) in order to pay the legal costs of an unsuccessful court action that she brought arising from her attack on the army and the authorities.

My sympathies went to both of the Castles for that, but my sympathies were also engaged by the troops who were at the receiving end of Barbara Castle's criticism. This was particularly so because I had myself inquired into charges levelled against the army by Greek Cypriots, and I had come to a different conclusion than the verdict at which she arrived. I doubted the veracity of many of the allegations, while she endorsed them, so lending to them political weight.

The affair began in September 1958, in the Paphos district of Cyprus, when men of the Argyll and Sutherland Highlanders were ambushed and Greek Cypriots complained that they were beaten up in searches afterwards. A tremendous anti-British propaganda campaign was launched.

Archbishop Makarios, later to become the first president of Cyprus, accused the soldiers of "indiscriminate massive retaliation". The mayor of Limassol complained to the International Red Cross about what he termed "British brutality".

Athens Radio excelled itself: troops were described as "felons" and as "filthy cannibals" who were "tearing the flesh from the people in the name of colonialism." It declared that compared with what it described as "British crimes" in Cyprus, "the late Hitler appears as a saint".

A senior Cyprus government official said that the Athens Radio output, with what he called "its daily dose of muck", was one of the larger difficulties with which the authorities had to cope.

Yet, as I reported at the time, "into the ears of every Greek Cypriot in a coffee shop go snatches of abuse and invective which would be funny if it were not so effective". Indeed, it was in fact occasionally humorous to the British ear, as when Athens Radio described the Argylls as "wild animals from England". An officer of the Highlanders complained, "They might get the country right."

So loud was the outcry that a government investigation team was dispatched to the villages in the area. An official statement was issued. This claimed that damage caused in the searches was largely of a minor character. It added, "It must be appreciated that not only were the soldiers engaged, following a terrorist ambush, in searching for the killers of one of their comrades, but that the villagers were uncooperative to the point of serious resistance in one case."

Feeling uneasy about it, because brutality, pillage, and even rape were serious charges to be levelled at the army, I made an on-the-spot inquiry of my own.

I drove to the scene of the ambush and afterwards to Kathikas, the village at the centre of the district alleged to have been terrorised. The simplest way of describing what I found is to reproduce relevant extracts from the report that appeared in the *Daily Telegraph*:

> *I was accompanied, for my own security only, by a military escort, but I was free to talk to whom I liked, both villagers and soldiers, without any official interference.*
>
> *It was in Kathikas that two of the Highlanders were seriously wounded by a Greek Cypriot who was shot dead after he had stabbed the pair. Greek sources declare that the man was defending his wife and children from rough handling by the troops.*
>
> *I interviewed the lance corporal who killed the man. At my request no officers were present as I talked to him and questioned him closely on the shooting. He said that he and his two companions went into the room where the man was, and he grabbed a knife from under the pillow. He attacked both of the lance corporal's comrades in the presence of his wife and children and the lance corporal withdrew to outside the building so as to avoid hurting the woman and her family.*
>
> *The two wounded men came staggering out with the Greek Cypriot after them, still brandishing his knife. The lance corporal said, "I took aim, shot him dead, and that was that."*

It was not, though, because apart from the row provoked by Mrs Castle's intervention, many other allegations had been made against the troops. I pursued inquiries and reported thus:

> I was also allowed to speak, unaccompanied by officers, to more "other ranks" who were engaged on the search operation after the ambush. None of them denied that they were in high tempers at the attacks on their comrades, but all stated emphatically that they had not ill-treated anyone.
>
> "After the stabbing, our company commander ordered us to keep cool and go on with the job we were doing quite properly," said one Highlander to me, "and that is what we did."

Into this dangerous political and military mess, while terrorism, murders, and countermeasures continued, there materialised the notoriously fiery Labour MP for Blackburn. I had met her years before, when she was allied with "Nye" Bevan and the left-wing "Tribune" group of the Labour Party, and I had reported some of the speeches for which she was noted. But by 1958, she was emerging as a politician who was more than just a red-haired rabble-rouser.

She had become vice chairman of the Labour Party and was due to succeed James Callaghan as chairman. She spent three days in Cyprus, most of the time with members of a Greek Cypriot body called a "Human Rights Committee", set up to publicise alleged offences by British forces.

On the day of her departure, she stoked up already smouldering furnaces of anger by alleging not only that British soldiers were being "permitted" to use "unnecessarily tough" measures against Greek Cypriots when engaged on anti-EOKA terrorist hunts, but that they were actually "encouraged" to do so.

There was immediate reaction by the authorities.

The director of military operations, Major General "Joe" Kendrew (himself lucky to survive an assassination attempt by EOKA when they detonated a mine which blew up behind his car) had previously issued specific orders on how soldiers should go about their duties. His chief of staff, Brigadier Paul Gleadell, showed me orders signed by himself on behalf of the director. They were quite specific:

Indiscriminate roughness, unnecessary destruction of property, discourtesy, and collective punitive measures have no place in internal security operations and merely make the task of the security forces harder by playing into the hands of the other side.

The last line of the order, which went to all units, was as follows:

Commanders will see that such instances do not occur and take disciplinary action should they do so.

When I study the terms of those orders to the British Army in Cyprus from half a century ago, I cannot help wondering if they are comparable with the shape of today's orders to the British Army in Afghanistan or elsewhere. I hope they are.

While formulating her accusations against the forces and the authorities, Mrs Castle had relied solely on what was produced as "evidence" from local inhabitants, being welcomed with cheers and bouquets in every village she visited.

She told me, "I received those because I had taken the bother to answer the villagers' telegrams and go to see the position for myself." It never seemed to have occurred to her that perhaps she was being manipulated and used by the "Human Rights Committee".

She made no bones about disbelieving governmental statements, just as many people today dismiss as whitewash any conclusions produced by a public inquiry, including inquiries headed by prominent men like Lord Hutton or Lord Butler. She told me, "I think the government investigations were incomplete and inadequate."

It was not long before she herself was at the receiving end of political "flak". As chairman of the Labour Party, James Callaghan, later prime minister, discreetly distanced himself from her position. Mrs Castle herself attempted quite quickly to tone down some of her comments by suggesting that she had not said, or meant to say, that the authorities were "encouraging" the troops in their "unnecessarily tough measures'.

By then, it was too late. The political damage had already been done, and propaganda use of Mrs Castle's outburst continued. The "Human Rights Subcommittee of Paphos", a branch of the Greek Cypriot Human

Rights Committee, issued a report on what it said was the "unprecedented cruelty" of British soldiers and claimed that accusations made against the Argylls had been confirmed by somebody described as an "independent investigator", namely Mrs Castle. She had, the Paphos report claimed, shown an "honest, human interest in visiting the villages concerned".

Back in England by now, Mrs Castle was conducting what would today be regarded as a damage limitation exercise on behalf of herself and her future. She said she had only visited the villages in a personal capacity and not, presumably, as vice chairman of the Labour Party.

It emerged that despite having been invited by the colonel of the Argylls to hear their side of the story, she had made no contact with them. This omission, I am convinced, told against her in the court action that she brought.

The case was against Chris Chataway, former athlete, television personality, and eventually Tory MP. It arose from events during the 1959 general election campaign. Chataway was campaigning for the Lewisham North seat, and he had made some remarks on television deploring the conduct of British politicians who went abroad and, by attacking the conduct of British forces, more or less offered aid and comfort to the enemy. This was disobliging to Mrs Castle, and she sued Chataway for libel.

Although I had returned to England to help in election coverage, and in the process had met Chataway as well as his opponents in Lewisham, his television attack had completely escaped me at the time. It was not until a year or so later, when I was back in the Middle East, that I received a call from the foreign news editor, asking me if I still had my Cyprus notebooks and if I could recall what Mrs Castle had said. Luckily, I did still have them, and I could clearly remember what had happened.

With another correspondent who had reported what Mrs Castle had alleged, I was summoned to the trial in London as a witness. Obviously, the cost of our airfare and hotel bills was going to add to all the other legal costs that would have to be paid by the loser of the case.

In this event, it was Barbara Castle. I took my hat off to her when, years later, I met her again, by which time she had become a minister in Harold Wilson's government. By that time, I was the BBC Commonwealth correspondent and she was the minister for overseas development. I had not seen her since appearing in the high court, when I suspect that my evidence about her not having responded to the invitation by the colonel of the Argylls to go and listen to their side of the story in Cyprus did not exactly help her case.

Somewhat hesitantly, I reminded her of the affair, because I did not want to start off on the wrong foot with a minister with whom I would have to deal in the course of my duties. She smiled, told me to forget about it, and even suggested that it had all been her own fault. We got along comfortably together after that, as she was a naturally warm person. I was astonished to read recently that people who could not have been her actual political opponents, but were merely descendants of her opponents, were objecting to a street, or something or other, in Blackburn being named after her as a memorial. This struck me as being mean-spirited, and it certainly displayed a meaner spirit than Barbara Castle herself ever showed.

Immediately after the Cyprus row over the behaviour of British troops, I received a letter from the commanding officer of the regiment concerned, Colonel Charles Anderson. It was dated 24 September 1958 and headed with the crest of the First Battalion, The Argyll and Sutherland Highlanders. I have retained the handwritten note as an honest record of what a soldier felt about the difficulties of his job and as an indicator and reminder of what soldiers probably still feel today when they find themselves on unpleasant internal security duties.

Colonel Anderson wrote: "Dear Osman, I should like to thank you for the support you have given to my Battalion in your paper. It is most gratifying to see that some people still stick up for the soldier of today. He has a practically impossible task to carry out."

Colonel Anderson's sentiments about the "practically impossible task" faced half a century ago by troops on "internal security operations" remain relevant today.

Presumably consideration of such difficulties as the colonel had in mind do still enter into the calculations of any prime minister or minister of defence thinking of committing British forces to such types of operation, but sometimes I wonder if this is so. The colonel concluded his letter by saying that all his men who were wounded "are now either recovered or on the road to recovery and no longer cause anxiety".

A colonel of quite a different sort beat up my television cameraman when I was reporting for the BBC from Nigeria during the Biafra War. This was Colonel Benjamin Adekunle of the Nigerian Federal Army. He became notorious as "The Black Scorpion" and did not disguise his contempt for journalists.

Nevertheless, faced with the job of covering a nasty war, we continued to try to report on what was going on in his sector of command, around Port Harcourt, with the Third Marine Commando Division. Aware of this particular "Scorpion's" sting, I went to some lengths in the former Nigerian capital, Lagos, to equip my cameraman, a Nigerian freelance, and myself with all the requisite army movement orders and authorisation before venturing anywhere near Port Harcourt. It made no difference to the colonel.

The cameraman and I walked down the steps of the military aircraft which had flown us to Port Harcourt, and the moment we set foot on the tarmac, a slight, wiry figure in officer's uniform took one look at the camera being carried by my cameraman, leapt forward in fury, and began to attack him physically.

"The Black Scorpion", for it was he, showered my unfortunate colleague with blows to his head and torso. The cameraman ducked and tried to ward off the assault inflicted by the colonel's fists as well as his officer's swagger stick. I protested loudly, producing my military bits of paper.

At this, the colonel stopped attacking the cameraman. Then he complained bitterly that nobody on the staff in Lagos had told him that we were to visit his sector. He ordered us to get back onto the aircraft forthwith and return to the capital. We did this with pleasure, especially the cameraman.

Trouble for me of a different kind, involving another Nigerian officer, followed a scoop TV interview I obtained following the collapse of civilian rule in Nigeria. That was in January 1966, when the giant African state first fell into the hands of military rulers.

The coup came six years after independence, just after the conclusion in Lagos of the first Commonwealth Prime Ministers' Conference ever to take place outside London.

Nigeria's first head of government, the doomed president, Sir Abubakar Tafawa Balewa, had barely said farewell to his presidential and prime ministerial guests, such as Harold Wilson, when the rebels struck. They seized Abubakar, drove him out of the city and shot him dead. His body was dumped in a ditch.

Other leaders were killed, including the key figure in the powerful northern region of Nigeria, with its Muslim majority population, the Sardauna of Sokoto, Sir Ahmadu Bello. The Sardauna's end came in Kaduna, when he was shot after an assault on his official residence led by a Sandhurst-trained officer, Major Chukwuma Nzeogwu. The major described to my BBC TV crew and me the circumstances and "accidents" of the attack he had led, resulting in the death of at least one woman.

We had managed to get into Kaduna after reports of disturbances began to trickle through to Lagos, but we knew little else about what had occurred.

We headed for the Sardauna's palace and ended up in front of it, with the major before our camera and microphone. My interview with the major was given prominence on BBC TV News, and part of it was reported verbatim by the *Times*, from which I quote because, in view of the critical reaction afterwards, it is perhaps worthwhile reproducing the transcript of the interview published by the newspaper.

I began, as I believe most professional reporters would have done, by asking him what had happened, as we had no real knowledge of what had gone on, despite many rumours:

> *Major Nzeogwu: "Well, when we went in there, there were a lot of guards, policemen, and some of us. Naturally, they tried to shoot us, so we shot them first."*

> *Osman: "Were there many casualties?"*

> *Nzeogwu: "Oh, not very many, no."*

> *Osman: "Can you give me an idea?"*

Nzeogwu: "I don't know. On our side, yes, one ... and our injured ... and the number of policemen, I think about three or four have been killed."

Osman: "Did the Sardauna himself attempt to fight?"

Nzeogwu: "No, we didn't see him until the time we actually shot him. He ran away from his house when we fired the first few shots from an anti-tank gun into the building. The whole roof was blown off and the place was still alight. Then we went to the rear of the house and there searched it from room to room until we found him among the women and children, hiding himself. So we took away the women and children and took him."

Osman: "Were the women and children safe, or did they die?"

Nzeogwu: "Oh, they were safe. No problem at all. We didn't bother much with them. We had to get them out in front because they tried to surround him and protect him. They were mostly the women of his harem, and children."

Osman: "There was one report that one of his wives had died. Is this true in fact?"

Nzeogwu: "Oh, that is possible because we fired so many shots, and in the darkness, you know, accidents are bound to occur, yes."

Forty years on, the major's account of events and his casual reference to "accidents" has a distinctly chilling effect on me, as it did at the time I put my questions to him and heard his matter-of-fact replies. It had a distinctly chilling effect on many other people too.

Horrified reaction took the form of criticism, from some quarters, of the way in which I had handled the interview. There were questions in the Commons and letters to newspapers. A former governor of Northern

Nigeria, Sir Bryan Sharwood-Smith, wrote to the *Daily Telegraph*, expressing outrage:

> *Sir,*
>
> *As scores of others must have been, I was shocked to see on BBC television news the principal murderer interviewed just as though he was a successful footballer, as he described the "operation" that he had conceived and carried out with so much ruthlessness and cunning.*
>
> *What effect is this apparent condonation of mass murder going to have on the more impressionable and less knowledgeable of its viewers in this country? Is this another example of BBC "realisms"? Is it suggested that this is merely the sort of thing that one can expect in Africa?*

Mercifully, I had no knowledge of such criticisms, for at the time they were being aimed at the BBC and me, I had already been dispatched elsewhere by my employers and was out of touch. If I had known about the criticism, I might well have responded. The suggestion that in some way I had condoned mass murder would have undoubtedly angered me. When I conducted the interview, I was seeking information on what had actually occurred, not trying to act as a prosecuting counsel against a soldier charged, in Sir Bryan's words, with "mass murder".

As for his point about it being wrongly suggested (as was his implication) that mass murder "is merely the sort of thing that one can expect in Africa", all I would add is that I might have been tempted to reply with what would have been, most definitely, a politically unfashionable affirmative. I could well have responded, "Yes! This definitely is the sort of thing that one can expect in Africa."

By that point in my life, I had already seen what had happened in the Congo, after Belgian withdrawal; in the Southern Sudan, after British withdrawal; and in Ethiopia, during the first abortive attempt in 1960 to overthrow the emperor; then subsequently in Somalia and Eritrea.

The harsh fact that blood was (and still is) far too easily and far too often shed in Africa has not always been accepted by well-meaning individuals such as Sir Bryan, who (to my way of thinking) are not only

high-minded but woolly-minded as well. They have often appeared surprised when blood is flowing. In my view, for a former governor of a big
African region apparently not to have realised that massacres in Africa
were (and are) all too possible would seem to be a sign of possible senility
or of downright incompetence.

I might have been tempted to say so if I had known about the row at
the time. Fortunately, though, by the time the controversy was brought
to my notice, it was academic as far as I was concerned, because it had
escalated to the level of the BBC Board of Governors where I had been
cleared of any charge of condoning mass murder.

The first I learned of it all, weeks later, was when I received a letter
in India from the BBC foreign news editor. He informed me that as a
result of criticisms publicly expressed about the TV interview with Major
Nzeogwu, the governors had taken a "highly unusual" step by arranging
for a special screening of my TV film report so that they could judge it
for themselves. Happily for me, the governors not only found nothing to
deplore in my work, but I was also sent a message of congratulations on it.

The active intervention of the BBC governors in the 1960s contrasts
oddly with what appears to have been their relative inaction, years later,
at a crucial stage in the Campbell-Gilligan affair over the alleged possession of weapons of mass destruction by Iraq and the consequent suicide
of David Kelly. That row resulted in the abolition of the old BBC Board of
Governors and the establishment of a different form of governing body.

Looking back on the fallout over my Nigerian coverage, I do not
think it would have done me much good with my employers if I had
contributed my own penny's worth to the controversy.

This is because, in broad terms, the governors were part of what has
become known as the "liberal establishment". My style of thinking, more
realistic than that of those who were shocked when African events spun
out of control, was unacceptable at the time to many of the powers that
be, including the secretary general of the United Nations at that time, U
Thant. His description of African political troubles, uttered at the time
of Congolese post-independence mayhem, has always stuck in my mind.
Africa, he said, was suffering from "teething troubles".

Here we are, fifty years on, and the "teething troubles" of Africa seem
to have perpetuated themselves far beyond the milk-tooth stage. Wars,

conflict, terrorism, corruption, crime, piracy, poverty, and disease prolif-
erate. Even the most industrialised state in black-ruled Africa (as distinct
from Arab Africa) has added itself to a list of states with a dubious future:
South Africa. It has an excessive crime rate; President Zuma seems to be,
at the very least, a somewhat self-indulgent leader if all reports about his
wealth and political behaviour are true (not least the Republic's baffling
diplomatic protection of Robert Mugabe in neighbouring Zimbabwe);
and there are, inevitably, acute worries about what will happen in South
Africa now that Nelson Mandela has died.

That list is painful for anyone who loves Africa. I spent some twelve
years or so of my life knocking about the continent, and I witnessed quite
a lot of the dismantlement of Empire. The after-effects have not always
been impressive, but it is simply not credible now to blame the colonialists
and imperialists for today's events. Too frequently, they are shameful for
Africa and for Africans.

When the imperialists were in charge, even though the territories
concerned were not democratically self governed, they were at least
efficiently and relatively honestly governed. In broad terms, despite colossal geographic problems, enormous health hazards, and technological
backwardness – and despite constant political, ideological, religious, and
moral criticism directed against those old imperialists and colonists – they
did achieve concrete and specific progress, whether they were British,
French, Portuguese, or Belgian.

Slavery had been outlawed and roads, railways, schools, and hospitals
built. Moreover, life expectancy for the ordinary African lengthened
as scourges like malaria and other diseases were attacked. Dedicated
colonial district commissioners, perhaps men like Sir Bryan, devoted their
lives to such tasks.

Even now, as Africa seems to stagger on from one disaster to another,
something of what the imperialists and colonists managed to construct
has survived; and, of course, much of what they achieved could not have
been done without African cooperation and support.

There are, and always have been, able, hard-working, and courageous
African men and women who try to improve the general conditions of
African existence and who dedicate their lives to the service of their
fellow human beings. The odds against their succeeding in the face of

widespread and endemic corruption, as well as poverty and disease, remain enormous, however. The right people, though, are still there.

In Uganda, for instance, their existence was proved to me – and personified for me – in the shape of an English-speaking Ugandan army paratroop officer to whom I have particular reason to be grateful. He saved the lives of my wife, Virginia, and me when threatened by his fellow Ugandan soldiers.

Once described by Winston Churchill, when he was under-secretary of state for the colonies, as "the pearl of Africa", Uganda has experienced more than its fair share of post-independence troubles. Independence from Britain came in October 1962, and I first visited the country in March 1963 with Churchill's son-in-law, Duncan Sandys, then the Commonwealth and Colonial Secretary, when Uganda was already passing through a period of uneasy constitutional transition.

Preparations were being made for the British governor-general, as the Queen's representative, to be replaced as Head of State. The first president of Uganda was the ruler of the Baganda people, the most influential of Uganda's several semi-autonomous tribal kingdoms. This was the Kabaka of Buganda, Mutesa II, a man known to British newspapers as "King Freddie". His prime minister was Milton Obote, who, in 1966, suspended the 1962 independence constitution.

Obote's troops attacked and captured the Kabaka's palace with an up-and-coming soldier, the late Idi Amin, personally active in the assault with a gun mounted on his Jeep. The Kabaka escaped to England, where he died three years later.

Amin overthrew Obote in due course, and his murderous military regime began. It was while under Amin's dictatorship of Uganda that one of his para officers protected my wife and myself.

It happened in 1972, when Amin launched his onslaught against Asians living in Uganda. I was in the process of being posted from the United States to South Africa, to report on Southern African affairs. The BBC suggested in the casual way which foreign news desks so often display when ordering a foreign correspondent onto an assignment, that I might like to "drop in" on Uganda on the way to Johannesburg and "have a look at things".

"Things" were unpleasant. Asians were fleeing; Uganda was plainly heading for crisis and chaos; and I advised Virginia to leave Kampala and head south. She was travelling with me for two reasons: first, because she was accompanying me anyway en route to a new posting; and second, because she wanted to spend time in Uganda gathering material for a book which she had been commissioned to write on East Africa.

As a journalist herself, as well as a woman of independent spirit, she declined my advice to leave Uganda, and instead of heading south, she drove westwards from Kampala towards the Ruwenzori, the Mountains of the Moon. An official of the Ugandan tourist organisation accompanied her, and the pair of them were equipped with all the necessary passes to enable them to do their work.

Meanwhile, things in Uganda worsened and rumours began to circulate about clashes on the border to the south between the Ugandan army and troops from neighbouring Tanzania, where Milton Obote had taken refuge. His host, President Julius Nyerere of Tanzania, loathed Amin and everything that a military regime represented, and he stood by his fellow left-wing politician, Obote. The Tanzanian Army eventually forced Amin out of Uganda in 1979.

As the atmosphere deteriorated, I began to worry seriously about Virginia, since she was in an upcountry area just north of the troubled frontier region, in a town then called Fort Portal. Trying, so to speak, to kill two birds with one stone, I decided at the weekend to head for the border area myself to find out what was going on – and at the same time look for Virginia. From the border, I planned to continue to Fort Portal and then to return from there with my wife to Kampala. This we eventually managed, but only as prisoners.

Attempting to get as near as I could to the frontier clashes, I drove south and west along the shores of Lake Victoria to Masaka and Mbarara. It soon became obvious that things were not normal, the towns being weirdly deserted. When I stopped to refill the hired car with petrol, at what looked like an abandoned and damaged service station, I hooted several times before a solitary scared-looking man crept out onto the forecourt to get the pump going. He said that soldiers had been there the day before, looting and rounding up Asians; and that some of the troops were in an ugly mood, having apparently been in unsuccessful action against the Tanzanians.

This caused me to worry even more about my wife. I pressed on to

Fort Portal, where, as I drove into the town, Asians were being forcibly rounded up by Ugandan troops and roughly loaded onto open army trucks to be driven off somewhere. Women in saris were crying, children were crying, and men were subdued. I took in as much of the scene as I could before heading for the Mountains of the Moon Hotel, feeling that I had to get out the news of what I had seen.

The pleasant old-style colonial establishment was deserted, except for one or two members of its staff and one visitor at the hotel: my wife. Her companion from the tourist office had made himself scarce as soon as he had heard about military action not far away and the Asian round-up had started.

I wrote a dispatch for the BBC on what I had witnessed and managed to get through by telephone to the BBC stringer in Kampala, a young free-lance journalist who later became a notable BBC correspondent, Philip Short. He transmitted my dispatch onward to London and advised me not to move from the hotel under any circumstances whatsoever – and especially not to try to get back to Kampala, because "things are going on". What was going on was that the entire corps of visiting foreign correspondents in Uganda was being rounded up and detained.

There was one exception. Either the Amin regime had decided that for some reason the man from the *Times* should remain free or, alternatively, the man from the *Times*, on learning what had happened to his colleagues, himself then did a disappearing act and sensibly kept changing his known whereabouts to avoid being picked up. An old friend and colleague from the United States, he had a pronounced sense of humour and was named Michael Knipe. After the success of his evasive tactics, he was dubbed "Knipe of the Nile".

Also escaping detention was Philip Short himself. As a resident corre-spondent, he was better known to the Ugandan authorities than the rest of the visiting journalists and so perhaps regarded by the authorities with less suspicion than the rest of us.

Anyhow, Virginia and I sat down that evening as the only guests in the Mountains of the Moon Hotel. As we had a drink, a group of Ugandan army officers came in and chatted amiably with us. They were quite friendly, even after I told them that I was a BBC correspondent. They sat down to dinner at their table, and we sat down to dine at ours.

One of them switched on a short-wave radio and tuned in to the BBC World Service and *Radio Newsreel*. Over the air came my own voice, with my dispatch, ending with the words "John Osman, BBC, Fort Portal".

Into the balmy evening and the hitherto friendly dining room, glacial ice descended. There was silence at the army table and silence at ours. The officers disappeared into the night, and we retired to our room. I told Virginia that we were about to be arrested.

The next morning, three or four men, all wearing what appeared to be in Africa the required gear for security officials in those days, civilian suits of a uniform nature plus sunglasses, burst into our room, shouting, "Here are the bastards!" and "Where have you hidden the weapons?"

They tore off the bed sheets and blankets, upended the mattress, and made themselves unpleasant without actually hurting us. We gathered our overnight bags (for we were both travelling light) and were hustled off in a truck to an army base, where we were questioned, politely but in an accusatory fashion, by a uniformed officer who commented that I seemed remarkably well informed. This I interpreted as being not a compliment but almost as a criminal charge.

He was momentarily disconcerted when Virginia produced her Ugandan tourist office permits and passes. These useful bits of paper undoubtedly helped us in what Victorian adventure writers would have described as a sticky situation or a tight spot. They helped especially per-haps myself, at the sharp end of army sensitivities about BBC reporting of the military round-up of Asians, although I too had Ugandan government accreditation as a journalist.

We were placed in a Ugandan army land rover with a driver and with an escort of a lieutenant and two soldiers to be driven off we knew not where. It was on the journey back towards Kampala that the lieutenant became our quiet and efficient saviour. To this day, I do not know who he was or (I hope and trust) still is.

We set off in the evening and drove towards the Ugandan capital. In darkness, we reached a place called Mubende, about halfway to Kampala. Just as Mary Tudor, Queen Mary I, declared that Calais was engraved upon her heart after England lost possession of that busy channel-port city in 1558, so my wife and I retain Mubende engraved upon our own hearts as a place where we nearly lost our lives in the African bush in 1972.

There was a sizeable Ugandan army base there, and as we drew up near its entrance, half of the army appeared to be present, much of it drunk. The place had a notorious reputation, and because two American journalists had disappeared inside just such a Ugandan army base never to be seen again, the last thing we wanted was to be dragged inside also. The rabble that was supposed to be an army gathered round our vehicle, which was brought to a halt. I was manhandled out of it while our escorting officer tried to talk to men who appeared to be the rabble leaders.

As he talked, he stationed his three soldiers travelling with us, including the armed driver, at key points outside the entrance of the base, as if positioning his men to open fire against anybody who tried to lay hands upon my wife or myself.

Nobody tried to molest Virginia, but I was pushed around a bit as loud debate reverberated among the rabble, and the lieutenant calmly replied to each point that was raised. This went on for half an hour or so (it seemed an eternity) as Virginia and I stood under the wonderful African moon, holding hands after our wedding of less than a year before.

Wondering how long we might have left to us to enjoy our marriage, we stayed quiet as the shouting and argument continued. Occasionally we squeezed our joined hands to encourage each other. Things finally simmered down. Our lieutenant and his firmness had won the encounter.

Begrudgingly the rabble released us back into the hands of our escort and I was given a hefty farewell kick to hasten my clambering body into the Land Rover. We sighed with relief, as did our escorting officer.

He had obviously gotten some idea beforehand of the state of affairs at Mubende because he had been tense, curt, and uncommunicative before we got there; and he visibly relaxed once we got away. I detected this and tried him with a question. I explained that neither of us understood the local language and we wondered if he could tell us what had been going on.

He replied, "Oh, they were discussing whether they should just beat you up or kill you."

He had dissuaded them from either course, telling them that he had specific orders to deliver us to State House in Entebbe, Amin's official residence. He fulfilled his orders to the letter, delivering us to the gates of State House. We arrived in Entebbe at midnight or so, and our escort communicated with the authorities inside. He was instructed to deliver us to Entebbe Police Station, where our existence became surrealistic.

A uniformed African police sergeant was at the desk on duty, and when the lieutenant handed us over, the sergeant asked if he could say upon what charges we were being held. The officer replied that we were in military custody and took his leave. He departed with our heartfelt personal thanks for having brought us at least as far as the police station safely.

The cells were full, so I lay down on the cement floor in the reception area of the police station and my wife stretched herself out on a wooden bench above me. I told the police sergeant that we had not eaten or had anything to drink all day and we would appreciate it if we could have something. He allowed us to telephone the nearby Lake Victoria Hotel and place an order. Within half an hour, a white-jacketed waiter arrived with tea, sandwiches, toast, and butter on a silver tray. He presented me with the bill, saying, "Cash or sign, bwana?"

I replied, "Sign." I took the bill, signed it, and scribbled on it a note addressed "To whom it might concern". I informed any possible reader that a BBC correspondent and his wife were being held at Entebbe Police Station. Could somebody call the British High Commission and ask for help?

Then, dirty and worried but at least re-victualled, we lay down again on our hard mattresses of concrete and wood to try to snatch some sleep, being rather tired by that point. At about three o'clock in the morning, there suddenly came the noise of a vehicle braking loudly to a stop outside the police station, and an army officer ran in shouting, "Where are they? Where are the bastards?"

As he came in roaring with anger, all he could see from the doorway were two pairs of trouser-clad legs with the feet pointing at him, one pair on the floor, belonging to myself, and the other pair on the bench, belonging to my wife. The officer upended the bench on which my wife was sleeping. She woke up and saved herself from tumbling down. She sat up, smiled at him sweetly, and asked him in Swahili, "Jambo! Wapi simba?" ("Hello! Where's the lion?")

This reaction reduced the furious officer to helpless laughter, especially as it came from somebody who, despite her trousers and her grubbiness from her adventures, was obviously a woman – and an attractive one too. He turned tail and left as suddenly as he had come.

We went back to sporadic dozing until a rather grim dawn arrived, in the shape of a battered-looking African police inspector who staggered into the police station to begin duty for the day. The inspector's uniform was torn, his face was bloody, he had a black eye, and he looked utterly drained of strength.

His first thought, however, was for us. Why were we being held? What was the charge? The police sergeant explained that we were in military custody, and the police inspector looked gloomy. "Look what our army has just done to me," he said. He had been beaten up on his way to work, and he told us that things were not looking good.

We were not encouraged by the fact that a Ugandan police inspector could be treated in such a way by the Ugandan army; and we were even less encouraged when, an hour or so later, we were collected again by soldiers and taken to the last place on earth to which anybody in Uganda wanted to be taken, the dreaded and dreadful Makindye barracks, infamous as a place of execution and torture.

The horrors of Makindye were immediately evident. We were shoved into a guardroom where a black prisoner stood, naked except for a loincloth. His back was scarred with fresh marks of flogging, and his wrists were tied behind his back. He was under questioning by a black interrogator. What we did not know then was that among the people also being held in Makindye were most of our journalistic colleagues.

The interrogator finished questioning the injured prisoner, who was dragged off somewhere or other, possibly to his death. Then we ourselves were questioned but not physically threatened, and our passports were seized.

I was familiar with this process, having endured previous occasions of arrest overseas during the course of my journalistic duties. On such occasions, I had established for myself the little habit of reminding the person depriving me of my passport that the document was the property of Her Majesty's government and anxiously asking the relevant official for assurances that the passport would be cared for properly. It was a point which sometimes gave the official concerned a slight pause for thought, but this was not the case in Uganda.

Instead, our interrogator sharply told us that the passports would be held until our departure and that we were to be deported. This we regarded as welcome news, but we were not so foolish as to say so.

We were driven under guard to our hotel in Kampala and ordered to stay there. Our room had been ransacked, our luggage torn apart, and various articles stolen.

Among the vanished items were pages of frank, informative, and sensitive notes on Africa, its politics, and its leaders, which my helpful BBC predecessor in Africa, Angus McDermid, had bequeathed to me. I have often wondered what officers of Amin's secret service and intelligence organisations might have made of Angus's reflections on Africa. Some of his thoughts must have provided them not only with fascinating reading but possibly with some uncomfortable moments as well.

Eventually, after being confined all day, we were driven with an escort from Kampala to the Entebbe airport. There, we joined five of our colleagues who had also been imprisoned and were being deported: Donald Wise of the *Daily Mirror*; Leslie Watkins of the *Daily Mail* (who was better known as a television critic than as a foreign correspondent); and three chums from BBC TV News, Keith Graves and his cameraman and sound recordist. We seven were the lucky vanguard of foreign journalists to be released from detention, the first to be freed and expelled from Uganda.

Exhausted, sweaty, smelly, and above all anxious to get away from Uganda, we made a nuisance of ourselves at the airport after receiving tickets paid for by the Ugandan government. We insisted on flying first class, and the deporting authority declined to pay more than the minimum fare.

So we produced our air travel cards and allowed our employers to foot the bill for the extra cost of upgrading us to first class for the flight to London. The East African Airways flight was empty because, apart from journalists, nobody in his or her right mind went anywhere near Uganda in those days. While still on the ground, we opened a bottle of Champagne and toasted our approaching freedom.

Back in London next morning, arriving at Heathrow, we found that we ourselves had become news. Off we went to our offices and broadcasting studios to fill newspaper columns, television screens, and radio airwaves with the accounts of our experiences.

Conscious of the inhibiting fact that a score or more of our unfortunate colleagues were still detained in Uganda, we had to choose our words with care. Uganda, however, reached out to us in London in another way, underlining the brutality and terror of Amin's regime, just the day after we had returned to England.

This time the victim was the chief justice of Uganda, Benedicto Kiwanuka. Only a week or so earlier, I had sat in the high court in Kampala watching him as he presided over a hearing which involved a British businessman held by the regime, whose lawyers had applied for a writ of habeas corpus to get him freed.

For the climate, the judge was ridiculously clad in full-bottomed wig and scarlet robe, superficially a figure of fun in an Evelyn Waugh kind of way. Yet the scene was not at all funny, and it possessed a dignity and a reminder of traditional values of justice that I like to believe are dear to most Englishmen and Englishwomen. Those values were being translated into public and visual action in an African setting and, more importantly, into judicial action. Again I was seeing something of what the old imperialists and colonialists had managed to build in Africa.

As chief justice, Ben Kiwanuka granted the writ of habeas corpus. The British detainee was freed. As a lawyer who had reached the peak of his profession, Kiwanuka was a respected public figure and had been the country's first prime minister when Uganda was first granted full internal self-government, only to be displaced by Milton Obote in later elections.

The *Daily Mirror*'s Donald Wise, a perceptive man and the only foreign correspondent with me in the courtroom, turned to me and made a comment that lives with me still: "The judge," he said, "has just signed his own death warrant, and he knows it."

Back in London a day or so after our deportations, a news agency flash of one sentence came through at the BBC. It said simply that the chief justice had been removed from his high court chambers at gunpoint and had disappeared. I called Donald at the *Daily Mirror* and, almost wonderingly, told him that his prediction about the chief justice signing his own death warrant had been fulfilled all too soon. Once again, we found ourselves reporting and broadcasting on Ugandan terrors, but this time from the safety of our London offices.

The regime of Idi Amin, the former Rifleman and Sergeant-Major who promoted himself to field marshal – and who awarded himself the Ugandan Victorian Cross, the Ugandan Distinguished Service Order, and the Ugandan Military Cross – lasted eight years, from 1971 to 1979. It was a regime which respected nobody and which killed anybody it feared or suspected of disloyalty. Holding high office was precarious. Victims of the regime included not only the chief justice and the country's Anglican archbishop but the entire country as well.

Although continuing to convalesce these days, sometimes controversially, under Yoweri Museveni's supervision, Uganda has still to recover fully from the severe injuries inflicted upon it by Obote and then Amin.

Those who fell fatally out of favour with Amin included those who administered the kind of medicine that Amin at one time or another wanted to dish out. One of them was his minister for internal affairs, A.C.K. Oboth-Ofumbi, the man who ordered our deportation from Uganda in 1972. He became one of his boss's victims. Five years after kicking us out, the minister, along with the archbishop of Uganda, was murdered. The deportation order he had signed hangs as another sombre souvenir on the wall of my study today.

Interviewing President Ayub Khan of Pakistan in 1959: an autographed copy.

My wife's glamorous mother, Molly Waite.

On the right of the sword-carrying Admiral, First Officer Molly Waite of the Women's Royal Naval Service (the "Wrens") acts as conducting officer to him at Greenwich during the war when he was making a tour of inspection.

"Wren" officer Molly Waite visits her daughter, Virginia (now and for the past 44 years) Mrs Osman, at a boarding school during the war.

Two pictures of Squadron-Leader Barry Waite, Virginia's father, during the war in RAF uniform. In the picture where the officers wear shorts he is on the right; and where they're in trousers he's on the left.

Virginia and myself in South Africa after having been arrested
in and deported from the late Idi Amin's Uganda.

CHAPTER 11

——

More Soldiers – and Politics

Three years after deportation, I found myself back in Uganda. By now, I had been upgraded (if that is the right word) by the BBC from being its Southern Africa correspondent to becoming its Africa correspondent. I presumed that this indicated in some way that the corporation felt that I had become "a good man in Africa", which was the title of author William Boyd's 1982 novel. In practice, it meant that I had to cover the problems of the entire continent in addition to those of what was still the white-ruled southern part of it (and they were more than enough).

I cannot say that I wanted to be anything like Boyd's comical disaster-prone fictional British diplomatist character, Morgan Leafy, any more than I wanted to be like the earlier, fictional correspondent character Boot of "The Beast" in Evelyn Waugh's *Scoop*, his classic satire on journalism and foreign correspondents in particular. However, reporting the troubles of the newly emerging independent states of Africa and the sometimes dubious proceedings of their pretty shambolic Organisation of African Union (OAU) was often surreal as well as hair-raising. There was more than enough scope for satire as well as raw news to keep me busily occupied gathering and interpreting that news both for radio and television.

It was an OAU annual conference in Kampala in 1975 that provided the reason for my return to Uganda, where I was still a prohibited immigrant. To its everlasting shame, the OAU had chosen Amin to be its president and thus its spokesperson for a year. It was widely viewed at the time as a disgrace to the OAU, and it was one of the many reasons that perhaps the organisation tried to remould itself and to project a new image to the world when it renamed itself the African Union in 2001. This embryo body has, in its first thirteen years, been somewhat more constructive than the OAU and has not yet discredited itself as much as its predecessor had.

Amin wanted to squeeze as much publicity as possible out of the conference he would be hosting. As an assiduous listener to the BBC World Service, he especially wanted the BBC to cover the proceedings of the conference, and, with an eye to publicity in the United States (as well as to all the countries around the world that the news agency served), he also wanted the Associated Press of America (AP) to be there.

He had a problem, though. Correspondents who were prohibited immigrants in Uganda represented in Africa those two news organisations, which both wanted to report the Kampala event in Africa. They were each a deportee from 1972: Andrew Torchia of AP and me. We were instructed separately by our editors to inform both the OAU and the Uganda government that our organisations naturally wanted to cover the conference but that they wanted Torchia and Osman to do the job. If that was impossible, then the two organisations would not be reporting the conference.

This show of firmness by the BBC and AP worked. On the very eve of the conference opening, Andy and I were informed that the prohibited immigrant orders against us had been lifted. So we found ourselves back in Kampala.

Towards its end, the conference took on an utterly unreal quality for me when I was summoned arbitrarily to take my seat in a black saloon car (always a dubious privilege in Amin's Uganda) to be driven to an unexpected interview with Amin himself, always referred to by officials and ministers as "H.E." -- "His Excellency". Andy also turned up, and he shared the interview with me.

Presumably aware that our background knowledge of Ugandan events, as previous deportees from the country, was more personal than most of the visiting correspondents at the conference, Amin made a point of trying to put us at our ease by opening with what he clearly hoped was a reassuring welcome: "Things are different now to what they were in nineteen seventy-two."

Well, they were, but not in the way he would have liked us to believe.

They were worse. They worsened still more until Amin fled some four years later and Uganda began its painful and still-continuing task of reconstruction.

Anyhow, we went ahead with our questions, and the contents of our encounter with Amin went around the world and reverberated, especially in Africa. This was not principally because of the content of his answers, but because of a question that H.E. had put to us.

We thought the interview had finished and were preparing to leave when Amin asked us not to go yet. Then he astonished us when, addressing me directly, he said: "You have been reporting that I am mad. Osman, do you really think I am mad?"

It was an awkward and possibly dangerous moment. He looked at me for a response. Taken aback and not really knowing what to reply, I tried to evade the question, just as politicians often do. I said simply that I had never reported such a thing, thus denying any implied assertion that I personally had reported that he was mad, while simultaneously suggesting that what newspapers were saying was none of my business. That answer did not content him.

He turned to Andy and addressed him directly also, trying to allow him no room to wriggle as I had done. "Well, you know what I mean ... A lot of newspapers and others are saying that I am mad. What do you think?"

By nature a contemplative man, Andy thought for a moment or two as I regarded him sympathetically. Then he answered in a slow American drawl, and, in my estimation, quite brilliantly, managing somehow or other to sidestep Amin's blunt query. He explained that he was not quite sure "in clinical terms" what madness was; therefore, he, Andrew Torchia of AP, was not qualified to judge.

Mercifully, Amin dropped the subject and we departed with relief. The BBC recording of Amin asking two journalists if we thought him mad may well be still in the archives because it was given much international broadcasting time. It was the only time in my life that a head of state ever asked if I thought he was mad. I think it is probable that it was the only time any head of state has asked reporters such a question, although I cannot be sure of that.

That somewhat fraught encounter with Amin was not the only

extraordinary journalistic experience I had at the Kampala conference. The other unusual one was my somewhat disconcerted personal involvement, together with the indirect involvement of the BBC, in letting another African soldier know that he had just been sacked – as ruler of the giant West African state of Nigeria. The ousted leader was General Yakubu Gowon, Sandhurst trained and known to everyone as Jack.

In the maelstrom of Nigerian internecine military politics after the initial collapse of civilian rule in 1966, Jack Gowon eventually emerged as something of a stayer. He was unable to prevent the Biafran civil war, which lasted until 1970, but as Nigeria's president and commander in chief, he survived it. He continued in control until fellow officers pushed him out in a bloodless Nigerian coup mounted while he was actually in Uganda at the OAU conference.

Of the many heads of government or state I have seen lose power by compulsion (some of whom were lucky enough, physically, to survive the process), Jack Gowon wins my personal admiration for relinquishing his own position of authority with the most grace. Upon learning that in his absence from Nigeria that his fellow officers had summarily sacked him as commander in chief and his country's leader, he promptly called a news conference in Kampala.

With the air of an actor familiar with the text, he quoted Shakespeare at us: "All the world's a stage. And all the men and women merely players; they have their exits and their entrances ..."

So Jack Gowon took his own exit. His manner of learning about his replacement as Nigeria's leader was, however, bizarre and reached him via the BBC, Idi Amin, and me. Here is how it happened.

I was in my bed at the New Stanley Hotel in Kampala as dawn was breaking when suddenly I was awakened by a knock on the door and called downstairs. Standing there was a Ugandan official who asked me to accompany him in a black saloon car. My heart sank as I thought of my 1972 incarceration and I thought, *No! Not again!*

A colleague, Gerard Kemp of the *Daily Telegraph*, was in the hotel lobby and keeping a thoughtful eye upon me. I was whisked away in the car to the Conference Centre, Kemp in encouragingly close attendance behind.

At the Conference Centre, I was escorted straight through the press room to another room at the far end, where Amin's foreign minister, another soldier, Major General Juma Oris, was standing. He handed me a cable from the BBC, which was addressed to me but which had never reached me.

He did not even bother to apologise for its interception. He simply asked me if I could tell him anything more. I read the cable, which, in Cablese brevity, said, "MONITORING HAS NIGERIAN RADIO GOWON OUSTED IN COUP STOP REACTION WELCOMED."

With Oris standing at my elbow and Kemp standing a few yards away discreetly watching and listening, I telephoned the BBC and spoke to the foreign duty editor, who was fast on the uptake. He grasped the position when I began with these words: "I am with the foreign minister of Uganda ..."

He rightly interpreted this as meaning that I was not wanting to waste time and that I would appreciate a prompt response from the London end. I asked him to tell me all that was known about what was going on in Nigeria, and he swiftly passed on everything that the BBC had in its possession by then.

I rang off after hearing the last words of the foreign duty editor to me: "Try to get an interview with Gowon, old boy."

Since I was, so to speak, helping the Ugandan government in its inquiries, I decided to put forward a request for a reciprocal favour. So when Juma Oris asked me for a summary of what I had been told, I gave it to him without any hesitation because it would have been counterproductive on my part not to have done so (I might even have been deported again, or worse). In any case, the Ugandans would have monitored the conversation with the BBC.

Thus, after briefing Oris, I seized the chance to say to him that if he could help in any way in persuading Gowon to give me a BBC interview, I would much appreciate it. Oris thanked me politely enough, said he would do what he could, and began to leave, still carrying the cable addressed to me.

I asked if I could have it, and he replied with a negative, saying that he was going to give it to H.E.

Amin then visited Gowon to tell him that he was no longer president of Nigeria, passing my cable to Gowon when doing so. The cable never did reach me, but I did get the Gowon interview. Off he then went to Warwick University to pursue academic studies before returning to Africa, at first to settle in Togo, not far away from Nigeria (in West African terms).

So blithe was Gowon's manner of departure that I suspected at the time that it had all been carefully stage-managed. I still wonder about that. At the time, everyone seemed genuinely surprised, and Amin's host government for the conference was apparently flabbergasted. Whatever the truth, Jack Gowon gave his exit news conference to appreciative, amused laughter from the hardened hacks of Africa, unaccustomed as we were to hearing Shakespeare quoted at us in such a way by a soldier-politician.

Four years later, Amin himself was out. He withdrew from Kampala after Tanzanian troops invaded Uganda and forced him to quit the capital. Nobody knew where he had gone, and once again I landed a sizeable scoop when I revealed that he had fled the country.

After weeks in Uganda, I was taking a break from what was quite difficult and sometimes dangerous work and travel. I returned to Nairobi and lunched with Virginia as guests of an old friend, the late "Gerry" Read and his wife, Audrey.

Gerry was the Shell boss in East Africa. He played squash with me at the Muthaiga Club every now and again and was a keen saxophone player. He was widely admired among the business community and his friends for the admirably cool way in which he tackled the difficulties of his task in serving an allegedly unpopular, beastly multinational oil company, without supplies of oil from which the whole of East Africa would have halted.

Among his most sensitive duties was the none-too-easy one of extracting from Idi Amin's regime the Ugandan payment of Shell bills for millions of pounds, dollars, or whatever currency was necessary for settlement of those bills. Every now and again, we would gather in the Muthaiga Club to wish Gerry good luck and Godspeed as he left for Kampala to beard Amin in person. Sometimes he had to spell out to the dictator that if he did not pay up, supplies of fuel would dry up.

We never knew if Gerry was coming back or not, but somehow or other he always managed it. If ever someone earned the CBE that came his way, it was Gerry Read.

Just before lunch, which he and his wife were offering us that day in

1979, his telephone rang. He listened, took a note, and rejoined us. He asked jokingly if I would like to know what Amin was doing.

He told me that Amin had just taken off from a remote Ugandan bush airstrip near the eastern border in a plane the pilot of which had filed a flight plan for outside Uganda. He said I was welcome to report the news so long as the source remained unidentifiable. We agreed that an "airport source" would be entirely accurate and would adequately protect Shell. The telephone call had in fact come from the Shell man at the airstrip who had re-fuelled the plane.

As the other guests began lunch, I wrote my script and then broadcast it to London over the same telephone that had conveyed to us the glad tidings of Amin's departure.

I joined the others for my own meal, and we sat around afterwards enjoying our digestifs, plus the news coming back to us from the BBC to the room from which it had emanated.

Amin's overthrow resulted in widespread relief throughout Uganda and, for me, a favourable bit of publicity in a book written by an American. So while on the subject of the book, as well as soldiers, Uganda and Africa in general, I should like to enlarge on a couple of other subjects quite close to my heart: the reputation of the BBC news operation and why being a foreign correspondent is a worthwhile occupation.

Colleague and friend David Lamb, then working in Africa for the *Los Angeles Times*, was the author of the book, published in 1983 in England by the Bodley Head and in America by Random House. It is called *The Africans – Encounters from the Sudan to the Cape*.

Lamb wrote:

> Before being transferred to Moscow, John Osman had bounced around Africa and travelling with him was something of a treat.
>
> He was as well known in Africa's English-speaking countries as Walter Cronkite was in the United States. Doors would open, presidents would vie for his ear (or, more appropriately, for his microphone), surly bodyguards would become gentle and respectful in his presence, knowing that the BBC had more clout than all the stations and newspapers of Africa combined.

Once, a few days after President Amin had been over-thrown in Uganda, John and I travelled up a dirt road to St. Teresa's Mission outside the town of Bombo. As our Land Rover went by, villagers dashed inside, to the safety of their huts. Then they would reappear cautiously, look again, and break into wild cheers, waving and dancing joyously. For them, the sight of white men driving without a military escort was their first confirmation that Amin had been overthrown.

From the door of the little mission, Father Emanuel Mbogo stepped unsurely, squinting into the sunlight. John introduced himself. The priest threw his arms around him, then stepped back and, star-struck, repeated, "John Osman? John Osman? Is it really you?" For three years, the priest said, he had listened to Osman's reports about Uganda on a short-wave radio he kept hidden under his pillow. If Amin's soldiers had caught him listening to the BBC or had found the radio, he surely would have been killed. "All this time," the priest said, "you were the only way I had of knowing what was going on in my own country."

The account clearly illustrates why I have always thought my job was worth doing.

CHAPTER 12

A Soldier: "Full of Strange Oaths"

My memories of Ugandan soldiery in general are none too pleasant. One sun-soaked scene on a green and beautiful lawn in Kampala sticks particularly in my mind. Three thousand or so baying troops, many bearded and uttering what were indeed "strange oaths", surrounded their prey: the primate of the Anglican Church in Uganda and two Ugandan government ministers.

The primate, the Anglican archbishop of Uganda, Janani Luwum, was clearly under no illusion about the brevity of his life expectation. He displayed true calmness as if he fully expected soon to be joining his predecessors, the Ugandans slaughtered in the nineteenth century and regarded by many as the first black Christian martyrs.

Another victim, Oboth-Ofumbi, the man who as interior minister had signed our 1972 deportation orders, did not appear to realise that he too was on Idi Amin's death list, although he had only a day to live. He appeared "smiling and relaxed", as I described him on BBC TV News after managing to have a brief chat with him. The third man about to die, the Minister for Land Resources, I did not recognise and did not know.

The archbishop and ministers were present because all government ministers, religious leaders, and diplomatists in Uganda had been summoned to attend what was described as a "rally". It was, in fact, a staged production of Ugandan military "justice" to denounce people whom Amin wanted out of the way. The doomed actors in it were compelled to perform their unhappy parts.

The setting for the open-air production was provided by the grounds of the Nile Mansions Hotel, a luxurious complex which possessed an air-conditioned modernity contrasting severely with the more familiar and traditional African landscape not far away: thatched huts of grass, reeds, mud, and tree bark, as well as shacks with corrugated iron roofs.

The Nile Mansions had been built with two objectives. One, understandable commercially, was to attract wealthy tourists wanting to stay in Uganda in comfort and to visit conveniently the game parks of the country as well as the nearby source of the White Nile at Jinja. This aim was certainly never attained during Amin's rule, when the place was eerily empty. The other purpose, understandable politically, was for it to be used as an impressive hostelry for African leaders attending the 1975 annual conference of the Organisation of African Unity.

On this particular day in 1977, the last full day on Earth for the archbishop and the two government ministers, the purpose at Nile Mansions was news manipulation on a scale of which Westminster practitioners of the doubtful art would never allow themselves even to dream (at least, I hope not).

The producers and directors of this propaganda show were seeking channels to present to the world an Amin version of events that would lead – as we learned later – to the "accidental deaths" of the archbishop and the ministers.

So an audience of two Western journalists was invited by the Amin government from outside Uganda to report on the drama.

I was one of them, representing one of the chosen channels, the BBC. The other journalist, representing the *Times* and Reuters News Agency, was the late Charles Harrison. The assembled gathering as a whole was not so much an audience as a supporting cast of "extras" for the lead actor, Idi Amin himself.

Charles was a respected freelance. In addition to his work for the *Times*, the BBC, and Reuter, he regularly produced pieces for many other news outlets. A former editor of the *Uganda Argus*, and a man who knew more about the country than any other Western journalist after years of living and working in Uganda, he had eventually been forced to quit the country when he was well into his sixties, because of its political and economic deterioration and the near-impossibility of producing an independently-minded newspaper.

Having lost his newspaper, his home, and most of his life's earnings, Charles moved himself to Nairobi, which was also my own base then for covering Africa. There he painstakingly reconstructed his life and career. I had known him for several years, and we worked closely together. He "minded the shop" for the BBC and me when I was absent from Nairobi.

He had arrived to live and work in East Africa after serving in the Royal Navy during World War II. Another wartime ex-serviceman, from the Royal Engineers, had also found his way to the same part of the world: Amin's "special adviser on British affairs", Bob Astles, who, when Amin died in Saudi Arabia in 2003, was living in Wimbledon at the age of eighty-one (until he ended his days there not so long ago at the age of at least ninety).

In practice, Astles became Amin's media relations representative, and it was through Astles that Charles and I had found ourselves in Kampala for the Nile Mansions "rally". Uganda Radio had announced that a plot had been discovered to smuggle arms into the country to overthrow the president, and accusing the archbishop and others, so Charles and I hired a charter plane to fly from Nairobi to Uganda to pursue inquiries.

We ensured in advance, through Astles, that we would be allowed to land, because movement in and out of Uganda was highly restricted. Astles and Amin's foreign minister, Major General Juma Oris, greeted us at the Entebbe airport. They took us to Kampala, and Astles guided us on foot from Nile Mansions to the scene of the mass parade of troops. On our way to it, we passed through a lobby crowded with soldiers. I caught a glimpse of the archbishop in the lobby and tried to move towards him to have a word with him.

Astles stuck his foot out in front of me, almost tripping me, physically halting me in my steps. He warned me against doing anything that might upset the soldiers. It might have been that his intervention really was genuinely protective, so febrile was the mood. Whatever the explanation, I failed to speak to the doomed prelate.

Both Charles and I were, however, able to do one thing for him: bear witness to his denial of the charges levelled against him. Once outside with the scene all set on the lawns, Idi Amin arrived to preside over what was really a kangaroo court, with a long list of accusations read aloud, in much the same way that Uganda Radio propagandised anything Amin so wanted. The archbishop and the government ministers, with others, were seated before the soldiers, who were told that arms had been discovered.

Alleged confessions were read out, and there were great roars and shouts for blood from the troops, worked into a frenzy by an oration from a senior officer.

There was no pretence at any defence, and neither the archbishop nor Ofumbi said a word. They were given no chance to do so. Charles and I watched the archbishop intently. He caught our eyes and probably our white faces in the frieze of mostly black faces surrounding him.

Looking straight at us as we looked straight at him, he shook his head silently as the accusations against him were read aloud. Suddenly, the show was over. Amin left, the troops left, and everybody else left. I managed to get a word with Amin himself, who told me that, as I reported at the time, "some of his government ministers and perhaps church leaders would be arrested". Within hours, they were.

Amin claimed that he had talked with the archbishop solely to ensure that he had not been beaten or maltreated. He added hypocritically that he felt it "improper" to try to make inquiries himself or to "interfere with the process of law".

Astles accompanied Charles and me back to a room in the Nile Mansions from where I broadcast to the BBC a description of what I had just seen and heard. Charles filed his dispatches. Astles stayed with us as we worked.

The two of us made a point of giving weight to the archbishop's gestures of denial. We realised that the ecclesiastical head shakings were probably the last public statements the archbishop would ever be making. We knew also that, together with the reports that we sent to the world, they were the only unscripted parts of the Amin production.

Not wishing to hang about in Uganda and expose ourselves unnecessarily to any hostile afterthoughts that Amin might all too easily develop about the publicity he was obtaining, we hotfooted it to the airport and back to Nairobi.

We were not there for long. Early the next morning, I talked by telephone to Astles in Kampala to try to find out what, if anything, had happened to the archbishop and Ofumbi. Astles asked me a significant question: did I know anything about Ugandan history and the Ugandan Christian martyrs?

These, I knew, were a group of twenty or more African youths who had converted to Christianity in the 1880s, when white explorers, missionaries, and traders were beginning to learn more about Uganda. Between 1885 and 1887, the young Africans were killed for their faith, as well as many others who suffered in that period of persecution. They were canonized in 1964 by the Roman Catholic Church and so had become widely referred to in Africa as the "first black martyrs".

I did not bother to reply to the question from Astles except to assure him that I did know about the martyrs. Immediately, however, I took his unusual question as a warped kind of hint that another martyr was to be added to the list and that the archbishop was probably dead. This feeling was strengthened when Astles added that I must be sure to listen to Uganda Radio at ten in the morning.

I called the BBC to alert them and to ensure that Uganda Radio was being closely monitored. I called Charles and said much the same. At ten o'clock, we duly learned from Uganda Radio of what were said to be the deaths of the accused in a road accident shortly after they had left the Nile Mansions the previous day.

How did the archbishop die? According to his son, Ben Luwum, he was executed in one of Amin's most notorious places of torture, the State Research Bureau. Mr Luwum was reported years later (in 2003, at the time of Amin's death) as saying that Idi Amin himself participated in the torture and execution of his father. Mr Luwum's view of his father's murderer was understandably bitter: "He was a madman. He killed so many people, and he never repented for what he had done."

Whatever the manner of the archbishop's death, there is no doubt that he was in fact murdered. Astles himself, referring to the whole affair several years later, talked of the "murder" of Ofumbi, with whom he had worked closely on anti-corruption duties. Even by the Ugandan government's own unbelievable version of events, Ofumbi had died at the same time as the archbishop, allegedly in the same car and in the same road accident, so the inevitable implication is that they were murdered at the same time.

All that was known at the time of the deaths, of course, was the Uganda Radio ten o'clock in the morning version of the road accident, following directly upon the carefully prepared charade of the day before. Ten o'clock in Nairobi time was eight o'clock in London.

I broadcast the news of the deaths into the morning bulletins and was interviewed by the *Today* programme. The world was horrified, and the churches, especially the bishops of Africa, reacted with condemnation of Amin.

Into Nairobi poured dozens of foreign correspondents and TV camera crews hoping to get into Uganda to report on developments. Having broken the news of the deaths, I followed it up with another call to Astles asking to be allowed to interview a Ugandan army officer, Major Moses Okello.

He was reported to have been in the car with the archbishop and the two ministers at the time of the accident. It was said that the major was injured and had to be in hospital. Astles said he would do what he could to respond to my request, and a few days later, together with scores of reporters from around the world doing the same, I chartered a plane again from Nairobi to fly into Uganda to report another staged event.

Astles accompanied journalists to hear Amin speak at a conference, where he denied killing the archbishop and denied atrocity reports. Then Astles took us to what they said was the scene of the accident, where there were skid marks and a piece of broken glass.

After that, they took us to a hospital, where Major Okello was wheeled outside to talk to us and to give his version of the accident to TV cameras and microphones. Seated in a hospital chair and wearing pyjamas and dressing gown, he wore bandages but showed few signs of damage apart from having metal crutches resting on his lap.

Almost incoherently, he told us that he was driving the car containing his prisoners when the steering wheel was seized from him and he knew nothing more until regaining consciousness some time later. The major was unconvincing, and few, if any, believed him.

Television camera operators and correspondents wanted to get back quickly to Nairobi to airfreight film, not to mention wanting to get out of Amin's unpredictable Uganda, where few people in those days wanted to hang around longer than was essential. I too was about to leave when Astles took me aside and said it might be worthwhile for anybody who so wished to stay on for a spell. He hinted that anybody who cared to remain in Kampala for a day or two might get an interview with H.E., which, as I have already explained, was how His Excellency, President for Life, Field Marshal Al Hadji Doctor Idi Amin Dada was always known among Ugandan officials.

The "Al Hadj" part of the title indicated that as a Muslim, he had undertaken the "haj", or pilgrimage to Mecca. The doctorate was non-medical and of an honorary nature, ill suited to a man who had decimated Uganda's Makerere University, previously one of Africa's most promising centres of education, after students there had dared to laugh at him when he addressed them.

His other titles and decorations were self-awarded: the Ugandan Victoria Cross; the Ugandan DSO, Ugandan MC, and so on, as well as the Ugandan CBE, although this was always spelled out in Ugandan propaganda not as "commander" of the British Empire but as "conquerer" of the British Empire. He also called himself "the last king of Scotland", which of course became the title of a riveting film.

Having already endured one spell as a prisoner in Uganda, and knowing how closely Amin monitored personally all BBC broadcasts including my own, I was none too keen on staying on alone in Kampala. I passed word round among colleagues, saying that I would be prepared to hang on in Uganda if somebody would join me.

One only volunteered to submit himself alongside me to the always-ambiguous embrace of the Amin governmental machine. Others, including Jon Snow, now the Channel 4 news presenter and then a reporter, sensibly got out of Uganda as quickly as they could.

The volunteer to join me in staying behind was not based in Africa covering African affairs full-time but was what we called a "visiting fireman". He was John Penrose, a lively reporter who was the Rome correspondent of the Daily Mirror. Plucked out of what we Africa hands regarded as his Italian "Dolce Vita", and deposited in Amin's Uganda, he was boldly determined to be undeterred. For those of us who, perhaps, had by then become overly deterred by "Big Daddy" (as Amin had been nicknamed by Penrose's newspaper), this was refreshing.

John and I were meeting for the first time, but we immediately hit it off, and I still recall his sardonic appreciation of our strange existence for the following week or so we spent in Uganda. I scratched around trying to form a picture of something of the repressed realities of life, accompanied more often than not by John and by Bob Astles, who had become what in the Soviet Union later I would have described as "our minder".

His more or less permanent presence with us turned out to be a circumstance that led to John collaring a front-page spread in the *Daily Mirror* about Astles, a man who was described as many things, from being an "apologist" for Amin to acting as a "henchman" to the tyrant. He gave his personal view of himself to John and me one evening when we sat drinking brandy with him in a room at the Nile Mansions. Each of us interviewed Astles and questioned him on his precise role in the Amin government machine.

The self-description Astles offered was, "I'm an odd job man." The *Daily Mirror*'s front page the next day duly carried a picture of Astles with a big headline: "The Odd Job Man".

Odd his jobs most certainly were, as were many of the perpetual curious scrapes in which he was involved. One, for example, occurred in 1979, just after Tanzanian troops had chased Amin out of Uganda. Late at night in my home in Nairobi, I received a call from somebody identifying himself as "Mr Mukasa". The caller had an African voice and said that Astles was in trouble. "He has no friends. Amin tried to kill him, and he does not have a lawyer."

It all sounded, well, a bit odd. The voice did not ring true. I challenged "Mr Mukasa", suggesting to him that he was really Bob Astles. The caller rang off.

A little later, the caller telephoned again, and this time any doubt was cleared up. The voice had changed. It was in fact Bob Astles, and he identified himself as such.

He disclosed that he was telephoning from the headquarters of the Criminal Investigation Department in Nairobi, where he was being detained. He had fled from Uganda, where a Kampala magistrate had issued a warrant for his arrest on a charge of murder. A delegation from Uganda bearing the arrest warrant and a claim for the extradition of Astles was awaited in Nairobi, and the purpose of his call to me soon became clear. He wanted at all costs to avoid going back to Uganda. He was seeking a lawyer to help him fight any attempt to extradite him.

The publicity that I promptly afforded him by broadcasting about his plight on the *Today* programme and on other BBC outlets produced what was the desired result for him: a lawyer. However, it was not entirely plain sailing for Astles, for he swiftly discovered that not only the new Ugandan government but the Kenyan government as well had an interest in him.

Some time previously, a former Kenyan cabinet minister, Bruce Mackenzie, had died on a Ugandan flight in a light aircraft that the Kenyans thought Amin had sabotaged. So Kenyan police were questioning Astles about Mackenzie's death, with Astles denying that he was in any way involved in such sabotage.

Astles told me all this over the telephone. Far from being implicated in any plot to kill Mackenzie, Astles claimed that he himself was the victim of a murder plot by the State Research Bureau, one of Amin's secret police units.

I asked Astles how he was able to make his telephone calls to me, and he explained that although locked in a room at the CID headquarters, he had "found a telephone in a cupboard" and was making use of it.

So extraordinary were his adventures and misadventures that it came as no great shock to me, though it was something of a surprise, when I heard from him once again from yet another prison. This was in 1980, after the BBC had posted me to the Soviet Union.

A letter arrived for me in Moscow from Astles, who explained in it that he was being held in the Luzira prison in Uganda, accused of murder, a charge of which he was eventually acquitted.

During his time in detention, he had heard me broadcasting from Moscow on his short-wave transistor radio that he had in his cell. From the gaol, without apparent difficulty, he had been able to send me the letter.

When studying obituaries published at the time of Amin's death, I was interested to read that Amin had ordered the death of Astles on at least four occasions. On one such, Amin reportedly telephoned the African wife of Astles to offer his regret for the "accidental death" of her husband and to inform her that she could collect the body from the city mortuary. In fact, Astles had evaded the attempted assassination.

Astles, generally referred to by Ugandans as "Mr Bob", was quoted as saying that survival under Amin largely involved staying out of sight until the dictator was in a better mood. Even after Amin's overthrow, and during his years of exile in Saudi Arabia, he maintained contact with

Astles via Mr Bob's Wimbledon telephone. Eventually, however, apparently irritated by the size of Amin's telephone bill, the Saudis removed his international dialling link.

Astles himself acknowledged in 1992 that he was "closely associated with President Amin and his regime"; that he "held a number of appointments under it"; and that he "gave credence and support to it". The acknowledgment came in a statement issued in 1992 after the resolution of a libel action brought by him against the BBC.

The statement also pointed out that Astles had been imprisoned in Uganda between 1979 and 1985, during which time fourteen criminal charges were brought against him, including two for murder. He was acquitted on both counts of murder, and the other charges were never pursued.

Astles lived to a ripe old age of ninety or so, dying eventually in Wimbledon not so long ago. He would certainly have been qualified to summarise his achievements like the French abbot and politician, the Comte de Sieyes, who, in recalling his life and deeds during the French Revolution, summed things up by saying, "I survived."

In that, I suppose, I have something in common with him after a lifetime often spent in covering wars, revolutions, and general mayhem at sometimes uncomfortably close quarters. Thankfully, though, I have never found myself compelled to sup with a spoon as closely to any devil as Astles supped with Idi Amin.

While Penrose and I were in Uganda and interviewing Astles, I continued to file news dispatches from Kampala, including reports on Amin's intention to visit London for both a Commonwealth Conference and to attend the Queen's silver jubilee celebrations. This horrified British politicians and led to the Liberal Party calling for Uganda's suspension from Commonwealth membership. The Liberal leader, the late Jeremy Thorpe, said Amin should be recognised as "the black Hitler".

Not content with only taking on the British, Amin decided to have a go at President Jimmy Carter of the United States, who had criticised Amin's regime. Amin fired off telegrams and messages to Washington, and I duly reported them, trying to assess Amin's policy motivation. No sign appeared of our half-promised interview with H.E., so Penrose and I decided to return to Nairobi.

Amin and Astles had other ideas, however. As "Mr Bob" drove us to the airport at Entebbe for our departure, Amin passed by on the other side of the road in his presidential Range Rover. We stopped, the Range Rover stopped, and then it turned round and joined us.

Amin ordered out of his vehicle his bodyguard, an Acholi of Milton Obote's tribe, whose people, it was alleged at the time, were being massacred in northern Uganda. Amin invited us into his own car, and the bodyguard got into Mr Bob's.

With Amin as our personal driver, and Mr Bob and Amin's bodyguard following us, John and I set off on a presidentially conducted tour round the bullet- and bazooka-shattered military section of the Entebbe airport, where, ten months before, Israeli troops had staged a stunningly successful raid in July 1976 to rescue hijack hostages from pro-Palestinian kidnappers, with whom Amin had colluded.

The control tower and buildings were battered, with smashed windows, blackened wood, and bullet and grenade marks everywhere. Amin sketched out for us his own account of how the Israeli forces had accomplished their mission, talking admiringly about their professionalism. He pointed out to us planes of the Uganda Air Force, including Soviet-made MiG-21s. He told us that some of them were armed with missiles.

At the end of the tour, he took us to the VIP lounge in the main civil section of the airport, where he received a telephone call from Washington, DC, apparently from his chargé d'affaires in the United States. During our conducted tour, Amin had made a point of taking us to meet a couple of Americans who, with a couple of dozen or so other Americans, were working for Uganda Airlines.

They assured him that they found Uganda a "beautiful, lovely country".

In reply to a question from Mr Bob as to what they thought of President Carter's criticisms of Uganda and President Amin, the couple not unexpectedly laughed and scoffed in reply, dismissing it all as "nonsense". It was rather obvious that the Americans suspected that they might be in a potential position of becoming hostages if they had said the wrong thing.

Amin was clearly satisfied with the American reply and equally clearly unsurprised by it. We journalists, needless to say, had another story, and as usual with Amin propaganda, the tale we had to tell served his purpose to some extent by reminding America of the vulnerability of its citizens in Uganda.

We telephoned our dispatches while Amin talked in another room to his chargé d'affaires in Washington. Eventually, we boarded our charter plane to take us back to Nairobi.

Just before we got into our aircraft to leave Entebbe, however, Amin appeared again on the airport tarmac in his car to insist on saying good-bye to us. He looked at his watch. "Ah!" he said. "Time for *Radio Newsreel*." He reached within his Range Rover for a transistor set, placed it on the car bonnet, and tuned in to London.

I was somewhat worried about his reactions to whatever it was I might have had to say. The programme led with my latest piece, an unvarnished report on the slanging match with Jimmy Carter, and Amin listened closely.

As I signed off from Uganda, Amin turned to me with a beam on his face and told me, "Osman, you very good reporter."

I was inclined to agree with him the next day when, safely back in Nairobi, I was offered five hundred dollars (quite a useful sum in 1977) to knock out a piece for *Time* magazine, interested in the American aspect of Ugandan affairs. The BBC gave me permission to do so, as was required in those days in accordance with the terms of my staff contract.

Not all listeners, however, were satisfied with my reporting of the end of the archbishop and of two government ministers. Echoes appeared of criticisms similar to those expressed eleven years earlier by the former governor of Northern Nigeria about my interview with Major Chukwuma Nzeogwu after the killing of the Sardauna of Sokoto: I had not been prosecutorial enough.

This time, however, the criticism came from one of my own bosses, one of the BBC governors. In the minutes of the BBC news and current affairs meeting of 18 February 1977, the editor of news and current affairs quoted a governor as having "felt that John Osman could have been more forthright in his report on the previous day of the deaths of the archbishop of Uganda and two Ugandan government ministers".

To my satisfaction, the minutes continued: "Some other governors had thought that John Osman had made his points very well." There was then further discussion at the news and current affairs meeting, and I was pleased to note from the minutes that the editor expressed the view that "Osman had expressed the right degree of scepticism".

Finally, I was gratified to note the conclusion of the meeting: "Later: The director general said that his comment to the Board of Governors had been that John Osman had done the only thing he could do. The editor said he had shown courage in going to Uganda in the first place."

In my doubtless prejudiced view, the succinct comment of the director general of the day, the late Sir Charles Curran, was entirely correct.

The following week I was further gratified when the minutes noted that the editor of BBC television news said that an interview I had conducted with Amin had "gone quite well" and that "both the editor of news and current affairs and the editor of radio news commended John Osman's work in the very difficult circumstances of the past fortnight".

Of the many soldiers of many lands I have met over the years, Amin was the most extraordinary. He was certainly the most extraordinary self-appointed field-marshal of my acquaintance.

The only other officers of that dizzyingly high rank I have ever met are (or were) genuine field marshals: the late Field Marshal Viscount Montgomery of Alamein; the late Field Marshal Ayub Khan of Pakistan; and two former British chiefs of staff, Field Marshal Lord Carver and Field Marshal Lord Bramall.

Ayub Khan, like Amin, was a Muslim, but an entirely different kind of man and soldier. I met him when he was ruling Pakistan. He was an impressive figure who managed to hold East and West Pakistan together, even through a war with India in 1965, which was my first actual war assignment for the BBC.

Montgomery I had met not long before that assignment. Our meeting was at the Royal Military College at Sandhurst, when I had just joined the BBC and was learning how to put a television news report together. Although contractually engaged as a BBC staff foreign correspondent, the BBC sensibly decreed that before I could be unleashed onto a wider world before a camera, I had to learn how to work for television by being attached for some months to a programme for the South East of England, called *Town and Around*.

I look back on that period of my life with immense pleasure. Charming men like Richard Baker and Michael Aspel presented the programme from Alexandra Palace, as part of TV News. I met there for the first time quite a few of my younger up-and-coming colleagues like Martin Bell. I wandered happily around London, Hampshire, Kent, Sussex, and Surrey compiling film reports broadcast after the 6 p.m. national news, and it was in this period that I met Montgomery.

I was at Sandhurst to cover a "Passing Out" parade; and there was the old warrior, the man who accepted the German surrender document at the end of World War II, as spry as ever. Spotting the cameras, "Monty", who was always a keen publicist, called me over during a reception afterwards and engaged me in vigorous conversation, interviewing me rather than the other way around.

His geniality and his piercing eyes are my abiding image of him. His gimlet eyes, I seem to remember, were icily blue, but my memory might be wrong because, as Shakespeare has put it, "old men forget".

Lord Carver – "Mike" Carver – I met in Cyprus when I was a young correspondent for the *Daily Telegraph* and he was the youngest major general in the British Army, commanding the British element in the United Nations Peacekeeping Force. Years later, when I was still a correspondent but he had reached the top of the military ladder, we met again in Moscow. He was taking part in heavily charged Anglo-Soviet talks on strategic questions of disarmament and international peacekeeping. He gave me an interview on the subject after his discussions with the Russians, and although by then he was a top ornament in the collection of British Top Brass, I found that "Mike" Carver remained quite human. So did the fourth real field- marshal of my acquaintance, Lord Bramall, chief of the Defence Staff during the Falklands War.

I have never met him in a journalistic capacity, only pleasantly and socially in the Travellers Club, where for some years he was our president. All four genuine field-marshals I have met certainly contrasted with the only self-appointed one of my acquaintance, with his disloyally acquired symbol of command.

What, I ask myself, would all four of them have made of "Field Marshal" Amin? If British military training ever created a soldier in the image of British military and colonial tradition, it was Idi Amin Dada, born in 1925 into a poor rural family of the small Kakwa tribe at Koboko in north-west Uganda.

At the age of eighteen, he joined the King's Africa Rifles and during World War II fought in its closing years with the Eleventh East Africa Division as a rifleman in Burma.

After the war, he went to the Fourth Uganda Battalion with which he was sent to deal with tribal marauders in northern Uganda. Later he served in Kenya on anti–Mau Mau operations. By 1957, he was a sergeant major. He played rugby and was a boxer. In 1959, seeking potential officers among African troops, the British Army established in East Africa the rank of "Effendi" for non-commissioned officers seen as officer material. Amin Effendi was one of the first.

By 1963, after Ugandan independence, he was a major, and by 1964 a colonel. More significantly, however, he had also become the deputy commander of Uganda's army and air force.

It was at this stage, I think, that the other field-marshals I have mentioned would almost certainly have decided that Amin was being promoted beyond his capacities.

It was Milton Obote himself, the man Amin overthrew, who was overseeing Amin's promotion. Allegations were made at the time that Obote, then prime minister, and Amin had misappropriated large sums, including gold, in dealings in or with the Congo (Zaire as it then was). The Ugandan National Assembly demanded Amin's resignation, and Obote, facing parliamentary defeat, used force to suppress those opposing him.

Instead of being sacked for corruption, as Parliament wanted, Amin was rewarded for his support to Obote by being given full command of the army and air force.

In 1966, Obote tore up the British-made constitution and tried to abolish the old tribal kingdoms. The largest and most influential tribe, the Baganda, rebelled. Their king, or kabaka, "King Freddie", who was also the president of Uganda, fled to England after his palace was attacked, with Amin prominent in the assault.

With discontent and corruption burgeoning, Obote began to worry about Amin and his ambitions. He sent Amin to Egypt to represent Uganda at Nasser's funeral, and while Amin was away, Obote purged the leadership of the armed forces in an effort to establish control of his own and to diminish Amin's personal support.

Two can play at that sort of game. Realising upon his return from Egypt that his position and perhaps his life were under threat, Amin bided his time until he could strike in Obote's own absence from Uganda. The moment for him to act arrived in January 1971, when Obote left to attend the Commonwealth Prime Ministers' Conference in Singapore.

Amin mounted a coup with key army and police units who were his supporters, and so began his eight-year reign. It started with joyous relief that Obote had been ousted, degenerated into abject terror, and ended with more relief at Amin's departure but also with justified and serious doubts about Uganda's future.

With BBC colleagues such as the late Brian Barron, I had covered the Tanzanian invasion of Uganda in 1979 and Amin's retreat northwards.

During this confused period of events, while Brian and I were shuttling between Uganda and Kenya every day to ship film and tapes to London from Nairobi, Britain reopened its High Commission in Uganda. The newly arrived high commissioner, Richard Posnett (later knighted), had no Union Flag to fly over his high commission, so he asked me to bring one in for him from the high commissioner in Kenya, Stanley Fingland (also later knighted).

Though it was almost midnight by the time I got back from Uganda to his official residence in Nairobi, Stanley Fingland duly obliged at that late hour by giving me not only a welcome beer but the Union Flag that flew from his own home. It was a generous gesture since he was not sure that Whitehall would provide him with another one.

It was during one of those periods when the Foreign and Commonwealth Office was acting with conspicuous meanness, even to the extent of clamping down on the traditional provision of strawberries and Champagne for embassy and high commission parties overseas on the Queen's official birthday.

This was a move which predictably annoyed British subjects abroad who rarely went anywhere near a British Embassy or high commission except to enjoy such occasions. Anyhow, carrying the precious flag, I returned to Uganda the next morning as fighting between Ugandan and Tanzanian troops continued around Jinja. I handed the flag to Dick

Posnett, who in due course hoisted it over the high commission in front of an approving group of Ugandans and, of course, in front of our television camera.

After fleeing from Uganda, Amin's host for a spell was Colonel Qaddafi in Libya. Then Amin left Libya to find a home in Saudi Arabia. There the royal family are not only secular rulers but also guardians of the Muslim holy cities of Mecca and Medina, with obligations to provide refuge if need be to Muslims in distress, just as Christian churches used to provide sanctuary for those in danger.

Thus in Jeddah, Amin died in exile in the King Feisal Hospital, a medical centre named after a Muslim monarch who was one of the braver reforming rulers of Saudi Arabia after World War II and a man I had previously met when he was trying to outlaw slavery in his kingdom.

Unloved by Islamic reactionaries, Feisal was assassinated, while Amin (who was backed for years by Islamic revolutionaries like Qaddafi and by Saudis who were less progressive than Feisal) died a natural death. The contrast between the life and the death of each man seems to me to have been ironically unjust! In my view, Feisal should have been luckier than he was in meeting his end; and Amin, I suppose, much unluckier than he was. However, I am not, of course, what both men would have called "Allah".

CHAPTER 13

A Soldier: "Quick in Quarrel"
Plus a Sailor or Two

Quickness in quarrel is not a failing unique to soldiers, nor is it universal among them. Most I have met are notable for quick calculation rather than for hot-headed action. They move swiftly when committing themselves to action but do not waste time quarrelling.

One was a notorious French mercenary, Captain Robert Dinard. Like the equally well-known British mercenary Major Michael Hoare, Dinard was active in the Congo, and for long after that, he kept cropping up all over the place in countries like the Yemen and the Comoro Islands. The Congo, with its endless troubles, is of course one of the most strikingly unfinished stories of my lifetime, and the country sticks particularly in my old mind because of the naivety, if not downright idiocy, of the remark made by the former secretary general of the United Nations, U Thant, who, back in the chaotic early days of Congolese independence from Belgium, described the bloodshed and confusion as "teething troubles". Nearly fifty years on, the "teething" continues.

Unlike the kind of soldier who appreciates publicity, Dinard was the type who tried to avoid it and sometimes positively discouraged it. He was not always successful, especially when his activities became too bold for the French authorities to ignore and he ran into trouble with them.

In a rare interview with a French journalist who once managed to extract a few words from him in the Yemen, the reporter asked Dinard why he had become a mercenary. Dinard looked at him pityingly and offered the most simple of responses: "C'est mon metier!" ("It's my trade!")

I encountered Dinard when he was involved in the 1960s with the mercenary troops of Moise Tshombe, the president of the breakaway Congolese province of Katanga, before United Nations forces, after three years, finally compelled Tshombe's surrender.

Working for the *Daily Telegraph*, I was in the company of an up-and-coming young cameraman who later went on to win international prizes for his television work for *Panorama* and other programmes. His name was Ernie Christie, and he was extremely tough.

The two of us bumped into Dinard while dodging bullets in the Katangan capital, which in those days was Elizabethville but is now Lubumbashi. Ernie raised his camera to try to get a few shots of Dinard, who turned to him and said, in English, "No pictures."

He spoke with a quiet menace, and Ernie lowered his camera. Ernie, however, was persistent, and he was keen on getting pictures of a man who was becoming something of a legend. So waiting for what he thought was a moment when he could film Dinard unawares, Ernie raised his camera again.

Dinard, with the reflex of an animal scenting danger, whirled around and put his hand on his holstered revolver. Addressing Ernie, he said, again in English, "Point that at me and I shall shoot you dead." He paused and added, in French, "Mort!"

That was Ernie's last attempt to photograph Dinard because clearly "Bobby" (as Robert Dinard was known) was not a man as cuddly as the diminutive version of his name. It was the only time I ever saw Christie too frightened to take a picture; and I watched him brave Chinese mobs in Hong Kong during the "Cultural Revolution" as well as seeing him at work in many sanguinary African locations.

One such was in Katanga in 1963, towards the end of the Tshombe attempt at secession, when we witnessed an ugly incident all too typical of life and death in the Congo.

It resulted in the Indian Army field commander issuing unusual orders that are still exemplary, in my view, for peacekeeping forces anywhere in the world today. The incident also provided Ernie with pictures that went round the world and catapulted him to the top of the league of international news photographers.

Ernie and I, with a couple of other correspondents, had been accompanying Indian troops of the United Nations along the road from
Elizabethville to the town of Jadotville, towards which Tshombe had
retreated. We were in the company of B Company, Fourth Madras
Regiment, and what followed is described by relevant extracts from my
dispatch in the *Daily Telegraph*:

> United Nations troops took Jadotville today. There was no
> resistance at all from the Katangan Army, but two Belgian
> women were shot dead by Indian troops.
>
> I was with troops advancing into Jadotville when two cars
> came down the road towards them. We ran into ditches in
> case armed mercenaries were in them. The Indians had earlier
> suffered some casualties inflicted by mercenaries as the UN
> force advanced towards Jadotville.
>
> The first car was a green station wagon, loaded with blan-
> kets and food, and the second a white saloon. Nobody waved
> the cars down, but as they passed, bursts of fire rang out from
> the troops beside the road. The saloon skidded into the side of
> the road, and bullets continued to rattle into it.
>
> Albert Verbrugghe, a Belgian cement factory worker,
> clambered from the car, his face pouring with blood from a
> deep cheek wound. With two other British correspondents and
> a photographer, I ran to the car as the Indians looked on.
>
> Verbrugghe's wife, Madeleine, and a friend, Aline van
> den Eyke, were both dying. The Indians looked on aghast at
> the scene, and Major Sami Kahn, the company commander,
> ordered a helicopter to be sent.
>
> Judging by the expressions of the troops, who have so
> far been restrained and efficient in action, they were feeling
> justifiably guilty. One officer said, "It is a shame. It should not
> have happened."
>
> Verbrugghe said an Indian major and the Mayor had
> driven round Jadotville saying that everything was quiet and
> people could go home. "That is what we were doing," he said.

His wife and her woman friend never got home and Verbrugghe disappeared into hospital. If he's still alive, I wonder what he thinks today about United Nations peace-keeping.

My news report was written in a hurry. It then had to be relayed by courier, driving through Katanga and into neighbouring Northern Rhodesia, because Congolese communications had been either destroyed or were broken down. From Northern Rhodesia, which a year later was to become the independent state of Zambia, the dispatch and pictures were transmitted onward.

This was all part of a chaotic day's work for any foreign correspondent before mobile telephones and satellite operations came into use. Even so, given the communication difficulties, the starkness of the account still makes plain the horror of the occasion. However, the details were worse. The "deep cheek wound" of the cement factory worker was a bullet lodged under his eye. He fell to his knees screaming repeatedly, "Ma femme est tue!" ("My wife is killed!")

An Alsatian dog travelling in the car jumped out howling, with its nose shot off. Finally, as we moved to the "saloon" (in fact a Volkswagen Beetle) to try to give help to its occupants, one of our group moved one of the dying women and the inner parts of her body fell onto his trousers.

Christie filmed the whole sequence of events, and his televised pictures, his graphic still photographs, and our eyewitness accounts of what had happened produced an international impact, especially at the United Nations. There, it was feared that attempts might be made to hold the organisation responsible for an unwarranted act of violence and so liable to compensation payment.

Efforts were immediately made to present the episode as merely an accident of war. I felt strongly about what became known as the "Jadotville Affair" and wrote a letter to the editor. This was unusual in that most reporters of those days preferred on the whole to write about controversies rather than to get directly involved in them, although obviously (as I saw it in this particular case), if a journalist had an interest in the truth and did not like to see dishonesty prevail, then he or she had a duty to speak up.

In addition, I was (and am) one of those perhaps old-fashioned journalists who regard with some contempt opinionated crusaders and campaigners who attempt to masquerade as reporters. I have no objection to their airing their opinions, but I become irritated when they pose as reporters. I have met many of them over the years, but few of them stay reporters for long because to do the job of a reporter properly is extremely demanding, much more demanding than columnar pontification.

I regard reporting, at its best, as a true vocation. The lines between honest reporting and slanted reporting are clear to a real reporter, if not always to readers and to some of the bosses who employ us, like editors, broadcasting producers, publishers, and former BBC Governors.

In any case, most reporters of my day were confirmed Johnsonians; that is, we firmly supported the maxim of Dr Samuel Johnson, who laid down what we regarded as a golden monetary rule: "No man but a blockhead ever wrote, except for money."

Despite my reservations about becoming a blockhead, I composed my letter, unpaid for and unsolicited, and the *Daily Telegraph* duly gave prominence to it. In it, I spelled out why the United Nations was responsible, beginning with the fact that people in Jadotville had confirmed what we had been told: a UN Jeep had gone round the town telling everyone it was safe to go home.

I responded to a UN claim that the car in which the women were travelling "failed to stop after being ordered to do so". I had been with the lead platoon of the troops, and I recalled:

> *The dual delivery of signals of which I was conscious were only abortive arm wavings from myself, dispatched from the semi-shelter of a roadside ditch, and similar wavings, from the ditch nearby, of Wing Commander Situ Mullick, press officer to the Indian forces in Katanga.*
>
> *After the incident, I turned angrily to Wing Commander Mullick and asked, "Wasn't that a bit unnecessary?" He, equally appalled, replied in immediate honesty, "It should not have happened."*

I asserted that the most damaging fact of all was that no clear signals to stop had been given by the troops involved. I stated bluntly, "Any UN claim to this effect is a lie."

The Indian forces in the Congo, for whom I had developed real respect, were largely instrumental in finishing the Tshombe rebellion, which ended two weeks later with the surrender of his last stronghold.

This was the town of Kolwezi. Its name cropped up in the final point I made in my letter because, as a result of what had happened outside Jadotville, one good thing had emerged: a determination by the Indians to ensure that no further unnecessary casualties should occur and that clear signals should be given to anyone approaching the troops to stop. The earlier omission to do this was underlined in the letter:

> Recognition of this failure was, I submit, made plain by ensuing orders from Brigadier Reginald Noronha, the Indian Field Commander, on the eve of the UN entry into Kolwezi.
>
> Determined that there should be no repetition of any such incident as that at Jadotville, he ordered not only that his troops were not to fire until fired upon, but also that they were not to fire until they themselves had suffered at least one casualty.

To my knowledge, the only other army in the world which has issued similar orders to soldiers under pressure is the British Army, although I am prepared to believe that other countries have also adopted similar stringent command procedures. I wonder what British – and especially American -- orders are today – say in Afghanistan or Iraq.

To those who have never been in the kind of situation where such orders are necessitated, I should perhaps stress that it takes courage for a soldier to wait to be shot at and possibly killed before being permitted to fire a shot back in defence.

Conforming to such orders is a sign of military professionalism and has been rarely if ever observed by many of the allegedly military forces that I have had the misfortune to encounter.

As a footnote to the Jadotville Affair and the reporting of Congolese events, I might add a funereal note about journalists involved and a happier memory about the soldiers.

One of the two correspondents with me was a Belgian, John Latz, who for some time was the stringer in Elizabethville for much of Fleet Street. With Christie, he was in the Congo on assignment covering yet another rebellion, in 1964, a year or so after the end of Katangan secession. The two of them were with a great friend of mine. They were ambushed while driving together near Stanleyville (now Kisangani), and my friend was hit between the eyes by a bullet, to die in the arms of Latz and Christie.

The victim was George Clay, Chief Correspondent in Africa of the American NBC television network. A South African who, when I first met him, was working for the *Observer* in London, Clay had been kind to me when I had been stricken down with fever on my first visit to the Congolese capital, Leopoldville (now Kinshasa), in 1960 during the immediate months after Congolese independence and the short-lived regime of Patrice Lumumba.

Clay had found one of only four doctors remaining in the chaos-stricken city to come to my aid; and Clay was the one who filed my dispatches for me for several days, together with Anthony Carthew, working in those days for the old *Daily Herald* before joining ITN.

Later Clay and I shared a house together in Nairobi, which we both used as our base for reporting African developments. As was reported at the time when he was killed, "He won an award for reporting the kind of situation that now, at forty, has finished him."

Christie lasted longer. He worked all over the world for major broadcasting organisations, including the BBC, and I worked on many assignments with him. He was a good-looking, swashbuckling character, popular with us all, especially women. He flew his own aircraft, and together we used to hop into and out of tricky bush airstrips in Africa when chasing the news.

He met his end when his plane crashed into a tower block of apartments in Johannesburg. An inquest was held, although I forget what the findings were (it was all a long time ago, and by then I was far away from Africa).

However, according to a mutual friend of Ernie's and mine, Ernie had been "ditched" by his last love, somebody far younger than himself, and she had gone to live with somebody else.

Already married and divorced, Christie was enraged and apparently maddened. He decided to put an end to himself and to the woman. So he flew his plane straight at the flat where he thought she was living.

He killed himself but not her. The final awful irony, according to the mutual friend, was that he also killed somebody in the wrong apartment into which his aircraft had crashed, namely the man who years before had given him his first job as an apprentice photographer on the old *Rhodesia Herald*.

A happier note can be appended on the subsequent careers of the Indian officers with whom I became involved in the Congo: the field commander, Brigadier Reginald Noronha; the press officer for the Indian Forces with the UN (including the Indian Air Force), Wing Commander Situ Mullick; and Major Rabindranath Seth, who was the press officer for the Indian Army in Katanga.

Some three years after we had all left the Congo, I found myself in India again after the 1965 war with Pakistan. By then, I was with the BBC and my dispatches from Pakistan and India had been widely broadcast. I received a telephone call from Situ Mullick, now promoted to group captain and head of public relations at the Indian Ministry of Defence.

Would I like to have a drink with him and with the commander of the Delhi region, Reggie Noronha, now promoted to major general?

Of course I would. Joining us for drinks was ex-Major Seth, now back in his post as a producer with All-India Radio and editor of a magazine dealing with international and Commonwealth affairs. He induced me as BBC Commonwealth correspondent to give him a long interview for the magazine.

Six years later came the next Indo-Pakistani war, resulting in the death of East Pakistan and the birth of Bangladesh. Back again in Delhi, after having left Mickey Mouse behind in Orlando, Florida, again I received a welcoming call from Situ and again I found myself having pleasant and extremely useful drinks with Reggie, by now a lieutenant general and later deputy chief of the Indian General Staff.

Over the next few weeks, the BBC profited by what was leaked to me on the war's progress. It was another illustration of how useful it sometimes is to a news organisation to have middle-aged, or even elderly, correspondents knocking about. Television went through a period when younger correspondents became more or less compulsory, and young women especially burgeoned all over the screen.

Some of them were and are very professional, not only short-term "goers" but, more impressively, "stayers" for a longer course. One of them, Kate Adie, a younger colleague with whom I had worked before she became such a household name, caused something of a stir in 2001 when, described as a "veteran" at the sprightly age of fifty-six at the time, she went so far as to accuse the BBC of wanting women reporters "with cute faces and cute bottoms and nothing else in between".

She alleged that television news was increasingly being glamourized and sensationalised in the quest for higher ratings. Describing herself as a "terribly old-fashioned old trout", she alleged that BBC bosses were more concerned about "the shape of your leg" than professional ability. She launched her assault from the Cheltenham Festival of Literature while answering questions about "dumbing down" at the BBC. The resultant headlines portrayed her as unleashing what was described as "uncivil war over BBC 'bimbos'".

Unsurprisingly, the BBC disagreed with her. A spokesperson said, "This is not a view of the BBC we recognise. The BBC's correspondents, male or female, are chosen for their skill as journalists, not how they look." Unkindly, other anonymous BBC "insiders" suggested that Kate was suffering from "professional jealousy".

I myself, as an ordinary viewer but as a former TV correspondent (and a reporter of fifty years or more), thought at the time that Kate had hit the nail on the head. However, solid evidence that televisual reporting life does not always end at thirty is provided by an assortment of my colleagues on the BBC, ITN, and Sky who have soldiered on splendidly. John Simpson, Michael Wooldridge, Michael Nicholson, Sandy Gall, Keith Graves, and the late Brian Barron among others all showed that it can be done; and the late Charles Wheeler proved that if the urge to work is strong enough, then one can go on until age and illness simply take one away.

In the 1971 Indo-Pakistani war, when I found my old contacts of such enormous help, there were BBC correspondents everywhere. Part of my duties, which included getting to the front if I possibly could, was to pull all the dispatches together each evening in Delhi from our team on the Indian side of the war and try to make sense of it all from at least one perspective.

One of the men in the field was another old chum who eventually became the religious affairs correspondent of the BBC, the late Gerald

Priestland. He was out on a desert limb in Rajasthan, contending with communication problems, but he still managed to file a useful dispatch every now and again. Afterwards he told me how difficult it had been and commented, rather enviously, "Yours, though, was the voice of the war!"

I had first met him in the Middle East, then later in the United States, where he had conducted a famous television interview with Martin Luther King just days before the latter's assassination. When that happened, I was in Canada as the Commonwealth correspondent, covering a Canadian election, and I was ordered to Atlanta, Georgia, forthwith to report King's funeral.

The murder affected Gerry deeply, and I remember sitting with him in his home in Washington and Gerry telling me that he felt he had to get out of foreign news reporting. He told me that he felt he could no longer maintain the objectivity required from a BBC foreign correspondent. So he returned to London, first to work for TV News in a special "slot" and later to distinguish himself as a broadcaster on religious subjects. Eventually, and much to my surprise, I succeeded to Gerry's post in Washington, working for three happy years alongside Charles Wheeler.

Gerry's early death was a blow to the BBC, which he had joined as one of the original BBC bunch of university graduate news trainees.

When I was able to get away from doing whatever was required of me in Delhi during the 1971 war, I managed to get to the Punjab front near Amritsar. With a Reuter colleague, Fred Bridgland, the subsequent author of books on Angola and Southern Africa, we came under fire from a Pakistani plane before nearby Indian gunners shot it down. A small metallic chunk of that aircraft adorns my study wall near my Buckingham Palace, 10 Downing Street, and various prison souvenirs.

Each time I look at it, it reminds me of the immediate aftermath. The Pakistani pilot had ejected successfully; had been taken along to the gunners' mess and entertained; and he and his Indian captors had animatedly discussed the whole thing afterwards as if analysing an India-Pakistan cricket test match. British traditions lived on for a long time in India and Pakistan, and I hope they still do.

One of the most charming memories I have of my relationship with my Indian Army chums (as they became) involved a presentation made to them by the assembled foreign correspondents who had covered the

LIFE, LOVE, LAUGHTER, LIBERTY

Katangan troubles. After the fighting had ended in Tshombe's defeat, the correspondents invited the media liaison officers of the Indian forces to dinner in a hotel in Kitwe, on the copper belt in what was still Northern Rhodesia.

As a thank you for their help in dangerous times, the foreign correspondents had clubbed together and we gave them each a silver cigar or cigarette case, inscribed to them personally, from those who had covered the 1960–63 Katanga campaign.

The Indians were delighted but also a bit worried. One of them quietly asked me later, "Is the gift personal or should we give it to the mess silver?"

I assured him that each gift was personal, for each to do with as he wished. I have never asked what happened afterwards, but my bet would be that the cases are now part of a silver collection in an Indian Army officer's mess.

One particular thank you which I had to offer them was for a scoop when Tshombe finally agreed to surrender. It happened late at night, when all communications had been cut.

I asked Major Seth, out of the hearing of my friendly but competitive colleagues, if I could send a short dispatch via UN channels to the United Nations Correspondent of the *Daily Telegraph* in New York, for him to forward on to London. I reasoned that the UN would have wanted the news out, one way or the other, so why not via the UN itself and through a big London newspaper?

I was told that there was heavy military and diplomatic traffic but that I could send a message limited to one hundred words. I wrote my piece; it winged its way to New York and the UN headquarters; and Geoffrey Myers, the UN correspondent, relayed it through to London. The next morning, the *Daily Telegraph* alone had a front-page report with this heading: "Mr Tshombe agrees to surrender." It contained ninety-five words:

> *President Tshombe of Katanga tonight agreed on arrangements for United Nations troops to enter Kolwezi. He will also ensure that the area's mining installations are not blown up.*
>
> *Beneath a portrait of Mr Hammarskjoeld, who died trying to solve Katanga's problems, Mr Tshombe signed away his*

> *last remnants of authority at a meeting with United Nations*
> *officials. The talks lasted four hours, twenty minutes.*
>
> *The agreement provides for United Nations occupation*
> *of Kolwezi, Mr Tshombe's last stronghold, by Monday. The*
> *gendarmerie will be disarmed, with the exception of two*
> *companies detailed to guard Mr Tshombe."*

It was the beginning of the end for Tshombe, who died at the hands of his enemies later in Algeria. For me, the scoop was a source of satisfaction, especially when the Reuter correspondent, Sandy Gall (later of ITN fame), asked me the next day how I had managed to get the news out. I cannot recall my reply, but I am quite sure it must have been somewhat complacent.

Soldiers in defeat, especially undisciplined troops, are not an attractive sight. From Kolwezi, just before Tshombe surrendered, I sent a dispatch conveying something of the reality:

> *I drew up in the town's centre, where an armoured car was*
> *stationed. Drunken Katangan troops perched on it, shouting*
> *and waving guns and bottles of Simba, the local beer.*
>
> *In and around the town are two thousand Katangan*
> *troops, mostly out of control, afraid of the United Nations and*
> *bold only with unarmed civilians.*
>
> *Two hundred white mercenaries remain, and of those I*
> *met, most are worried about two things. What will the United*
> *Nations do with them if they are captured? What will the*
> *Katangans do with them if Mr Tshombe loses control of Kolwezi?*
>
> *I talked to General Norbert Moke, commander of the*
> *Katangan army. He refused to give me a permit to visit his*
> *troops' positions, saying, "We don't want journalists running*
> *all over the place at this time."*
>
> *Four officials of Union Miniere (the big company con-*
> *trolling mineral assets in the region) are forbidden to go on*
> *their own into their own installations. One Kolwezi official of*
> *the company said to me, "They are the masters with their guns*
> *and their dynamite."*

A Belgian mercenary in paratroop uniform and wearing a tamoshanter of the Cape Town Highlanders said, "If Mr Tshombe says, 'Blow the lot up', then phfoot!"

He and others said that they were determined to fulfil their contracts with Mr Tshombe to the last, though some mercenaries have already started to flee. At Mwinilunga, on the North Rhodesian border, seventeen have arrived.

The Federal authorities" (that is, the authorities of the short-lived Central African Federation of Northern Rhodesia, Southern Rhodesia, and Nyasaland, created by and then abandoned by Britain) "have disarmed them and are holding them in custody for immigration officials to question.

Among the tougher nuts I met among the mercenaries, some of whom were as drunk as the Katangans, was Alex, a bearded white Russian who fought at Dien Bien Phu and in North Africa with the French Foreign Legion.

Accompanying him, an astounding sight in this trigger-jumpy town, was his Belgian wife, Yvette, in para commando's uniform, carrying a nine-millimetre Italian Astra automatic in a shoulder holster and wearing Red Cross chevrons on her sleeve.

She was well made-up and had her blonde hair tied in two ponytails. She said, "This is not quite like Brussels, but it has been exciting." A resident told me that on Friday after Jadotville fell, Katangan troops in Kolwezi commandeered cars from civilians to flee from the United Nations.

Captain Jean-Marie, a French mercenary with a leg injured in the September 1961 Elizabethville fighting, declined to allow me to visit six hundre Katangans in position facing the United Nations. He explained, "It is as much as we can do to look after ourselves, let alone you."

I heard little praise from the mercenaries for the behaviour of the Katangan soldiers, except for a compliment for forty of them. These Africans fought with thirty Europeans in "Red Group" against advancing Indians and helped to blow up the Lufira bridges.

*In active command at present is a Frenchman, Captain
"Bobby" Dinard, who is at the front.*

Dinard's "metier" of the mercenary soldier is a trade still exercised in
Africa, although judging by the difficulties in which, not so long ago, the
old Etonian Sandhurst-trained ex-SAS officer Simon Mann found himself,
in Zimbabwe and in Equatorial Guinea, it is not exactly a flourishing occupation. The job was to some extent glamourized by the film *The Wild Geese*.

From what I have observed of most mercenaries, it would seem a
dubious choice of career; even though new and different kinds of opening
for it have arisen in, for example, Iraq, where security officers are or were
keenly sought.

Of all the troubles on which I have reported over the years, those in
the Congo and in neighbouring areas of Africa were among the worst.
Death was so casual. It was simply a matter of luck as to whether or not
one survived.

Once, for instance, I was leaving the Congo to drive to Northern
Rhodesia, crossing the ill-defined and amorphous so-called "front lines"
between the United Nations on one side and the Katangans and mercenaries on the other.

The car in which I was travelling got through with no problem;
the one behind did not. A Swiss was killed; and a friend who was a
correspondent and who later joined the BBC, the late Jim Biddulph, was
wounded in the head. The UN troops who fired on the car were Swedish.

On another occasion, in Zambia, I had visited the border where
Rhodesian forces had attacked Zambian troops and had filmed interviews
with the soldiers there before returning to Lusaka to dispatch my report.
A journalist who had covered the war in Vietnam, Anthony Joyce of the
Australian broadcasting organisation, ABC, decided to visit exactly the
same scene the next day. There he was shot dead by one of the Zambians.

With BBC colleagues and the BBC itself, we tried to help with the
aftermath, including dealing from afar with Tony's widow and helping
to make funeral arrangements. It had been a fatal day for one foreign
correspondent and a bad day in the life of other foreign correspondents.
Competitive though we are, we do not wish to see our competitors dead.

The mercenary soldiers so familiar upon the African scene tended to be different to another kind of mercenary soldier. Some of these I met in the Middle East in particular.

They tended to follow in the tradition of Lawrence of Arabia, (Lieutenant Colonel T. E. Lawrence); and Glubb Pasha, (Sir John Bagot Glubb), commander of the old Transjordanian Arab Legion. Essentially, they were British officers on British secondment to friendly Arab countries, serving British interests as well as the interests of the country where they held command.

One of the most fascinating of them, and one of the most romantic figures I have ever met, was the commander of the Trucial Oman Scouts, Colonel Stewart Carter. He entered into my field of acquaintanceship in 1960, before the United Arab Emirates had been born and when they were known as the Gulf Trucial States, all of them British protectorates.

In each of the British protectorates there was based a British political agent, usually a youngish Foreign Office career diplomatist. The immediate regional boss of the agents was a senior diplomatist, the Political Resident, based in Bahrein, and in those days, the real ruler of the Gulf States insofar as their defence and foreign policies were concerned. For many years, the post of Political Resident had been occupied by Sir James Belgrave, leading inevitably to the whole of his Gulf "empire" being known in the Foreign Office as "Belgravia".

Stewart Carter was an unlikely-looking inhabitant of the real Belgravia, a plush part of London. A tall hawk-faced man wearing a Bedouin headdress, Colonel Carter frequently bore on his wrist a bird of prey which looked just like him. His Arab soldiers loved him, just as the men of the old Arab Legion had loved Glubb Pasha.

There was a minor war going on around Buraimi Oasis and the Colonel drove me there from Sharjah in a Land Rover with sandbags on the floor to protect us in case we hit a mine and blew up. There was no road, just the desert and occasionally a track.

We approached a wadi, a dry riverbed, in which, squatting in a circle on the ground, were half a dozen Bedouin with their camels. To my astonishment, the colonel called out to one of them, "Good morning, Julian." One of them stood up and replied, "Good morning, Colonel."

I looked more closely, and beneath the beard and the Bedou garments was an Arab who was English. He was a Foreign Office Arabist who had spent months in the desert, visiting every palm tree, every bush, every tiny spring or oasis, consulting with tribal Arab leaders on the ownership of every square inch of the barren landscape.

The reason for this was that the end was in sight for the British protectorates. Formal borders had to be established for the different sheikhdoms. The desert might be just that, but there could be oil underneath it. On departing from the area, Britain did not want to leave behind disputed borders, whether between the sheikhdoms themselves or between the sheikhdoms and their far bigger neighbours, such as Iraq or Saudi Arabia.

Despite the far-sightedness of the Foreign Office, the Kuwait-Iraq border in particular has become a frontier now familiar with war; and the strains between Bahrein and Iran have displayed themselves with riots in the island, possibly encouraged by Iran.

The low-key conflict over Buraimi, involving principally Oman and Saudi Arabia and to a lesser extent the Gulf States, was nevertheless at the time a nasty little war, with Nasser trying to exploit any anti-British feeling. Cairo radio, for example, reported on no fewer than four occasions during his command of the Trucial Oman Scouts that Stewart Carter had been killed – before he eventually retired to become a public relations officer for a brewery in England.

Another remarkable character was the former commander of the armed forces of the sultan of Muscat, Colonel David Smiley. The colonel of the Royal Horse Guards, "The Blues", introduced me to him in London, in which regiment Smiley had served earlier and which I had come to know in Cyprus. As we sat down to lunch in his club, his opening words across the table to me were, "Do you know anybody who wants a good assassin?"

I asked him why he should think that I could help. He replied that I seemed to know many curious people (like John Simpson, whose book, *Strange Places; Questionable People*, immediately struck a chord with me). David Smiley thought that I might just be able to recommend him to somebody or other.

I gathered that he was contemplating the role of assassin for himself, so I asked him who, for example, he was thinking of killing. Only half-jokingly, he answered that he would quite like to begin with Nasser. It was a jolly interesting lunch.

I understood that he was looking for some sort of active well-paid work, as his service for the sultan had ended and he had a Scottish estate to maintain. I said I would do what I could, and I did. I invited him to meet the editor of the BBC TV programme *Tonight*, the predecessor of *Newsnight*.

This was Derrick Amoore, who was also an extraordinary character. He was a highly imaginative, constantly restless journalist and filmmaker who later became editor of BBC TV News. The colonel, the editor, and I had lunch together at the old BBC TV Lime Grove premises, and I have rarely seen two such contrasting personalities click with each other so immediately as those two men did.

On one side of the table was the raffish, almost Bohemian, intellectual Amoore; on the other was the tough soldier associated in wartime Balkan adventures with men like David Stirling, and he was just back from Arabian adventures. The upshot was that Amoore commissioned Smiley to go off with a BBC TV team to the Yemen, where there were endemic disturbances throughout the 1960s.

I had my own, earlier, souvenirs of the Yemen. In 1963, accompanied by a Yemeni guide, Tagi, I walked one hundred miles or more from the Red Sea town of Jizan, in Saudi Arabia, into the deep and mountainous interior of the Yemen, the "Arabia Felix" ("Happy Arabia") of the Romans. It was anything but happy in 1963, with twenty-five thousand of Nasser's Egyptian troops trying in vain to subdue Yemenis loyal to their prince and ruler, Imam Mohammad al-Badr. The Egyptians employed tanks, rocket launchers, and artillery; they had complete control of the air, but they could not break the Yemeni resistance.

A coup mounted fifteen months earlier in the capital, Sana, by Yemeni officers, and backed by Nasser, had failed to get rid of the ruler. From his cave headquarters, and with the support of thirteen other Yemeni princes, five of them brothers, he fought back for some years while the Egyptians became confined to the main cities and main roads, rather as the Russians were later in Afghanistan. Eventually, like the Russians in Afghanistan, the Egyptians too pulled out and the Yemen continued existence in what seems to be its normal state of turmoil.

After a ten-day journey through northern Yemen on foot, and sometimes seated on the back of a pack mule named Juma, I finally reached the imam's cave. There was a radio link there from which an operator using a Morse key was able to send short dispatches from me via Saudi Arabia to the *Daily Telegraph* and also to the recently founded *Sunday Telegraph*. In fact, an Arab territorial dispute of the kind engaging the energies of men like "Julian" formed the subject of a dispatch from me from Bahrein, which appeared in the very first issue of that newspaper on 5 February 1961.

Just a couple of years later, I was reporting upon not just the potential for an Arab dispute but also a vicious and virtually unreported Arabian civil war. The Yemeni fighting was largely uncovered because of the difficulties of travel and movement in beautiful but wild country, as well as the obstacles set up by the Egyptians and their Yemeni puppets to access by correspondents to the shaky new republic. This was because Nasser, in particular, wanted nobody from the outside world to see what was really going on as his forces strafed, bombed, and shelled Yemeni villages. The brutal tactics employed would not have improved Nasser's already decaying international image.

There was also a pronounced reluctance in the West, especially on the Left and among liberals, to accept that Nasser was a military dictator just as much as an Arab nationalist hero. He had particularly engaged the sympathies in England of the *Observer*, to such an extent that one of the most brilliant of that newspaper's correspondents, the late Rawle Knox, parted company from it because (he informed me) his employers simply did not want to hear from him about what was going on in the Yemen, despite his attempts as the Middle East correspondent to report on the Yemeni realities. So he joined the *Daily Telegraph* instead.

While I was in the Yemen, the royalists held two hundred Egyptian troops as prisoners; and Egypt was attempting to negotiate their release against freedom for the wives, children, and sisters of the royal family detained during and after the coup.

The imam told me that nineteen women relatives and eight children were held in Cairo and elsewhere and that Nasser was trying to force him into releasing the Egyptian prisoners of war by threatening to harm the royal detainees.

"But I shall make no special consideration for my family in this case," he declared, including in that his two wives and his mother, who were held in the Yemeni capital of Sana. Then aged forty-four, the imam was, as I reported in the *Sunday Telegraph*, "bearing up well to revolution, attempted assassination, bombing, shooting, war and discomfort".

The Nasserist policy was supported by the Soviet Union and by Algeria, while the Saudis helped the royalist forces of the imam. Further in the background were the Americans, playing a far from clear role. They had recognized the republic and seemed to be sympathetic to Nasser, to such an extent that the commander of royalist forces on one Yemeni front that I visited, Emir Abdullah ibn Hussein, commented to me, "We cannot help wondering who is paying for all this, the Russians or the Americans."

The Yemenis in those days were not especially anti-American. The prince himself, just fifteen months before, at the time of the coup, had been studying at the American University of Beirut. When I met him, he was twenty-five, long-haired, and wild-looking, fighting for his life and his beliefs, one of the five princely brothers holding sector commands.

An American doctor who later became a colonel in the US armed forces, Dr William Bartlett, accompanied me on my journey into the Yemen, together with a British medical assistant, Arnold Plummer.

The two-man team, later joined by another British doctor, were working for the British Red Cross, and they stayed in the Yemen to establish some rudimentary medical facilities. As I reported at the time:

> The imam normally works in his cave by night, receiving and sending messages and orders. Movement by daylight for the royalists is difficult because of Egyptian air activity. The imam broke this rule, however, to visit the cave field surgical unit which the British Red Cross has established in a valley near his headquarters. In the first three weeks of their work, the team has already treated 950 patients.

Asleep in our tent one night, our Arab guide, Tagi, awoke us and addressed himself sorrowfully to Bill Bartlett. President John Kennedy had been assassinated. We tuned in on our transistor radio to listen to the news. The Yemenis were full of sympathy for the American doctor in his country's loss.

After I had said my farewells to the imam and my Red Cross friends to start the long walk back to Saudi Arabia, I was asleep one night in a house in a small Yemeni village when an Arab messenger awoke me. He emerged from out of the darkness and the surrounding wilderness with a letter for me. It had taken him two days to reach me. I opened the envelope, and using a torch, I noticed that it bore an Arabic princely insignia and, in English, my handwritten name and my address: "Beit Ethageh; c/o El Nagib Nezan; Elme'mery". So that's where I was! (In Arabic, "beit" means a house).

Inside was a piece of paper also bearing the insignia. It was handwritten, dated 2 December 1963, and signed by the young prince I had visited in his sector of command:

> Dear Mr J. Osman,
>
> I hope that you didn't find any difficulties on your way to Beit Ethageh. Humbly, I enclose with this letter a small present, hoping that you will accept it. It is just a humble souvenir of your visit to my headquarters. I hope that you will arrive at Garrah well and without facing any difficulties.
>
> Until we meet again, I wish you Merry Christmas and Happy New Year, although it is early for that, and full success in your work.

Well, we never met again. I had no alternative but to accept the "small present" because to decline it would have been an impermissible insult. So I sat down and wrote a letter in return. Regarding his wish for "full success" in my work, I tried as diplomatically and politely as I could to assure him that I would report upon the situation in the Yemen as honestly and accurately as I could, but making it plain that I would not be committing myself to support for the royalists.

In due course, prominence was given by the *Sunday Telegraph* to my long and detailed final dispatch that I think I can claim opened the eyes of many people in the West to the realities of the struggle in the Yemen. If the prince ever survived to read the report, I hope that he was pleased.

Dealing gracefully with gifts in the Arab world, or elsewhere, can be tricky. A year or so before receipt of my own unexpected gift, I had reported on the presentation of another one, in Cairo, to a departing British diplomatist, Mr Colin Crowe (later Sir Colin).

The manner of presentation demonstrated the status and influence of one of Nasser's closest confidants, Mohammed Hassenein Heikal, the editor in those days of the major Cairo newspaper *Al Ahram*.

He was a man commonly referred to in the Arab world as "His Master's Voice;" and Colin Crowe was British chargé d'affaires in Egypt for a year or two preceding the arrival of the first fully fledged British ambassador after Suez, Sir Harold Beeley.

As charge, Crowe had fulfilled the sensitive task of picking up the broken diplomatic pieces and beginning the restoration of normal diplomatic relations. In fact, he became something of a master of that particular art, being chosen by the Foreign Office during his career to reopen closed embassies not only in Egypt but also in two other countries that had severed relations with Britain: China and Saudi Arabia.

At this particular Cairo farewell party for him, things went like this (according to what I reported shortly afterwards):

> *Heikal, a handsome and ambitious man, came up to Mr Crowe, placed an envelope in his hand, and said, "A parting gift."*
>
> *Somewhat embarrassed, since the Queen's servants do not accept presents, yet unable to refuse without offending Arab rules of behaviour, Mr Crowe began to murmur something about "giving it to charity".*
>
> *Heikal interrupted him to say, "Open it."*
>
> *Inside the envelope on a piece of paper was written "Zarb".*

The name was that of James Zarb, who had been imprisoned for allegedly spying for Britain. His release was Nasser's parting gift to Colin Crowe.

What was my own "small present" and "humble souvenir"? Out of the envelope, when I opened it to read the prince's letter, tumbled twenty-five British gold sovereigns. I carried them back to England with me and took them into my bank in Fleet Street, the National Westminster, in the old Reuter building. Like the newspapers for which Fleet Street was famous and which have long since moved elsewhere, both NatWest and Reuter have now disappeared from that building, where many thousands of pounds must have been lent to indigent journalists across the years, including myself.

I pushed the sovereigns across the counter, and within minutes I was invited into the office of the manager. Had I declared the gold when I entered the country? No, I had not. I explained that I had never had occasion before this to import gold into England and I simply did not know that it was necessary to declare it. He pointed out that ignorance of the law was no excuse.

However, he would speak to "the authorities" and would look after the gold for me. A week or two later, he asked me to call in. He had sorted things out with the authorities, and there was no problem. He then told me something that I found romantic and delightful.

The sovereigns were all dated 1917, and they had been minted to be used by Lawrence of Arabia in encouraging the Arab revolt against the Turks in the Great War. So they had returned home to England as an Arab gift to a British journalist.

I wish I had been able to afford to keep them, as obviously they were going to appreciate in value, but I was hard up at the time, so I sold most of them for three pounds each.

I kept some, however, and had a couple turned into earrings, hoping that my elder daughter, a beautiful mezzo-soprano, might perhaps wear them when singing an operatic role. As for the princely letter, that too is among my souvenirs.

Apart from things like diaries at Christmastime and an occasional bottle of something or other, the only gift of any consequence which I remember accepting during my years as a reporter came to me many years later during my last staff job as the BBC diplomatic and court correspondent.

It was Christmastime in 1984 that I was presented with this gift. I had just returned from a seven-day trip round the world with the prime minister, Mrs Thatcher. She had first flown for twenty hours to Peking (or Beijing) to sign the agreement to relinquish British sovereignty over Hong Kong to China; then she visited Hong Kong itself; then she flew on via Guam and Honolulu to Washington for talks on what were known as "Star Wars" with President Ronald Reagan.

By the time we were taking off from Andrews Air Force Base to return to England, I was pretty tired, and I note from my diary that our man in Washington at the time, Martin Bell, bought me "a Big Mac hamburger, chips, and Coca-Cola lunch". He told me he adored junk food.

Back in London at 4.45 a.m. on 23 December, just before Christmas, I had to "wrap up" for the news bulletins the implications of the Thatcher odyssey. Then I later went to TV Centre for the strictly private viewing of the Queen's Christmas Day television message to the Commonwealth, with the monarch sitting in the viewing room next door watching the finished recording before putting her imprimatur on the Crown copyright product.

This annual preview was a regular job for accredited court correspondents, and it was good of both Buckingham Palace and the BBC to let us see the broadcast and write about it, under strict embargo, before Christmas, thus enabling us to take the day off on Christmas Day itself.

Unfortunately, some time later, this benevolent arrangement came under threat when one of my TV successors indulged in a pre-Christmas lunch with some tabloid journalists belonging to what was known as the "royal rat pack". He let slip a few remarks about the content of the broadcast that were turned into headline news before the broadcast was actually screened and aired.

There was a great row, and my unfortunate colleague Michael Cole, who had won tremendous plaudits for his coverage of the IRA Brighton bomb explosion, found himself in trouble because he had trusted his colleagues a mite too much. He subsequently left the BBC and became a spokesman for the former owner of Harrod's, Mohammed Fayed, father of the man who died with Princess Diana in the Paris car accident.

I have no idea what precisely the arrangements are these days for court correspondents, or any other journalists, to have prior knowledge of the contents of the Christmas broadcast; but I hope that arrangements still exist so that the Christmas Days of reporters might remain uninterrupted.

Having completed on that Christmas Eve my court and diplomatic news duties, I was about to leave the office when my telephone rang. It was the Soviet Press attaché in London, Gennadi Chabanikov. He invited me to meet him for a Christmas drink at the Soviet Embassy in Kensington Palace Gardens as he had done the previous year.

Just as I had done the previous year also, I told him I was too tired to get out to "Millionaires Row" and then find my way back home to Islington. I asked if he could come down to the old BBC Club in Langham Place (now the Langham Hotel) to have a drink with me.

He accepted, and half an hour later, we were toasting each other's health: "Nazdarovya!"

He said, "I have a present for you, John," and I replied, "Oh, good!" because I remembered that he had given me the year before a highly acceptable bottle of Stolichnaya vodka.

But no, the gift this year, he explained, was from the Soviet ambassador himself. The reason for this was that earlier in the year, on the occasion of the sixtieth anniversary of the establishment of diplomatic relations between the Soviet Union and Great Britain, I had conducted for the *Today* programme an interview with the ambassador which had gone down well with all concerned: the Foreign Office, the Soviet Union, and even Buckingham Palace. The Queen was laying plans well in advance for an eventual historic visit to Moscow and, of course, an equally historic visit to London by Mr Gorbachev to meet Mrs Thatcher, or the "Iron Lady", as the Russians called her.

I was pleased by such unanimous approval from those on high, for such commendation is a rare thing for a journalist to experience. I was also pleased, but a bit taken aback by, the ambassador's Christmas present. It was a silver hip flask from the royal silversmiths.

I accepted because it was impossible not to do so, but I was uneasy about it. The BBC had reasonably clear rules on such matters, and I was aware that this was something rather more than a diary, a bottle of vodka, or a fountain pen.

So after Christmas, I went in to see my editor, Larry Hodgson. I told him what I had received, and he asked me to show it to him. "Very nice," he said. Then he asked me, "Would you like to see what the Russians have given me?"

He produced an enormous crystal bowl of succulent caviar; it must have been worth thousands of pounds. I reacted by saying, "Larry, I think we're being got at."

He agreed. I asked, "Well, what are we going to do?" His reply was the reply of a good editor: "We wait until they come round to us one day carrying bags with thousands of dollars in them, then we tell them to ... go away."

His last two words, of course, were not "go away".

We then had a drink and tucked into some of the caviar. I use my hip flask occasionally and sometimes wonder what has happened both to the Russian ambassador and Chabanikov, as well as to Larry Hodgson.

Both the Russian and the Yemeni gifts were, I think, simply genuine expressions of appreciation by their donors to a journalist who had bothered to report their side of things in an always changing and uncertain world.

On the other side of the Arabian Peninsula from Yemen, I met another princely soldier, still in power in 2014, who is another remarkable man.

This was Sultan Qabus ibn Said of Oman, the largest country of the Arabian Peninsula after Saudi Arabia. In few countries of the world has change been so dramatic in so few years. Up until 1970, the sultanate (formerly better known as Muscat) was little known because, until then, the old sultan had deliberately kept the country isolated in mediaeval squalor. This was Sultan Sayyid Said bin Taimur al-Said, the present ruler's father.

Prohibitions were the order of the day: travel was rigidly restricted, and no woman or government official could leave the country without the sultan's permission. Coastal tribes could not visit the interior; desert and mountain tribes could not visit the coast. Dancing, music, singing, smoking, and alcohol were forbidden, as was the wearing of Western clothes – and spectacles! People owned slaves, and black Omanis of slave descent walked with their eyes downcast. There were no roads and no proper airport, and electricity and telephones existed only for a privileged few.

There was only one hospital of twelve beds, run by American missionaries. There were only three primary schools for boys in the entire country and not a single girls' school. The infant mortality rate was thought to be the highest in the world, at an estimated rate of 80 per cent.

The inevitable result was a mass exodus by thousands of Omanis who fled to find work and education elsewhere. Rebellion inevitably followed, with support from newly independent Aden and South Yemen. The old sultan remained closeted for the last fifteen years of his reign in his palace in Salalah, in Dhofar, not far from the South Yemen border.

His son, Sultan Qabus, returned from Europe, where he had been educated at Sandhurst and had become an officer in The Cameronians. On getting home, he found himself under virtual house arrest for some time and was almost helpless. Eventually, though, he was approached by the governor of Dhofar, the Wali, and by other leading Omanis for his approval of plans to install him as sultan in his father's place.

He was fond of his father, and at first he hesitated. In time, he realised he had no choice if the country was to survive and therefore agreed to the deposition of his father in a bloodless coup. The old man went to Claridge's Hotel in London, where he spent the last three years of his life. From the moment his son took over, Oman has been transforming itself.

From the word go in July 1970, Qabus set about building a new Oman. He promised his two million or so people his best personal efforts to secure a better future for all. The Omanis responded, including many of his father's opponents. One of them, who had become a minister in the sultan's government, told me that when Qabus spoke from his heart it struck into the heart of most Omanis.

I was there in 1980, just ten years after the Omani renaissance had started. The first years were difficult. The sultan told me, "We had to run to catch up." Nevertheless, by 1980 the old restrictions had been largely swept away; there were no slaves, plenty of roads, hospitals, schools for girls as well as for boys, and no problems over spectacles.

Evidence of Omani progress has continued to be unmistakeable. Oil has been exploited, although on not such a large scale as in other Arab states, and attempts have been made to diversify the economy, including the tapping of water resources discovered not so long ago. As the sultan put it to me, "When the oil dries up, we don't want to dry up with it."

The real threat has been external, because Oman holds a strategic position at the entrance to the Gulf, commanding the Straits of Hormuz. Therefore, the sultan also has a navy which, when I was there, consisted of four gunboats, two missile boats, a freighter, a three-masted topsail training vessel, a dhow called a "boom", which had a pointed stern to make it sail faster; several landing craft; and the sultan's royal yacht, armed with two machine guns.

The navy is by now, I am sure, larger and more sophisticated, but I enjoyed sailing with it after an interview with the sultan which he gave to myself and another correspondent, my wife (then working for the *Nairobi Times* as well as freelancing for many newspapers round the world). Our meeting ended with him commanding an aide, "Give them the navy!"

So off we went to meet the navy's commander, Commodore Harry Mucklow, who was on secondment from the Royal Navy to the Omani Navy.

We took off from a flight deck on the royal yacht in a helicopter and flew over a Soviet warship in the centre of the Straits of Hormuz, waving down to the Soviet sailors below as they waved up to us. This was at a time when the West and the sultanate itself were worried about Soviet troops moving into Afghanistan. All were concerned generally about Soviet activity in the Gulf area and on the Arabian Peninsula.

Because I was about to be posted to Moscow, I was glad to see personally, before heading there, something of Soviet activity in the Middle East. In Russia a few months, later one of the first events I had to cover was the opening of the 1980 Olympic Games, controversial because of the American boycott imposed due to the Russian involvement in Afghanistan.

Like Commodore Mucklow, a sailor through and through, another of my varied military and naval acquaintances was another nautical officer. However, on the only occasion that I ever met him, he was in fact a soldier for the evening. This was Admiral of the Fleet Lord Louis Francis Albert Victor Nicholas Mountbatten, first earl Mountbatten of Burma; supreme commander in South-East Asia from 1943 until the end of World War II (when he received the Japanese surrender in Singapore); last British viceroy of India; then first sea lord and later chief of the defence staff.

It has become fashionable in recent years for critics to denigrate his career and achievements, but whatever alleged mistakes he might have made in performing his duties (for example, for the loss of life in the Dieppe Raid during World War II, when he was chief of Combined Operations Command), the fact remains that his entire life was dedicated to British public service. He was a handsome man with close royal connections, and that glossy combination encouraged anyone of an envious nature and with republican leanings to detest him doubly. Not only was he lucky enough to be good-looking, but worse than that, he was uncle to the Queen's consort, Prince Philip, and great-uncle to the Prince of Wales.

His deeds, his good looks, and his life were finished off in a spectacular display of Provisional IRA terrorist inhospitality in 1979, when he was blown to death while he was fishing near his summer home in Ireland. Well before his unhappy end, however, I encountered him for a happy evening in Windsor.

The setting for our meeting there was in the officers' mess of the Life Guards. Mountbatten was not wearing his usual impressive naval uniform as an admiral of the fleet but was even more gorgeously clad (if that is possible) in the scarlet tunic of a colonel of the Life Guards. The evening was the kind of night often described as "glittering", with the regimental silver doing exactly that and regimental hospitality ample. With another journalist, the late Donald Wise of the *Daily Mirror*, I was there as a guest after the regiment had got to know the two of us in places like Cyprus and Aden.

In our dinner jackets, we were the only black-and-white "penguins" in a sea of scarlet, although Donald displayed his World War II medals to add just a touch of adornment to his garments that my own unadorned suit lacked.

We had been invited to join in the celebrations to mark Mountbatten's "dining in" as honorary colonel of the Life Guards. I was placed next to the guest of honour, and through the mists of time, not to mention the wine of the evening, I remember that we had a long conversation about India and Pakistan, from where I had just returned after reporting for the BBC the 1965 Indo-Pakistani "Rann of Kutch" War. Mountbatten had obviously listened to many of my war dispatches and was eager to talk about it all.

Inevitably, our discussion turned to the 1947 independence of India and Pakistan, when Mountbatten as viceroy had presided over events leading up to partition, implementing as best he could the policy of Clement Attlee and the British government.

Speaking to me with a frankness that surprised me, Mountbatten blamed himself about how he had "got things wrong". He recalled his memories of the horror of communal massacres and of ensuing Indo-Pakistani tensions and conflict.

For my part, I responded by telling him that I truly doubted if any other viceroy could have done any better. I argued that if the fault was anyone's, it was not just his but the fault of the Hindus or Muslims them-selves – and of the British government for not having thought things through somewhat more clearly before proceeding to impose policies that precipitated the tragedy. I suggested that he had really been the government's fall guy.

I spoke with all the spurious authority of somebody who had not been in India at the time of partition but who had at least read about it and who also had some up-to-date knowledge of what was happening in the subcontinent.

What was more, I had sympathy for this great public figure who, at the age of sixty, was anguishing himself over what he might or might not have done better, years earlier and thousands of miles away. All this on an evening of celebration!

Mountbatten was not to be consoled. To this day, his own judgement on how he had performed in India rings in my ears and in my memory.

As one who dislikes the tasteless use, in writing, of the dictionary's "vulgar slang" word, I shall permit myself an exception this time because it is the only honest way of reporting accurately what the last Viceroy of India thought about the way he had done his job: "I fucked it up."

Pandit Nehru, the Indian Prime Minister, gives a news conference in
the Indian hill-town of Mussourie in 1959 after his first meeting with the
Dalai Lama following the Tibetan leader's flight from his own country to
become an exile in India. I was among the journalists who questioned him
following his four hours with the Dalai Lama. Nehru, a keen horseman,
rode a snow-white mare to meet the Dalai Lama in his place of refuge and
I reported Nehru's appeal to us not to exacerbate the growing tensions
between India and China. It did no good and not long afterwards the
two countries experienced a short but nasty Himalayan border war.

At the jungle muddy track entrance to India's forbidden North-East Frontier
Agency, NEFA, not far from Tezpur in Assam. It was – and remains – a
sensitive and geographically-difficult border region in neighbouring India
and China. Entry was forbidden without authority and hazards to any rare
traveler actually allowed access included elephants, tigers, mosquitoes
and, higher up, difficult mountain terrain. The notice on the tree warned
visitors to stay out. The Indian with me (I'm in shorts) was my nervous
Indian guide. The Dalai Lama and his entourage had a long and hard
month-long journey to make down this track through NEFA from the
mountains above to reach the plains of Assam and the town of Tezpur,
where he made his first public appearance after his flight from Tibet.

Three pictures of Indian refugee camps being built near Tezpur
for Tibetan refugees fleeing Chinese oppression.

The late James Cameron (then working for the old "News Chronicle) in Tezpur, looking rather jaded at the bottom of the picture, with a BBC TV cameraman, and myself in shorts.

Two pictures of me interviewing Afghan Mangal tribesmen in tribal areas of the north-west frontier between Afghanistan and Pakistan in the Kurram tribal agency near Parachinar in 1959. Even then, 20 years before the Soviet Union moved troops into Afghanistan, they were complaining about Soviet influence.

Defying municipal orders in Lahore in 1959, I sit on Zam-Zammah: "Kim's gun." The gun stars in the opening paragraph of Rudyard Kipling's great novel, "Kim." The paragraph reads: "He sat, in defiance of municipal orders, astride the gun Zam-Zammah on her brick platform opposite the old Ajaib-Gher – the Wonder House, as the natives call the Lahore Museum. Who hold Zam-Zammah, that 'fire-breathing dragon,' hold the Punjab, for the great green-bronze piece is always first of the conqueror's loot." The newspaper on which Kipling worked as a journalist, the old "Civil and Military Gazette," was still being published when I was first in Lahore. Like other visitors I looked in at his old office and, like many interested in his work, sat happily for a moment or two in his chair.

CHAPTER 14

"Seeking the Bubble Reputation" And the Dalai Lama

My own less than viceregal experience of India and Pakistan began in an unexpected way. It started at my home in London in 1959, whence I had returned from Cyprus and a six-month initiation into foreign correspondence. I was trimming my garden hedge on an early April afternoon when I received a call from the foreign news desk asking me if I knew where Kalimpong was. I did not.

I was informed that it was in the Himalayas, south of Tibet, tucked away between the mountain kingdoms of Nepal, Sikkim, and Bhutan, on the ill-defined and mountainous north-eastern frontiers of India. Would I mind going there because rumours were seeping out of Tibet that there had been a rebellion against Chinese rule?

That night I left England to undertake one of the most fascinating assignments of my life: covering the flight from Tibet of the Dalai Lama. Now, more than half a century on, the Dalai Lama is still compelled to exist in exile and is talking of "retirement", having already relinquished the political role he formerly held to a much younger Tibetan. He remains the spiritual leader of Tibetans, however, and in 2011, when he was seventy-six, he indicated that when he reached the age of ninety or so, he would probably decide on the reincarnation process leading to the choice of the next Dalai Lama.

This reminded China that the last word on the matter, so far as Tibetans are concerned, still belongs to the Dalai Lama and not to the Chinese government, no matter what efforts might be made by China to establish its own approved monk as the Dalai Lama.

Meanwhile, the election (also in 2011) by the Tibetan government in exile of a younger Tibetan political figure to relieve the Dalai Lama of the political role from which he wanted to rid himself anyway has the advantage of helping to diminish any possible political leadership crisis in the event of his death before he reaches ninety.

In his years of exile, he has won the admiration of millions around the world, not to mention the Nobel Peace Prize, and he has attracted the fury of the Chinese government for his steadfast and peaceful campaigning on behalf of the Tibetan people. Despite the visit to China last year by the British prime minister and other British leaders, diplomatic relations between China and Great Britain remain sensitive because of the Tibetan problem, and when David Cameron met the Dalai Lama in London in 2012, the Chinese made plain their disapproval. Things have been patched up for economic and wider political and strategic reasons, but underlying tensions remain over Tibetan human rights.

Nor did the Chinese like it when the Tibetan spiritual leader was earlier received by the Prince of Wales, one of his admirers. The apparent Chinese colonisation by Han Chinese of Tibet; the reported repression of Tibetans by China; the waves of protest (and even self-immolation) by Tibetan Buddhists; the growth of package tourism in Tibet with the construction of a high-altitude railway; and the prolific philosophic and moral activities (never far from the international spotlight) of the Dalai Lama himself ... Well, all these ingredients add up to present a picture of an uncertain future for Tibet and its people, and they form one more of my many unfinished stories.

When I left London in April 1959, there was no knowledge of the flight of the Dalai Lama from the Tibetan capital, Lhasa. There had been a clampdown on news by Tibet's Chinese communist overlords, but it was plain from the accounts of Tibetan refugees arriving in India that something serious was happening.

I got into Calcutta (as Kolkata still was), checked in for the night at a hotel, and by one of those strokes of luck that sometimes befall a journalist, I met in the bar an Indian pilot I had previously met when he was flying with UN forces in the Middle East. He told me over our whisky nightcaps that, incredibly, he had just flown in the brother of the Dalai Lama, Gyalo Thondup, who was upstairs in a room in this very hotel.

Early the next morning, I knocked on the door of Gyalo Thondup's room and talked with him. He told me that there had been an uprising in Lhasa and that since then he had received no news of his brother. He was one of the Dalai Lama's four brothers. He asked me not to disclose his own whereabouts but informed me that a close friend, a senior Tibetan government official, Pangda Tshang, one of the first Tibetans to seek asylum in India, had arrived from Tibet in Gangtok, the capital of Sikkim. It was a welcome pointer for me.

I thanked him and headed for Gangtok. I flew from Calcutta to Bagdogra at the edge of the Himalayan foothills. From there, I travelled up through the hills to Kalimpong (I now knew where the town was).

I booked into the one tolerable hotel of those days, in which I stayed again fifty years later. By then, in 2009, it had become a very comfortable establishment indeed, but still with its tranquil garden, hot water bottles, coal fires with scuttles by the fireside, and bearers to lay and light those fires and refill those scuttles. The place was owned by the same family, proprietors since 1920. It is the Himalayan Hotel.

I hired a Jeep for a further drive of four hours or so along the hair-raising road from Kalimpong, past tea plantations, through forest and over rickety bridges, to Gangtok, with its six-thousand-foot-high hilltop palace and its Buddhist monastery glistening in the sun.

The Chinese border was only twenty-five miles away at Chumbi. In Gangtok, I struck journalistic gold. The Indians were represented in Sikkim, then an Indian protectorate but now subsumed into India, by a political agent, Apa Pant (later one of India's Commonwealth high commissioners). He had a diplomatic radio connection with the Indian consulate general in Lhasa, and the raw information arriving daily in Gangtok direct from Lhasa was transmitted straight to New Delhi and the Indian prime minister, Pandit Nehru.

Through a decision taken by Nehru himself in consultation with Apa Pant, an arrangement was made whereby news emerging from the Tibetan capital was leaked to myself and three other correspondents in Kalimpong, provided that we disguised our source. Since the Lhasa consulate was the only non-communist reasonably reliable source from inside Tibet of news developments there, neither the Indian government nor we journalists wanted to risk losing it.

So we agreed to a proposal by which our dispatches should not be filed from Gangtok nor appear under Gangtok datelines. If such a dateline had appeared, the Chinese authorities would quickly have cottoned on to how information was being obtained and they might have closed the Indian Consulate in Lhasa.

The upshot was that for some days, my colleagues and me made the challenging four-hour drive from Kalimpong to Gangtok each morning in order to spend ten minutes at the Indian Political Agency being "filled in" on Tibetan developments.

Then we drove back again in the afternoon for another four hours to Kalimpong, in India, to file our cables from there. In today's era of Internet, satellite, and mobile telephone communication, it is hard to believe that this was then all part of the day's work. We handful of correspondents and Apa Pant agreed that in addition to avoiding the use of a Gangtok dateline, we should further steer clear of using phrases attributing information to "diplomatic sources".

Since the information that we were getting was from the Indian prime minister's own source, we felt that it carried just as much weight, if not more, than some accounts offered by refugees, although those of course we reported as well. Essentially, a reporter has to act according to personal judgement. Overall, a good professional gets things right, although mistakes inevitably are sometimes made. The result of my own decision was this sort of front-page headlined dispatch that appeared under a Kalimpong date line on 4 April 4 1959:

HEAVY BATTLE REPORTED IN TIBET.

CHINESE DRIVE TO SMASH KHAMBAS.

Reports filtered through here today of heavy fighting in Tibet. Artillery fire has been heard for two days in a region thirty-five miles south of Lhasa.

It is believed the Chinese Communists are doing their utmost to wipe out the resistance of Khamba tribesmen. They have been sending thousands of troops to Tibet by air as a precaution against fresh rebellion.

I reported on "principal fighting" in an area "south of the Brahmaputra river" in Tibet with Khambas being in complete control of south-central Tibet. The Chinese were trying a pincer move in south-east Tibet to isolate a rebel pocket and were said to be employing paratroops. Khamba guerrillas were reported to be systematically ambushing the Chinese and killing large numbers. The Chinese were forced in some areas to do their patrolling by night and were watching the Sikkim and Bhutan trade routes with spotter planes. More than two thousand Tibetans had been killed, with many more dead of wounds or starvation.

All of this came from the Indian official but surreptitious source. The reason for the discretion was in fact twofold: not only did the Indian government want to maintain in operation its invaluable consulate, but in addition Jawaharlal Nehru was playing for time while being compelled to revise his policy towards China in unseemly and uncomfortable haste.

He was experiencing real difficulty over China and Tibet. The 1955 "Bandung Spirit" of "Afro-Asian solidarity" was still high on the list of popular causes, with Indian and Chinese friendship officially propagated. The communists, however, were not being helpful. India had made unsuccessful approaches to China about Chinese cartographical encroachment on territory regarded as Indian. Parts of the Indian state of Assam and the whole of India's restricted border region of the North East Frontier Agency (which the Dalai Lama and his entourage eventually traversed on their way to Assam after their escape) were marked on Chinese maps as Chinese. The Indian government had tried to play down such differences.

When rumours of trouble in Tibet began to leak out, similar efforts were made to minimise the impact. The Indian Press, with official encouragement, scoffed at Fleet Street attempts to find out what was going on; and Nehru himself complained about "exaggerated reports". At first, India even strengthened its border check posts to try to keep Tibetan refugees out of India. Eventually, though, with the flow of information reaching him proving beyond doubt that Tibet was in turmoil, Nehru could no longer turn a blind eye towards events. Tibetan refugees were permitted into India, where there was a lot of public sympathy for them.

Finally the prime minister announced to the world, several days after the event, that the Dalai Lama, aged twenty-three; his mother, Gyuam

Chemo, aged fifty-seven; his sister, Tsering Domme, aged twenty-six; and one brother, Ngari Rimpoche, aged fourteen, together with an entourage of eighty, had arrived in the North East Frontier Agency of India, and that they were to be granted political asylum. The Dalai Lama would be treated as an honoured guest.

The announcement was greeted by cheers in the Indian Parliament, except from the communists. The flight from the snows of the Buddhist god-king of Tibet made front-page news everywhere, as did the fresh flow of information about fighting in Tibet.

Nehru started to adjust his policy from appeasement of the Chinese to one of greater firmness. As I reported at the time, India realised that "the Tibetan revolt is Asia's Hungary, and Asia knows it" (this comparison being a reference to Soviet communist repression three years before of the 1956 Hungarian uprising).

A year or two later, India and China had a brief but unpleasant mountain border war due to growing strains. One of the new realities to which the Indian authorities had to adjust themselves was unprecedented international interest in what was happening. Above all, every major news organisation in the world wanted to find the Dalai Lama. What did he look like? What might he have to say? Where, exactly, was he?

In the ensuing hunt, I was well ahead of the pack, together with my three colleagues (and competitors) in Kalimpong: an Indian journalist, Nair, working for Reuters; the late Noel Barber of the *Daily Mail*; and the Hong Kong correspondent of the *Daily Express* at the time, Bertram Thomas. Competitors or not, between us we worked out roughly where the Dalai Lama – if he had in fact fled from Lhasa – might cross from Tibet into India. We knew that he had no real geographical choice, if he was travelling by land, other than to descend from the mountains to the plains of Assam.

I returned to Calcutta to head for Assam, in the company of Barber and Thomas. In those days, both the *Mail* and the *Express* were broadsheet newspapers, not tabloids; and they possessed what they do not seem to possess now: serious foreign news staffs, with correspondents in major capitals covering news other than gossip about film stars, footballers, so-called celebrities, and all of their affairs.

Rivalry between the newspapers of Lords Rothermere and

Beaverbrook was especially direct and intense. The biggest news story of the day began to assume bizarre journalistic characteristics of the kind immortalised by Evelyn Waugh in his novel about foreign correspondents, *Scoop*.

The first hint of this came when Barber, Thomas, and I chartered a plane to fly about eight hundred miles, from Calcutta to Tezpur.

We had correctly calculated that this Assamese town amid the tea plantations would be the Dalai Lama's eventual place of arrival, possessing both a railway station and an airfield built during the war for use against Japan in Burma and for flying into China "over the hump" of the Himalayas.

We left on a Sunday morning after the *Daily Mail* man had disappeared on the Saturday evening, an occurrence which had the *Daily Express* man biting his nails with anxiety. His fears were not lessened when, in mid-flight to Tezpur, Noel joked to Bertie and me that he hoped we would not mind, but that he had "done a bit of flying". What he had been up to on Saturday night, he revealed, was an hour or two's study of an old explorer's guide to the North East Frontier Agency. This he had milked to provide an account of the country through which the Dalai Lama still had to pass on his difficult journey down to Assam from the mountains. The *Daily Mail* gave Barber's description of the country, allegedly from the air above it, some prominence.

Noel's narrative did not worry me as much as it did Bertie. When we got to Tezpur, there was enough hard news to file that provided us with columns of material. Helicopters were standing by, ready to pick up the Dalai Lama. The escaped party was in a Buddhist monastery at Tawang, just south of the Tibetan border in the North East Frontier area. The group still had to undertake a gruelling journey of one hundred miles or more through some of the most challenging, largely unexplored terrain in the world. An escort of Assamese riflemen had been provided to protect the Dalai Lama from Chinese agents; Indian government officials had gone to greet him; and security precautions were being imposed everywhere.

All this provided a solid dispatch spiced with a dash of history. I recalled that this was the second time that a Dalai Lama had sought asylum in India, the previous occasion being in 1910, when a Chinese force entered Tibet. The Dalai Lama at the time, the thirteenth of the line, fled to India and was granted asylum by the British Raj. He stayed in Darjeeling until 1912, when a Tibetan rebellion threw off the Chinese yoke and he returned to Lhasa to rule until his death in 1933.

A regent then governed Tibet until his resignation in 1950, when the present Dalai Lama was enthroned as the fourteenth "living Buddha". With the given name of Lhamo Dondup, he was born into a modest family in July 1935 in Tsinghai, in the Amdo province of Tibet. He was discovered and recognised by the Buddhist authorities as the new Dalai Lama when only two or three years old and taken to Kumbum Monastery. There he was given a titular name, Tenzin Gyatso. Expert linguists (including an old Mongolian chum of mine) say that the word "Gyatso" is the Tibetan equivalent of the Mongolian word "Dalai", which in English means "oceanic".

Since the word "lama" means (according to the Oxford Dictionary) "a Buddhist priest of Tibet or Mongolia", a loose translation would be that the words "Dalai Lama" mean "Oceanic priest" in English, with the word "oceanic" being used in a religious and poetical sense, implying the universal vastness of the Buddhist authority of the priest. In fact, though, for many years the Dalai Lama, receiving almost divine honours, was known to Europeans as the "Grand Lama".

However, the Mongolian word now universally used, "Dalai", has been attached to the Tibetan leader for nearly five hundred years, according to Mr Alan Sanders of Reading in a letter published in the Times not so long ago. According to Mr Sanders, it was a title bestowed upon the Tibetan head lama in 1578 by the leader of the Tumet Mongols, Altan Khan. I find the Mongolian connection interesting for two reasons.

First, long ago, the other great Buddhist, "Grand Lama", was the Mongolian "Teshul Lama", once ranking just below the Dalai Lama. Second, my Mongolian chum who first told me all about the "oceanic" linguistic and religious connection with the Tibetans was, at the time, an official of the foreign ministry of what was then the communist government of the Republic of Outer Mongolia.

His knowledge and his willingness to share it with me as the first BBC correspondent ever to visit his country displayed the depth of Buddhist cultural and historical education and memory among Mongolians despite years of communist religious oppression and the attempted rewriting of history. To me, it is just another indication of what Chinese communists are probably up against in dealing with Tibetan cultural and religious folk memories.

The first official act, at the age of sixteen, of today's Dalai Lama after the resignation of the regent, was to grant a general amnesty to all political prisoners in Tibet. Preaching his creed of non-violence ever since and winning the Nobel Peace prize in 1989, he has pricked the conscience of the world and hopefully even that of China. For example, in June 2013, reports were emerging from Beijing that suggested a crack in the fifty-year-old Chinese campaign against the Dalai Lama, with some monasteries saying they were no longer being forced to denounce him.

Monks were reportedly told that they could venerate the Dalai Lama as a spiritual leader, provided they did not regard him as a political leader, something of a contradiction to previous Chinese propaganda describing him as a "wolf in sheep's clothing" who wanted to split Tibet from China.

Whatever Chinese motivation for any current tentative softening of the policy line against the Dalai Lama, he has for years been a thorn in China's political side, with China protesting against his visit to Britain in 2004 and trying to get it cancelled.

The Chinese did not succeed. Although partly appeased when the prime minister, Mr Blair, was unable to meet the Dalai Lama because of "diary pressures", they were less than pleased when the Prince of Wales hosted a reception for him as a guest at St. James's Palace. A spokesperson for the prince explained: "For many years, he has been concerned about the situation of the people of Tibet and has been impressed by the Dalai Lama's efforts to seek a peaceful resolution."

Well, when I first saw the Dalai Lama in Tezpur in 1959, he was a boyish-looking man of twenty-three with a charming smile and dressed in magenta-and-cinnamon coloured robes with a pair of serviceable-looking brown brogue shoes on his feet.

Among the thousands who turned out to welcome him to Tezpur was his old tutor, Austrian climber Heinrich Harrer, the author of *Seven Years in Tibet*, whose arrival in India in an attempt to see his former student was not accomplished without difficulty.

This was partly because of Indian official reaction to Noel Barber's "bit of flying". Back in London, his editor, William Hardcastle, who later became much better known to the public as the first presenter of the Radio 4 *The World at One* programme, had conceived the idea of engaging Harrer to fly out to India in the hope of obtaining an exclusive *Daily Mail* interview with the Dalai Lama.

A well-known feature writer for the newspaper, Rhona Churchill, was assigned to help Harrer obtain a visa to accompany him and, if need be, to help with English-German translation.

When, a week or more later, she arrived in Tezpur with Harrer, she described to me what had happened when she went to the Indian High Commission in London to apply for his visa. It was pointed out to her that Herr Harrer had last left India illegally.

That was twenty years before, in 1939. He had been in the country on a climbing expedition when war broke out between Britain and Germany. Since Austria had been taken over by Hitler, Harrer was promptly detained and imprisoned as an enemy alien by the Raj. Almost as promptly, he escaped from his prison camp and walked in a pair of tennis shoes across the highest range of mountains in the world to reach Lhasa, resulting in his bestselling book and a later film.

Indian officials still had this illegal departure acutely in mind. They also raised a further problem. They produced a copy of the Daily Mail and showed the front page to Rhona, complaining that it seemed that the Daily Mail correspondent already in India had broken Indian law by overflying a restricted area of the country without authority.

It says a lot for Rhona's diplomacy that she managed to persuade the Indian authorities to abandon their objections and to obtain a visa for Harrer. Whether or not he ever got an interview with the Dalai Lama, I do not know. I doubt it, because the Tibetan exile was cocooned in security for a long time afterwards. What I do know, though, is that Heinrich Harrer borrowed a shirt from me and I never got it back. I have always planned to look in on him one day while skiing in Austria, where at one stage he was running a bed and breakfast in Kitzbuhel. Regrettably, I never got around to it.

The comic side of the journalistic aspects of reporting the Dalai Lama's flight was highlighted by the intense battle for publication of the first pictures. By the time the Dalai Lama reached Tezpur, two weeks after I had arrived there, hundreds of other correspondents and photographers were camped on the banks of the Brahmaputra. The major news organisations had spent enormous sums to charter aircraft and equip them with dark rooms. This was for the development and printing of photographs while in flight from Tezpur to Dum Dum airport outside Calcutta.

There the Indian Post Office had set up a special transmission point to relay wired photographs to the rest of the world. In especially fierce competition were the two major American news agencies of the day, Associated Press (AP) and United Press (UP).

Pictures were taken of the formal ceremony at which the Dalai Lama was welcomed and an official statement by him was read. The news agency photographers clicked their cameras and dashed to their planes. The race to Dum Dum was won by UP.

What happened next was described to me by the losing AP photographer, a friend of mine called Don Royle. The UP team plonked a dozen pictures down on the transmission desk, knowing that each transmission took about twenty minutes for the revolving drum to complete its work. Effectively, they were blocking the line for use by anyone else for several hours.

Gloomily, Don recognised that he was beaten but managed to persuade the Indian operator to slip in among the UP photographs just one of his own AP pictures at number three or four down the list. Then he went to his hotel to await inevitable criticism and drown his sorrows. An hour or so later, the first cable arrived from AP complaining: "Opposition leading Japanese mornings with Dalai Lama. Where's yours?" He had another drink.

An hour later, a querulous second cable arrived: "Opposition in New York evenings. Still awaiting yours." He had another drink.

A third cable arrived: "Yours now arrived but your Dalai Lama bald. Opposition has long-haired Lama. Why?"

Royle cheered up. He sent a reply that has become a classic in the history of photojournalism. It said simply: "My Dalai Lama right Dalai Lama."

The UP photographer and team, supervised by a corporate vice president who had flown in to oversee operations, had taken a series of pictures of the wrong man: a Tibetan official with braided hair and pigtails. He was the one who had read the Dalai Lama's arrival statement, not the Dalai Lama himself.

Royle dined out on his story for a few years. I worked with him in other parts of the world, including the Congo. He survived various wars and disturbances but died in a helicopter crash while on a routine job.

When the Dalai Lama fled his homeland, I was not a broadcaster but was already friendly with the late Charles Wheeler, then the Delhi correspondent of the BBC (we had met earlier in Cyprus). He too had his difficulties with Tibetan coverage, a job he shared with Rene Cutforth, distinguished Korean War reporter for the BBC. Like the cameramen, the broadcasters also had to get back to Calcutta from Tezpur in order to be able to move their broadcasting material.

The BBC had set up an expensive radio circuit to All-India Radio and kept it open until Charles managed to get to the studio tired, dirty, hot, and much behind the expected time of arrival. A senior woman news traffic manager in London rather sharply said to him over the circuit, "Charles, you are late!"

His reply, almost as legendary as Royle's about his "right Dalai Lama", was, "I am terribly sorry, Cecilia, but my elephant was delayed."

This was not merely a joke. Some correspondents did hire elephants in an attempt to get into the forbidden North-East Frontier Agency. They had no more success than I did. A terrific game of hide-and-seek had developed between the Indian authorities and the journalists of the world. Reporters did their utmost to evade security measures, and the government placed every conceivable obstacle in their way.

My dispatches recall the flavour of all this. On 8 April 1959, I reported that food and medicine were being dropped daily by Indian Air Force Dakotas to the Dalai Lama's party. There had been an unexpected influx of people creating a supply problem in the desolate area of Tawang, at ten thousand feet in altitude. An official of the Indian Foreign Ministry was on his way to meet the Dalai Lama, taking with him a personal letter from Mr Nehru.

Of course, I also wanted to try to get to the Dalai Lama, so I drove on a mud track to what was called "The Inner Line", through forest and jungle in the mountain foothills between Assam and Tibet. It was a line marked only by a small notice fixed to a tree at the side of the track.

This banned entry to the area without a permit issued by the Indian authorities. I recounted:

Last night I gained some impression of the difficulty of trying to penetrate the wilderness of this part of Assam when I set off in search of the Dalai Lama. After spending a day purchasing supplies, I drove after dark from a tea planter's bungalow for one and a half hours over dusty, pitted roads to a spot near the border. Fireflies flashed vividly in the darkness as we drove along. My Assamese driver wanted to stop because of tigers' eyes he had seen in the jungle nearby.

I persuaded him to continue to the place where I had arranged to meet some guides, but it was all in vain. The guides refused to accompany me. Their objections were twofold. First they said they were afraid of elephants in the dark, not to mention tigers. Then they said they had been ordered by the Headman of their village not to take me along the jungle paths across the line which marks off the North East Frontier Agency from the rest of Assam. I was thus forced to call it a day.

The tea planter's bungalow was my comfortable lodging and base for my stay in Tezpur, having been accepted as a guest by the hospitable British couple who lived there, Ron Brown and his wife. I was luckier than scores of my colleagues who arrived later and endured the discomfort of primitive accommodation, some sleeping if they were lucky on the billiards table in the Tezpur Club. Others dossed down at the railway station, consisting of what I reported was "a dirty white building with waiting rooms for the 'Upper Class' and 'Lower Class.'"

To the displeasure of Indian officials, the former Tibetan prime minister, Lu Khang Ha, made his appearance there. I described him in my dispatch as "venerable and dignified", but the Chinese had named him as leader of what they called the Tibetan "revolutionaries". As such, he was an embarrassment to India.

I reported that the arrival the night before of the ex-premier's party from Kalimpong "was most unwelcome" to the Indian authorities, as was obvious from the "somewhat rude reception they were given". I wrote:

The former Prime Minister was discovered sitting on the platform of Tezpur's decaying railway station. The local Assam officials took this line: "He's just another Tibetan and nothing to do with us."

It was not until an Indian foreign ministry official was approached that a roof was found for the aged minister. This in itself was uncomfortable enough, a native boarding house called The Hindu, where I met Mr Lu Khang Ha this morning. With a goatee-type beard and long grey hair, he sat fingering his beads on a wooden-planked bed while parrots screeched outside the small and dark room. He wore voluminous grey-blue and golden robes and greeted me quietly and courteously, raising his hands to his forehead before shaking my hand.

Through an interpreter, he stated that he wished to see the Dalai Lama if possible but was not sure if he would have the opportunity to do so. But he indicated that wherever the Dalai Lama went, his government went too.

Subsequently a ban was imposed on journalists using Tibetan interpreters. We learned of it when interviewing a group of Tibetan refugees. I was talking through my interpreter to the first woman to complete the 450-mile journey from Lhasa over the mountains and through the bush.

I reported:

She is Rinzi Chuki, aged forty-eight, and with her was her son of eleven, Tenzing Khetoo Jigmi Nymgal, an incarnate lama from Sera Monastery.

Smiling and diminutive, this dark-haired woman in a green and black Tibetan dress, with a single diamond on each ear, looked as if she had just been on a pleasant country walk rather than on one of the world's most arduous and dangerous journeys.

Her first task, after drinking a large enamel mug of tea at the forest hut where the party rested, was to wash her son's beaming silk-smooth face.

The Chota Lama (small lama), as the Indians called him, was then examined by a doctor, who found he was suffering from conjunctivitis. I started with my interpreter to interview Rinzi Chuki when Major K. J. Thomas, commanding the Assam Rifles Engineer battalion stationed in the foothills, walked up to him and ordered him to stop questioning. "I have received strict instructions to let reporters talk directly to Tibetans but not through interpreters. They are not allowed."

This in effect has the immediate result of preventing any communication with the Tibetans. When I asked why the ban had been imposed, the answer I received was, "You caught them out. You caught New Delhi on the wrong foot. They did not expect you to bring private interpreters."

Journalists then found Indian official obstacles placed on access to Tibetans close to the Dalai Lama. For instance, when his brother, Gyalo Thondup, the man I had met in Calcutta two weeks earlier, arrived in Tezpur, I was blocked from any contact with him. I duly and faithfully reported the Indian obstruction:

Armed guards in plain clothes stood outside the bungalow on the edge of Tezpur, where Mr Gyalo Thondup, the Dalai Lama's brother, is staying while awaiting the Dalai Lama's arrival. Mr Thondup arrived last night. Earlier he had gone to Calcutta after being refused permission by the Indians to enter the Agency to meet his brother.

Getting in touch with him is most difficult. Guards refuse to accept messages. A Government spokesman said, "He is not feeling too well." In effect, he is being held incommunicado.

So the uneven contest continued between the Indian government and the world's reporters. At the same time, the Dalai Lama himself set out by pony from Tawang on a trek over the passes of Assam towards Bomdila. The journey of sixty-two miles was expected to take five days along mountain paths, crossing at one point the Sela Pass, at an altitude of fourteen thousand feet. Before leaving Tawang, the Dalai Lama blessed all the inhabitants at a special audience held in the monastery. When he got to Bomdila, he and his party rested for a couple of days before they were able, for the first time, to use road transport, continuing towards Tezpur in a caravan of Jeeps.

The Dalai Lama's last halt in the wilderness of the North East Frontier Agency was spent at night in a camp at Khelong, ten miles inside the "Inner Line" of the agency. Roads were closed and security tightened even further. In Tezpur, impressive preparations were made for receiving him and the expected crowds on the sports field of the Darrang College.

The school was smartened up for the occasion with its long, low buildings whitewashed and the woodwork darkened. I reported that "even the open drains opposite the school mud hut tuck shop were being cleaned out". Tree trunks were painted white, and the metal posts of a barbed wire fence were painted silver.

A temporary classroom of wattles and mud plaster on the sports field was knocked down, and a ten-foot-high dais of bamboo and other woods was put up to enable the Dalai Lama to mount it and to bless from it the crowds and the devotees of Buddha. Before going there, he would stop on the north bank of the Brahmaputra in the circuit house, where he could wash and refresh himself. The roof of the circuit house received a coat of fresh red paint, and its wicker chairs were all freshly painted green.

A special air-conditioned train with first-class accommodation was waiting in the station to convey the Dalai Lama and his party across India to his first hill station refuge in that country, in Mussoorie, 120 miles north of New Delhi. The Indian authorities said that they would have provided him with the Presidential train but that was not possible on the narrow-gauge railway to Tezpur.

The Dalai Lama arrived in Tezpur just a month after he had fled from Lhasa. In the text of a statement issued on his behalf, he said that the Chinese had broken the seventeen-point agreement of 1951 between China and Tibet guaranteeing Tibetan autonomy. There was none, said the statement. It went on to say that as a result, a struggle broke out in the Kham province, assuming serious proportions in 1956.

The Chinese armed forces had then destroyed monasteries, killed lamas, used monks as forced labour, and had interfered in the exercise of religious freedom. By February 1959, the relations of Tibetans with China were "openly strained".

Then, after the Dalai Lama had agreed earlier to attend a cultural show in the Chinese headquarters in Lhasa, a date was "suddenly fixed" for 10 March 1959. This became an important date in Tibetan history, and I can do no better than repeat the official Tezpur version, issued under the authority of the Dalai Lama, of what then happened. This was the statement:

> The people of Lhasa became apprehensive that some harm might be done to the Dalai Lama, and as a result, about ten thousand gathered round the Dalai Lama's summer palace, Norbulingka, and physically prevented the Dalai Lama from attending the function. Thereafter, the people themselves decided to raise a bodyguard for the protection of the Dalai Lama. Large crowds of Tibetans went about the streets of Lhasa, demonstrating against the Chinese rule in Tibet.
>
> Two days later, thousands of Tibetan women held demonstrations protesting against Chinese authority. In spite of this demonstration from the people, the Dalai Lama and his government endeavoured to maintain friendly relations with the Chinese and tried to carry out negotiations with the Chinese representatives as to how best to bring about peace in Tibet and assuage the people's anxiety.
>
> While these negotiations were being carried out, reinforcements arrived to strengthen the Chinese garrisons in Lhasa and Tibet. On 17 March, two or three mortar shells were fired in the direction of the Norbulingka palace. Fortunately, the shells fell in a nearby pond. After this, the advisers became alive to the danger to the person of the Dalai Lama, and in those difficult circumstances, it became imperative for the Dalai Lama, the members of his family, and his high officials to leave Lhasa.
>
> The Dalai Lama would like to state categorically that he left Lhasa and Tibet and came to India of his own free will and not under duress. It was due to the loyalty and affectionate support of his people that the Dalai Lama was able to find his way through a route which is quite arduous. The route which the Dalai Lama took involved crossing the Kyichu and the Tsangpo rivers and making his way through Lhoka area,

Yarlung Valley, and Tsona Dzong before reaching the Indian frontier at Kanzey Mane near Chutangmu.

On 29 March 1959, the Dalai Lama sent two emissaries across the Indo-Tibetan border, requesting the government of India's permission to enter India and seek asylum there. The Dalai Lama is extremely grateful to the people and government of India for their spontaneous and generous welcome as well as the asylum granted to him and his followers.

India and Tibet have religious, cultural, and trade links extending over a thousand years, and for Tibetans it has always been the land of enlightenment, having given birth to Lord Buddha.

Expressing himself as "deeply touched" by the kind greetings extended to him, the Dalai Lama set off in his train across India. He was enthusiastically greeted at stations along his route, and at none more so than at Siliguri, in West Bengal, where he received a tumultuous welcome.

Meanwhile, the Chinese prime minister, Chou En-lai, had claimed that now that the Chinese were in control in Tibet, the Tibetans were clamouring for social reforms. He alleged that Tibetan "reactionaries" had turned the country into "a hell on earth".

The scene in India, however, did not indicate that the Dalai Lama was a Satan presiding over such a hell. Far from it: he appeared as a heroic divinity.

My dispatch from Siliguri gave my own impressions. Here are extracts:

Seven thousand Tibetans gave a noble and moving welcome to the Dalai Lama here today. From the mountainous Himalayan borderlands, they travelled to this humid town on the Bengal plains to pay homage to their living Buddha and to offer thanks for his deliverance.

It was an occasion so tremendous that observers had the rare experience of seeing the normally impassive Tibetans displaying their emotions quite openly. Women relatives of the Dalai Lama, reunited with him in the privacy of a coach on his special train, came out onto the hot platform with tears running down their faces.

For hours before the Dalai Lama's train arrived, the Tibetans, with about four thousand Indians, gathered outside the white modern railway station in low-lying swampy fields. Many came from Kalimpong, forty miles away, the town claimed by China to be a centre of Tibetan intrigue.

Lines of Bengali Police in khaki drill shorts and green berets carried long sticks to control the crowd and the pedicabs, bullock carts, Jeeps, and cars. All along the single narrow-gauge railway track, soldiers and police were on guard. A little hand-operated truck carried officials along the line. It was making sure that no obstruction could block the way of the thirteen-coach train with its steam engine at each end.

A Tibetan orchestra played a selection of outlandish instruments, including a long horn called a thun chen and a type of reed flute called a gyaling. Shaven lamas in robes of saffron and red knelt humbly behind bamboo barriers praying and whispering. A group of Tibetan women stood under a huge golden doo, or parasol. Multicoloured gyaltsen, religious and secular banners and streamers produced on auspicious occasions, were held high in the air as the sun gleamed dazzlingly down.

The dignitaries began to arrive. First, in a large American open car, came Prince Thondup Namgyal of Sikkim, a slim man of thirty-six, in splendid scarlet kho robes. With him was his porcelain-charming sister, Princess Phunkhang, and his mother, the Maharanee of Sikkim. A gorgeously dressed palace guard, wearing peacock feathers in his conical hat, waited on the prince.

The Indian political agent from Gangtok, the capital of Sikkim, Mr Apa B. Pant, stood with his arm round the shoulder of a young boy, the Dalai Lama's nephew. The Dalai Lama's sister, who has been at school in Darjeeling, and his niece were among other waiting relatives.

Mrs Tes Jigme Dorji, wife of the prime minister of Bhutan, was also in the group of graceful women and colourfully dressed men who waited on the platform. Prince Thondup took cine camera shots of the scene and chatted with me about the event, which he described as "momentous and historic". He said the Dalai Lama was travelling with a gift from Sikkim, consisting of a small image of Buddha, a prayer book, and a miniature stupa, a cone-shaped religious symbol. To Buddhists, the image represented "the body"; the prayer book represented preaching or "the word"; and the stupa "the faith". He would also be presenting the Dalai Lama, more materially, with Sikkim orange juice "to help ward off the unaccustomed heat".

At 9.30 a.m., the blue-and-red train, with "North East Frontier" painted in yellow on its sides, pulled in to finish the first five-hundred-mile leg of the journey from Tezpur. The Tibetan music was weirdly amplified over the station loudspeakers. The crowd grew quiet as the relations and friends of the Dalai Lama entered the train to meet him.

After fifteen minutes, the Dalai Lama emerged in his russet-and-golden robes to be given a gay bouquet by the stationmaster. Broadly smiling, his boyish, bespectacled face reflected something of the excitement of the event. He posed and waved courteously to a voracious horde of photographers and then, with his leading ministers and family, walked out of the station to be received by the people.

Cries and chants went up. "Dalai Lama! Dalai Lama!" was repeated with spiritual fervour. Kneeling in the forefront of the rejoicing Tibetans with an expression of utter rapture on his face was Siling Trotro, a leading anti-communist guerrilla. He wore a pink neckerchief and was surrounded by clouds of burning incense.

As the Dalai Lama surmounted a blue and white striped dais twenty feet high, the crowds began to throw katas, white silk scarves, into the air, so many being exuberantly tossed up that they formed a white mist over the heads of the people. The presentation of katas is a Tibetan form of ceremonial greeting

equivalent to an English handshake. From the officials meeting
him, the Dalai Lama received an extra-long kata, a nangdzok.

He stood smiling and waving while the shouts and chants
grew greater. Then he left the dais to walk nearer to the throngs,
showing himself to his devotees and his followers. Behind him
filed his stately entourage: his mother, brothers, and sisters;
his Senior and Junior Tutors; three Cabinet ministers; his Lord
Chamberlain; the Master of Ceremonies; the Master of the
Robes; the Master of Tea; an Incarnate Lama of Draye, and
representatives of Sera and Drapong monasteries. It was a rare
and wonderful sight.

An hour after the train had reached Siliguri, it pulled away
again to the west, across the burning plains of India, carrying
with it the refugee God-King who has left the snows behind him.

A couple of days later, I caught up again with the "refugee god-king"
in Mussoorie. From there, I reported that his first act on settling into his
temporary residence was to retire to the privacy of his room and kneel in
prayer. He was occupying the bedroom of a rich and prominent Indian
woman, Mrs Birla, who with two days' notice had moved out of Birla
House, her home, at the request of the government.

She told me that it had been a pleasure to do so. "I felt rather sorry for
him. He is very nice. I am only too pleased to help in any way." She said
she had left some of the staff, including gardeners and bearers, to help. She
added smilingly that in the dining room, there was an image of Buddha,
saying, "But my children chipped it slightly last year."

She and her family, along with others of her staff, were staying in a
nearby hotel taken over for the season by the government. Barbed wire
put up around Birla House was briefly removed a day or two later to
permit the Dalai Lama's brother, the man I had not been allowed to see
in Tezpur, Gyalo Thondup, to move in with him.

Mr Nehru arrived in Mussoorie and had a talk of four hours with
the Dalai Lama, their first encounter since the Tibetan leader had fled
his country. Always a keen equestrian, the prime minister rode to Birla
House on a snow-white mare.

Afterwards, he gave a news conference attended by seventy or so journalists, among them me. He said that discussions had centred on the possibilities of creating an atmosphere for a solution of the Tibetan problem. He said there was no intention to muzzle the Dalai Lama, but at the same time, "We do expect him to keep in view the difficulties of the situation and to speak and act accordingly."

Mr Nehru explained: "These events are important and have far-reaching consequences." He urged journalists: "I beg of you, therefore, not to allow your hunger for news to override other considerations. I would like these matters not to become the subject of heated exchanges and heated debates, but that they should be considered quietly with a view to avoiding the situation becoming worse."

His appeal was unsuccessful. Matters did become worse, with Tibetan refugees pouring into the Tezpur area where refugee camps were set up by the Indian authorities to accommodate them. The Chinese alleged that Tibetan "rebels" were receiving help from inside India.

In August, just four months after his meeting with the Dalai Lama, Mr Nehru said that Chinese troops had entered the North East Frontier Agency. They also entered south-east Ladakh, farther west in the Himalayas, and clashed there with an Indian patrol. China advanced extensive territorial claims that India rejected, and in 1962 hostilities erupted between the two countries in the mountains. An uneasy truce followed.

During the fifty-five years following his flight from Tibet, the Dalai Lama has steadfastly pursued the course to which he committed himself then: seeking what he calls "the middle way", with Tibet enjoying autonomy within China.

His brother, Gyalo Thondup, the man who was my first lucky "contact" on the assignment, on several occasions visited China for discussions that seemed to have been sterile. As for Tibet itself, it was reported in April 2005 that environmentalists and British tourist operators were highly critical of Chinese plans published the previous month for a ninefold increase by 2020 in the number of tourists visiting Tibet.

The United Nations Educational, Scientific, and Cultural Organisation, UNESCO, which lists the Potala Palace in Lhasa and other Tibetan buildings as World Heritage sites, has also expressed concern, with UNESCO representatives calling upon the Chinese authorities to halt the "demolition of Lhasa's urban tissue" and to ensure a "buffer zone around the listed buildings".

Journalists allowed working visits to the Tibetan capital have reported that China was trying to reconstruct the country with the building of new towns as well as the railway.

A concomitant of all that, as Richard Spencer stated in the *Daily Telegraph*, was what he described as "prostitution on an industrial scale". He reported that in the new town Taiyang Dao (Sunny Island), on the edge of Lhasa, everything was provided that "Chinese immigrants" into Tibet could possibly want. "On every corner is a glitzy 'karaoke' bar, where scores of Sichuanese girls await their customers. At one, sixty girls were waiting to be picked to accompany a businessman upstairs. The doorman said two hundred worked there altogether and this was just one of several establishments on the block."""

Spencer also offered as long ago as 2003 his own analysis of Chinese government strategy, which sounded then, as now, about right. He defined it as "reinvolvement with the Dalai Lama". He said that while officials still criticised the Dalai Lama for "insincerity", the Chinese rhetoric was milder than before. The Chinese had an eye to world opinion and, with the internal security situation contained, felt little need to make compromises.

They would most likely offer a deal they knew would be unaccept-able: the status quo with the Dalai Lama allowed to return to a figurehead position, but possibly being restricted to Beijing itself.

The exiled Dalai Lama himself encourages tourists to visit Tibet, but he urges them to acquaint themselves with his country's troubled history and ancient culture before going there. For half a century now, his home in exile has been in the remote northern Indian town of Dharamsala.

His flight from his homeland and the ensuing brief but dangerous war between India and China, plus continuing border tensions between these two great nuclear powers, resulted in the annexation in 1975, by India, of the Indian protectorate of Sikkim. China did not recognise the Indian claim to the territory, although more recent reports have suggested that Chinese maps no longer show Sikkim as Chinese.

When I revisited Sikkim in 2009, it was still necessary to obtain a special permit from the Indian government to do so, and movement near the border with Tibet was still restricted.

In 2003, Mr Vajpayee, former Indian prime minister, visited China, and relations improved somewhat, with an agreement to open up the trade route through Sikkim across the 2,500-mile-long mountain border between the two giant Asian states. The Chinese, however, would not formally accept at that stage that Sikkim was part of India, even though, for its part, India confirmed in the agreement that Tibet was part of China.

India also said it would not allow Tibetans to engage in anti-China political activities in India. The security of Sikkim, where thousands of Tibetans live, appears then to remain as essentially delicate as the security of nearby countries such as Nepal and Bhutan, all three mountain states squeezed uncomfortably between the Indian and Chinese giants.

Whatever the future brings to this complex region on the roof of the world, the Dalai Lama's efforts to retain the world's interest in, and concern about, his native land have never ceased. From afar, I have followed his courageous course with admiration and as much fascination as I felt when reporting, over half a century ago, the "rare and wonderful sight" of thousands of Tibetans rendering him homage.

CHAPTER 15

"Seeking the Bubble": Reporter to Correspondent

What's in a name? That which we call a rose
by any other name would smell as sweet.
—Juliet, in Shakespeare's *Romeo and Juliet*

With the Dalai Lama settling down to his existence as an exile, I too changed my way of life. The *Daily Telegraph* offered me the chance to leave the reporters' room and to become a staff foreign correspondent. I seized the chance, and for the rest of my working life, some forty years or so, I roamed the world, first for the newspaper and then for the BBC.

When asked what the difference was between a reporter and a correspondent, the author and former foreign correspondent Ernest Hemingway famously answered, "Oh, I guess about a couple of hundred dollars a month." The response was not inaccurate, but I have my doubts about Andrew Marr's description of a foreign correspondent.

In his book, *My Trade: A Short History of British Journalism*, the BBC's former political editor (who now has his own Sunday morning TV programme) calls the foreign correspondent "the aristocrat" of the craft of journalism. I cannot say that I ever felt especially aristocratic when I found myself either cowering in a hole being shelled or dossing down uncomfortably in some other sort of hellhole. I felt closer to a less salubrious description employed among journalists themselves for a foreign correspondent: "a district reporter with dysentery".

My first posting was to cover the Middle East, based in Cairo. Now, as then, the Middle East remains another unfinished story, together with the occupancy of the Islamic Caliphate, in formal limbo since an international Muslim conference in 1926. In Cairo, I was the first British daily newspaperman to take up residence, together with my family, after the Suez Crisis; and it was not an easy place in which to work, nor for family existence (because of many basic shortages).

Neither was my newspaper the regime's favourite British publication. President Nasser and his acolytes preferred newspapers sympathetic to him, like the *Observer*, and were wary about hostile newspapers like mine, which for a long time after Nasser came to power, continued to refer to him as Colonel Nasser, even after he had promoted himself to general.

My family consisted then of my first wife, Anne (who died in 2010), and two young daughters. One went to school in Zamalek and the younger had an Egyptian nanny-cum-maid. My wife did her best to adjust to a Cairene existence, but I know that she would really have liked to stay in Somerset, where I first met her, surrounded by dogs, horses, chickens, and children. I did not and do not blame her for that.

It is quite possible, I suppose, that if I had opted for Yeovil as the *Bristol Evening Post* district reporter and not for Fleet Street, we might even have remained married for longer than the seventeen years we actually spent together. Who can tell? In any case, I have never regretted the Fleet Street move. As for Anne? Well, after our divorce she remarried and remained so until her death forty years later.

For much of 1959, before leaving England to live abroad for most of my working life, I wandered through the northern mountainous regions of India and Pakistan.

I returned to Assam and Sikkim and ventured into Nepal well before its development as a tourist attraction and then its less happy transformation, not so long ago, into a land of troubling problems (yet another unfinished story).

My arrival at the airport near Katmandu was over-exciting. I was on board an old Dakota DC-3 aircraft of the Royal Nepalese Airlines, and as we neared the end of the flight, an eagle or vulture flew into the port engine just by my window seat.

The view was blotted out by scarlet bits and pieces stuck to the exterior of the glass, and the engine conked out. The pilot steadied the juddering plane and landed it with just one engine. To this day, I believe that the Dakota DC-3 is the safest aircraft ever to have been built. I never worried about flying in it anywhere.

In Katmandu, there was then only one tolerable hotel, previously a royal palace of the reigning Rana family. I enjoyed using the bathroom because of the immense proportions of the bath. The only baths of such size I have seen anywhere else are those at the MCC, (Marylebone Cricket Club, in London) which appear to have been designed for substantial Victorian cricketers of the stature of Dr W. G. Grace.

But the Rana palace bath was exceptional in ways other than its proportions. Its taps were gold-plated. No water came out of them, however. Instead, a bearer brought in pails of water at different temperatures, from which I chose the water with the temperature that suited me. The bath was then filled for use, a team of the bearer's assistants bringing in dozens of pails of water at the desired temperature until the required level had been reached. Then the bearer, a turbaned and moustachioed giant, would say, "Tikhai, sahib" ("OK, sir") and permit me to immerse myself.

A White Russian exile named Boris had set up a pioneering modern-style bar in Katmandu, the original "Yak and Yeti" bar. Around a central log fire, a few people, mainly mountaineers, sat toasting their toes, enjoying a drink, and chatting with Boris's glamorous young Danish wife. Tourism on a popular scale had yet to start.

As for problems with pro-Chinese insurrectionaries, with which Nepal has been concerned, I reported that the prime minister at the time, Mr Koirala, in an interview with me, said he feared "internal subversion" by communists more than external aggression by the Chinese. He did all he could to play down fears of Chinese aggression.

In order not to offer the Chinese any chance to complain, he refused permission for the Dalai Lama to visit Nepal, where there were three thousand Tibetan refugees. The Dalai Lama's representative in Nepal, the Chinai Lama, told me that the reason for the refusal was that the Nepalese government was "frightened of making enemies of the Chinese".

At the other, more westerly, end of the mountains, on the North-West Frontier in Pakistan, I found my way to the Khyber Pass and into the Kurram Tribal Agency at Parachinar on the wild Afghan border, in an area nowadays affected by the Taliban. I was the first foreign journalist for many years to be allowed into this forbidden tribal area, and there I interviewed and photographed leaders of 3,500 Mangal tribesmen.

They had fled over the border into Pakistan to complain of growing Soviet Russian activities in Afghanistan, long suspected but vigorously denied in both Moscow and Kabul. The Afghan story is also unfinished, although the problems these days appear to be not the Russians and communist expansion but the Taliban, internal conflict, corruption, endemic opium-poppy cultivation, and apparently uncertain government.

From the tribal areas, back I went to Peshawar to file my dispatch and send off my pictures; then off I flew up to Gilgit in the Karakorum Mountains. It was a more frightening flight than the Nepalese trip had been. I was in a Bristol air-freighter of the Pakistan Air Force, the pilots of which regularly made the hazardous trip with supplies to Gilgit and to the Karakorums frontier region with Sinkiang, China, and Indian-held Kashmir.

The terrifying peaks culminate in the mighty K2 (Godwin Austen) summit, the world's second highest mountain, with its altitude of 8,611 metres or 28,251 feet (lower than Everest by 239 metres or 784 feet).

The Pakistani pilots called the flight "the most dangerous milk run in the world" because much of it was flown actually below the peaks, with a point of no return at one particular place in a valley where pilots had to keep going even if cloud came down.

Happily, it was a sunny day when I flew there. I stayed in Gilgit for several days with the Northern Scouts, whose hardihood in the snows was legendary. The soldiers were tribal mountain men who knew the area, and their officers were seconded from the Pakistani Army, controlling disputed sections of the frontier. The Scouts were known as the "Snow Leopards", after their silver badge in the shape of the animal, much feared by the mountain people.

The weather was so good that my regimental hosts decided to stage a cricket match, in which I was invited to play. I have never been much of a cricketer and told them so, but they insisted that I should participate, and of course I did. I responded somewhat ungraciously to the regimental hospitality by bowling out the colonel for a "duck," (no score), which amused the entire regiment, including the colonel himself.

On another day, the regiment staged an incredible polo match, with wild tribesmen riding bareback matched against the officers, seated more conventionally on saddles. Both sporting events remain vividly in memory, set spectacularly as they were in the remote valley beside the fast-running but freezing waters of the Gilgit River, with mountains towering above.

Those mountains, irresistible to mountaineers, have been a source of border arguments involving India, Pakistan, and China. During my travels around Pakistan, I interviewed President Ayub Khan and the foreign minister, Manzur Qadir, who both talked about such problems as well as about their fears of growing Russian involvement in Afghanistan. This was fifty-five years ago, well before the Soviets openly moved troops and tanks into Afghanistan twenty years or so later.

During my travels, Pakistanis expressed interest in my surname. Many asked me outright if I was a Muslim. The question was not new to me because in Cyprus and the Middle East, I had already discovered that the Islamic and Ottoman connections of the name were a source of concern to my Greek-speaking friends, who promptly Hellenicised me and nicknamed me Osmanides.

Almost inevitably, I had labels pinned on me by my colleagues. They included Osman Pasha, Osman Bey, and Osman Effendi. Some chums downgraded me to a mere "Ali Bin Osman".

I became curious about the name's origin, so I checked on family records and looked it up in an etymological dictionary of English names. Despite its Islamic links, the name seems to go back into Oxfordshire for at least a couple of centuries, with several of my father's family lying buried in a wind-swept Oxfordshire churchyard at Ipsden.

According to the etymological dictionary, the name either is a simple corruption of the word "Norseman" or is derived from the Norse or Viking word "os", meaning "divine". I particularly like the latter, although I have never felt divine – far from it. I am more comfortable with a colleague's view of me: "as English as a pub". That is the phrase used about me by the late Christopher Munnion in his 1993 book, *Banana Sunday*, a funny and sometimes hair-raising work about foreign correspondents who slaved away in Africa covering the epoch of decolonisation.

I was delighted to see the book, eleven years after its publication, described in 2004 by a reviewer in the *Spectator* as "a classic". I am not so sure, however, about another description used by Munnion about me: a "bouncing, perennial Boy Scout roving reporter".

As the dictionary has it, the somewhat banal origin of my name is a bit disappointing. I rather fancy the idea of being descended perhaps from a crusader who went wrong, joining himself, say, to an exotic Arab lady. Equally, I would be delighted to find that I was descended from one of Saladdin's followers who went just as wrong and, after capturing Constantinople, found himself a lovely Byzantine Christian girl and subsequently moved westwards to end up in the Chilterns. Alas, there appears to have been no such romantic liaisons among my rural labourer forebears.

Osman I (who died in 1326) is regarded as the founder of the Ottoman Turkish state, and Osmanli was the tribal name of the Turks of the Ottoman Empire. Even earlier than Osman I though, there existed another leading Muslim, an Arab. In Arabic, he was Othman; in Turkish, he was Osman.

He was the third caliph, ruling from 644 to 656. The caliphate had been established after the death in 632 of Mohammed, the prophet of Allah, who departed this world without leaving instructions for the future secular government of Muslims. So by subsequent choice of the Muslims of the holy city of Medina, where Mohammed's tomb is in the Prophet's Mosque, the first leader to hold Mohammed's political functions after his death adopted the title of "kalīfat rasūl Allāh, the "successor of the messenger of God".

From kalīfat came the terms "caliphate" and "caliph". There were many caliphates over the next fourteen centuries: the Omayyad caliphs; the Abbasid caliphs; the Almohads, or Western and Spanish caliphs; the Fatimids, or Egyptian caliphs; and endless Ottoman claims to the caliphate.

Eventually, after the collapse of the Ottoman Empire, an international caliphate congress was held in Cairo in 1926. It decided in effect that until all Islamic peoples could join in establishing a new caliphate, the office should remain in abeyance. This has sometimes been crudely compared to a Roman Catholic Church existing without a pope.

In such a limbo, I have occasionally asked myself the following: did the late Osama bin Laden perhaps ever see himself as the next caliph of

Islam? Do any of his followers imagine that they could be caliph? I should not be surprised if such ambitions exist and the current ambitions of the terrorist ISIL caliphate movement in Syria and Iraq are displayed by the very use of the word caliphate.

When questioned, often by immigration officials in predominantly Muslim states, about my surname and my religion, I have developed a stock answer. I describe myself as "a failed Christian". Sometimes the response is a smile; sometimes a scowl.

The scowl has occasionally provided early indication of an unwelcoming kind of country, in which it is dangerous to make even the mildest of jokes about religion. Taking note of this, I would try during my stay in such a place to behave as carefully as possible and not to provoke over-zealous religious reaction of the dangerous "fatwa" variety pronounced against Salman Rushdie.

My name was much confused at one stage with two well-known correspondents, both of them now deceased: James Mossman, one of the earliest BBC *Panorama* reporters, and his brother, John, who over the years worked in Fleet Street for the old Labour paper, the *Daily Herald*, and then for the *Daily Mail* and the *Daily Telegraph*. I knew them both, and I was as shocked as most British journalists when, in youngish middle age, James committed suicide.

He had a reputation as a homosexual in the days when that could still be difficult. He was a brilliant reporter and a loss to BBC television. His brother, John, remained one of my friends for many years until his death in 2001.

When we first met, in Cyprus, John was still with the *Herald*. Although his employers were on the left and mine were on the right, our association became close enough to become a bit of a joke among our colleagues. This led to one of our number, the late Rawle Knox of the *Observer*, writing a funny piece of doggerel about the assembled International Press Corps in Nicosia.

It started with these lines:

"Osman and Mossman the terrible twins,
Sold their souls for a couple of gins ..."

To my astonishment, this was recalled forty years on at John Mossman's funeral service, when it was quoted in a memorial address. From accounts offered to me by those present, largely survivors from the old Fleet Street, appreciative laughter almost brought down the crowded church. John would have liked that, as I did.

In the almost claustrophobic world of the Ledra Palace Hotel in the 1950s in Nicosia, then occupied almost entirely by foreign correspondents (in much the same way as the United Nations later occupied it, on the dividing line between Greek Cypriots and Turkish Cypriots), the swift delivery of cables to the right name and not the wrong one was an important matter.

John Osman and John Mossman occasionally got muddled up, leading both of us to check with each other that we were receiving the right messages. These were delivered to the hall porter's desk, presided over at night by Savas, a legendary member of the hotel staff.

He was known to us all as the "night news editor", so efficient was he in tipping us off in the middle of the night when things were happening. Only once, to my knowledge, did he ever make a mistake (apart from a long-lasting tendency to lose his money on racehorses).

We all had him on our payrolls, and he made a lot of money out of Fleet Street over the years. One day, though, he overplayed his hand. He had taken aside the correspondent of the *London Evening Standard* to whisper to him that a competitor from the old *London Evening News* had received an interesting cable. The *Standard* man, Mark Wilson, a keen golfer who later became a successful golf correspondent, was naturally curious to learn what the opposition was up to and quickly cast an eye over the contents of the cable.

An explosion of wrath followed. Savas had inadvertently confused the *Evening Standard* man with the *Evening News* man and had tried to sell to Wilson the contents of a cable actually addressed to him.

The aggrieved Wilson stormed into the bar swearing that Savas would never again get a penny out of him. Savas was suitably contrite, relations were restored, and the journalistic merry-go-round rotated as usual. I remained on that roundabout for many years, finding that the fallout from it is unpredictable, even to the extent of influencing the names given to people.

Thus somewhere in India today is a forty-five-year-old man who had my name inflicted upon him, poor blighter. I say that because the name is so apparently Muslim that it would be unusual, and perhaps unwelcome, for any Hindu to bear such an apparently Islamic identification. I hope he has not suffered from it.

The first I learned of this far-flung namesake was in February 1972, when I had returned home from covering for the BBC the 1971 Indo-Pakistani War. I received a letter from Evan Charlton, an authoritative British journalist who had been editor of one of the major newspapers in India. He wrote, "You will (I hope) be pleased to know that a distinguished Hindi writer has named his newborn son after you! This is as a tribute to your coverage of the war."

Two months later, I received confirmation of this by way of a letter from Patna and the father of the child. He wrote, "We would never forget the days when we used to wait for Ratnagar Bharti [an Indian broadcaster] to read out a dispatch from you. John Osman had become a household name. During the same period, we were looking for a name for the young one. He was to be named on Christmas Day." The family, he added, in deciding on a name, "found none better" than mine.

Well, it is pleasant, I suppose, to possess a name that a stranger finds "none better" rather than "none worse". People who, for some reason or another, did not like what I wrote or broadcast never hesitated to say so as the years passed by, and I came in for my share of the sort of "stick" against which most journalists become inured.

This happened predictably enough in Nasser's Egypt. It was not easy going there because the *Daily Telegraph*, once described by Malcolm Muggeridge as "the repository of the soul of the Tory Party", was not Nasser's favourite newspaper.

Our local freelance stringer was an Egyptian Copt called Maurice Fahmy, and he ran into trouble during my tenure in Cairo, being arrested in my absence from Egypt and imprisoned in The Citadel. I was never able to establish what it was that he had done wrong, but I felt always that it was probably because he worked too closely with journalists like me, who declined to be Nasser propagandists.

Maurice was married to a Scottish woman, Donelda, and they had a son who later became a journalist working for an American news agency.

After having endured several rough months in detention, Maurice was released. His ordeal had not improved my relations with the more dictatorial side of the Nasser regime, because, with the support of the newspaper, I had done what I could to get him out of jail. In the process, I might have trodden on the toes of a few officials who were not accustomed to being challenged.

They did not like my reporting on the Middle East anyway, simply because I did it as dispassionately as I could, giving the bad news about Nasser's Egypt as well as the good. Any initial honeymoon period (of which there was little) between Nasser's regime and myself wore thin until, after a couple of years, my Egyptian visa was withdrawn. Looking back, it is surprising that I lasted that long.

I fired off a couple of tremendous main leader-page pieces summing up Nasser's credits and debits. I rebased in Cyprus and continued to cover the Middle East and a lot of Africa as well. There, too, it was not long before I ran into trouble.

It came in Ghana in April 1960, when Kwame Nkrumah, the prime minister, won a plebiscite to change the constitution. It turned the recently independent state into a republic, with himself as its first president with dictatorial powers. He won easily.

His veteran opponent, Dr "Joe" Danquah, who claimed to have been the man who originally chose for the old Gold Coast colony the name for the new state of the ancient Ghana Empire, expressed doubts about his own behaviour back in 1947, when he had been one of the first politicians to call for independence.

There was a good deal of organised thuggery at the polls in 1960, and Dr Danquah said he was beginning to feel ashamed of himself for saying in the past that "we were fit to govern ourselves". He added, "I was wrong. Although I would do again what I did in 1947 in asking for the country's independence, I am beginning to feel ashamed of the things that are being done in the name of democracy here. Evidence is beginning to show that power is being flagrantly abused. Why should we do things this way? We are making it appear to the world that authoritarian rule is natural for the African. But it is not true."

These were strong words for a respected and experienced campaigner for Ghanaian independence. Another critic was the deputy leader of the party opposing Nkrumah, Mr Joe Appiah, who had married Peggy Cripps, daughter of Sir Stafford Cripps, Chancellor of the Exchequer in Attlee's post-war government.

Mr Appiah said, "This has not been an election but a big national joke. It is pathetic." He alleged widespread violence and intimidation. The national chairman of the opposition party, Mr Solomon Odammten, went even further and in an interview with me came straight out and expressed the belief that the plebiscite was being "rigged". This brought me into my first personal contact with political, legal pressures.

First, a Ghanaian government spokesman "vehemently refuted" the accusation that the election was being rigged. Then, ten days after the interview, Mr Odammten himself issued a statement saying he felt an "unfortunate misunderstanding" must have arisen during the course of the interview because he had said that the election "could" be rigged and not that it actually "was being" rigged.

A day after that, I was "requested" by the assistant commissioner of the Criminal Investigation Department in Accra, the Ghanaian capital, to make a statement to the police about the interview. I stood by the accuracy of my report, but knowing that Mr Odammten had come under great pressure, I added this in my report on the row to the *Daily Telegraph*:

> *My own view of Mr Odammten's denial is that he is making it in good faith and that he genuinely feels I misunderstood or misquoted him. His position is an extremely difficult one, however, in a country where uninhibited and often robust political utterances, particularly those of the Opposition, are closely watched.*

This minor clash between the Ghanaian government and a correspondent of the *Daily Telegraph* passed off swiftly, unlike a much more important dispute not long before between the government and my *Daily Telegraph* colleague and friend, the late Ian Colvin. This had become a "cause cèlebré". Ian had been unsuccessfully charged in Ghana with contempt of court, and a man heavily involved in that case was also involved in my own lesser contretemps.

He was a British QC and former Labour MP who became attorney general of Ghana, Mr Geoffrey Bing. He had been savaged in the Colvin court case by Colvin's counsel, another British QC, Christopher Shawcross. Shawcross accused the attorney general of being solely responsible for a move against Colvin that, said Shawcross, "smacked of Star Chamber methods". So when, some months later, I found myself invited to have a chat with Geoffrey Bing, QC, at much the same time as I had been requested to make a statement to the police, I was extremely wary.

Nothing happened afterwards, but the encounter underlined the Ghanaian atmosphere in those days of "Big Brother is watching you!" This persisted and worsened under Nkrumah in Ghana as the years passed and a one-party state was established. Declining to bow to dictatorship, unrepentant foreign correspondents sometimes irritated the Ghanaian authorities by singing in the old Black Star Hotel to the tune of "I Got Plenty o' Nuttin'", a ditty which began "I've got qualms about Kwame, and Kwame's got qualms about me."

It was the work of two of my journalistic chums, the late John Ridley of the *Daily Telegraph* and the late George Gale of the *Daily Express*. Gale was the origin of two *Private Eye* magazine characters: "George G Ale" and "Lunchtime O'Booze".

Not only we foreign correspondents were among the journalists in trouble. As always, the most immediately affected by the thought police and the writers' commissars were brave indigenous journalists. One of them with whom I worked was Ben Dorkenoo, who ran into trouble and later removed himself from Ghana to work at the United Nations as a press officer.

Nkrumah was eventually overthrown by a military coup while he was away in China. He sought asylum in what was then another left-wing state, Guinea, where he was given the status of co-head of state. He died in 1972, having damaged his country almost beyond repair and turning a place intended by his backers in the West to be a showpiece of the brave new post-colonial world into a despotic and corrupt state requiring prolonged convalescence.

Nkrumah, who called himself "The Redeemer", possessed an unattractively enormous ego, well summed up by Nehru at a Commonwealth Prime Ministers' Conference in London. After an especially wearing session dealing with South Africa and Apartheid, Nehru turned up at a background briefing for a few selected correspondents and made no secret of what he thought about Nkrumah. Reaching for a recuperative whisky, "Panditji" sighed irritably, saying, "Oooh dear! Kwame does think he is sooo important!"

I was back in Ghana again at the end of 1960, during which I had been all over the place: Egypt, Syria, Lebanon, Gaza, Turkey, Iran, Ethiopia, Djibouti, Aden, Bahrein, Sharjah, Togo, the Congo, and Nigeria. As a change from bloodshed and upheaval in the Congo, and troubling problems in the other countries, Iran provided an unusually pleasurable assignment.

It was reporting the birth to Queen Farah, the third wife of the late shah of Iran, of the couple's son, Prince Reza. This event was prematurely hailed as securing future stability for the shah's rule and as being a fillip for the Pahlevi dynasty.

The ayatollahs had yet to emerge from their comfortable places of exile, such as Paris, or from their mosques, to claim for themselves the seats of power. In so doing, they deprived Prince Reza of any inheritance and established an oppressive religious regime that to this day remains unsavoury, despite recent developments towards an agreement about Iranian nuclear activity. It rather looks as if the rest of the world is placing the ayatollahs on probation, so to speak.

Back in 1960, though, interest in the birth of the shah's child was such that I was even commissioned to write my first piece for my newspaper's "Woman's Page". In it, I explained how a nation had been delighted by the achievement of a pretty twenty-two-year-old ex–Girl Guide and architecture student in delivering a long-awaited boy as heir to the occupant of the Peacock Throne.

Troubles were not then hitting Iran, but they were affecting the country next door, Turkey. There, at the less pleasurable end of the journalistic scale, a military coup had toppled the Menderes government and surprised the world. It was an extraordinary revolt organised by an unusual combination of senior officers and young officer cadets. It succeeded, and I was kept busy reporting Turkish developments for some time in Ankara.

At the end of the year, an attempt elsewhere by politically motivated military plotters to change the state of affairs in their country came to a bloody and unsuccessful conclusion. This was in Ethiopia, where a group of officers and soldiers tried to dethrone Emperor Haile Selassie while he was on a State Visit to Brazil. As a result, I got one of the biggest scoops of my life.

I was in Ghana when news came through that rebels had "deposed" the emperor and had declared his son as king. Ethiopian air space was closed, but scores of correspondents tried to get into Ethiopia by heading for the French-ruled port of Djibouti in the Horn of Africa and then taking a train to head for Ethiopia's capital, Addis Ababa (a railway itinerary immortalised by Evelyn Waugh in *Scoop*).

However, I beat my competitors by several days through the expedience of joining the emperor on a royal escort aircraft and flying back with him. In the process, I got a magnificently uncompromising imperial interview with him. For several days, my dispatches led the front page of the *Daily Telegraph*.

Of course, getting onto the plane was not that simple. When I first heard the news in Accra of the attempted coup, I had a gut feeling that the emperor, who had stood up to Mussolini, would not acquiesce quietly in any attempt to get rid of him. So I boarded an Ethiopian Airways plane flying from Accra to the Sudan, one of Ethiopia's neighbouring states.

While in flight, I learned via the Ethiopian crew and their radio contacts with a plane on which the emperor was travelling that he was not continuing with his state visit in Brazil, as had been deliberately publicised, but was in fact being flown as secretly and as swiftly as possible back towards Ethiopia.

He was scheduled to land in the Sudanese capital, Khartoum, which is where I too was heading. On arrival, I asked the British ambassador, Sir Edwin Chapman Andrews, who was known to the emperor and was hoping to speak to him, if he could suggest to the beleaguered head of state that if he attempted any return to Ethiopia, then I should accompany him.

The ambassador was marvellously helpful. We came to an arrangement as to how I should get onto the plane if the emperor agreed to take me with him.

Although few people knew what the position was inside Ethiopia, the emperor was still formally the ruler, and he was received at Khartoum Airport with appropriate honours: a military band, a red carpet, a guard of honour, and a line-up on the tarmac of Sudanese ministers and foreign envoys. I watched from the roof terrace of the main airport building in a scorching temperature, along with thousands of Sudanese.

I saw His Imperial Majesty deep in conversation for some minutes with His Excellency the British Ambassador. A few moments later, as the emperor moved on along the line of diplomatists, the ambassador turned towards the airport building, where he knew I would be watching from the roof, and raised his arm above his head. His thumb pointed upwards.

I was overjoyed and relieved that he was not signalling with his thumb turned down. I grabbed my bag and my portable typewriter and not long afterwards was flying on an aircraft escorting the emperor's plane towards Asmara in Eritrea. That night when we were there, the emperor gave me an interview that went round the world via the columns of the *Telegraph*, announcing his intention to return soon to his capital, Addis Ababa. "Soon" turned out to be the next day.

Thousands of people streamed along the road behind Haile Selassie's slow-moving car, from which he smiled and waved at them. I reported from Asmara:

> Tonight the Emperor talked to me in a drawing room of the Imperial Palace and said, 'I shall be going soon to Addis Ababa to lead my people and soldiers for the purpose of quelling the revolt.'
>
> The Emperor, calm and dignified as always, said, 'It is difficult to say now whether this coup was provoked from within, but it appears that it was planned by people rather irresponsible and immature, and by people of ambition. The plotters have tried to deceive the people with propaganda not acquainted with the facts.'
>
> I asked him if he thought that Crown Prince Asfa Wassen (the Emperor's son) was a plotter or if he was being held under duress. The Emperor replied, 'I do not think with suspicion of him. The rebels have tried to use him as a 'front'. Such an act of treachery is in no way worthy of him.'
>
> The Emperor wore the uniform of the commander in chief of the Ethiopian army. He said that Sir Chapman Andrews, the

British Ambassador in Khartoum, and the British Ambassador
in Rio de Janeiro, had been 'of considerable assistance' after the
news of the coup had reached him in Brazil.

The emperor did not linger in Eritrea. He flew on to Addis Ababa the following morning, and I flew into a military airfield outside the capital, where fighting continued. Somehow I managed to find my way into Addis Ababa itself. Machine gun and rifle and mortar fire went on for some days; bodies were hanging from lamp posts and trees; there was a battle in the hills with rebel remnants; cabinet chiefs were among the many dead; members of the royal family were held hostage, including the crown prince and the empress, and then they were later rescued or released.

All of this I reported plus the fact that "three English women played a notable part" during the shooting. They had helped to "keep going smoothly an African Women's Conference despite bullets breaking up a meeting and injuring people". One of the three women was the director of the World Bureau of the Girl Guides, Dame Lesley Whateley.

I recounted: "A bullet went through the skirt of Dame Lesley, who was unperturbed, saying, 'A miss is as good as a mile'."

One of the luckiest survivors of what was a bloodbath, with thousands dead, was the American ambassador, Mr Arthur Richards. He was in the Imperial Palace at the request of the rebels and of the emperor to help in trying to arrange negotiations.

As they realised that their hold on events was slipping, the rebels panicked and massacred fifteen government ministers among twenty being held as hostages.

Mr Richards said, "I was in a palace room with the ministers when the shooting broke out. They began firing at the ministers, and I beat a hasty retreat through the window. The window was open, so I did not even have to stop for that."

He explained that he was in the room as an intermediary and a carrier of messages, "just like the Red Cross". He added, "Someone always has to do these things like message carrying in such circumstances, and this time it just happened to be me." He had been in Ethiopia for only three months and was learning about diplomacy in Africa the hard way.

A survivor of the palace massacre, a vice minister of state, who had been wounded in both legs, said that the rebels had come into the room where the hostages had been held and added, "They shot us four times to make sure we were all dead. I lay silent and was lucky to live."

My last dispatch of 1960 was from Addis Ababa, and it was published on 23 December. It struck a seasonable note, but not much of a note of good will.

I recounted how a British Embassy official, Mr James Mcleod, had spent a dangerous night at home with his wife and their two children, Patricia, aged ten, and Michael, eight. Their house was at the centre of a skirmish, and Mr Mcleod said, "We turned out the lights, and I pulled Patricia from the window where she was enjoying watching the gun flashes. Bullets hit the house, so we kept our heads down. But by the firelight, I managed to complete decorating the Christmas tree."

A problem in covering the sanguinary sequence of events was filing dispatches, for communications were unreliable. Telephones were cut off, and the cable office was barely operative, with unseen censors at work in a rear room. So I handed in my dispatches for transmission without much hope of them getting through and made what I regarded as necessary alternative arrangements.

One of them was to send a copy of my dispatches by an air link to the British consul in Asmara, who had helped me on the emperor's first night back in his country by filing from an American communications base in Eritrea the report of the interview with Haile Selassie. The other method was to send a second copy of my dispatches via a Royal Air Force flight to Aden, for a press officer acquaintance of mine there to cable on to the newspaper.

A couple of weeks later, I received a letter from the foreign news editor full of praise for my exclusive coverage but complaining about the cost of my dispatches. Every method used to get the news to London had worked, and the cabling cost for the *Daily Telegraph* had tripled!

Fourteen years after the 1960 abortive coup, another attempt to dethrone the emperor succeeded. It fell to my lot, as the BBC Africa correspondent at the time, to write and broadcast his obituary. Born as Prince Ras Tafari Makonnen in 1891, he had, as regent and heir to the throne, westernised the institutions of his country; resisted in 1935 and 1936 Mussolini's Italian conquest of Abyssinia (as Ethiopia then was known in the west); was restored to the throne in 1941 after British liberation of his country; and was a founding member of the Organisation of African Unity, now the African Union.

Famine, economic chaos, industrial strikes, and mutiny among the armed forces led to his 1974 deposition and detention. Just a year later, while still a prisoner, the deposed emperor died at the age of eighty-four in unclear circumstances, believed at the time to have been a result of suffocation by pillow.

Among those taking part in the 1974 coup was Colonel Haile Mariam Mengistu, who, three years later, led yet another coup. He seized power and maintained it, with help from both Russia and the West, throughout the difficult 1980s – harsh years of drought, guerrilla fighting, problems with Somalia and Eritrea, and perennial economic confusion and disorder.

I reported from the country on and off from 1974 until in the late 1970s I was refused entry into Ethiopia because of what I was broadcasting on the BBC about what was happening. In 1987, Mengistu established what was euphemistically described as "one-party civilian rule" under the Marxist-Leninist Workers Party with himself as president. His regime lasted until 1991, when rebel groups closed in on the capital. His government fell, and he fled.

The last I heard of Mengistu, who is now about seventy-nine, is that he was living in Robert Mugabe's Zimbabwe, afforded refuge there as a gift from one African left-wing dictator to another. Mengistu's name is not remembered with much affection in Ethiopia, black Africa's oldest Christian country and one which has endured more than its fair share of hideous problems. However, Haile Selassie, the first real moderniser of Ethiopia and the brave opponent of Mussolini's Italian Fascist invaders, remains still an honoured name among Ethiopians as well as a name revered further afield by groups such as the Rastafarians and respected by old foreigners like myself.

CHAPTER 16

Slavery and Women

Of the many Ethiopians I have met, two particular individuals stick in my mind. The first is the emperor himself, who received me and talked to me on several occasions over several years, not least at that 1960 moment of crisis when he flew back to Addis Ababa, put down rebels trying to overthrow him, and reoccupied his throne.

The other man I met only once, but long hours spent drinking tea with him one day are especially memorable. Our encounter occurred in Taif, a hill town in the Red Sea east coast mountainous hinterland behind the Saudi port of Jeddah.

An Ethiopian captured by Arab slavers, he became a slave, and eventually the Saudi public executioner. By now, he must long since be dead, but in 2013 the job he did was being publicly advertised within the Saudi kingdom because, it appears, the authorities have been having difficulties in recruiting a new swordsman.

Because of the nature of the butchery involved, I was not surprised when I read about this. Nobody could describe it with more authority than an actual executioner.

This is what I had to say about him and the nastier aspects of his formal duties in March 1963, just fifty years before candidates for the less-than-coveted post were being openly sought in March 2013:

> Aged fifty, born an Ethiopian and slave to Emir Feisal for most of his life, Said el Feisal meditates regretfully on his past in his house at Salamah, Taif.

He told me that although his existence had been "the will of Allah", he would have changed it if he could have. Stocky and studious-looking when wearing spectacles, Said assumes a different fearsome dimension when he holds a long sword inlaid with silver and gold, a serpent engraved on its gleaming blade and a Koranic inscription: "I give you a good start; may you gain fortune and success."

For with that sword, he has cut off 150 heads as Saudi Arabia's public executioner. Said has now retired from his post. "I got bad dreams," he says.

He drives a red Chevrolet car, listens to his Philips wireless set ("I like the London Arabic programmes"), and enjoys his Lipton tea. All has been provided for him by the man he refers to as "my kind and strong master, to whom I am a son". The master, Emir Feisal, was the man who turned Said into an executioner – "Al Sayyaf", the swordsman.

Said told me that he was captured at the age of eight in Ethiopia by slavers and sold into Arab ownership in Yemen. He was presented to Feisal, who clothed him, fed him, and led him in battle when Feisal's father, King Ibn Saud, the founder of Saudi Arabia, was fighting to establish his authority in the region. Then, when Said reached the age of twenty, he was ordered by Feisal to perform a public decapitation in Mecca. Said continued:

For three days, I could not eat. I did not want to do the job. But my father [meaning Feisal] said to me, "I have given you a gun and sword and horse. You can use them. If you don't, I might as well have a woman by my side."

I remembered I am from the Wolumu, the fiercest tribe in Ethiopia. So I told Emir Feisal I would do it, to show him I was obedient and loyal. He said he wanted me to be the lion by his side. After my first execution, Emir Feisal told me, "You are my right arm." I cut through the man's torso by mistake and went mad when I saw the blood and could not get the sword out. Afterwards, they always placed a ring of other slaves around

the execution spot, in case I went wild. It's not always easy to
cut off a head. I would not do it again.

The executioner now is Eid bin Fadala, a younger slave
who watched me at work. I began to get bad dreams, and people
became frightened of me. Emir Feisal retired me, and I am now
his bodyguard in Taif.

My destiny is in Saudi Arabia. If I went back to Ethiopia
as a convert to Islam, I would be killed. My tribe is a proud one,
and I am of good blood.

That chilling account of what it means to be an *official* executioner possibly explains why it is not too easy these days for the Saudis to find a new one, despite the current practice in disturbed Islamic countries elsewhere by *unofficial* executioners – extreme Islamic terrorists – of decapitating their victims and then displaying the results of their terrorism on television and the internet.

As for Said's successor in the official post, the "younger slave", Eid bin Fadala, I suppose that by now he also has retired; and I wonder how many heads he hacked off and if he too experienced bad dreams.

Said's "kind and strong master, to whom I am a son", was at the time the crown prince and prime minister of Saudi Arabia who soon afterwards became king. He ruled from 1964 to 1975, when he was assassinated. I respected him as a serious and honest reformer, something that possibly played a part in the motivations of his murderer. Soon after coming to power, King Feisal outlawed slavery in his country, but not without difficulty.

The abolition of slavery in many other parts of the world was marked in 2007 in England by the two hundredth anniversary of British legislation that led to the end of the practice in many places. A government advisory committee chaired by the deputy prime minister of the time, John Prescott, was reported in 2006 to have considered issuing "a statement of regret" on the actual bicentenary of the date upon which the Slave Trade Act was passed by Parliament, in 1807.

This idea led to controversy, with people arguing that Britain should not apologise for something so long ago, especially in view of the fact that Britain led the world in outlawing slavery. Lord Gisborough, for example, argued that there should be no British apology unless African nations apologised on behalf of those Africans who, with Arabs and others, captured their own kind and marched them off to sell to the slave ships. Another critic deplored the idea of the government "making the same meaningless apology for slavery that the Church of England unwisely made some months ago".

Despite all the efforts to erase slavery, it still exists in some countries in varying forms, apparently even in Brixton (if one is to judge by court proceedings that were in course as I write, involving a so-called Maoist cult). I note, too, that my old newspaper, the Telegraph, has teamed up with the Home Office today and is currently trying to raise awareness of what it terms "Britain's hidden shame", headlining its publicity for its efforts with the words, "Slavery is happening right under our noses."

Wherever and whenever it exists, I can claim a modest part by having helped to persuade one important Arabian King, Feisal, and his important oil-rich country, Saudi Arabia, to outlaw it there.

My involvement began back in January 1961, when I found myself in that country for the first time. Like Egypt, Saudi Arabia had severed diplomatic relations with Britain but, unlike Egypt, had yet to begin to restore such state ties. The breach with Britain had come about not because of the 1956 Suez Crisis but because of a frontier dispute between the Saudis and the British-supported sultan of Muscat and Oman over the Buraimi Oasis.

Argument had dragged on for eight years, and relations had been broken five years before my visit. Signs were appearing that both sides were getting tired of the row, and after six months of waiting, I managed to acquire a visa from the Saudi Ambassador in Cairo to go to his country. On my first of several journeys there, I travelled over a month or so from Jeddah in the Hejaz, on the western Red Sea coast, to Dammam, on the eastern Gulf coast of Arabia.

At the time, Saudi Arabia was one of the most difficult places in the world for a non-Muslim journalist to visit. The Saudi state had been established only thirty years earlier, after the redoubtable first ruler, Ibn Saud, had carved out his desert kingdom with his sword – and with British support.

That kingdom was discreetly beginning to seek an end to the Buraimi dispute, and by my reporting, I played a minor part in bringing this about. When I last visited Saudi Arabia with the British foreign secretary in 1983, in my role by that time as BBC diplomatic correspondent, I could not help comparing the highly active British Embassy in the capital, Riyadh, in the heart of the Nejd Desert, with my first impressions, twenty-two years earlier, of the old British Embassy, still housed on the edge of the Red Sea in Jeddah.

Without an occupant, the building had been closed and shuttered, and it was being cared for by Pakistan in the absence of any envoy from Her Majesty. A Pakistani official and a Saudi interpreter escorted me into the embassy, where everything was carefully covered by dust sheets. I blew the accumulated sand and dust off the unprotected visitors' book and duly placed in it my signature, with the date, below the last visitor's signature of five years before. That signature was also from a journalist, Richard Beeston of the old News Chronicle, who had been in Jeddah when diplomatic relations between Saudi Arabia and Britain had been severed. We reporters are a ubiquitous species.

I left my visiting card on the silver tray beside the book. My escort and my interpreter approved of this observation of the formalities, and a day or two later, to my mild surprise, I found myself invited to speak at a luncheon arranged for various dignitaries by the Saudi Ministry of Information. After it, I headed for the interior and Riyadh and was rewarded journalistically with an exclusive interview with King Saud.

A father of 133 children, including 60 sons, he was the elder of the 40 sons of King Ibn Saud, so deeply admired by Winston Churchill "because of his unfailing loyalty to us" during both world wars. According to Britain's wartime leader, the first Saudi king was "always at his best in the darkest hours".

When Ibn Saud died in 1953, Saud succeeded him. The king made it plain to me during an hour-long audience that he wanted to resume relations with Britain. He talked warmly of the British, saying, "I am waiting for better times again. We think the British are a good-hearted and good-natured people with whom we have always had a traditional friendship."

Then he gave a clue as to why the dispute over Buraimi had dragged on for so long. He explained that he felt that his personal honour and dignity were involved "because the action taken by the British against us was launched in the year that I ascended the throne". The action in question had been the occupation of the Buraimi Oasis by British troops acting on behalf of the sultan of Muscat and Oman. The king argued, "The action of the British has not been normal over Buraimi." He claimed, "We have shown great patience all this time waiting for a solution." Well, it eventually arrived, and diplomatic links were restored in 1963.

My dispatch that helped to prepare the way for the resumption of relations was published the next day on the front page of the *Daily Telegraph*, the Saudis being so keen to ensure that my work was not wasted that I was invited to type it out in a room in the royal palace. From there, I was able also to telephone it to London without any of the routine problems usually encountered in those days of getting a call through.

In the scarlet-carpeted corridors outside, veteran Bedouin guards with rifles and golden scimitars sat on cushions or leaned against the walls, quietly maintaining guard. The king himself, talking to me in his private study, wore dignified and classic Arab robes and fingered a turquoise circlet of beads such as are used by many devout Muslims in "telling" their prayers. His conversation with me was the first occasion for several years on which the monarch had received a journalist and, as with Emperor Haile Selassie just a month beforehand, both my newspaper and me made the most of the scoop.

It was not an insignificant dispatch in foreign policy terms, but for me personally, it had greater importance. Because of the contacts I made on my first venture into Saudi Arabia, I was unknowingly putting down some groundwork for one of the greatest assignments of my life. This began the following year and was completed in 1963. It was an investigation into slavery that resulted in King Saud's successor, his half-brother, Emir Feisal, outlawing the practice a few months after I had produced evidence to him about its horrors inside Saudi Arabia.

In 1961, however, I had no idea of what was ahead and I continued with the usual peregrinations and prolific output of a hard-working daily newspaperman whose beat was the Middle East. In that year alone, I filed dispatches from Egypt, Iraq, Kuwait, Bahrein, Dubai, Syria, and Lebanon; from Somalia and Ethiopia in the Horn of Africa; and, deeper into the continent, from the Sudan and the Congo.

In the process, I built up a store of knowledge about aspects of slavery in Arabia and Africa that proved useful when I was later asked to go more profoundly into the subject.

One important aspect was the position of women in Muslim-dominated and highly traditionalist societies, and my journey into Saudi Arabia was helpful in casting light on this. The establishment of girls' schools had been authorised by royal proclamation for the first time in 1959, only two years before I went there, and I managed to produce what I think was the first foreign report ever to appear about one of the schools.

It was in Jeddah, and it was a private establishment called "Daral Hanan", or "House of Charity". As a man and as a non-Muslim, there was no question of any access to a girls' school for me, and the information I gleaned came from an embryo official organisation called the Department for Girls' Education.

The department came not under the control of the Education Ministry but of the Grand Mufti. This was an arrangement that led reformers to argue that education would take second place to learning the Koran.

There was some truth in this argument, but the reality remained that the women and girls of Saudi Arabia were overjoyed at being offered any sort of education. There was, though, no chance of talking to any of them about it. In my month or so in Saudi Arabia, the only woman I met (apart from the wives of diplomatists) was the Malayan-born and English-educated Muslim wife of a leading Saudi executive. He, in the privacy of his home, invited her to join us in our conversation. Through her, I managed to learn more about the first educational steps towards a brighter future for Saudi women; and I managed even to acquire one of the first pictures ever taken in a Saudi Arabian girls' school of unveiled girls and of their unveiled woman teacher too.

It was taken in a kindergarten in Mecca, the holiest of holy Muslim cities, and the photographer was, of course, another woman. Once again, an article by me appeared on the "Woman's Page" of the *Daily Telegraph* under the headline: "Saudi Girls Can Now Go to School; Emancipation Gets Men's approval". The piece occupied almost the entire page, complete with the relevant picture. It contained plenty of doubts about the headline word "emancipation", but broadly I reported that "limited but genuine moves at last are being made for 'education of the females of the kingdom', as the appropriate royal decree so grace-lessly puts it."

One of the prime movers, I suggested, was the founder of the Daral Hanan school, Princess Sara, daughter of King Feisal. Arabian princesses and educated Arabian women have for a long time supplied much of the motivation for women's education in Islamic societies as well as offering spirited resistance to any government foolish enough to try to bully them.

One such was Princess Amatullah, sister of Imam Mohammad al-Badr of the Yemen. She was one of his women relatives being held captive by President Nasser as a bargaining chip to obtain the release by Yemeni royalists of two hundred Egyptian prisoners of war. Under the heading "Capture an Arab Princess and You've Trouble on Your Hands!" this is what I wrote for the "Woman's Page" in February 1964, in a series asking, "How free are women today?"

> Arab women can be as difficult as any in the world, as President Nasser of Egypt is now finding out with an intransigent feminine political prisoner. Aged thirty-seven, Princess Amatullah is held captive in Cairo with eighteen other women, eight children of the Yemeni royal family, and two servants. The party includes two young brothers of the imam, two sisters, two mothers-in-law, four aunts, and nieces and cousins.
>
> Princess Amatullah's husband was killed by Yemeni rebels in the coup d'etat fifteen months ago and, furious, she seized a gun and fought the rebels until they managed to capture her. They then put her in shackles to keep her quiet.

Explaining how the party was flown to Egypt on the pretext of being transferred to another city in the Yemen, I described how Nasser was offering back to the imam his family in exchange for the Egyptian soldiers held prisoner:

> This is where the Egyptian President's bargaining has back-fired, with a bit of help from Princess Amatullah. She has written to the imam, with all the authority of being his eldest

sister, to instruct him: "Put us out of your mind. Forget us completely. Do not give Nasser his soldiers back just for us."

At one interview in Cairo, witnessed by a Red Cross official, the princess insulted Egyptian officers and dared them to do their worst.

I reported that the imam "laughed with sympathy for his enemy". He said he knew what a will Amatullah had and just how difficult she was likely to be. He reemphasised what he had told me earlier: he would not be blackmailed into releasing the Egyptian prisoners. He said, "I should get a tremendous telling-off from Amatullah, who would accuse me of weakness if I got her back in this way."

Another Arab woman who boldly broke with tradition actually chose to do it in Saudi Arabia on another of my journeys into that country. Here is the account that appeared on the "Woman's Page" in April 1964 under the headline "Out of the Kitchen: Samira Dares to Talk to a Man":

I have met remarkable women who labour unceasingly for the good of their sex. But rarely have I met one such as Samira Mohammed Khashaggi, who enforces her drive for feminine emancipation with beauty and bravery.

She is a lovely, pale-skinned Arab beauty, with shining black hair and deep brown eyes. She is twenty, married, and comes from the holy Muslim city of Medina.

In an uncompromisingly conventional Islamic background, she is one of the first Saudi women to attempt to behave in her own country as anything other than a veiled and hidden household possession.

With careers and education closed to them until very recently, Saudi women have previously fallen into two categories of chattelhood: perfumed, pampered, and dressed by Dior in the enervating atmosphere of the harem; or overworked and worn out by childbirth, degenerating into beasts of burden.

Samira dared to talk to me at her brother's house in Riyadh in the desert-bound heart of Arabia a few weeks ago. She was behaving in a revolutionary manner, breaking all routine

*norms by receiving and chatting with a man – and an infidel
journalist man at that!*

*Samira is perhaps the best known among a group of Saudi
women who are, in her own words, "trying to elevate the social,
educational and religious standard of Saudi women".*

*Educated at an English school in Alexandria, this beauty
from Medina has produced three novels in Arabic, on sale
throughout the Middle East, with unrestrainedly romantic
titles – Farewell My Hopes, Tearful Memories, and Spark in
Your Eyes. The more down-to-earth side of Samira's character
is shown in a thesis she has published, "Awakening of the
Saudi Girl".*

*She is the co-founder of a woman's club called "Society of
El Nahdeh". Its establishment was a major victory for Saudi
womanhood, and similar clubs are being set up all over the
country.*

*The society publishes a woman's magazine, has estab-
lished an institute for girls aged six to eighteen, is setting up
an institute for the blind, is teaching illiterate women to read
and write, and is establishing a health-care centre.*

*Finally, films are being shown at the club, another revolu-
tionary step in a country where for centuries the reproduction
of any living image has been banned by religious forces.*

I wonder what has happened to Princess Sara, Princess Amatullah,
and Samira. If they remain alive, they are doubtless formidable old ladies,
forerunners of today's Saudi women, who have recently been campaigning to be allowed to drive cars, their country being the only one in the
world where women are forbidden to drive.

I also wonder what has happened to the Daral Hanan school and the
Society of El Nahdeh. Those bodies might have survived and flourished
or they might have disappeared with the apparent rise of Islamic fundamentalists who oppose the very idea of feminine emancipation.

One of the more appalling aspects of traditional treatment of women
in a number of Islamic, Middle Eastern, and African communities is
the practice of what has now become a familiar abbreviation in today's

newspaper headlines: FGM, or female genital mutilation. Fairly unusual publicity about it in the British Press has developed over recent years because the barbaric practice has found its way, with some immigrants, into England.

Despite the practice being illegal in the United Kingdom since 1985, not a single prosecution had been brought until quite recently, according to the *London Evening Standard* (which has been campaigning on the issue). The newspaper reported in November 2013 that an official inquiry is to be launched by one of Parliament's committees, the Commons Home Affairs Select Committee, in an investigation as to why no charges had been brought against persons known as "cutters", or others arranging for girls to be mutilated.

It is estimated that at least 66,000 women in the UK have already been mutilated, and estimates of those at risk of mutilation range up to 24,000. Nobody has publicised the experience more commandingly and gruesomely than a woman who described her own "snipping" of the "scissors down between my legs" – Somali-born former Muslim and former Dutch liberal politician Ayaan Hirsi Ali, writing of her experience in her extraordinary autobiography, *Infidel: My Life*.

The publicity given to the practice these days in newspapers and by broadcasters contrasts sharply with the nervousness with which my editors reacted to my questions about it fifty years ago, when I conducted my inquiry into slavery for the *Sunday Telegraph*, the results of which were published in 1963, seven years before Ayaan Hirsi Ali's birth.

Consideration of female genital mutilation was confined in those days to clinical or medical studies and never got far beyond desiccated documentation at the proceedings of United Nations committees or of other concerned bodies dealing with the vast general subject of human rights. Female circumcision was not classed as slavery as such, although it was closely connected with it.

One problem in attacking the practice was a pronounced reluctance by political reformers campaigning for the end of colonialism, especially among those urging independence for African territories, to accept that such practices actually existed. What was worse, for the reformers' case, was that where such practices were indeed discouraged, the discouragement came from the allegedly oppressive imperial or colonial authorities.

There were instances where the known practice of female circumcision was to some extent excused by campaigners (say, for sub-Saharan African independence) as being something that should not be criticised or opposed, because to do that would be to "interfere" in what were viewed as different "cultures". One prominent writer who came under fire for such thinking in 1999 (when she was professor of comparative literature at Warwick University) was Germaine Greer.

She argued that an attempt to outlaw the practice represented an attack on cultural identity. She said in "The Whole Woman" that "one man's beautification is another man's mutilation … If an Ohio punk has the right to have her genitalia operated on, why has not the Somali woman the same right?"

I imagine that her question would get a forthright answer from Ayaan Hirsi Ali. In any case, a Commons Select Committee on International Development said it was absurd for the feminist writer to seek to compare female genital mutilation forced on young girls with voluntary body piercing by Western teenagers.

Real reform thus appeared to have its limits in the eyes of some regarding themselves as reformers. Whatever the reason, though, there existed a general conspiracy of silence about the practice, in several countries, of the deliberate disfigurement of women's bodies.

I first became aware, in the Sudanese capital of Khartoum, of the deep difficulties of the problem when, during the course of my inquiry into slavery, a Sudanese doctor and surgeon who had qualified in England told me about the kinds of challenges he faced. He had, he informed me, performed a clitoridectomy (the excision of the clitoris) on a girl at the request of her mother and her grandmother.

I asked him why he had done it. His answer was that he had been given no choice. The grandmother and the mother of the child were devout Muslims and had each suffered themselves, when young, the operation. He told me that he had at first declined to perform it, and then the grandmother, who was what he described as "an old crone like a black witch", made a terrible threat. She said that if he did not do it clinically and hygienically, then she would employ broken glass herself to perform the excision. So he gave in to the old crone's menaces, as he feared she would do what she threatened.

One of the things about the practice that has always puzzled me is why men (and apparently some women like the "old crone") should insist upon such mutilation. The explanation I was given by the Sudanese doctor was that by removing the clitoris as a source of sexual pleasure for women would make women less inclined to offend against strict Islamic religious and moral rules by indulging in premarital or extramarital sex.

In short, the specific objective was to deprive women of at least one source of sexual pleasure. Since the excision of the clitoris is perhaps the most common form of female genital mutilation, I am compelled to ask why a man should be thought to derive pleasure from sexual congress with a woman who has been deprived of her clitoris. I cannot conceive of a full sexual union between a man and woman when one of the partners has lost a source of bodily sexual fulfilment.

My editors in 1963 considered at length the question of how far a newspaper could possibly go in publicising practices like female circumcision. The result was that it was decided that the subject would be considered by readers to be too upsetting, too uncomfortable, and too delicate for us to tackle. So we concentrated instead on other aspects of slavery, many just as appalling but less directly of a sexual nature.

The change of public and editorial climate between 1963 and now, enabling a taboo subject to be openly considered, is overdue, and I was pleased to note that in 2004 the former prime minister's wife, Cherie Blair, publicly addressed the question when speaking in the United States. On an autumn tour, she asserted in Detroit that the biggest human rights crisis the world now faced was "attitudes to women".

Mrs Blair explained: "It's frightening to think that women still have to endure being treated like their father's property, still have to put up with female circumcision."

Also overdue is a campaign against more contemporary forms of slavery involving women, such as the organised import into Western Europe from Eastern Europe, or elsewhere, of women who are encouraged, if not compelled, to become prostitutes.

Equally obnoxious practices include the imposition of forced marriages (especially among Muslim groups) upon young British women by religious or cultural extremists, including the families of the women. Some of those guilty simply ignore British law, and there seems to have been official hesitancy about upholding it for fear of accusations of cultural bullying, of racism, or (shamefully) of losing immigrant votes.

Having become interested in, as well as upset by, the problems that beset women in various parts of the world, it came as something of a surprise when in 1978 I found myself being criticised by a woman, Ann Jones, in the *Times Educational Supplement*, for laughing at some aspects of sex discrimination as publicised in England.

The reason for her attack was a fifteen-minute talk I had given for Radio 4, called "Coming Back". After many years overseas, the BBC had asked me simply to unburden myself during a three-month stay in London of a few personal impressions of how the place seemed to me to have changed. I was unwise enough to stress that "certainly" I had noticed some things:

> For instance, some of the laws against race discrimination and sex discrimination strike me as being trivial compared with much more fundamental issues in the great wide world outside. I find it hard, for example, to take seriously a court case over whether or not a woman should be allowed to have a drink standing up at the bar of El Vino's.

Now, El Vino's was a Fleet Street bar that I knew well, not to mention several of the women journalists who at the time were fiercely, if not fanatically, fomenting fights of one sort or another about fashionable feminist "freedoms". As they saw it, one of those was their right to stand like men at the bar and drink, rather than sitting down comfortably to drink away from the bar, as many sensible men preferred to do anyway. That, of course, depended upon whether a man could find a chair in which to sit, for the old El Vino's was the sort of bar where a woman, always then regarded as a "lady", was expected to be seated and where a man, or "gentleman", would have offered his chair to a person of the opposite sex.

In expressing my mild amusement over the El Vino's case, I felt that the efforts of my journalistic sisters could have been better exerted in other directions. Instead of campaigning for the right to stand with the men in a London bar and booze, they could, for example, have been campaigning for the provision of uncontaminated water supplies to millions of other women, in Africa and elsewhere, who were condemned to spend much of their lives at frequently polluted wells, drawing water in order to survive.

However, I made the mistake of not spelling out precisely why I had found the El Vino's row so irrelevant to existence. As befitted a columnist in the *Times Educational Supplement*, Ann Jones swiftly took it upon herself to educate me.

"I don't find sex discrimination funny," she declared, after castigating me for finding trivial some of the results (that I listed) of race and sex discrimination. She went on to quote me, slightly inaccurately but not importantly so, as saying, "You can't help laughing, but you don't quite know what you're laughing at."

Writing about news and current affairs on Radio 4, Ann Jones described how she enjoyed "the sense of immediacy given by those crackling tapes, which bring to mind a beleaguered BBC correspondent filing his report while civil war, flood, and famine rage at his studio door". (I react: So far, so good).

Then she asked: "What sort of men are these who speak with the BBC's voice of authority?" (I react: Even better.)

And why are they all men?" (I react: Hang on a bit. Is there some axe grinding here?)

"I refuse to buy the idea that women have less authority." (I react: What does this have to do with news and current affairs? Probably a plug for more jobs for women in news and current affairs.)

"The only woman I heard discussing current affairs during the week was Mary Goldring, and it would be impossible to fault her authority or competence." (I react: I agree about Goldring, but I sense that men are about to get it in the neck.)

Sure enough, so they did. I was astonished, though, to be singled out specifically for attack. "Some hint of those iron-nerved, well-spoken foreign correspondents was given in a talk by John Osman, who recently returned to England after some years abroad. I must confess that I was by turns irritated, infuriated, and incredulous." (I react: Good! As the old journalist's saying goes, "Love me or hate me, but for God's sake don't ignore me!")

"Unfair perhaps to be so irked by a personal opinion. But one is so used to hearing an impartial account in the same measured tones that personal opinion seems to be given official sanction." (I react: Flattering that Ann Jones seems to think that my views had BBC approval, though it is not true. In fact, I had to argue many of my points through with my producer, a lovely man called Tom Read. The truth was that the BBC, a hard taskmaster in those days, was getting fifteen minutes of its airtime filled from an already overworked correspondent, without paying anything extra for it.)

By now, though, the columnist was really getting into her stride. "Anyone who claims that he chose to live abroad because it rains a lot here and drinking is expensive" [she was quite right: I did say that, and I still think the same] "does lay himself open to some criticism. [Yes. From whom? The envious?] "Never mind, I thought, he must be a jolly sort of chap." (So my friends tell me too.)

After that came her blast at my observations on race and sex law in the London of those days, followed by a crushing dismissal that sounded a bit odd, coming as it did from a writer in an educational supplement that would never have thought of me as a teacher: "A lot of people living in London don't need Mr Osman's schoolmasterly strictures to look around them."

Well, that put me firmly in my place. Still, in my time, I have been called much worse than "schoolmasterly".

I was overseas again before I read the views of Ann Jones. Another woman thoughtfully drew them to my attention by sending me a photo-copy of the article. The sender was Paddy O'Keefe, who for many years was the producer of *From Our Own Correspondent*, which Ann Jones rightly admired as being "a serious programme which does not lose its common touch".

Paddy, for whom I have always had great respect and affection, added a little footnote to the photocopy: "Thought you might like to see this. As ever, Paddy O'Fooc." Paddy had acquired her nickname because in those far-off days when correspondents were commissioned to write a piece for the programme, we were asked in cablese, or over a circuit or satellite, if we could "do a FOOC" (pronounced "fook"). The programme is still on the air in parts of the BBC, and for all I know, the same working shorthand still exists. When Paddy O'Keefe became the producer, she was inevitably transformed into Paddy O'Fooc. When I last heard of her (and we still exchange Christmas cards), she was living in Cornwall as a widow, Mrs Powell.

Ann Jones ended her onslaught on my opinions by saying, "Finally, I disagree with his remark about growing disrespect for the law." Ignoring examples I had cited for my assertion, she quoted me disapprovingly for saying, "Civilised men and women support the law when they understand it." I still feel that, and I wonder what Ann Jones thinks these days about the point.

Clarity in the law is important, and legislation can sometimes be ambiguous or difficult to understand. Even definitions of "slavery" differ. In 1956, the United Nations defined traditional chattel slavery as "the state of someone over whom any or all of the powers attaching to the right of ownership are exercised". That is a lawyers' definition, wider and less pungent than the Oxford Dictionary meaning: "A person who is the legal property of another and is forced to obey them."

The first direct personal knowledge I gained of slavery came when I stayed in the early 1960s as a guest in the house of a young British political agent, Donald Hawley, in the Gulf. In the due course of time, he became an ambassador and was eventually knighted for his services. He had in his garden, which overlooked Dubai Creek, a tall pole from which flew the Union Flag. Moored at a quay at the end of the garden, he kept a vessel to help him in his duties in the Gulf, with a crew of half a dozen Arabs. Trying to smarten up this rather motley-looking bunch of sailors, he persuaded the Foreign Office to allow him to kit them out with uniforms for their duties.

Hawley arose one morning and found, to his astonishment, one of his sailors on his knees in the garden, with his arms wrapped around the flag pole. He was seeking his release from slavery by way of a traditional method of manumission established during a worldwide British crusade against slavery after the passing of the Slavery Abolition Act.

The sailor was merely Hawley's employee, not his slave, but, quite unknown to Hawley, the man was in fact a slave belonging to somebody else. It emerged that each week, the sailor had gone home and handed his wages to his owner, but when his owner wanted to appropriate the sailor's uniform as well as his wage, the slave-sailor rebelled. He fled to the British Agency, enfolded the flagpole in his arms, and was duly granted British protection.

My subsequent involvement in the *Sunday Telegraph*'s investigation into slavery began in 1961, after my first visit to Saudi Arabia and after Lord Maugham had written a book called *The Slaves of Timbuktu*, in which he recounted how he had purchased a slave in West Africa.

This had attracted public attention, with the Anti-Slavery Society lobbying hard in Fleet Street, Parliament, and elsewhere, urging more countries to sign and to implement various international slavery conventions more efficiently.

These developments were unknown to me when I received a letter from the *Sunday Telegraph* asking me if I thought anything could be done in the new political situation in Africa to see how freshly independent states admitted almost daily to the United Nations were either fulfilling or ignoring their international obligations on slavery.

It was a difficult question to answer because of its sheer scope. The *Sunday Telegraph* had been founded only a month or two earlier, in February, while I was still in Arabia. The founder and proprietor, Michael Berry, later Lord Hartwell, had a tremendous personal commitment to the success of the newspaper and was prepared to spend money on exciting journalism if there was a reasonable chance of bringing challenging projects to successful completion.

I pondered deeply about the possibilities, which offered wonderful journalistic opportunity but which entailed serious investment of money and time. Considerable correspondence ensued between my editors and myself. At that stage, there was no suggestion that I myself should receive the assignment; I was merely being asked what I thought of the idea and how best the newspaper should go about it.

I pronounced the task of getting hard, well-documented material on the slave trade as an "excellent" idea but added that it was a job "that has to be done properly or not at all". I was then asked to give specific plans as to how to tackle such an assignment and to take it on for myself.

I estimated that it would take from four to six months and that an investigator would have to work his way from West Africa across the continent along traditional Muslim pilgrimage (and slavery) routes to the Sudan and to the Horn of Africa, then continue to the Arabian peninsula. I wrote:

Distances and communications difficulties are immense, and contacts will not be easy to make. I would want it clearly understood that it would be impossible to work to a deadline, although obviously I should want to get the job over as soon as possible (I would point out that none of the areas to be visited are holiday centres).

In the Arabian states, of course, it will be strictly a question of "playing it by ear". I think I am the only British journalist since 1956 to have been into Saudi Arabia and to get on any sort of terms with King Saud (three dinners and an interview with him!) I could probably pull off another visa, but without a trip, it would be pointless. Slavery without Saud is rather like Hamlet without the prince.

The size of the project rather overwhelms me, and the possibilities of failure are great; for example, if I start in West Africa and work my way across one is almost bound to be uncovered before reaching Arabia. No one trying this task could promise success, and this is a hard thing to swallow when thousands of pounds and months of effort are at stake.

However, if Mr Berry decides to take the quite considerable risk involved – and I hope he will – I can promise to do my best if the project matures. It's a great challenge for a newspaper and a newspaperman. I feel complimented by being considered for the job.

On the cost, I would say that this will obviously be more than that involved in pursuing my usual duties, but not all that much more. I should, of course, produce odd news stories and features while en route; this would help provide first-class cover for my real purpose.

Looking back, I am impressed by my own temerity in more or less laying down the conditions upon which I would accept the assignment: no time limit, expenses more than usual, acceptance of the possibility of failure. I stressed that it was no easy task to get into Saudi Arabia legally and that obtaining a Saudi visa was "a highly personalised business". However, I thought I stood a good chance of getting one.

Michael Berry decided to go ahead, and I was instructed to give priority to the project, with the *Daily Telegraph* accepting that the flow of daily news from me would be necessarily diminished. I returned to London to bone up with the Anti-Slavery Society on the international legal, economic, and political aspects of slavery, getting a lot of help from the secretary, the late Commander Thomas Fox-Pitt.

Founded in 1823 to campaign against slavery, the society had been dissolved in 1833 with the passing by Parliament that year of the Slavery Abolition Act. The man whose life's main work it had been to bring this about, William Wilberforce himself, died just one month before the act became law.

It was not long before the society resumed its work again under different names, such as the Aborigines Protection Society and the British and Foreign Anti-Slavery Society. Both were incorporated into the later body, the full name of which was the Anti-Slavery Society for the Protection of Human Rights. Armed by the society with a lot of useful background material about slavery, I set off to look for the real thing.

I started my inquiries in a region where Lord Maugham had finished his: in West Africa. I headed first for Timbuktu, the remote town that is the meeting place of Arab and African, desert and bush, Algeria and Mali. The first European to have reached there, in 1825, was a Briton, Major Alexander Gordon Laing of the Second West India Regiment. Still standing was the mud house where this pioneer had lived for a few months before he was killed in 1826. A plaque placed on the wall in 1930 by the Africa Society, London, commemorated him.

The French did not arrive in any strength until 1893, when their colonisation spread south from Algeria through vast areas of central and western Africa, including Mali. All traces of French imperialism were, however, being scrubbed out as quickly as possible, and a new name had been attached to Fort Bonnier, the French Foreign Legion *Beau Geste*–style fort where Field Marshal Joffre, victor of the Marne in the Great War, had served as a subaltern at the end of the nineteenth century. It had become Fort Sheikh Sidi Bekaye. The expanse of sand in front of it, formerly Place Joffre, had been relabelled Place de l'Independance.

I spent some time in Timbuktu, staying in a government rest house, where I bought a postcard of an African woman captioned "Slave of a Targui chief". It expressed a social truth acknowledged by all eight thousand inhabitants of Timbuktu except for government officials and party politicians: that there were two predominant local castes, master and slave. I wrote:

> It is the dark-skinned Bella who do the heavy work around Timbuktu. I saw them sweat over pumps watering livestock while the fair-skinned Tuareg supervised. They heaved at labouring jobs while the Tuareg performed little more than traditional nomadic duties of saddling and loading camels. The veiled masters are dignified and warlike, armed with swords, rifles, and religion; the slave caste are as they always have been: friendly and smiling, of immense endurance, but ignorant, superstitious, and vulnerable. Many Bella live in filthy lean-tos on the edge of Timbuktu.
>
> I watched similar shacks reappear on town fringes as I followed the pilgrim route across Africa: outside Gao on the Niger; near Kano in northern Nigeria; at Port Sudan and Suakin on the other side of the continent; and in Saudi Arabia itself. It is from these shacks that slaves are obtained.

I took plenty of photographs illustrating the realities of existence at the southern edge of the Sahara. From Timbuktu, I went on to Gao, then a mosquito- and toad-ridden mud hovel town on the River Niger. In the Mali capital, Bamako, I was received by President Modibo Keita, head of state, prime minister, foreign minister, defence minister, and the secretary of Mali's one permitted political party.

Mali was a slave source country like near and neighbouring states such as Mauritania, Chad, Senegal, Ghana, Liberia, Togo, Guinea, Niger, Dahomey (now Benin), and Upper Volta (now Burkina-Faso). They were mostly newly independent states and had recently joined the United Nations Organisation. Yet none of them were then parties to the UN Slavery Convention.

"Why not?" was my question to President Modibo Keita. His far from convincing reply: "Even if we haven't signed the convention, we support it. Slaving is a question that needs a more international approach. It is a question of practical application and study."

The place where I found at least some practical application in action, months later, was in the Mali Embassy in Jeddah, in Saudi Arabia. I had arrived there after my long journey across Africa along the Muslim pilgrimage and slavery route into Arabia. In the embassy, over one hundred escaped Malian slaves were sheltering. Most of them had fled from Mecca, where they had been taken on pilgrimage. With the help of Mali's chargé d'affaires, M. Doucoure, I painstakingly interviewed and photographed them, using interpreters, and so built up a formidable dossier of evidence that I presented to Emir Feisal and that was then published by the *Sunday Telegraph*.

Whatever the lack of enthusiasm displayed by his government about signing the anti-slavery convention, M. Doucoure himself worked with dedication to recover African slaves. I reported:

> *By luck, I had the chance to watch him in action in his office when in walked a plump Saudi merchant, Said Adham, of Jeddah, who was acting for his partner, Ali Zahrani, of Taif. Clutching his sunshade handle, Said Adham complained that Zahrani's slave, Mohammed, aged about thirteen had fled. He believed he was hiding in the embassy. "I have come to get the boy," he said.*
>
> *M. Doucoure told his visitor politely but vigorously, "This is our countryman; this is our soil. Neither you nor anybody else shall harm a hair of his head. We will not allow our people to be bought or sold in any country."*
>
> *Splendid words – but would they not stand a better chance of fulfilment if firmer policies on slavery were followed by African governments, including M. Doucoure's own?*

The runaway slave who sticks in my mind most vividly from the fugitives in the Mali embassy was a woman named Kumu bint Edwal. This was her story:

> *Aged thirty, she sat before me in Jeddah, shyly suckling her slave daughter, Najat, aged six months. The child, with infected eyes, looked ill. Kumu drew her ragged headscarf decently over*

her breast as she told me of her trans-African journey into
bondage.

"Two years ago with my son Akli, then aged two, I came
with Mohammed Ibn el Hatab to Saudi Arabia. There were no
police or government officers in the Gao area of Mali, where
I lived, and Hatab came by one evening to my house. He left
and returned later that night with another man while I was
sleeping. He tied me up and bundled Akli and me into a car
and drove off.

"We went onto a camel and again into a car and drove to
Sudan. In Suakin, a Sudanese official asked who I was. The
Shangiti El Hatab said I was his sister, but because I am black
and the Shangiti white, the official said, "Impossible.'

"The Shangiti swore I was his sister, and I said nothing,
as I was afraid. After a month, he managed to arrange for us
to leave, and we came by dhow to Jeddah. After the pilgrimage
season, I went to Medina and Hatab handed me to a slave
agent, Mohammed Ahmed.

"Ahmed took me to Hail, Medina, and Mecca with several
other people whom he sold. I shouted, "I am not a slave" and
cried, and nobody would have me. Ahmed took me back to
Hatab, who sold my son and me to two sisters in Mecca, one of
whom died and one who lives. She is Asma. They paid eighteen
thousand rials (fifteen hundred pounds) for us.

"Sometimes I could not work and was ill treated. Asma
gave me to a man slave working for her, called Hamam, and I
bore him Najat earlier this year. I quarrelled with Asma, and
she ordered Hamam to hit me. He beat me on the head with a
pot, my head bled, and I went to hospital."

Kumu showed me her still-bruised head.

They beat Akli and even Najat. It was very hard to escape, and
I did not want to leave Akli. But I could not stand it any longer
and decided I had to leave him. I could barely escape with
my own life and Najat. I fled at night and walked on my bare

feet, carrying Najat fifty miles to Jeddah. I reached the Mali Embassy three days ago.

Kumu bint Edwal's description of her experience of twentieth-century slavery illustrated the inhumanity of the practice. The "Shangiti" she mentioned were Muslims posing as missionaries for Islam in Africa, whose favoured method of slaving was to lead pilgrims to Saudi Arabia, after having equipped them with the necessary documentation that they then destroyed on reaching the country. Essentially, they thus blackmailed unsophisticated Africans into submission through fear of transgressing immigration rules.

Many of the slaves also arrived illegally by being actually smuggled into Arabia. They came from the Sudan, Ethiopia, Eritrea, Somalia, and Djibouti by way of the long African coastline of the Red Sea. The smugglers used maritime methods similar to those often employed nowadays by smugglers of immigrants into Western Europe from the Balkans, the Middle East and north Africa into Italy or Spain.

After visiting Suakin and Port Sudan, I described how it worked:

> *The main centre for transit is the modern town of Port Sudan and Suakin, the Sudan's old, dead port where Solomon once met the queen of Sheba.*
>
> *Suakin, which before Port Sudan was built had a population of thirty thousand is now a ghost town falling into ruins, with six thousand nomads, fishermen, and fellaheen as inhabitants.*
>
> *It comes to life only for the six-month pilgrim season, when the quarantine station opens. Most of the smugglers are Gehenia from Saudi Arabia, small, hardy men with monkey-like faces. I met some of them at Flamingo Bay, a stinking creek north of Port Sudan, where they bring in sacks of mother-of-pearl for a twice-weekly auction. "The Gehenia are all smugglers," explained my official guide. "They bring in gold from Saudi Arabia and take out animals and human beings."*
>
> *The deputy commissioner of police in Khartoum outlined the same story. The Sudan police are fighting smuggling with*

Land Rovers and camel patrols, but distances are huge, and
as the pilgrims' officer noted, smugglers make a lot of money.

Whatever happened to Kumu bint Edwal and her daughter Najat in later life, I do not know. Moreover, I do not know if she ever became aware of the fact that she was chosen in England by the Anti-Slavery Society to be publicised as sad proof of the necessity to maintain the work of such organisations. After the appearance of my series of articles, "Slavery Lives On", in March 1963, the society used my photograph of her and her daughter for its Christmas card at the end of the year. It also made me one of its members, though it is many years since I have had any contact with the society. Nearly two hundred years after its original foundation, it is still active and is linked with the American and the Australian Anti-Slavery Societies.

Official recognition of the need for such bodies is provided by the fact that 2004 was chosen by the United Nations as Slavery Remembrance Year, that year having been the bicentenary of the creation of Haiti, a state symbolic of slaves' resistance and the first black independent state in the New World of the Americas.

The official commemoration of the struggle against slavery was launched at a ceremony in the Ghanaian port of Cape Coast, once one of the most active trans-Atlantic slave-trading centres. Well before it became what it is now, an official "World Heritage" site, I visited it in 1960 for a reason other than slavery but one strongly linked with the kind of moralities opposed to the practice.

Despite the anti-slavery activities over a couple of centuries or more by all sorts of Christians, from Quakers to Catholics, the churches in Ghana at that time were coming under fire from the government of Dr Kwame Nkrumah. He was building himself a cult as the "Gandhi of Africa", "The Redeemer", and "The Saviour". The churches particularly disliked the biblical comparisons, and as a result, the Roman Catholic archbishop of Cape Coast and Metropolitan of Ghana, Dr. W. Porter, attacked what he termed "blasphemies" in the official government press.

The Anglican bishop of Accra, Dr R. Roseveare, supported him, telling his congregation that the use of scriptural allusions reserved for over two thousand years for our Lord was "deeply offensive" and came "dangerously near to blasphemy".

Nkrumah's government was worried because there were then well over one million Christians in Ghana, six hundred thousand of them Catholics and the rest Anglican, Presbyterian, and free church. So the *Ghana Times*, the organ of the ruling party, struck back at the archbishop, abusing him as "ignorant" and as a "religious imperialist agent". I went to interview the archbishop, a Liverpool man who was retiring after serving as a priest in West Africa for over forty years. He was straightforward in saying that Nkrumah's party had "a definitely Marxist stance" with an "un-Christian philosophy". He felt, however, that the Christian community would be steady enough to withstand any hard blows and would not submit too easily to regimentation from the government in any new form of slavery.

His prognostication seems to have been entirely accurate, with the churches in Africa remaining as vigorous as any in the world, certainly as vigorous as any church in England. I hope I am wrong and that the Church of England, for example (of which I am, I suppose, a flawed product), can manage to display a clearer idea of what it stands for these days.

At the Cape Coast opening ceremony in January 2004 of the United Nations "International Year to Commemorate the Struggle against Slavery", the head of UNESCO (the United Nations Educational, Scientific and Educational Organisation), Koichiro Matsuura, said that the UN wanted to express solidarity "and commitment towards those who still did not enjoy basic human rights".

A representative of Slavery International, Beth Herzfeld, added that chattel slavery involving a class of hereditary slaves still existed in parts of Africa and that bonded labour remained common in South Asia. New forms of abuse such as the trafficking of women and girls for the sex trade in Europe had also appeared.

One of Ghana's leading tourist attractions now is the old castle at Cape Coast, featuring a "Door of No Return" through which slaves boarded ships taking them away from Africa. The emphasis on remembrance is understandable and is not misplaced but could not more emphasis be placed on countering modern forms of slavery?

However, I note that the United Nations and various anti-slavery organisations do continue to campaign against emerging types of slavery as well as the reported revival of the slave trade routes across West Africa, the sort that I investigated.

According to the Anti-Slavery Society in 2003:

> *Slavers have reappeared following the old slave routes, except
> that trucks, Jeeps, and modern four-wheel-drive vehicles and,
> on occasions, aircraft, have replaced the camels. The slavers
> often carry mobile telephones.*
>
> *Some things, however, have not changed. Cunning, deceit,
> the use of drugs to subdue the children, and the whip remain
> part of the essential equipment of the professional slaver. The
> trade involves most states in sub-Saharan West Africa.*
>
> *The children are kidnapped or purchased for $20–$70 each
> by slavers in poorer states, such as Benin and Togo, and sold
> into slavery in sex dens or as unpaid domestic servants for $350
> each in wealthier oil-rich states, such as Nigeria and Gabon.*
>
> *These children are bought and sold as slaves. They are
> denied an education, the chance to play or to use toys like other
> children, and the right to a future. Their lives are at the mercy
> of their masters, and suicide is often the only escape.*

This paints a bleak picture. The varieties of human exploitation might tend to turn would-be reformers into faint hearts. But despair is not permitted to those determined to avoid John Bunyan's "Slough of Despond". A reminder of the force of William Wilberforce's legacy that I personally found encouraging came in March 2004, when the Hull-born reformer, who lived from 1759–1833, was named "the greatest Yorkshireman". This was the choice of a panel of judges from nominations submitted by the public to a BBC North TV programme called *Yorkshire Greats*. If slavery lives on, so it seems does the spirit of Wilberforce.

In the year or so of my life that I spent investigating the subject of slavery, I was depressed by the overwhelming amount of human misery I witnessed and the proof of human brutality that I accumulated. I was pleased, however, with the journalistic result of my labours. So were many others, including my employers. Editor Donald McLachlan wrote to me to say that my articles had been much commented on. "I think you did a very impressive piece of digging and travelling," he commented. Assistant editor Ralph Thackeray wrote, "We thought the slavery articles made a very good show, thanks to your patient digging and the excellent pictures." Letters were published which praised my inquiry as being "compelling journalism" and my articles as being "magnificent".

The old *Punch* magazine expressed the hope that the editor of the *Sunday Telegraph* would "continue to give preference to such features as John Osman's excellent series on slavery".

Did my work achieve anything? I think I can say it did, especially in Saudi Arabia. In outlawing slavery completely in that country, Emir Feisal acted, partly at least, upon the evidence about slavery that I presented to him. It remains one of the most satisfying things I ever did as a journalist.

The emir himself was internationally and quite properly praised for doing what he could to eliminate the practice. Not only did he outlaw it, but official action also went much further: thousands of slaves were freed after being purchased by the government from their owners.

At that time, the brother of the king and of the emir, the governor of the Riyadh central region, Prince Salman Ben Abdel Aziz, said that 1,682 slaves were bought in that region alone for £1,785,000, an average price of £1,061 each for an individual's freedom.

Economic problems are always associated with slavery abolition, and Emir Feisal explained to me in fascinating detail such considerations:

> *Emir Feisal realistically outlined the internal difficulties as we sipped mint tea and bitter coffee in the old Hashemite palace of Shoubra. Enormously charming, subtle, and strong (although physically now frail), Emir Feisal was concerned over problems arising from people losing money on their "investments", the word he employed for the human beings who are slaves.*
>
> *"Slaves are a great social and economic problem representing thousands of pounds of investment to some owners. If we release them, we create two economic problems: how to find jobs for the slaves and how to compensate owners for loss of cheap labour. Settling of compensation may lead to all sorts of dishonesty, since we shall inevitably get people pretending they were slaves to someone, compensation gained being subsequently divided between 'owner' and 'slave'."*

As well as economic considerations, religious beliefs also often come into play in trying to abolish forms of slavery, whether in an Islamic society or, say, in a Hindu temple. When the British ruled India, they not only outlawed the Hindu practice of "suttee", by which a widow would immolate herself on her husband's funeral pyre, but they also made it a criminal offence under the 1860 Indian Penal Code to procure women or girls for the purpose of child prostitution.

The move was an effort to suppress it altogether, and according to the Anti-Slavery Society, child prostitution was in fact in decline throughout the earlier part of the twentieth century under British imperial rule. However, fifty-six years after the end of the Raj, in 2003, the society reported a revival of religiously sanctioned practices involving sacred temple slaves and child prostitutes in the Indian states of Karnataka and Andhra Pradesh, as well as in Nepal.

The society stated:

> *Historically, these girls served as hierodules, or sacred temple slaves or temple dancers, who were engaged by the priests to provide sexual services to male supplicants or male worshippers at the temple.*
>
> *However, nowadays, this original purpose has gone and, after dedication – usually at the age of five to seven years – the child is often deflowered by the priest and sold to the highest bidder, who keeps her as his child concubine. When she grows older and loses the bloom of youth, her buyer usually gets rid of her. The girl then has to work in a brothel which often has a shrine at the door to symbolise her original dedication to Hindu cult prostitution.*

As for the Islamic approach, Emir Feisal spelled out to me what he thought:

> *The prophet laid down rules about how slaves should be treated, and it is difficult to say it is against religion. If we moved too fast and finished slavery too soon, people would revolt.*

Slavery has gone on throughout the history of Islam, and here it goes on still. Show me one Muslim state where there are not still slaves!

Feisal told me that he did not remember ever buying a slave but that he had many times been presented with them. As a progressive ruler, he tried to overcome opposition to his reformist measures during his eleven years as king, but reactionaries hated him, and his assassination was no great surprise. The murderer was his nephew.

Two pictures. The late King Saud of Saudi Arabia gave me an
interview on my first journey into Saudi Arabia in 1961 that
helped to lead to a resumption of diplomatic relations (which
had been severed) between his country and Great Britain.

In 1962 President Modibo Keita of Mali gave me an interview during an investigation lasting for well over a year that I made into slavery for "The Sunday Telegraph." I questioned him as to why his country, a slave-source country, had not signed the UN Anti-Slavery Convention.

Two pictures (including the Christmas card). My picture of a Mali woman slave, Kumu bint Edwal, and, her child, taken in Jeddah, Saudi Arabia, in the Mali embassy there, after she had fled from her owners in Mecca. The picture was used by the Anti-Slavery Society as its 1963 Christmas card.

This photograph was taken at a kindergarten in Mecca. It is one of the first official pictures ever taken in Saudi Arabia of unveiled women — not only of the pupils but the teacher too. The photographer was, of course, another woman !

The first picture published in the west (on the Woman's Page of "The Daily Telegraph" in 1961) of Saudi girls at school. The establishment of girl's schools had been authorised by royal proclamation only two years beforehand and one of the first of them was the school attended by these young pupils, Daral Hanan, or House of Charity. A prime supporter was Princess Sara, daughter of the late King Feisal. The photograph was taken by a Saudi woman and handed to me together with a report about the school.

The Saudi public executioner, Said el Feisal, whose sword had lopped off some 150 heads in public executions over the years. A former slave, he talked to me at length about his job during my investigation into slavery. Now-a-days the Saudi authorities are reported as advertising the post because of difficulties in finding swordsmen capable of fulfilling its duties.

Five pictures (all my copyright although some were used by
"The Sunday Telegraph.") The scenes are from Timbuctoo in
Mali during my 1961-62 slavery investigation. They show Arab
masters, including slave-owning Tuaregs, and black slaves.

Plaque in Timbuctoo erected in 1930 by the Africa Society to the memory of Major Alexander Gordon Laing, of the 2nd West India Regiment, "first European to reach Timbuktu, 1823, fell here in 1823."

CHAPTER 17

===

"Seeking the Bubble" (continued)

From Saudi Arabia across the Red Sea lies what was (geographically speaking) the biggest state in Africa: Sudan. Whether or not it remains the biggest geographic African state, after recent recognition of the independence of South Sudan, I simply do not know. Only a geographer-mathematician could work that out. Whatever the answer, both states bearing the name of Sudan have for years provided another of my troubling "unfinished stories"; and things in that African region – and not all that far from it (in African terms) – do not look immediately as if they are getting much easier.

Quite apart from the continuing saga of problems in the southern Sudan, its near neighbour, the Central African Republic, is enduring (as I write) sanguinary disturbances between Christians and Muslims that newspaper headlines are describing as near-genocidal. Farther north, in Darfur, on the western borders of Sudan itself with Chad, what has been described as an "ethnic cleansing process" has reportedly been pursued by proxies of the Khartoum government, known as the Janjaweed; and Chad itself has suffered its own troubles.

As the first correspondent to report as long ago as 1963 from the Southern Sudan about developing conflict there, I have followed events both by revisiting the region later and, from afar, as a newspaper reader, radio listener, and television viewer. As the years pass, the world will doubtless learn how Southern Sudanese independence unfolds. I do not wish to be too pessimistic, but the depressing possibility is that peace in the south, such as it is, might vanish as completely as a Sudanese town that I went to in 1961 on my first visit to the Sudan: Wadi Halfa.

That, too, was not accomplished without riots and difficulties. The town is now beneath the waters of Lake Nasser, following the construction of the Aswan High Dam, but when I was there, more than sixty thousand inhabitants existed in the area, some eleven thousand Halfawi in the town itself plus fifty thousand or so other Nubians who eventually lost their homes and who lived in nearby settlements along the palm-shaded banks of the Nile. The mighty river had been the source of life for them and for their forebears for thousands of years and, as the Sudanese District Commissioner explained to me, "They are even more reluctant than most human beings to be forced to change their homes."

Nevertheless, that was what happened, and inevitably people at the time feared for their future. The Sudanese government mounted a somewhat belated information drive to explain to the Nubians the benefits they would receive if they moved to a region of which most had never heard. This was a place one thousand miles away, called Khashm el Girba, in the eastern Sudan, near the Ethiopian border.

So I went there too, driving from Khartoum 250 miles east, in desert heat, to the banks of the River Atbara to see the start of a £30 million resettlement scheme. An Italian company was building a dam to help irrigate 150,000 acres of a semi-arid region. It possessed excellent soil but had only three months' unpredictable annual rainfall. A further 150,000 acres was to be opened up in a second stage of the scheme, originally conceived by the British before departing from the Sudan in 1956.

Gradually, the Sudanese government was persuading the Halfawi to accept the move.

Parties of tribal leaders and village elders were conducted around the nucleus of the scheme, and samples were exhibited of the produce already grown by a pilot farm: splendid onions, beautiful maize, excellent beans, fine wheat, and an abundance of other crops. The local eastern Sudanese tribes, chiefly nomadic people with grazing stock, said they looked forward to the Halfawis' arrival, but it was clear that they were far more concerned with their own hopes for greater prosperity than they were with the arrival of the newcomers.

The same went for the Halfawis, one of them summing up the prevailing consensus: "Well, Aswan may end our old way of life, but we might get a better one." They eventually had to quit their own drowned town, the only place of any size in a part of ancient Nubia that was rich in antiquities. It was of course when I was there before its submersion, the centre for archaeological teams working to excavate and preserve valuable remains.

I seized the opportunity to visit the mighty temple of Abu Simbel in its original position on the banks of the Nile before UNESCO moved it and so preserved it from inundation. To this day, that successful project remains perhaps the greatest single achievement of an occasionally controversial organisation.

The breathtaking plan entailed lifting three hundred thousand tons of rock, together with the temples encased in it, some two hundred feet up the granite and sandstone Nubian hillside, eventually to stand above the man-made lake for future generations to see.

In June 1961, I reported from Cairo President Nasser's decision to adopt the elaborate twenty-five-million-pound Italian scheme, plus plans for salvaging other Nubian monuments, costing a further ten million pounds. One of them, Philae, was among seventeen other temples it was decided to dismantle and preserve. Now the results of the historic transformation are there to be enjoyed by tourists.

I was back in the Sudan later in the year to report on a visit to the country by a rising Soviet political star, Leonid Ilyich Brezhnev, who only a few months before had been made the chairman of the presidium of the Supreme Soviet. I accompanied him and his Sudanese host, the general who headed the military regime of the day, President Ibrahim Abboud, on their engagements in Khartoum and in Omdurman. I travelled with them out into the western Kordofan desert area, neighbouring the troubled Darfur region of today. The "jovial communist leader", as I described him, was treated with the rest of the Sudan's guests, including myself, to a spectacular cavalry demonstration by sixty thousand warlike tribesmen near El Obeid.

Mounted on camels and horses under the stifling sun, many of the riders were nevertheless clad in heavy chain mail as they charged past us, their turbans flying, hooves pounding, swords waving, lances extended, dust and sand billowing, with many of the warriors bellowing the Islamic slogan: "God is great."

I reported that "healthy scepticism" was displayed by the Sudanese towards "a communist state which is officially godless". The Russian head of state, however, missed no propaganda chance. Members of his entourage were busy at every stop, handing out lapel badges, one showing a mosque with a minaret topped not with a crescent but with a red star.

Nowhere in the world have I ever seen such a massive equestrian and camelid display, with so extraordinarily mediaeval a flavour, as that which I saw at El Obeid.

A similar sight must have presented itself sixty-three years earlier to Kitchener's army when, in 1898 (with young officer Winston Churchill among the British force), the Battle of Omdurman was won. The defeated were the Islamic followers of the Khalifa, successor to the notorious Mahdi, whose hordes thirteen years earlier had conquered most of the Sudan, captured Khartoum, and in the process had killed General Gordon.

It was an episode that was costly for Britain's great statesman of the nineteenth century, William Ewart Gladstone, four times prime minister. As the *Encyclopaedia Britannica* puts it, "The worst mistakes he ever made were to allow General Gordon, whom he had never met, to go to Khartoum; and then to fail to rescue him."

The Mahdist theocracy lasted seventeen years in the Sudan. It was on the island of Aba, in the White Nile, on 29 June 1881, that Mohammed Ahmed ibn al-Sayyid Abdullah had proclaimed himself as the expected Mahdi, divinely elected to restore Islam. Just four years later, he had completed a triumphal series of successes. Then he died, probably of typhus, in the place he had named as his capital, Omdurman, having finished off Gordon a mere five months earlier.

Mahdist rule continued for another thirteen years until the Khalifa, Abdullahi ibn Mohammed, lost at Omdurman. He got away but lasted only until the following year, when he was killed in the Kordofan by an Egyptian force commanded by a British officer.

Forms of Mahdism, however, still survive, not only in the Sudan but, as the world has witnessed via its television screens, in, for example, Iraq. There, Shia Muslim militiamen loyal to the cleric Moqtada al-Sadr were at one stage, before Iraqi elections, labelled by newspapers and broadcasting organisations as a "Mahdi Army". In Arabic, "Mahdi" means "the divinely guided one", although the Koran does not mention him and theologians are divided over the origins of Mahdism.

No matter what religious experts might say, many among the Muslim masses have continued to hope for the arrival of a messianic deliverer to herald the arrival of a golden Islamic age before the end of the world. The doctrine of a Mahdi dates back for more than a thousand years, especially among Shia Muslims. Many have claimed the title over the centuries, and it has often attracted social revolutionaries aiming to seize power from governments.

When I was last in Omdurman, the Mahdi's tomb had been restored and the Khalifa's house had been turned into a museum. I talked in Khartoum to the great-grandson of the Mahdi, Sadiq al-Mahdi, who had studied at Oxford and who was the leader of six million Ansari Muslims. Then in his twenties, bearded and turbaned, he possessed a striking presence reflecting his position as the most powerful man in the Sudan outside the government.

After living a dangerously up-and-down political career, in April 2005, he was banned, at the age of sixty-nine, by the Sudanese military regime from addressing political rallies and his headquarters were raided. Dozens of officials working for his Umma Party, the largest opposition movement in the Sudan, were arrested, and Umma itself was barred from political activity. He clearly remained a force and was then developing it. He told me that he thought the old Abboud military regime had "outlived its usefulness", and he had no hesitation in claiming the following: "I am the only man in this country who could raise a war or rebellion, but I would not do it." He added, "I do not advocate violence for a moment, although our good friends the British are helping the regime with arms and thus encouraging them."

Not long afterwards, he came into the political limelight directly when he played a significant role in wide public discussions that led to and accompanied a 1964 uprising against the army and the restoration of democracy in the Sudan. In 1966, at the age of thirty-one, he became the country's youngest elected prime minister but was overthrown after nine months.

Detained for several years, he was forced into exile until 1985, during which period I met him again in Tashkent, in Uzbekistan, where he was attending a Soviet-approved Muslim conference. Returning to the Sudan, he was again elected prime minister in 1986 but was toppled in 1989 by another military coup, which was bloodless and which brought to power President Omar Hassan Ahmed al-Bashir. He is still in power.

Sadiq was kept under house arrest for seven years until he escaped in 1996 to Eritrea to become leader of what was regarded as "the Sudanese opposition in exile".

Allowed eventually to return, he blamed government policies for the crisis in Darfur, where conflict caused the deaths of hundreds of thousands of people and forced another couple of million into primitive refugee camps.

Sadiq called on the Bashir regime to abide by United Nations resolutions on Darfur, and he upset the government by telling it that it should cooperate with the International Criminal Court in The Hague. In 2005, after that court had been handed a sealed list of fifty-one people suspected of carrying out atrocities in Darfur, Bashir pledged that no Sudanese citizen would be handed over to a foreign court. Rallies in support were organised all over the country. Sadiq's opposition to the president on the issue was seen as a "step too far", and it led to a ban on his party and himself. The last I have heard of him is that he had apparently returned to the country, where he leads a relatively quiet existence after his former high-profile political activities.

Covering Arab and African imbroglios provided daily journalistic material throughout 1961, and I found myself moving from Kuwait to Katanga as troubles erupted in one place or another. Until becoming immersed in the slavery investigation during 1962, I continued to cover run-of-the-mill news with upheaval in Syria, although not on today's scale; a political crisis in Turkey; and an uprising by the Kurds in northern Iraq.

The "Kurdish problem", as it became known, was just beginning to emerge into the light of day, and I was one of a handful of foreign correspondents who helped to focus the light.

It was difficult for foreigners to get into General Kassem's Iraq and almost impossible to enter northern Iraq, except for workers in the oil industry whose movements were closely controlled. I managed, however, to obtain access by entering the country through Turkey and northern Syria.

That also had its difficulties. The British ambassador to Turkey, Sir

Bernard Burrows, explained them to me in Ankara. He was just as keen as I was to learn anything possible about Kurdish activities because the Kurds were a problem for the country to which he was accredited as well as for Iraq, Iran, and Syria.

Three countries (Turkey, Iraq and Iran) were experiencing outbreaks of disorder in border regions where Kurdish militants were active, the Kurdish people having historically suffered the misfortune of being divided by frontiers in such a way as to live in sizeable numbers in different countries.

A call by some Kurds for the creation of an independent Kurdistan was seized upon as an opportunity in the 1960s by the Soviet Union to stir up trouble in the region, especially for Turkey, a NATO ally of the West. The Russians had trained and were backing Mullah Mustafa Barzani as leader of the Kurdish revolt.

In addition to the three countries mentioned, Syria also had experienced difficulties with Kurds, though on a lesser scale. I told Sir Bernard of my own plans to get into northern Iraq via Syria to see things for myself, and he immediately assumed his formal ambassadorial role by warning me against trying to go to the affected region. He pointed out that I would be passing through a region of Turkey forbidden to foreigners without specific permission.

Upon being told that I intended to make an attempt anyway, Sir Bernard took off his jacket, rolled up his sleeves, and rolled down a wall map. He then told me all that he said he knew. I left the embassy with his last warning ringing in my ears, as well as his wishes of "Good luck!"

I headed first for the ancient city of Diyarbakir, located in Turkey and enclosed by its great, grim black walls; then I pressed on to the town of Mardin, where a power station was being built and which was not far from the Syrian border. From Mardin, I filed a report about frontier animosities boiling up, with Syria arresting hundreds of Turks, and Turkey detaining Syrians in retaliation. Describing it as a "wild and jumbled area of the Middle East, where Turkey, Syria, Iraq, and Iran meet", I reported:

> *The detentions, the Kurdish uprising, traditional Turkish-Arab friction, and a nasty riot recently in this mountain fortress town display clearly the strains in the area.*

Then I took one of the more interesting railway journeys of my life, from the Turkish border town of Nusaybin into and across north-east Syria and so into northern Iraq. I reported:

> *I reached Mosul by train. As the "Taurus Express" chugged slowly along its single-track line, now and again smartly overtaken by an old woman on a donkey, I had ample time to view the minefields stretching for fifty yards each side of the line. At intervals of three hundred yards, army frontier posts are manned by armed guards. On the barbed wire, notices display scarlet skull-and-crossbones signs, and even less edifying are a couple of sun-blenched skeletons lying in a minefield.*

I managed to spend a couple of days in Mosul, a city banned to all diplomatists from the embassies in Bagdad. I soaked up a lot of information, mainly from Christian refugees from the directly stricken and disturbed area around Mosul and north of it. I was under constant surveillance by the Iraqi secret police. I slipped my police shadows as much as possible until, inevitably, I was detained on Wednesday, 23 May 1962 and placed on a train for Bagdad with a police escort.

I was surprised, relieved, and delighted when, with the "heavies" escorting me, I stepped onto the platform at the Bagdad railway station and a dapper man in a suit approached and introduced himself as the British ambassador.

He conducted me to a waiting Rolls-Royce with an ambassadorial flag on it and drove me off before my disconcerted escort could decide what to do. We left them standing behind on the pavement. Once in the embassy, the ambassador and I agreed that I was in a bit of a spot. He put to me a proposition: if I gave him a rundown of what I had learned, he would help me get safely out of Iraq.

I did not have much choice except to agree, but I did so subject to a condition. This was that if I told him what I had learned, he would guarantee that there would be no leak at the London end from the Foreign Office to any Fleet Street chap sitting at the comfortable desk of the diplomatic correspondent in a newspaper office, who had not actually travelled, worked, and to some extent risked his neck as I had to get the story. (Naturally, my perspective changed, when years later I became the BBC Diplomatic Correspondent!)

The ambassador assented and was as good as his word. He got me to the airport, saw me safely away, and from Beirut on Sunday, 27 May, I filed a dispatch that appeared in the *Daily Telegraph* on the Monday morning with an unusual dateline: "Mosul, Northern Iraq, Thursday (delayed)."

I had not filed from Mosul because I did not want to risk being arrested earlier than I actually was. The ambassador, alerted by his colleague in Ankara, had known that I was heading in his direction; and he was warned by an Armenian contact of mine in Mosul that I had been detained and put on the train, hence his most welcome one-man diplomatic reception at the Bagdad railway station.

So five days after detention, and the day after I had left Iraq, my dispatch appeared:

Pillage and Murder in Northern Iraq
Two Hundred Killed: Thousands in Flight from Tribesmen

Law and order have broken down in northern Iraq. More than five thousand people, mostly Christian, have fled from their villages, and many deaths are reported in clashes between rival factions after a revolt of Kurdish tribesmen. Recently Iraqi Army and Air Force attacks have been launched against the Kurds. In these and in Kurdish villages, the known civilian death toll is now well over two hundred. To the north and east of the half-dead city of Mosul, for a radius of one hundred miles, pillage, rape, murder and sacrilege are going on despite Iraqi government attempts to restore order.

The "Kurdish problem" is still with us. So is the ambivalent and dubious attitude of Syria towards the West and the United Nations, as President Assad's Syrian government employs brutal repression against internal opposition. A military coup had occurred in Syria just two months before my excursion into Mosul, and I remember it because of two particular journalistic aspects.

The first was that I managed to get into Damascus, the Syrian capital, a couple of days before other Middle East correspondents, most of whom were based in Lebanon, in Beirut, just down the road from Damascus. The Syrians closed their frontier with Lebanon when the coup took place, so when, belatedly, my colleagues eventually arrived in the Syrian capital after the border had reopened, they wanted to know how I had managed to get there before them.

I did not tell them, largely because I did not want anybody in Syria to know that I had reached the country through Israel. This brings me to the second reason that I remember the story particularly: it was the only occasion in my life upon which I used three British passports in one day!

Like other British correspondents and businesspersons, I was accustomed to the possession of two passports, issued upon request by the passport office if the Foreign Office agreed. The reason was that if an immigration official of one country, say Syria, in dispute with another country, say Israel, found a visa from Israel in a passport presented upon arrival at the immigration desk, then entry to Syria would be banned. So over the years I carried separate passports for use in Arab countries or in Israel, for use in white-ruled countries like Rhodesia and South Africa, or for use in the black-ruled countries of the continent.

When the Syrian coup occurred, I happened to be in Cyprus. Syria had closed its airports as well as its border with Lebanon, but it appeared that Syria had not closed its southern frontier with Jordan. So I decided to try to get into Syria through Jordan.

The quickest way of doing this was via Israel, so I chartered a plane from Nicosia to Tel Aviv, using my ordinary "All countries" passport on departure from Cyprus. I used my second passport, employed for access to Israel, when I arrived in Tel Aviv. There I took a taxi through Israel to Jerusalem and crossed the border on foot into Jordan, then still ruling old eastern Jerusalem.

On entering Jordan, which permitted border crossings from Israel, I had to employ my "All countries" passport again, and this created a problem, because the entry stamp into Jordan showed that I had arrived from Israel. The Syrians, I knew, would regard that as a reason for not being allowed into Syria. However, in old Jerusalem at that time, there was a British consulate, and the consul cheerfully equipped me on the spot with a new, third British passport that showed I was in Jordan but had no indication on it of any visit to Israel.

Off I drove to Damascus, encountering no Syrian border difficulty. Within hours, I was filing dispatches about the ring of Russian-built tanks surrounding the Syrian capital; the unknown leadership of the so-called "officers' revolution"; the imposition of a curfew upon Aleppo as pro-Nasser officers fled; and as much as I could gather of the confused events always following any coup d'état.

Once again I enjoyed the satisfaction of receiving congratulations from my employers on winning the latest match in the unending tournament of foreign news competition. Even more satisfying, I savoured the annoyance of my competitors and colleagues when they eventually joined me in Damascus. It reminded me happily of similar imprecations directed at me in Addis Ababa the year before, after I had flown in with the emperor when he crushed his rebellion.

Other correspondents had then arrived days after me, following an uncomfortable train journey from Djibouti, and I was at the receiving end of a curse from a chum of mine, Robin Stafford of the *Daily Express*, that I remember with especial pleasure: "To hell with people who fly in on emperors' aeroplanes!"

Such were the joys and sorrows of foreign correspondence in the 1960s. Some of my colleagues of the period were a wild lot, and alas, many of them have now passed on. One, though, a good companion on my sortie into northern Iraq, and until recently playing a leading role with an English-language weekly newspaper in Cyprus, was a Greek Cypriot journalist of Russian descent, Alex Efthyvoulos, who died not long ago. A third man with us on that Kurdish venture I have long lost touch with: Harry Scott Gibbons, formerly of the *Daily Express*, who, I am told, has just written a book on Cyprus that I look forward to reading.

Eventually, my reporting of things that President Nasser did not appreciate about the effect in the Middle East of Egyptian policies, led, after nearly three years, to the withdrawal of my Egyptian visa. It was perhaps surprising that I had lasted in Cairo for as long as I did.

I continued with Middle East coverage but was drawn more deeply into Africa, where the decolonisation drive was in full throttle and the flow of news in full spate. Covering the run of events for the *Daily Telegraph* also gave me a chance to dig away quietly on the slavery inquiry for the *Sunday Telegraph*.

By the end of 1962, I had completed most of the investigation and my employers decided to repost me to Africa. I set up a new base in Nairobi and followed the achievement in swift order of full independence for the whole of British-ruled East Africa: British Somaliland, Uganda, Kenya, Tanganyika, Zanzibar, and, later, Mauritius and the Seychelles.

Elsewhere, too, Harold Macmillan's memorable winds of change were blowing, sometimes with disastrous effects, as Belgian, French, and Portuguese colonial withdrawals proceeded more or less in accompaniment with the British imperial retreat. With the exit of Belgium from the Congo, the long-drawn-out agony of that part of Africa affected its neighbours and sucked the United Nations into a political, tribal, and economic morass that, among other horrors, resulted in the death of the UN secretary general, Dag Hammarskjoeld, in an air disaster. A state of virtual civil war prevailed in several parts of the country.

I watched as the British Union Flag, France's "le drapeau Tricolore", and other national ensigns were lowered in several places and as fresh oblong pieces of cloth were raised bearing colours other than red, white, and blue. The ceremonies were not always flawless, but one of them offered Prince Philip the chance to crack perhaps the very best of his sometimes controversial spontaneous jokes.

It happened in Kenya; as the new flag was hauled under floodlights to the top of the flagpole at midnight, it momentarily declined to open. There was an awful, embarrassed silence from the enormous crowd. Prince Philip turned to President Jomo Kenyatta and asked him, "Changed your mind?" There was an immediate, tremendous roar of delight, and Kenya began its new existence.

There was also a flag problem on the other side of the continent, where I witnessed the former French colony of Togoland become what was then the smallest African state of Togo. I reported how it "started life at midnight as the national flag was hoisted slowly upwards to become firmly stuck at half mast in the floodlit view of thousands". I continued:

*A dignified Togo chief standing near me muttered half-seriously
as a French gunboat fired a 101-gun salute, "French sabotage."*

*A conspicuous omission from the planned proceedings was
the lowering of the Tricolour, which was to have been hauled
down as the "Marsellaise" was played. The French objected,
and this part of the day's chaotic proceedings was deleted.*

*One diplomatist among the forty foreign delegations
present explained why: "After all, we're attending a birth, not
a funeral, aren't we?"*

As ritualistic post-colonial births and imperial funerals were cere-
moniously extended into future years, I found myself still covering such
occasions but also working increasingly on major assignments for the
Sunday Telegraph. Each took weeks or months to complete, but to any
journalist worth his salt, the work was wonderfully satisfying.

The newspaper more or less gave me my head to go where I wanted
and do what I liked. Literary agents began to ask me to write books for
publishers they had lined up ready. It was a flattering prospect, but I never
had time to pursue it because I could not resist travelling and writing for
my kind -- but calculating -- employers.

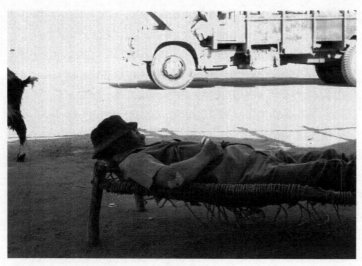

A mid-day break in the eastern Sudan in 1961, somewhere between Khartoum and Khashmel-Girba: - the destination for thousands of people losing their homes in and around Wadi Halfa, on the Nile, as their ancient town was being covered by the rising waters of the Aswan High Dam.

A rising Soviet political star in 1961, the late Leonid llyich Brezhnev, then recently appointed chairman of the Presidium of the Supreme Soviet, when I photographed him taking aim with a rifle in the Kordofan region of the Sudan at a special demonstration arranged for him by the Sudanese. He went on to rule the Soviet Union for 21 years until his death in 1982 when, as BBC Moscow Correspondent, I broadcast despatches for over 12 hours suggesting that he was dead before any official announcement was made. It was a worrying twelve hours for me.

Typing a dispatch as the BBC Africa Correspondent,
in 1978, on a Nile steamer in the Sudan.

CHAPTER 18

"Seeking the Bubble:" It Bursts

I received a stunning assignment in 1963, when I was in London between African and Middle Eastern commitments. The *Sunday Telegraph* had published a remarkable exclusive story by its communist affairs correspondent, the late David Floyd, about the great black American bass singer Paul Robeson, whose magnificent rendering of "Ol' Man River" is still recalled by millions.

He was sixty-five, ill, and in London. For many years, he had been linked with communists and left-wingers in the United States and elsewhere; and a controversy had developed over reports that he had "broken with Moscow".

Access to him had been barred, and his wife, Mrs Eslanda Robeson, had refused interviews, arguing that his views were of no political interest. This was in marked contrast to his earlier days as a campaigner for Negro rights in America and as a professed admirer of the Soviet Union. The comrades, however, were doing all they could to keep him incommunicado when I became involved.

Floyd had been tipped off that there were plans to "smuggle" Robeson out of London to somewhere behind the Iron Curtain, which was still very much in existence. On the morning when Floyd's story was published, I was asked by the *Daily Telegraph* to go to the London airport to try to find Robeson if possible and to follow up the story. I was asked to clarify what exactly his current political views were. Did he still hold opinions formerly so publicly expressed or had he lost faith?

Sure enough (just as Floyd had suggested would happen, and as Mrs

Robeson herself confirmed later as being the plan), Robeson was taken secretly to the airport, in a bubble car, with help from the Polish Embassy. He appeared from discreet shelter in a private room to board a Polish Airlines flight to East Berlin. He wore a dark suit and a grey hat and was accompanied by two women and a Polish Airlines officer carrying a copy of the *Sunday Telegraph*. One of them was Robeson's wife, and the other, also speaking with an American accent, was a friend, Mrs Hurwitt. I booked myself onto the plane and watched as the three Americans settled down into their seats in the first-class compartment and as Mrs Robeson handed the *Sunday Telegraph* to her husband to read.

Once the aircraft had taken off, I approached Mr Robeson, presenting my card and introducing myself. He smiled charmingly and seemed about to talk to me. At that point, Mrs Robeson, a couple of years older than her husband, angrily intervened and called members of the aircrew. She said, "I can disorganise the plane if necessary. No one can go near him. It is my job to keep questioners ..." She broke off and corrected herself: "I mean, it is my job to protect him."

I reported from Berlin later:

> *Mrs Robeson is a formidable "protector". She claimed: "I know judo. I learned it to keep people away from him, and I will happily kick them in the groin or break their glasses.*
>
> *"I told the crew I had thought they were friends and did not expect this, with one of the enemy aboard! They said you were a fare-paying first-class passenger and they were sorry, but you had every right to be here."*
>
> *She said she would like to "explain the situation" to me. Mr Robeson was "not up to making statements". He had been "crucified" in America. "It is worse now there under Kennedy than it was with Eisenhower or McCarthy," she stated. By this time, she was sitting beside me declaiming earnestly that in the United States, "The great Negro revolution has begun."*
>
> *On her husband's political views, she commented, "It has never been proved that he is a communist. He has always been a friend of Soviet Russia." I asked, "Is he still?" She declined to reply.*

*I asked her if she would permit me to ask him that without
causing a scene, and she declined emphatically. At the end
of the flight, she stood over me when I had at last persuaded
her to permit me to speak to Mr Robeson himself. He sat like
an effigy in his window seat and said only two things: "The
Sunday Telegraph article is vicious misrepresentation." His
wife beamed. "The turning point has come for the American
Negro people in America." His wife beamed again.*

*As soon as I tried to ask another question, she interrupted
me and beckoned me away while her husband looked on stolidly.*

*Just before I left this unique pair at the Schönefeld airport
for West Berlin, Mrs Robeson informed me that I should find
West Berlin "very Nazi".*

The *Daily Telegraph* led the front page the next day with my dispatch
from West Berlin telling the story of the flight and Mrs Robeson's determined defence of her husband. I described how Mrs Robeson had
described to me "with gusto" some "extraordinary details of the way
he was smuggled out of a south-west London nursing home a few hours
earlier to be spirited behind the Iron Curtain". She said that his strange
exit from London had been arranged with the help of the Polish ambassador and air attaché, and, as she put it, "There has been a lot of cloak and
dagger about all this."

She was not understating the case. Reaction was immediate, with the
British communist newspaper of those days, the *Daily Worker*, attacking
the *Sunday Telegraph* for making "a disgraceful exhibition" of itself and
for its "phantasmagoria of innuendo or insinuation". The *Worker* opined
that the "sincerity" of the *Telegraph*'s "alarm about the future of Paul is
somewhat suspect in view of the *Telegraph*'s hostility towards all that he
has stood for."

However, elsewhere there was a lot of favourable comment on our
scoop. Even the Socialist *New Statesman and Nation* conceded that Robeson
"did leave for East Germany in curious circumstances" and that rumours
had been published for some time that he had "broken with Moscow".
The *Statesman* concluded:

> *In all these circumstances, it seems far-fetched for Mrs Robeson to claim that her husband's views "are no longer of public interest". How can that be true of a man whose whole life has been dedicated to propaganda for a cause? Unless, that is, he is too sick to express his views.*
>
> *But that doesn't square with his alleged statements to the East German press – or for that matter with his demeanour as observed by the Daily Telegraph reporter who travelled with him to Berlin but was not allowed by Mrs Robeson to chat with him.*
>
> *I have no wish to defend press intrusion – and it may be that the Robesons have grounds for complaint. But so I think has the public. The fact is that, from whatever motive, Mrs Robeson's refusal to offer even nominal cooperation to the British press, whose interest does not seem to have been un-reasonable, has created a mountain of suspicion and mistrust out of what may have been only a molehill of gossip. She has also, I fear, unwittingly injured her husband's reputation and his life's cause.*

Even more gratifying for my employers and myself was a column in the *Catholic Herald*. It commented that the "combined op" of The Daily and Sunday Telegraphs was a fine example of "quietly finding scoops under everyone else's noses" and showed "a considerable amount of initiative". Then it went on:

> *More than that, it gave readers a fascinating insight into the way a big news story is collected – in this case, John Osman's attempt to interview Paul Robeson on the Polish jet taking him and his wife to East Germany.*
>
> *So many of the complaints laid in the lap of the Press Council involve cases of intrusion by reporters who care little for the feelings of the people they are pursuing that this pen portrait of an experienced reporter at work was doubly valuable.*
>
> *When I first tried to approach Mr Robeson …,' Osman says civilly, 'his wife called members of the crew'. Later she asked*

him angrily to return to his seat. But she could not resist the
opportunity to talk to one of the reporters who, she claimed,
have consistently misrepresented her husband, and in a matter
of minutes, she was sitting down beside Osman chattering
away non-stop.

The *Catholic Herald* said the report was "one which gave readers a rare
sight of efficient journalism at work". It concluded:

It was a good story, and although this, in itself, would not be
sufficient justification for printing it if intrusion or "yellow
press" tactics had been used to secure an interview, the signs
are that, for once, politeness paid.

David Floyd himself weighed in with a letter to the *Daily Telegraph*,
wondering why Mrs Robeson had turned to the Polish Embassy for
"cloak-and-dagger" assistance, pointing out that Robeson was free to go
anywhere he wanted. Floyd wondered what the Polish government and
the communist press of Poland would have said if they had discovered
that the British ambassador in Warsaw had engaged in similar activities
to put someone on a British aircraft leaving Poland.

Other commentators picked up the point about politicians and crusaders for a cause welcoming publicity when it suited their books but
presenting themselves as victims of intrusion when such publicity did
not suit them. One wrote: "This desire to have things both ways is, of
course, common among public figures. They want all the smooth but
none of the rough."

Floyd dropped me a nice note saying "what a wonderful job" I had
made of the Robeson story, saying, "I take my hat off to you for doing a
very tricky job so brilliantly." The foreign news editor of the *Daily Telegraph*
sent me a note that declared the following: "I want you to know how
much your efforts in the Robeson story were appreciated. Your initiative
in getting on the plane at the last moment, your persistence in pressing for
the story once on board, and your good writing at the end all added up to a
first-class effort. It paid off in the display you had in the paper, which put us
out in front of all the competition. Thank you for an excellent job of work."

As for the managing editor of the *Sunday Telegraph*, the late Brian Roberts, who had stuck his neck out by leading his front page on Floyd's inside tip, well, he wrote the following:

> My dear Osman,
>   Congratulations on your Paul Robeson story in yesterday morning's paper. It not only stood up admirably to the Sunday Telegraph exclusive, on which I had taken a large-sized gamble, but was a first-class piece in its own right.

Finally, and most satisfyingly in the material sense, I received a memo from the managing editor of the *Daily Telegraph*, Peter Eastwood, saying simply, "Mr Michael Berry (the proprietor) has approved a bonus of £20 for your good work in the Paul Robeson story last weekend." It was a useful sum in 1963.

For the moment, I was riding high, but I soon took a tumble. Off I went back to Africa, and after the publication of the slavery series, I produced major pieces for the *Sunday Telegraph* in October, November, and December.

October found me filling the front page and a whole page inside with revelations about "Corruption in the Congo Cabinet", made by a Congolese cabinet minister whose accusations against his ministerial colleagues I described as marking "a remarkable moment, even by the uninhibited standards of African politics".

Regarded by the Congolese as a "clean" minister, his allegations had an immediate effect. There was a stormy meeting of the Congolese cabinet; he was not allowed to leave the country; and he was attacked by other ministers for making "gratuitous accusations" against them and against high officials of the republic. He was accused of betraying the interests of his country and of smearing the moral integrity of his colleagues. He did not last long as a minister after that, but I shall record his name as a memorial and personal compliment to an honest African who did his best against overwhelming odds to establish decent government in his country: Alphonse Nguvulu.

He was the Minister for Labour and Social Security. His theme was simple and expressed with force:

"It is an unhappy thing," he declared, "but it must be said that corruption has been institutionalised here and people can be bought for nothing, 'pour un rien.' People have received money, packets of dollars. I have heard of one person who is buying a sixteen-room villa near Rome. Other people have received Mercedes-Benz cars, and another man is building a villa for £210,000, with ceilings made of material imported from Italy." Others, he alleged, had been given holidays in Europe.

"In Brussels, you will see buildings belonging to Congolese worth several million Belgian Francs. These have been bought by misappropriation of public funds and by trafficking in diamonds and copper. There are people who were nothing three years ago and who have suddenly blossomed into Congolese millionaires. This disgusts the public in general and the unions in particular."

Mr Nguvulu's reference to the sudden acquisition by politicians of Mercedes-Benz cars was joked about all over Africa as people talked about the birth of a new tribe known as the "Wabenzi".

His open attack on the cabinet to which he belonged came after I had been recommended by a contact in a major oil company to talk to the minister, if I could. The firm for which my source worked had been involved in negotiations for a major Congolese oil contract and had lost it at the last moment, the bid failing because of what the company was pretty sure had been a large inducement offered by a rival foreign oil company to a Congolese minister more powerful and less honest than Mr Nguvulu.

It was a murky area and the general corruption, on a massive scale, unfortunately involved the United Nations. In some ways allegations against UN officials and representatives in the Congo were echoed years later in Iraq, with accusations about profiteering from the application of oil contracts while sanctions were in force against Saddam Hussein.

In the Congo, I reported on how UN officials were themselves undermining monetary policies that the UN itself was trying to impose:

United Nations officials are involved in the general corruption. Despite the establishment of a Congolese Monetary Council by

the United Nations and its issue of banknotes in an effort to
effect financial improvement, UN officials help to subvert their
own organisation's operation.

With other, less hypocritical people, whose responsibility
is not so elevated in international terms, the UN men and
women indulge in currency exchanges which increasingly un-
dermine the Congolese franc. I saw this for myself one day when
I went with a friend to a backstreet grocer's shop to discover
the realistic, unofficial rate of the Congolese franc against the
dollar. The money changer provided francs by the thousand to
any applicant who could deposit hard cash in a bank outside
the country.

As we walked through a curtained door behind the shop's
counter into the room where transactions were made, a UN
official and his mistress walked out. 'Well, well', the official
joked to my companion, 'is this your source, too?'

The one thousand Congolese franc note issued by the
Monetary Council is known ironically as "Un Conseil". The
old one thousand franc note, still in circulation, with the head
of the King of the Belgians on it, is known as "Un Baudouin".
Such is the financial reputation of the UN that the Congolese,
when changing a "Baudouin" for a "Conseil", insist on re-
ceiving twelve hundred francs in the new money for the one
thousand francs of the old. It seems there is still more African
confidence in Brussels than in the United Nations.

This kind of reporting did not endear either the *Sunday Telegraph* or
myself to UN supporters who were reluctant to admit that the world
organisation could do anything wrong. Nevertheless, it was painfully
true. Six years later, when I arrived at the UN as the new BBC United
Nations correspondent, I came in for a good deal of ribbing from old UN
hands who recalled the newspaper reporting that had in 1963 somewhat
embarrassed the international body.

Well, that was the Congo in October. In November came the Sudan,
with the *Sunday Telegraph* again filling a couple of its pages, including
the front page, with a despatch from me in Juba, in the Southern Sudan.

There, the long-running war between the African South and the Arab North was developing.

My dispatch was trumpeted by the newspaper, accurately, as being from "the first newspaper correspondent to visit the Southern Sudan since the attempted revolt", although the "attempted revolt" turned out to be the harbinger of a much longer war to come.

From the Sudan in November, I crossed the Red Sea to more war in December in the Yemen, described already. Then, in the following year, 1964, something happened that changed my life yet again. Conflict had broken out once more between Greek Cypriots and Turkish Cypriots, just four years after Cypriot independence. The EOKA leader and former Greek Army officer, George Grivas, had arrived in the island. He was calling for a referendum on ENOSIS, union with Greece. Thousands of EOKA men emerged to parade publicly past the Cypriot president, Archbishop Makarios.

Turkish Cypriots objected; bloodshed began; and United Nations troops, including British and Canadian forces, were increasingly drawn into difficult security duties. Eventually, in a badly deteriorating situation, the Turkish Air Force attacked Greek Cypriot positions. It was something of a forerunner for the Turkish invasion of Cyprus ten years later, when, in 1974, there was a failed attempt to overthrow Makarios by a coup encouraged by the ruling military junta in Athens of the Greek colonels.

His Beatitude escaped from the conspirators and saved his own life by fleeing through a window of the presidential palace to jump into a British helicopter. It had landed on his lawn to ferry him to safety. So the archbishop who had always declined publicly to condemn many killings of British men and women was rescued by those who might easily have been on a hit list of targets for his unrebuked flock. The rescue of Makarios from his fellow Greek Cypriot would-be killers was an illustration of humane British diplomacy and armed services efficiency. For Makarios himself, perhaps, it was an unusual lesson in practical Christianity.

During this steadily escalating crisis, the Greek and Greek Cypriot authorities had been openly challenging United Nations efforts to maintain order and to control the supply of arms entering the island. Newspaper correspondents like me, as well as BBC correspondents, reported all this as faithfully as we could and inevitably made ourselves unpopular with the authorities responsible both for the import of weapons and for their failure to control the bloodshed.

In the process, the Cyprus government decided to deport a number of BBC correspondents whose reports were not appreciated. The trouble for the government was that the BBC picture of events differed often to that painted by the government; and the trouble for the BBC (then as now) was that its reports were monitored closely as they were swiftly broadcast on the BBC World Service.

The expulsion of BBC journalists outraged other journalists, including newspapermen, and as one of the latter, I became involved in compiling a petition by media representatives that we sent to organisations like the Commonwealth Press Union. This was done in the feeble hope of trying to persuade the Cyprus government to halt its policy of discouraging independent news coverage.

While this went on, yet another BBC man arrived on the island to do a stint there, the Corporation's Commonwealth Correspondent, a charming Irishman, the late Lionel Fleming. In between excursions to watch riots, skirmishes, or fights in different parts of the island between Greek Cypriots, Turkish Cypriots, and the UN, he and I were seated at the bar of the Ledra Palace Hotel one day when, to my surprise, Lionel asked me if I had ever thought of broadcasting. I had not.

He asked me if I would be interested if the BBC offered me an opening. Dearly though I loved my work with the *Daily Telegraph* and the *Sunday Telegraph*, I answered that of course I would be interested.

He and I had met previously in the Congo, where Lionel, with two American correspondents, had narrowly escaped death in the break-away Congolese province of Katanga. Events surrounding that unpleasant episode illustrated not only the tribulations encountered by journalists in the Congo but also underlined darkly comic aspects of their work that Evelyn Waugh, the author of the original satire on foreign correspondence, could not have bettered. In *Scoop*, Waugh had his fictional character "William Boot, Countryman" sent to cover a war in Africa after being removed from his normal task of editing "Lush Places", a "bi-weekly half-column devoted to nature".

Boot's counterpart in real life, twenty-five years after the first publication of *Scoop*, was one of the two American correspondents who ran into trouble, a music critic of the Baltimore Sun. He had been covering the opera season in Milan when his employers instructed him to go to the Congo. In a continent full of physical danger, the Congo was overflowing with it at that stage, but nevertheless the music critic found himself on his way to Africa for the first time (just like Boot), even though the only approach to physical danger known previously on the American journalistic music circuit had surfaced when the father of a woman singer threatened to punch the nose of a critic who had savaged his daughter's performance.

Since the singer was Margaret Truman and her father was President Harry Truman, quite a bit of publicity had been attracted to the critic himself, Paul Hume.

Anyway, unfortunate *Baltimore Sun* man Weldon Wallace, a charming but understandably worried man, found himself seated beside me on a plane from Rome headed for the Congo and chaos. He questioned me closely about things and quickly understood that I myself, with considerable experience already of Congolese mayhem, was not looking forward with any great enthusiasm to a return to the place.

As I passed on a few tips for survival, his face got longer and longer. I warned him that if he went into Katanga with an American passport, he could well run into trouble because the Americans were opposed to Katangan secession and were backing the UN.

He tried nevertheless. He teamed up with a fellow American, a broadcaster named Arthur Bonner, and with Lionel Fleming, whose Irish nationality was perhaps even more dangerous for him than their American nationality was for the Americans. This was because Irish troops were playing a direct part in the UN operations against Katanga.

Inevitably, the three men were arrested. They were stripped, roughed up, and were being led away into the bush to be shot when, miraculously, another correspondent passed by at the crucial moment: Peter Younghusband of the *Daily Mail*.

Equipped with Katangese credentials, considerable physical presence, and enormous courage, Younghusband helped persuade their captors to release the three men and accompanied the trio over the border to the safety of Northern Rhodesia (now Zambia).

Both Fleming and Bonner remained in good enough shape to be

able to write and broadcast their stories, but the music critic was in no condition to write. White, shaking, and in shock, he was sedated by a doctor summoned from a nearby copper mine, who ordered him to bed. Again Younghusband helped out, together with his colleague – and direct competitor from the *Daily Express* – John Monks.

These two "good men in Africa", one South African (Younghusband) and the other Australian (Monks), listened to Wallace muttering just before he went under from sedation that he had to write a story and file. They told him not to worry, and the critic went into a deep sleep. The two of them then composed a dispatch for him.

It began with these words: "My American passport today nearly cost me my life." Later that evening, when I myself had reached Northern Rhodesia with my eyewitness account of the killing of the Belgian women (described earlier), Younghusband and Monks showed me the dispatch they had written on the American's behalf and which they had just cabled.

The *Baltimore Sun* gave the dispatch great prominence, and it was nominated for the Pulitzer Prize for Journalism. We old Africa hands waited with breath proverbially bated to see if it would win. To the music critic's everlasting credit, though, he recounted the whole story to his employers and the Pulitzer nomination was withdrawn.

Younghusband and Monks even tried to persuade Wallace, after he had regained consciousness, that he had written the story himself and that they had merely filed it for him; but he knew he had not, and he was not to be fooled. One of the two authors of the dispatch commented regretfully that the withdrawal of the Pulitzer nomination was "a pity because that's the closest either of us ever came to winning a prize".

Because of the complications and difficulties of communication problems, correspondents on the ground in the Congo often came to ad hoc arrangements among themselves to help each other out. Younghusband, Monks, and I had arranged to provide each other with an account of whatever we saw or experienced in different areas. Thus that evening in the Edinburgh Hotel in Kitwe, a student of journalism could have witnessed journalistic brotherhood on full glorious display, with Younghusband and Monks writing their American colleague's dispatch for the *Baltimore Sun*, then writing their own *Daily Mail* and *Daily Express* dispatches, incorporating my *Daily Telegraph* account of the killing of the Belgian women; and with myself writing my own Telegraph dispatch, incorporating the joint *Mail/Express* account of the ordeal of the Americans and the Irishman.

Although competition among journalists is ever present, so often in difficult conditions, mutual support for each other emerges. Equally important in confused conditions is the possession of correct credentials: holding the right piece of paper is sometimes a matter of life or death.

This was very much the case in the Congo. To survive, a correspondent had to acquire UN accreditation, Congolese government accreditation, and Katangese accreditation. The relevant piece of paper had to be produced depending upon where you were and who was checking it. It was all too easy to produce the wrong piece of paper, a mistake that might be fatal. Thus many of us kept passes which we thought would not be required at the next control post in our shoes under our heels, to be taken out for use only when we anticipated necessity for their production.

Lionel Fleming and I recalled with satisfaction and relief our survival of various journalistic antics in the Congo as we sat a year later in the Cyprus bar, itself a scene of correspondents' camaraderie and competition.

It was in this very bar, for instance, that Donald Wise, one of the more flamboyant foreign correspondents ever to roam the world, told me one morning how, the evening before, he had poured a pint of beer over the head of Randolph Churchill, son of Sir Winston. As a result, he was being offered a job with the *Daily Mirror* at twice whatever salary he was then earning with the *Daily Express*.

Randolph had flown to Cyprus to write some pieces for the *Evening Standard*, which, like the *Express* of those days, was part of the Beaverbrook group. Donald, as the Beaverbrook man in Cyprus, gave a party in his Nicosia apartment for Randolph, who, rather the worse for wear, began to insult Donald's other guests.

Donald warned him to behave himself or be asked to leave. Randolph took no notice, so Donald "doused the soused" with beer and kicked him out. One of the other guests was the political editor of the *Daily Mirror* at that time, Sydney Jacobson (later Lord Jacobson). He watched and enjoyed Donald's performance; recommended Donald to great powers at the *Mirror* like Hugh Cudlipp and Cecil King; and Donald left the *Express*, where he was earning fifteen hundred pounds a year, for the *Mirror*, earning three thousand pounds.

Financial calculations came into my own head when Lionel sounded me in the Ledra Palace bar on the possibility of quitting Fleet Street to join the BBC.

He explained that he would be retiring the following year; that he had followed my work for some time; that he thought I might make a reasonable broadcaster; and that he would put in a good word for me with his BBC bosses as a possible successor to him if I was at all interested. He stressed that of course he could not promise me anything. Would I let him know?

Aged thirty-four, I had never even thought of leaving the *Daily Telegraph* until that moment. I considered the idea overnight and decided that looking ahead, there were only two jobs on the newspaper that might interest me in the long term (diplomatic correspondent or defence correspondent). Those jobs were both occupied by able journalists who had plenty of years of work in them yet, so I asked myself, Why not at least think of doing something else?

I indicated as much to Lionel the next day and forgot all about it. Months later, I was invited to meet the BBC foreign news editor, who informed me that Lionel's job would be advertised in a few months and that I would be among those invited to apply for it. In effect, I was being put onto a short list.

At about this time, the bubble of my own burgeoning reputation was pricked and sharply deflated. The thorn was provided by legal action brought against the *Daily Telegraph* after a row over a front-page piece that I had written following an abortive military coup in Tanganyika (not yet Tanzania) against the late President Julius Nyerere.

The kerfuffle implicated the Tanganyikan minister for foreign affairs and defence, Mr Oscar Kambona, who, it had been suggested to me, was "undoubtedly the chief communist spearhead operator in East Africa". This was the phrase employed by my informant on the story, which I attributed directly and accurately to him. I described him as "an author-itative intelligence source" and as "a man with a deep knowledge of East Africa". This was entirely accurate, but the trouble was that the source himself appeared to have got it wrong.

Questions were posed in Parliament, with Denis Healey (later Lord Healey) asking "by what authority a government intelligence officer" had given me the interview. The prime minister, Sir Alec Douglas-Home, replied that no authority had been given to a government intelligence officer to talk to me (and nor had I claimed that this was so).

A Tory MP said that the article had gone a long way to enlighten the public on the communist menace in Africa and asked if there was not "every merit in the public being made fully aware" of it.

Meanwhile, Mr Kambona began libel proceedings, and the upshot was that the *Daily Telegraph* published an apology and explained: "We published the report in good faith believing it to come from a reliable and responsible source, but we are now satisfied that the statements we published were untrue."

"We desire to express to Mr Kambona our sincere apology for having published them, and we have agreed to pay him an appropriate sum of damages and his costs."

I had egg spattered all over my face, but I was saved from being further boiled and scrambled by my excellent gentlemanly source. Immediately the row broke the *Daily Telegraph*, through me, asked the source if he would be prepared to go into a witness box in our defence. He was unable to do that, but he welcomed a chance to explain things further, coming into the *Daily Telegraph* office to join me in a talk with the proprietor, Lord Hartwell (then the Honourable Michael Berry, the same man who had dished out to me not long before the twenty-pound bonus on the Paul Robeson story).

The proprietor accepted that there was a lot in what the source had passed on to me and a lot in what I had written, but that, between us, the pudding had been over-egged.

Except for Lord Healey and me, those participating in the affair are now dead: Oscar Kambona, Michael Berry, Alec Douglas-Home, and my source. He had been, in fact, Kenya's last British minister of defence.

Such a source then was not actually a British government intelligence officer, so the prime minister had been quite correct in telling Denis Healey that no authority had been given to such an officer. He was, however, as Kenya's defence minister, on an important intelligence body established by Britain: the East African Intelligence Committee, formed jointly between the governing authorities in Tanganyika, Uganda, and Kenya. The committee met regularly, but the Tanganyikan minister responsible for defence, Oscar Kambona, never attended any of the meetings, leading my source to tell me: "He always gave some excuse. His position was always suspect as a result."

The things that a journalist gets wrong are remembered quite as much as, if not more than, the things he gets right. That is why, when I was a junior reporter learning my job on provincial weekly, evening, and morning newspapers, there was usually on prominent display in the newsroom admonitory lines from "The Rubaiyat of Omar Khayyam":

> *The moving finger writes; and, having writ,*
> *Moves on: nor all they piety nor wit*
> *Shall lure it back to cancel half a line,*
> *Nor all they tears wash out a word of it.*

It would not be a bad idea, I think, if the same lines were on display in offices and newsrooms of broadcasting organisations these days, including those of the BBC. I think especially of the Hutton Report, criticising the corporation's journalism, and also of the somewhat dubious journalism displayed by the corporation during the horrible saga involving the late Jimmy Savile and the *Newsnight* programme.

Anyhow, regarding myself as a journalistic sinner after landing my newspaper in a libel action, I was reminded of my sin a quarter of a century later at a farewell party given for me at the Foreign Office upon my retirement as BBC diplomatic correspondent.

My host, the foreign secretary at the time, Sir Geoffrey Howe (now Lord Howe), joked that he believed there was "still an orphanage in Dar-es-Salaam built on funds from a certain libel action". It produced a good laugh and proved that diplomatists possess long memories.

Three pictures of the war in the Southern Sudan (still cruelly
afflicted by bloodshed despite its recent independence)
when, in 1963, I reported the start of conflict there.

Continued from Page One

CONGO BRIBERY

position is "handicapped by his entourage, certain people among whom are constantly fiddling and After a stormy Cabinet meeting, which took place immediately after my interview, a statement MR. NGUVULU, Congolese Minister of Labour, talking with John Osman, Special Correspondent of THE SUNDAY TELEGRAPH. On the wall is a portrait of President Kasavubu.

The Congolese Minister for Labour and Social Security, Alphonse Nguvulu, who did not last long in office after he gave me an interview accusing his cabinet collegues of colossal corruption soon after Congolese independence.

Three pictures of our shot-up hired car in the Congo in December 1961 in the fighting between the breakaway republic of Katanga and the United Nations. The pictures show the late John ("Jack") Starr of the "Daily Mail" peering through the bullet-damaged windscreen and looking at the bullet-stricken door; and the late John Bulloch of "The Daily Telegraph" holding open the damaged door.

Peter Younghusband of the "Daily Mail" and myself in Manono, Katanga,
in the Congo, at the time when he saved from death three of his colleagues,
(two American correspondents and an Irish correspondent), when they
were being led away to be shot. Younghusband was the co-author with
John Monks of the "Daily Express" of a dispatch for the correspondent
of the "Baltimore Sun" that was about to be nominated for the Pulitzer
prize for Journalism after they'd written it for him while he lay under
heavy sedation following his rescue. The nomination was withdrawn
when the American journalist told his employers what had happened.

CHAPTER 19

"Seeking the Bubble": It Floats Again – In America

If a major unfinished story of our times is the struggle against international terrorism, the greatest blow struck by terrorism in America has
been undoubtedly that of 11 September 2001 against the World Trade
Centre in New York. It has become known, because of the terminology of
the American calendar, as "9/11". That mass murder of innocent civilians
not only shocked America and the world; it helped to lead to whatever is
now going on in Iraq, Afghanistan, and elsewhere.

Well, as long as forty-five years ago, a New Yorker predicted the
horror of the blow. His prophecy was offered to me shortly after I arrived
in that city in 1969 to assume my first overseas posting for the BBC as
its United Nations correspondent, after five years as its Commonwealth
correspondent.

There had been a series of minor explosions in the city, and as I
reported for the Radio 4 programme *From Our Own Correspondent*, an
immediate indicator of the effect on New Yorkers was plain and direct:
bomb scares, evacuation of premises, and extra security precautions all
over the place. Then, in a prophetic comment in view of what happened
later in 2001, I reported the following:

> *The psychological impact of the bombings has been much
> greater than the physical damage. A remark made to me by
> one perceptive office evacuee who stood chatting to me on the
> pavement in Park Avenue was that 'all these revolutionary nuts*

*have read the classic terrorist handbooks, and if their tactics
have worked in jungles and wild places, they'll certainly work
in overcrowded cities.'*

*He was making a very telling point, for if a bomb should go
off in the packed anthill of a New York skyscraper by design or
by accident when people are actually working there, the vision
conjured up is quite horrible. So far, it hasn't happened, but
what's worrying everybody is that it might.*

The comments of that "office evacuee" were broadcast in 1970, and, of course, the reality of what happened thirty-one years later was even worse than the "quite horrible" vision conjured up. Another evacuee from the earlier minor bombings episode marked my arrival with a sardonic New Yorker kind of quip: "Welcome to Fun City and check who your apartment neighbour may be. He could be a capitalist!"

Although I had left Africa (and a good deal of terrorism there) behind me for two or three years, I nevertheless soon found myself reporting, in America, yet more murders and more problems with a distinctly African aspect, involving Americans of African descent as well as white.

My first assignment, in fact, in the United States was in Atlanta, Georgia, covering the funeral of Martin Luther King after his assassination. I accompanied his funeral procession and, in the same year, attended another funeral ceremony, in Arlington Cemetery, of yet another murder victim, Senator Robert Kennedy, brother of the assassinated President John Kennedy.

Another early assignment for me in America involving somebody's unnatural death was reporting the inquest in 1969 into the demise of Mary Jo Kopechne at Chappaquiddick, on the island of Martha's Vineyard, offshore from the state of Massachusetts. She had drowned there as the result of a car accident in which the brother of John and Bobby Kennedy, Senator Edward Kennedy, was involved.

Although he remained a United States senator, that accident finished any chances he might have thought he had of becoming a United States president.

When I got to the snow-covered beauty of Martha's Vineyard with many other journalists, I quickly discovered that a rotund elderly reporter from the *New York Times* had (as we used to say) "got the place sewn up". He knew everybody, and everybody knew him: the coroner, the police chief, the politicians, the local councillors and church officials, TV and radio representatives, and other American newspaper people.

To this list of Americans should be added foreign journalists such as myself, to whom Homer Bigart was something of an exemplar: a figure today who would be described as a role model. Back in the early days of the 1950s, he had covered with distinction the Korean War and had won the Pulitzer Prize for Journalism, not once but twice.

He was an admirer of the BBC, and I was fortunate as a newcomer to the States to be taken under his wing and helped by him. He did this not only at Chappaquiddick but later at Fort Benning, in Georgia, where once again we found ourselves covering yet another kind of legal proceeding: the court martial of Lieutenant Calley, the officer involved in the notorious My Lai incident in Vietnam in 1968, when several hundred inhabitants of the village were killed by United States troops.

If Homer admired the BBC, I admired him. I was, however, unwise and immature enough to ask him at Chappaquiddick how it was that he, an internationally known war correspondent, found himself covering a mere inquest.

He quickly put me right, explaining that what was going on in Martha's Vineyard was the top story in American politics and, given the power of the Kennedy family, was likely to remain so for many years to come. This was borne out ten years later, when, in 1979, memories of Chappaquiddick caused the withdrawal of Teddy Kennedy's presidential nomination.

Homer boasted to me that he was proud of the fact that throughout his long and distinguished career, he had never declined a reporting assignment, a reminder of the versatility required from a true top reporter. It was a reminder, too, for me, of a historic memo that for long was preserved in Fleet Street and which had been addressed to George Augustus Sala, a famous Victorian journalist. It read as follows: "Please write a leading article this morning on the price of potatoes in Covent Garden and proceed this afternoon to report the coronation of the tsar of the Russian Empire in St. Petersburg."

Having reminded me of the essential truth that a reporter is never more important than his assignment, Homer then delivered himself of the observation to be found at the front of this book: "We all start off as young, unknown reporters, and we all end up as old, unknown reporters."

Versatile though a professional reporter has to be, certain kinds of assignment are inevitably more enjoyable than others are. My least favourite kinds of assignment were about show business and publicity-driven events involving awards for writing books or for producing so-called works of art. My idea of journalistic hell is to be condemned to report for eternity contests such as those for the Turner Prize or the Booker Prize. I love the theatre, opera, reading, classical music, old-fashioned jazz, and occasionally a good film; but I simply detest hyped-up events such as, say, the Oscar Awards ceremony.

On the only occasion on which I was called upon to cover that event, which was in Los Angeles, I made such an indifferent job of it that, happily for me, I was never asked again to try my hand at it.

I had originally gone to Los Angeles to report on a crisis involving Rolls-Royce, threatened with bankruptcy, and Lockheed, the huge American aircraft manufacturers who were buying Rolls-Royce engines. After I had completed that assignment, an earthquake struck the area and, I reported that too. It had been a tiring few days, culminating in filming the wreckage of buildings and of human beings. I was about to head gratefully for bed when the *Today* programme asked me to report the Oscars ceremony that evening for the programme.

Even though I had been given no time to do any homework, it was difficult to decline the task. I had no idea who was involved – which actors, producers, and so on – and I had even less idea of the contestants' films. I found it hard to take the whole razzamatazz seriously, and the result was predictable. I was, as one of my editors told me, "absolutely awful".

Other types of assignment involving less-obviously hyped show business events I quite enjoyed, however, and my coverage of them was well received both by my editors and producers as well as by listeners and viewers. I think, for example, of amusing encounters with Mickey Mouse, Donald Duck, and other Disney characters at the opening of Disney World in Orlando, Florida, or of an auction by the MGM studios of garments worn by famous stars, such as the dancing shoes worn by

Judy Garland in *The Wizard of Oz* and an old hat and raincoat worn by Humphrey Bogart.

Perhaps the most enjoyable of all the "light" stories that I did in the United States, though, was the opening of the former London Bridge at Lake Havasu City, near Phoenix, in Arizona. An enterprising American millionaire had purchased the bridge, and it had been exported to America, where it was laboriously rebuilt, stone by stone, with the encouragement and participation of the city of London.

I began my TV report from Arizona by stopping a red London bus at a bus stop in the desert next to a large cactus and asking for London Bridge. I ended it by hailing a London taxi on the bridge itself, to be driven off into the Arizona desert again.

At the time, some tabloid newspapers suggested that the millionaire had purchased the old bridge by mistake, thinking it was Tower Bridge that he was buying. This, however, was far from the truth. He knew precisely what he was after and how he was going to make money out of it. When the bridge was re-erected in Arizona, thousands of tons of stone were removed from its interior, beneath the bridge road surface, and the empty space was turned into a museum and show gallery.

The stone thus extracted was cut into souvenirs for sale, ranging from large fireplaces to small ashtrays and chess sets. A certificate signed by the Lord Mayor of London accompanied each item sold, vouching for its authenticity as a piece of Portland stone which had once been part of London Bridge. The souvenirs sold like hotcakes.

Offbeat news like this provided a pleasant change now and again from covering serious news. The two biggest international news stories I reported during my two or three years in the United States were the Nixon decision to establish links with China and his decision to end the fixed link between gold and the United States dollar.

Even with heavyweight news, however, it was possible sometimes to strike a less-than-serious note.

Nixon had employed Henry Kissinger to arrange his historic presidential trip to China by sending him on a secret exploratory mission to set it up. The Russians, as suspicious about their huge Chinese neighbour as they always were about America, were concerned. They watched closely everything Kissinger was doing.

In 1972, for instance, this is what I broadcast from Washington about Kissinger, then President Nixon's national security adviser:

> *Down in the basement of the West Wing of the White House is Dr Kissinger's office. In it, there are two minor bits of clutter which underline the importance of both the man and the job. One is a rather elderly globe of the world with a notice on it saying, "Do not touch – fragile." It's a thought which most of us hope the President's National Security Adviser always keeps in mind.*
>
> *And the other object is a photograph which Kissinger had admired at a Russian exhibition. On the back, and this time the writing is for the man perhaps more than the job, is a message from Mr Dobrynin, the Russian ambassador here. "Henry," it says, "don't be too serious. Take it easy. Relax."*
>
> *Kissinger does, in fact, relax. The press celebrate him endlessly as "the secret swinger of the White House" or "the Playboy of the West Wing". As one of his women friends understandingly puts it, "If you're with Golda Meir all day, you don't need Indira Gandhi all night."*

Even with difficult economic and financial news, like the abandonment in 1971 of the fixed link between the dollar and gold, I found it possible to get in a light touch. The announcement came on a Sunday night, and it shook the world's economists and markets on Monday morning. It was in effect the abandonment of the twenty-seven-year-old Bretton Woods economic system, set up in 1944 at an international conference, to stabilize world currencies and establish credit for international trade in the post-war years. Forty-four nations, including the United States and Great Britain, had then agreed to fix exchange rates for members in terms of gold and the dollar.

The rate set was, for all of that time, at thirty-five dollars for an ounce of gold. That ended when Nixon disconnected the two, leading to the introduction of floating exchange rates.

I reported on Radio 4:

Most Americans are painfully picking their way through all the technical jargon associated with the dollar crisis. From all accounts, the leaders who made the decisions were also pretty perplexed. One story going the rounds, and not denied, is that after the vital planning session at the President's mountain retreat in Maryland, a lot of tired men gathered at dinner to let off steam. "After this," one of them said, "everybody here should get a PhD in economics."

"Yes," came back a reply, "and everybody who already has one should turn theirs in."

The complexity of the 1971 economic development prompted BBC TV News to ask me to address myself in a satellite TV report answering this question: "Has Nixon devalued the dollar?" Not being much of an economist, I was reluctant to commit myself to any judgement confirming that this was precisely what he had just done, especially since Ron Ziegler, Nixon's press secretary, had gone out of his way at a briefing on Sunday night to emphasise to us that the dollar was not, repeat *not*, being "devalued" but was simply being "set free".

Fortunately, the *Wall Street Journal* came to my aid. I reported accurately to the camera and the watching millions the White House assurance that this policy move did not mean dollar devaluation. Then I unfurled to the camera the front page of the *Wall Street Journal* so that viewers could read it, and I continued, equally accurately, to say that the headline produced by the Voice of High Finance and Capitalism was "Nixon devalues dollar".

Since the price of gold now (in 2014) has reached well over one thousand dollars an ounce, compared with the previously fixed rate forty-two years earlier of thirty-five dollars an ounce, I suppose that the *Wall Street Journal* was, in the long run anyway, more reliable than the White House.

TV News was delighted to such an extent with my *Wall Street Journal* flourish that it wanted a follow-up in the shape of an interview with the director of the International Monetary Fund, which had been established by the Bretton Woods system together with the World Bank. These two organisations are still in operation, even though the monetary system itself has changed.

The trouble for me at the time, though, was that the subject was overly complex for a journalist not versed in economics other than those required in compiling his expenses. I simply did not know what questions to ask.

Again, help was at hand. The economics editor of the BBC at the time, the late Dominic Harrod, compiled a list of questions for me, all of which I put to the IMF boss. He answered them to everyone's apparent satisfaction.

It was, though, the only interview I conducted in a lifetime of reporting in which I did not understand the questions I was putting, let alone the answers received.

Difficulties of a different kind arose when, in 1972, the programme *From Our Own Correspondent* asked me to produce a piece on the influence of the pro-Israeli lobby in American politics, a subject of enduring and contemporary interest. It is also one that nearly always leads to any journalist trying to tackle it dispassionately to be accused of pro-Arab bias.

So it turned out after my own broadcast, although the BBC staunchly defended me and accusations levelled against me faded away. Since the issue remains with us as acutely as ever, I think perhaps it is worth repeating here the essence of what I said, although allowance should be made concerning any figures mentioned in 1972. They have changed: among other things, for example, I believe that many more Arabs now live in the United States than did so at that time.

The piece was reprinted in the now-extinct BBC magazine the *Listener*, under the heading "Wearing the Yarmulka":

WASHINGTON: As every Arab knows, twice as many Jews live in the United States as in Israel, and – as most Arabs think – Israel's greatest protector is the United States.

This, they feel, has been the case ever since Harry Truman, way back in the forties, made a bid for the Jewish vote in New York and asked, in the most hard-headed way, how many Arab votes were there in Manhattan.

This happened well before I came to this part of the world, and I gather that the Truman quotation has since been argued over. Nevertheless pretty well every educated Arab I've spoken to, either here or in the Middle East, believes it. Many of them honestly believe that the government of the United States is essentially in the Israeli pocket.

Well, any American will tell you that this simply isn't true, and Israeli lobbyists here feel that the opposite is the case: they say it's vital for them to work all the time against the allegedly pro-Arab bias of State Department professionals as well as against the mighty American oil industry with its Arabian links.

One thing is certain: the astonishing success of the Jewish community in this country in raising funds and sympathy for Israel. There is a substantial case for arguing that Jews in America, only 3 per cent of the population, constitute the most powerful minority in the world. Their influence on American politics is generally acknowledged to be out of all proportion to their numbers.

They are among the major financiers of the political parties, especially the Democrats, just as they are major backers of the State of Israel itself. Their donations last year for Israel and Israeli institutions totalled 600 million dollars – an average of 100 dollars a head for every man, woman and child who's Jewish American. This is impressive proof of dedication and hard cash; it's therefore no surprise that American politicians admire it as well as understand the leverage which such efficiency brings to bear.

So, one gets the sort of comment from the Florida Primary recently when, in wooing Jewish voters in Miami, one Presidential hopeful was said to look as if he didn't want to be in the White House so much as in the Knesset, Israel's parliament.

And from the days of Lyndon Johnson's Presidency, a story recently published in the Washington Post ... illustrates the importance of Jewish support in a highly Johnsonian way. It *tells how Supreme Court Justice Abe Fortas was photographed in the yarmulka, the Jewish skullcap, and the picture was sent to LBJ from his Jewish Affairs Adviser, Harry McPherson, together with a note suggesting that not enough political mileage was being got by the President from that sort of thing.*

"Listen, Harry," was Johnson's answer, "I've had that little hat on more times than Abe has."

One way or another, then, it's easy to appreciate why, in the opening months of this Election Year, Presidential contenders have all displayed such concern for Israel. Mr Nixon has agreed to sell the Israelis more warplanes, and he's authorised a $50 million loan to help house Soviet emigrants to Israel. Similarly, his opponents, Senators Edmund Muskie and 'Scoop' Jackson, have introduced bills to provide American money to help resettle Russian Jews. On a different tack, Senator Hubert Humphrey proposes that the United States should formally recognise Jerusalem as the Israeli capital.

All in all, it's not difficult to understand why Arab Ambassadors in this capital sometimes have a look about them of bewilderment, if not of despair.

Reaction to my broadcast quickly followed, and the *Listener* published a letter from Rosella Piazza, writing from Koch, Missouri:

Mr Osman's "Wearing the Yarmulka" is a bit disquieting. It seems we have heard such comments before, and they led to things of which I am sure he would disapprove.

In his memoirs, Albert Speer mentions that he was in part influenced in joining the Nazis by his belief that the Jews had a disproportionate influence on the cultural life of Germany. The argument is an old one indeed, and in a great many instances preceded the overt acts of persecution. A "climate of opinion" is first created: the pogroms and the extermination camps come after.

Factually, Mr Osman is not altogether veridical. He would lead one to believe that the Jews in America have the

US Government in their collective vest pocket. This is simply
not so. Nor is it true that the Arabs have no friends in the US.
Our State Department, influential Senators (Fulbright, for
one), and the oil industry are all quite pro-Arab. Perhaps it is
also germane to mention that the Arabs have received far more
military and other aid from the communist world than all the
combined aid that Israel has received from our Government and
from American Jews.

But assuming that Mr Osman's article were factually
impeccable, it would still leave me with a 'So what?' Should
minorities refuse to exercise whatever political leverage they
may have? He leaves the impression that the help that American
Jews give to Israel is somehow lacking in propriety. I happen to
be non-Jewish, but I have not forgotten the abuse and cruelty
perpetrated by my 'Christian' brethren against the Jews, most
particularly in recent memory.

The world forgets too easily, and even men of good will, as
Mr Osman very probably is, lend themselves to stoking the fires
for the next holocaust."

Phew! "Stoking the fires for the next holocaust", eh? – because I was examining as honestly as possible, as requested by my employers, the influence and activities of pro-Israelis in America.

What's more, I was accused of being "factually" not altogether "veridical", which means "truthful or coinciding with reality". Nowhere did my assailant, however, inform me of where my facts were wrong.

Still, I shrugged my shoulders and decided not to respond, especially when I noted, with satisfaction, the following note printed beneath Rosella Piazza's attack:

We have received other letters which also seek to establish a
connection between John Osman's account of pro-Israeli in-
terest groups in American politics and the Nazi death camps.
Readers who wish to study Mr Osman's article will see that
there are no grounds for doing so.

Editor, Listener

Despite the undoubted influence of pro-Israeli groups in American politics, I was astonished when I was posted from New York to Washington to find that fellow Americans discriminated against American Jews. My wife and I had set up home in a charming, colonial-style house in Bethesda, Maryland, where our neighbours welcomed us and invited us to join a local tennis club.

There we discovered that Jews were unwelcome as members. We also discovered, when we gave a house-warming party to which we invited three or four sets of neighbours, that a family of American Jews who were our immediate neighbours had never before met any of the others.

From the expressions of surprise that we received from those others when all met in our house, we concluded that it was unusual for non-Jewish Americans in our district to mix with Jewish Americans. Virginia and I were apparently breaking down some sort of barrier against Jews in the district.

Anyhow, for the rest of the couple of years or more that we lived in Maryland, we all happily mixed together occasionally, either in our house or in the home of one or other of our neighbours. I like to think that Virginia and I made our little contribution towards breaking down a kind of unwritten "apartheid" separating Jews from non-Jews in that particular small corner of the United States of America.

Statutory "apartheid" itself, of the South African variety, was of course already familiar to me; but just a couple of years after my 1972 broadcast that had so upset Rosella Piazza, I was interested to learn even more about apartheid and about the vigour of South African Jewish support for Israel: greater in "per capita" terms than American Jewish support.

I had been reposted to Africa, and upon my return there, the programme *From Our Own Correspondent* once again asked me to report on the extent of the influence of pro-Israeli groups, but this time in South Africa, not in the United States.

The assignment followed the Yom Kippur War, when many South African Jews dug into their pockets to support Israel and many South African Jews went off as volunteers to fight for Israel. I was helped in my inquiries by the secretary of the South African Board of Jewish Deputies, who informed me that, man for man and woman for woman, South African Jews contributed even more per head towards Israel than American Jews did.

When we got around to talking about race policies, Hitler, the Holocaust, and apartheid, he referred me to the *Encyclopaedia Judaica*, and what I found there was fascinating. There was round condemnation of apartheid as the sort of thinking that led to Nazi concentration camps and mass extermination. At the same time, however, acknowledgment was expressed that because of apartheid, the general sense of South African Jewishness had been strengthened and encouraged rather than weakened and discouraged. This reminded me forcibly of the old claim that nothing encourages the Church more than vigorous oppression of Christians.

Anyhow, I warmed to my helpful Jewish official informant because he laughed uproariously at my script of the *From Our Own Correspondent* broadcast, which I had sent to him later, as promised. His laughter was in response to a closing quip that I allowed myself.

This was to point out that devout Jews and certain devout Old Testament–style Afrikaners both believed themselves to be the one chosen people of God, so at least one of them had to be wrong.

Joking about religion is always fraught with danger, of course, for a writer or broadcaster, but that is no reason for a writer or broadcaster to be frightened away from a touch of irreverence. Although I might well be doubtful of, or even opposed to, the beliefs of a person, I would not necessarily condemn that person for the beliefs held.

Nor would I mock God (after all, God may exist). Wary though I am about being blasphemous, I strongly believe that a little mockery aimed at religious organisations and at the representatives of such organisations probably does them nothing but good, in just the same way that a little mockery helps to remind all organisations and all of us that we are but human and fallible.

Most critics attacking me over the years have done so in published letters, such as that quoted from Rosella Piazza. The American senator mentioned by her, the late J. William Fulbright, was, when I met him, the chairman of the Senate Foreign Relations Committee. As such, he was without doubt, as she accurately commented, one of the most "influential" people in American politics.

He was also one of the most interesting examples I ever came across personally of the deliberate duplicity it required to be a successful politician in the United States. He became noted for his criticism of the

Vietnam War, but in addition to that, he had also been admired by many for his effort to produce a basis for peace between Israel and the Arabs. He was an outstandingly liberal and constructive influence in international affairs. Who has not heard, for example, of the international "Fulbright Scholarships"?

Yet when I went into his office in Washington, I was stunned by the coarseness of his Arkansas election literature. This presented him as "Bill" Fulbright, a sort of "redneck" backwoodsman, with the emphasis placed heavily on local issues, with no reference to his international reputation. When I raised the point with him, he just laughed and explained that his image in Arkansas had to be different to his image at the United Nations.

It reminded me of a meeting I had experienced a few years earlier with Dr Hildegard Muller, foreign minister in John Vorster's South African government. Dr Muller was a gentlemanly former Rhodes scholar and was striving hard to present South Africa as something other than a pariah state when he received me in Pretoria soon after I had become the BBC Commonwealth Correspondent. It was a strictly off-the-record briefing on South African policies.

He began our chat by swearing me to absolute secrecy because, he explained, if the Afrikaner electorate in his constituency even suspected that he had been talking to a man from the hated BBC, he would be out on his neck at the next election.

Politicians really are extraordinary people. So are secret agents. Not long after I had arrived in Washington, I was present at a big official dinner for something or other and the guest sitting next to me gave me his visiting card. It bore upon it the badge of the US Secret Service and his name and position: "Assistant Director, US Secret Service".

The card also had on it his office address and telephone number. I have often asked myself: in what country in the world other than the United States could such an open introduction of himself have been made by an assistant director of a secret service to a newly arrived foreign correspondent? Such a thing has certainly not happened to me anywhere else, although I have met a few spies in my time, including the late "Kim" Philby, granted Soviet citizenship when he disappeared behind the Iron Curtain in 1963.

By the time I bumped into him, in the late 1950s in the Middle East, while he was working for the *Observer* and for the *Economist*, he was most certainly not going round like the American officer, handing out visiting cards printed by his employers (from either the KGB or the British Secret Intelligence Service, for both of which services he worked; with Philby even now – still, in these days – being described in reputable encyclopaedias not as a "traitor" but as a "double agent").

However, at the stage when I met him, Philby had acquired a specific American connection in the shape of his third wife, Eleanor, formerly married to Sam Pope Brewer of the *New York Times*.

Sam and Philby had first met in Spain during the Spanish Civil War, when both were correspondents and when Sam already thought that Philby was working for British intelligence. Eleanor acquired a divorce from Sam in Mexico in 1958; Philby married her; they lived together in Beirut; and she became estranged from him when he fled to Moscow.

Poor Sam seemed to me never to have recovered from the blow of losing his wife to the most notorious British traitor of the twentieth century (to whom a memorial was recently, in 2010, unveiled in Russia). When Sam (still with the *New York Times*) and I worked as colleagues at the United Nations, he seemed to me a sad and broken-looking man. As for Philby, he always appeared to me much as he did to many who met him in those days in the Middle East: a more or less charming drunk with the label already attached to him of being the "Third Man" of the Guy Burgess-Donald Maclean-"Kim" Philby trio.

Apart from the assistant director of the United States Secret Service and Senator Fulbright, other prominent Americans I enjoyed meeting during my years in America included the former vice president, Senator Hubert Humphrey, the Democrats' unsuccessful candidate against Richard Nixon in 1968; Henry Kissinger, Nixon's national security adviser and later secretary of state; Senator George McGovern, the Democrats' unsuccessful candidate against Nixon in 1972; and Milton Friedman, the monetarist "guru" and winner of the 1976 Nobel Prize for Economics. Much later, in my final years as BBC diplomatic correspondent, I had also the immense pleasure of meeting and shaking hands with President Reagan when he gave a state banquet for the British prime minister, Mrs Thatcher.

One prominent American I did not enjoy meeting, principally

because she amazed – and indeed almost shocked me with her strident views! – was militant feminist leader Betty Friedan. Now, I suppose, she has become accepted as being, like Germaine Greer, more or less a member of The Establishment.

The most memorable encounter of all for me, though, in America, was with the late Dean Acheson, President Harry Truman's secretary of state and formulator of the post-war "Truman Doctrine", under which countries threatened with communist interference were provided with economic and military aid.

Acheson also helped to shape the Marshall Plan, after the 1939–45 War, to help put Europe back on its feet; and he promoted the establishment of the North Atlantic Treaty Organisation, NATO, that has preserved Western freedom for most of my lifetime.

However, he is chiefly remembered in Great Britain these days for his percipient and entirely correct summary of our national quandary, a succinct analysis that he offered in a speech at the West Point Military Academy in 1962: "Great Britain has lost an empire and has not yet found a role."

The occasion of our meeting was a relaxed luncheon at which I entertained him, together with his wife and mine, in one of the smartest Washington restaurants of the early 1970s, Le Provencal. (I wonder if it is still there.)

It was conveniently close to the BBC office in the CBS Washington building, and I had been assigned the delightful duty of acting as his host before the private screening of a film that the BBC had made about Acheson's career and his life.

Our lunch continued for three hours or more (an extremely unusual event in the United States!), and he talked amusingly and uninhibitedly about many of the great men he had dealt with: Truman, Churchill, de Gaulle, and John Kennedy, to name only a few.

He was the kind of American who embodied in his civilised way a complete answer to all those critics of the United States who lump American politicians together as being stupid and crude. In my experience, they are no more so than politicians anywhere else; and the best of them are as good as, if not better than, many of their foreign critics.

It is not just controversial American policies that really motivate the resentment of anti-Americans but jealousy (as well as fear) of American power. Nowhere have I noticed this more than in the two countries where today I live most of the time: in France and in my own country, the one that has "not yet found a role".

Two pictures of the former American Vice-President, Senator Hubert Humphrey, on his campaign plane during the 1972 California contest for the Democrats' presidential nomination. Humphrey was defeated in the nomination battle by Senator George McGovern but McGovern was defeated by Richard Nixon in the presidential election.

CHAPTER 20

The "Floating Bubble Reputation": Aloft Again

Starting a fresh job in 1965, trying to build a new reputation as a broadcaster, required new skills for writing and presenting news both on TV and on radio. On the radio side, I first spent days working in a studio with an experienced newsreader who, like others then, had earlier been an actor. He got me to read in the studio a script I myself had written and then played back the recording for me to hear. I thought it did not sound too bad.

Then he took the same script, *my* script, into the studio so that I could hear him read it. This was humbling because he illustrated precisely how a professional presenter could broadcast *my* scripts a great deal better than I myself could. He then gave me many tips that I took to heart and applied for the rest of my broadcasting career.

After that came an attachment to TV News, learning to produce a bulletin piece spoken to camera of, say, 150 words, requiring just under a minute of screen time. Then came the craft of writing to pictures, at an average of three words a second spoken over a piece of timed film. The course included exercises in handling and presenting film so as not to produce a distorted perspective of the news, for alas, in the hands of an incompetent TV journalist – or a skilled propagandist – one picture alone can all too easily be deployed to distort the truth.

The simplest of examples that I remember among several which we trainee TV correspondents were given to handle consisted of dealing with three different film versions of a large demonstration in Trafalgar Square. One piece of film, a long shot, showed a vast crowd of peaceful demonstrators with nothing out of the ordinary happening. A second piece of film, a medium-distance shot, showed a similar crowd with a scuffle going on at one spot. A third, a close-up shot, showed a couple of faces in anger and blows being exchanged, so producing an overwhelming image of violence that the demonstration itself did not produce. What piece of film should be used and what sort of words should accompany it to convey the truth about the demonstration?

Wordsmiths tended and still do tend to regard many pictures as wallpaper, while picture addicts played down the importance of words while stressing the significance of film. The experienced television journalist somehow or other marries the two strands to produce a fair report, while the inexperienced TV journalist (or worse, the deliberate propagandist) produces an unbalanced report.

Having learned the technique of the job in the studio and the newsroom, we trainees then went out on exercises with a TV cameraman and TV sound recordist to compile a film report of our own.

Finally, before trainees such as myself were allowed out into the whole wide world, we did a stint working on local but real news stories with the former "Town and Around" regional news bulletin for London and the south-east.

This, as I have already said, was fun; and a news report sent from overseas to "Town and Around", rather unusually for such a local news outlet, constituted my very first dispatch to the BBC from abroad.

The assignment was coverage from Dieppe of the Sussex-Normandy Trade Fair. One of the Sussex exhibits showing its paces in the French port resort was an old Southdown double-decked, open-roofed bus of the kind that were once used to carry tourists along Brighton seafront.

Its larger modern descendants are now employed on sightseeing trips around London and elsewhere. My cameraman had the bright idea of me performing my piece to a camera on the top of this open-decker as it progressed on its jerky way through the narrow streets of Dieppe. I just about managed to say what I wanted to say, and to remain standing upright on the top deck, as the bus did everything it could to make me lose my balance: starting and braking, turning and slowing, stopping and setting off again.

It was my introduction to a dimension of television journalism that

I always found trying. The insistence of TV editors that their correspondents should be in some sort of appropriate setting for the story sounds reasonable enough, but it sometimes leads to unpredictable consequences.

For example, on one occasion, when Harold Wilson's government was deciding to withdraw British forces from bases east of Suez, I found myself standing outside the door of 10 Downing Street broadcasting live into the evening news as the prime minister of Singapore, Lee Kwan Yew, was inside talking to Wilson about the issue. At precisely the same moment, a government van carrying material for delivery to Number 10 reversed closer and closer towards me until, with barely a second to spare, I completed my piece to the camera and was just able to leap sideways to avoid being run down.

The noise of the van approaching relentlessly nearer must have distracted viewers as much as it disconcerted me, yet somehow or other I managed to mouth my words and keep going. My own view is that I could have presented my piece with less distraction (let alone the threat of an accident) from the studio – and that to decide that I should speak from outside Number 10 just because the subject was being discussed inside the house was simply childish.

However, TV editors seem to favour such childishness, and this editorial immaturity seems to me as a viewer to have worsened in recent years. I note that people like poor Nick Robinson, BBC political editor, still have to stand outside the door of Number 10, gallantly trying not to look miserable as the rain descends upon them, as they do their best to inform the nation of what might be going on behind the door. The presentation seems to me to add to the difficulties of a journalist trying to explain a serious news development and to interfere with the journalism rather enhancing it.

On a quite different kind of occasion, while covering the 1965 Indo-Pakistani war, I had made a long and difficult journey from the front back to Karachi so that I could make a broadcast and, on arriving dirty, unshaven, and exhausted at the port city, I found waiting for me there a BBC camera crew. They insisted that I talk a piece into the camera straight away, before I could get to the studio to get the actual news out, before I could write a script, and certainly before I had shaved or tidied myself up.

To them, the pictures they got of somebody who had plainly had an uncomfortable time actually took precedence over my own priority, which was to report the news. As the TV foreign news editor explained later, "We like our war correspondents to look as if they've had a rough time."

Welcome to showbiz!

When I was eventually unleashed as the corporation's Commonwealth correspondent after my TV induction, inevitably I had to report events in Commonwealth countries, including, of course, Tanzania, where my earlier coverage of certain aspects of an army mutiny that could have led to the overthrow of its president, the late Julius Nyerere, had led to libel action against the *Daily Telegraph*.

Despite the doubts I had cast upon his ministerial colleague, Oscar Kambona, and the ensuing legal proceedings, President Nyerere (like Dame Barbara Castle before him with her libel case) remained always civilised in his attitude towards me.

However, Nyerere enjoyed occasionally teasing me. One such occasion occurred when Dr Henry Kissinger, President Nixon's secretary of state, visited Dar-es-Salaam during international efforts to resolve the Rhodesian problem. Afterwards, Nyerere gave a news conference. One of his staff asked correspondents not to address him as a head of state but as *mwalimu*, meaning "teacher". This was a title that his image makers had dreamed up as a gimmick in domestic Tanzanian politics.

I did not think much of this, and when I rose to put a question to *mwalimu*, I started as usual, formally, when questioning a head of state or government. My first words: "Mr President …"

He interrupted me with a smile. "Ah!" he chuckled. "Bwana Osman!" The occupants of the conference room collapsed into laughter, me included. The word "bwana" ("boss"), was used in colonial times by blacks when addressing whites; and Nyerere had turned the tables on me for not calling him "teacher".

With its undertones of respect for somebody, the word "bwana" had been officially replaced in common usage in Tanzania by a more egalitarian word: *ndugu*, meaning "comrade". It was rather like the replacement in Russia of the old Tsarist word *gaspodin* (roughly equivalent to "sir") by the communist *tovarich* (or "comrade").

While working later in the Soviet Union, I was always addressed by Russians as "gaspodin", just as many Africans continued to address me (and other white men) as "bwana". I can only conclude that some of us simply do not look like natural "comrades".

In any case, I dislike the enforced employment of forms of address for blatantly political reasons; and I reserve the word "comrade" for people who are personally and genuinely precisely that, especially comrades in adversity. Political and ideological semantic exercises compelling the use of egalitarian forms of address started, I suppose, in modern history with the French Revolution. Then, everybody in France, at least in theory, became a "citizen" for a while, until Napoleon made the word "emperor" fashionable again.

An echo of frustrated French imperialism presented itself to my attention on my first visit to North America. I was visiting Canada in my new role as Commonwealth correspondent, traversing the country from Quebec to British Columbia over a month or so. Earlier, visiting Quebec, President Charles de Gaulle had provocatively cried out at a public meeting, "Vive Quebec libre!"

This had been used by secessionist French Canadians to provide what they interpreted as French presidential support for an independent Quebec. I talked to quite a few of them on my trip, notably at the Laval University.

However, when I reached the Pacific Coast and British Columbia, I was assured in Vancouver by the premier of the province at that time, the late "Wacky" Bennett, that British Columbians were far more likely to secede from Canada than the Quebecois.

The reason, he argued, was that if Quebec ever tried seriously to "go it alone", then BC would opt to join the United States as a new state, virtually delivering a death blow to Canada. It would, Bennett argued, result in the isolation of an independent French-speaking Quebec. Such a state, he asserted, would probably end up being surrounded by unfriendly English-speaking new member states of the United States, all previously Canadian.

It is, I suppose, still a remotely possible scenario, unlikely though it might sound; and it could probably only be envisaged if the Quebecois really did try to secede from the Canadian confederation. On a recent visit to British Columbia, I found it still extraordinarily British, living up to the British part of its name in many ways, despite the North American scenery, the Pacific Ocean, and the burgeoning Canadian Asiatic population. Many of the Asians, of course, were formerly in Hong Kong and so are well acquainted with echoes of empire.

In any case, my exploratory visit to Canada paid off handsomely because it was not long before I was back in the country again covering, first, the rise to power of Pierre Trudeau in 1968; and second, the kidnapping of a British subject, Mr Cross, and the murder of the Quebec Minister of Labour, Pierre Laporte, in 1970, by Quebec separatist terrorists. The development underlined that Canada – and not only its more populous neighbour – had (and has) its own security problems.

Both events produced sizeable BBC scoops. The first came on the eve of the 1968 general election in Canada, when I persuaded Mr Trudeau to give the BBC a television interview before he had actually been elected prime minister, but conducted on the basis that he was in fact the prime minister. The reason for this was the time difference between London and Ottawa. I knew that if we waited for the election result the next day, we would not get Trudeau, the favourite to win, onto the screen in time for the next night's bulletins.

I gave him my word that the interview would not be broadcast if it turned out that he had lost the election, and he accepted my promise. I did the interview; airfreighted the film to London; he won the election; and we had our scoop.

Trudeau, who was born in French Canadian Montreal but was strongly anti-secessionist, looked wildly unorthodox for a prime minister. He dressed casually, with a leather jacket; was keen on judo; and thought nothing of doing a handstand or a somersault if political meetings became a mite boring.

A tremendous cult developed in Canada among youngsters, who became known as Trudeauniks, indulging in Trudolatry or Trudomania. He contrasted extraordinarily with his predecessor, the internationally respected but less exhibitionistic figure of Lester ("Mike") Pearson.

However, although Trudeau looked unconventional, in his use of power he was both orthodox and effective. Quebec secessionists hated him and nicknamed him "Lord Elliott", mocking him for his English-sounding second name (he was Pierre Elliott Trudeau).

Before his election, some Quebec separatist leaders had been arrested; there had been riots in Trudeau's home city, where he had been professor of law at Montreal University.

Despite his youthful and maverick personality, with young people attracted by it and older people rather dubious, he was elected mainly because he took an uncompromising stand against Quebec separatism. Canada gave him a strong confederal hand to play, and this was useful for him two years later, when in 1970 the "Front for the Liberation of Quebec" (FLQ) turned to terrorism.

This produced my second BBC scoop from Canada. After the discovery of the body of the murdered Quebec minister in a car boot, I was covering events in Montreal, while political developments were moving fast in Ottawa. I got a useful insight, though, into what was happening at the top there from an old friend of mine, Philip Noakes, who for years had been a senior official at the Colonial Office before that department of state was subsumed into the Foreign and Commonwealth Office as the Department for Dependent Territories.

With the disappearance of the Colonial Office, Philip had been given a new diplomatic job in Canada, taking with him his enormous constitutional knowledge. This paid off for me because he gave me one of the hottest news tips I have ever received.

Many of my colleagues used to view Philip as being long-winded, so they tended not to listen to him as closely as they should have done; but from long acquaintance, I knew how Philip went about things. It was no different when he gave me my magnificent tip-off.

I had fallen into bed at 1 a.m. or so, extremely tired after broadcasting by satellite on the latest Montreal developments for both TV and radio. I had to drag myself painfully out from sleep when the telephone in my hotel bedroom rang at 3.00 a.m. or so.

It was Philip, and his opening words were, "John, what do you know about the Canadian constitution?"

I nearly replied impolitely (3.00 a.m.!), but knowing Philip's roundabout way of getting to a point, any point, I managed to avoid cursing him. I tried to switch on my brain; thought a little; and ventured a hesitant reply. "Well, I think it's got something to do with the 1931 Statute of Westminster."

Like a patient schoolmaster questioning a slow pupil, Philip commented encouragingly, "Good! Now what status did that confer on Canada?"

By now, my brain was engaged and I was beginning to think. I replied, "It is a dominion."

"Yes, splendid," said Philip approvingly, and I sensed that he was starting to approach the point. "As one of her dominions," Philip continued, "Her Majesty the Queen is informed by her representative, the governor general, of Canadian cabinet decisions.

"Furthermore," Philip continued, "as a matter of courtesy, the representative of the British government in Canada, the British High Commissioner, is usually also informed about what is going on."

I felt that now, at last, he might be getting warm in his run-up towards any offer of news. Perhaps I was about to be rewarded for my painful but accurate answers to the history test he was administering in the early hours. So I tried a question or two of my own on him.

"Where are you, Philip? What is going on?" He replied that he was in the British High Commission in Ottawa and that an emergency meeting of the Canadian cabinet was being held in the Canadian capital at that unlikely hour.

"Would you like to know what has been decided?" he asked. By now I was agog, but I patiently indicated that yes, I would like to know.

Philip then announced, "The Canadian cabinet has decided to bring into force a War Measures Act."

"What does that mean, Philip?"

He then produced his stunning punchline: "It means that at the stroke of a pen, civil liberties in Canada are suspended!"

They were too. Before ringing off, he advised me to look out of my hotel window, and I did. Down the road came a column of armoured cars moving into Montreal. Detentions were made of FLQ activists, and Trudeau extricated Canada from a growing threat of terrorism by his uncompromising actions. He shocked a number of Canadians, including quite a few liberal journalists, by saying that he did not mind upsetting a few "bleeding hearts".

I was broadcasting to London over the hotel telephone within minutes of getting the news, and out my dispatch went all over the globe.

Meanwhile, in Ottawa, word had spread about the pre-dawn cabinet meeting and TV reporters were waiting on the doorstep for the prime minister to emerge. Asked what he was going to do, Trudeau answered, "Just watch me!"

It was all very dramatic, and the truly amazing aspect of the whole episode, looking back on it, is how long it took before the Canadian authorities acted against the FLQ. If tougher action had been taken earlier, it might have saved the life of the Quebec minister and prevented the kidnapping of Mr Cross (who was eventually released).

Being a democracy, however, and not having experienced anything for a long time that involved political murder and kidnapping, any Canadian government would have hesitated before taking drastic action of the kind that Trudeau took. As it was, a genuine "casus belli" had presented itself to Trudeau, and most Canadians felt he was justified in his introduction of the War Measures Act, a move which worked.

Quite a lot had been known about the FLQ before things had become so bad. It began operating in 1963, mainly motivated by Quebec separatism. This was exacerbated by Gaullist French nationalism. These elements quickly became exploited by other disruptive forces in a classic demonstration of how a political movement can be used for purposes other than its original purpose and, much more sinister, of how it can be turned into a cloak for terrorism.

In what I believe is still the longest single broadcast ever put on the air by BBC Radio's *From Our Own Correspondent* programme, I talked for eight minutes about "Les Felquists" and about how much of what had been known about them had been deliberately hushed up.

What was learned then is still pertinent in dealing with today's international terrorist groups, especially on their methods of operation and their links with other so-called "liberation" movements. For example, a ransom note from the FLQ expressed support for the "revolutionary Catholics of Northern Ireland" (meaning the IRA); for "American and African blacks"; and for the so-called liberation movements of Latin America, Asia, and Palestine, where a handful of "Felquists" had been found a few months before the Montreal troubles training with Palestinian guerrillas.

The FLQ worked with cells of four or five people operating separately from other cells, with as little contact between them as possible and little knowledge of each other, so that if one cell was caught, the entire ring would not be badly damaged.

The year before the Montreal troubles, a report was made by a royal commission on security in Canada, and it was specific about communist and Trotskyist influences in the movement "exploiting French Canadian feelings and real economic and social dissatisfactions".

So explosive were the contents that a large part of the report was suppressed, and only after months of delay was a heavily edited version published. Among other things, it disclosed that Canada's armed forces were worried about infiltration, and it was recommended that separatists who had made their way into the services should be immediately discharged. In my piece for *From Our Own Correspondent*, I reported:

> *Les Felquists range from real French Canadian nationalists, through radical socialists and communists and intellectual anarchists, to downright thugs, barely disguised as political activists. The list of the so-called political prisoners, all convicted in open-court proceedings, whom the kidnappers want released, is itself indicative of the variety of types engaged in terrorism, or what they prefer to call "Operation Liberation". They include, for example, a Hungarian-born former French Foreign Legionnaire and paratrooper found guilty of murder; a former philosophy student guilty of robbery; and a former social science student, college dropout, and self-styled Marxist-Leninist revolutionary guilty of bombing the Montreal Stock Exchange and of other bombings.*
>
> *The kidnappings were carried out by two different FLQ cells. One of them, which seized Mr Cross, calls itself the "Liberation Cell". The other, which seized and murdered Mr Laporte, originally called itself the "Chenier Financing Cell". Chenier was the name of a French Canadian killed in 1837 while leading rebels against the Crown.*
>
> *As for the financing part of the cell's name, it is suggested that the cell is one that specialises in raising FLQ finances – that is, by bank raids. Another cell name has since cropped up, giving evidence of a warped and murderous sense of humour.*

When the kidnappers left a message indicating where Mr Laporte's body was to be found, they signed themselves as being from the "Royal Twenty-Second Dieppe Cell".

This was a jeer at the famous French Canadian regiment, the Royal Twenty-Second, the very men who were first moved into Montreal to help police in their guard duties, as well as a reference to the Dieppe raid in World War II, when Canadian troops suffered their bloody defeat.

An interesting thing about FLQ revolutionaries is that they differ from other revolutionaries like Mao and Castro in that while accepting Maoist teaching in many respects, they reject the tactic of organising their movements in remote hills and wild country.

On the contrary, the FLQ has tried to create what some of its captured documents describe as "urban guerrilla warfare". One of the most extraordinary aspects of the whole history of the organisation is that a complete trunk-load of these documents was taken to the Canadian capital last year and dismissed by federal officials as worthless, as some sort of local political ploy.

Well, the mood is different now, and the FLQ's challenge is widely seen as an attempt to destroy Canada's existence as a nation.

That spasm of violence in Canada occurred in the autumn of 1970, just nine months after New York had experienced the unusual wave of explosions that I have already mentioned.

Before that, in my five years as Commonwealth correspondent, I had trotted about all over the world, from Hong Kong, during the Chinese Cultural revolution, when I fled from Maoist mobs in Macao and in Hong Kong itself, to a much happier sort of occasion on Independence Day in British Guiana, when the colony became the new state of Guyana.

My first major job, though, for the BBC was covering the 1965 Indo-Pakistani war from the Pakistan side, when, for the first time, I had to deal with direct military censorship of my broadcasts. When war broke out, I could use only one radio studio to communicate with London, and that was in Karachi, nearly a thousand miles away from the military action inland, with fighting in areas well east of Lahore, Rawalpindi, and Islamabad.

The BBC flew an engineer to Karachi, and we managed to extend radio circuits as far as Rawalpindi. As a result, for some weeks, the corporation was the only international broadcasting organisation in the world offering war dispatches on air. Indeed, the BBC agreed to American networks using our facilities and coming into the studio after I had finished my BBC labours. Later, TV crews arrived, and I did the usual double act as and when required in those days for both radio and TV.

Before hostilities had started, but when it was plain that they were going to, I had met in Karachi the military censor, who was not a soldier but a sailor, Commander Hussein of the Pakistan Navy. He informed me that my scripts would have to be presented to him before being broadcast and that he would sit beside the microphone and me just in case I departed from them.

I left Karachi to head for Rawalpindi and the old Flashman's Hotel (they were wonderful, those old Raj period establishments: Dean's in Peshawar, Faletti's in Lahore, Flashman's in 'Pindi. Do they still exist?).

I was in Rawalpindi when war broke out and endured the usual adventures of a war correspondent, including one brush with death when my colleague from the *Daily Telegraph*, the late John Ridley, jumped into the slit trench where I cowered as Indian jets attacked the Pakistani column with which we were travelling. An Indian Air Force rocket landed a hundred yards away and fortunately failed to explode, but Ridley's leap into my funk hole had ended on top of my tape recorder, putting it out of action for the rest of the war.

I was sadly reminded of this when, nine years later, Ridley died. He had become a good friend over the years, and I was one of those who always appreciated what an obituarist described as "his highly idiosyncratic brand of melancholy wit". This applied despite the fact that I myself had been one of the victims of his mordant sense of humour after he had taken refuge in my slit trench.

The obituarist recalled the event as an example of what Ridley found funny:

> *One notable example came from the Rann of Kutch fighting*
> *between India and Pakistan a few years back. Firing became*

heavy, and Ridley jumped into a slit trench, where John Osman of the BBC was dictating his own report into a tape recorder.

The instrument was not improved by this sudden irruption, and Osman's feelings were far from assuaged when he arrived for a drink before dinner that evening to hear Ridley telling the bar his own version of the episode: "And there, at the bottom of the trench, was poor John Osman, simply babbling to himself with fear."

It was, of course, half true. I was scared at the time, like Ridley himself, but I was also trying to do my job, which he very well understood. However, I had to laugh at his droll account that evening, complete with his description of the microphone into which I was allegedly "babbling" as being "a penis-like object".

Although Ridley had put the machine out of action, I had lots of material and headed for Karachi via Lahore. I drove nearly a thousand miles across the Punjab and Sind in a taxi with *Guardian* correspondent Peter Preston, who later became, for many years, the newspaper's editor.

Commander Hussein passed my scripts without comment and sat beside me while I broadcast them. I was instructed by the BBC to state the following at the beginning and the end of the broadcast: "This dispatch has been censored and cleared." This was so that the listener would appreciate the position. It was a good rule.

I continued to report from Karachi for a few days before returning towards the front because there were newsworthy internal political developments in Karachi itself. Anti-American and anti-British demonstrations were growing, some deteriorating into riots, and I covered these. Suddenly, I ran into trouble with Commander Hussein.

I had made a practice of getting to the studio a bit before my broadcast time so that he could read the scripts and clear them, and on this particular day, as I approached the Pakistan Radio building, I came across a banner over the street attacking the Americans and the British: "Out and down with America and Britain, running dogs of imperialism." I noted it down and added it to my script as an indication of the sort of thing that was happening.

Commander Hussein said, "We can't have this." He simply did not want to believe that such a banner had been put up. Since we had a quarter of an hour or so to spare, I asked him to accompany me and see the banner for himself. He did, and he was angry.

As we got back to the studio, he turned to me and said, "I am not going to let you broadcast that." Then he added, "I will, though, make a deal with you. If you take that bit out of your dispatch, I shall see that the banner comes down!"

Since there was not anything much I could do about it anyway, I accepted his offer and edited out the offending item. He fulfilled his promise, and by the next day, the banner had vanished.

As politics entered more and more into the story, he became increasingly unhappy, and eventually he threw down his censor's pen in disgust and exploded. "What am I doing here?" he asked. "I should be standing on the bridge of my ship fighting the enemy!"

I tried to console him but without much success. Anyhow, after this he never removed a word from any of my dispatches. I hope Commander Hussein eventually got back to sea, because he was plainly not cut out for the task of censoring.

On our long journey back from the front to Karachi, Peter Preston and I had first gone from Rawalpindi to Lahore, then the biggest city in West Pakistan, which Indian forces were threatening. As we drove into the city, columns of refugees were moving out and the sound of artillery could be heard.

We made a quick tour of the city, talked to several people, and could feel the fear of enemy occupation. I could not make a broadcast; the telephones were unreliable at the best of times, and at that moment, they were out altogether with the prevailing uncertainty. In a desperate attempt to get something away, I went to the Pakistan Telegraph Office and found that cables were still possible but had to be kept short. I managed to file a few paragraphs informing the BBC that refugees were fleeing Lahore in their thousands, that the sound of guns could be heard, that Lahore radio was still on the air, and that the city was still held by Pakistan.

That short cable, I was told later by the foreign news editor, John Crawley, was one of the most valuable dispatches I sent throughout the conflict. Unknown to me, a news agency had reported from New Delhi that Lahore had fallen to the Indians, and BBC Television News had broadcast that wrong piece of information.

Pakistani immigrants living in Britain had overwhelmed the BBC with anxious inquiries, and in the middle of immense confusion, my brief cable arrived saying that Lahore was still Pakistani. I was glad I had managed to get the news through, even though at the time I sent it, I thought it was a rather anaemic dispatch.

Other vivid memories of my spell as Commonwealth correspondent included, of course, coverage of various bush wars in Africa and my detention and expulsion from Ian Smith's Rhodesia, together with the two-men BBC TV crew who had accompanied me from Portugal for three months or so, around Angola, Mozambique, South Africa, and eventually Aden.

They were a wonderful pair of professionals, and the three of us were afforded the relative luxury of an individual cell each when we were jailed in what was then Salisbury and is now Harare. The cameraman was the late Bill Baglin, MBE; and the sound recordist, then a young novitiate and nowadays a prize-winning cameraman in his own right, was Eric Thirer. I knew that he would go far when, upon our release from the cells, Eric turned round and cast a last look over his grimy lodging for the night, with its green wall covered with disgusting dirt. To the astonishment of our burly police guardians, Bill Baglin, and me, Eric reflected a little and then said, "Rather a tasteful pastel shade, don't you think?"

Bill Baglin was with me again on another memorable African occasion after the assassination of the rising Kenyan politician Tom Mboya. Working with Bill and with the late Mohamed Amin, another award-winning cameraman who later filmed the Ethiopian famine with Michael Buerk, we covered riots in Nairobi and elsewhere in Kenya as we accompanied the funeral cortege and the coffin containing the corpse of Mboya for several days across country to Lake Victoria.

Every evening at last light, we made our way to the nearest bush airstrip to place our film and my recorded report onto a chartered plane that then flew back to Nairobi for the material to be airfreighted to London to be screened.

We stayed en route at upcountry lodging houses or in mission stations. Having reached Lake Victoria, we hired dugout canoes and were paddled precariously across the murky waters, filled with bilharzia, crocodile, and hippopotamus, to Rusinga Island, to join thousands of Luo tribesmen and women trudging along bush tracks, sweating our way up and down a steep hill in the blazing sun, with Bill lugging his camera and muttering, "Conservation of energy! Conservation of energy!"

I was told later that in the news cameramen's room at BBC Television Centre, a map was put up on the wall showing Lake Victoria and Rusinga, with the hill on the island marked as "Mount Osman".

As we slogged our way along the paths, a rickety bus appeared on the one dirt road, and we thought we might get a lift on it. Rioters quickly made it useless, though, stoning it and smashing all the windows, with passengers hurriedly jumping out to join the streams of people wending their way through the bush in endless single files towards Tom Mboya's burial place. It was an amazing sight, of the sort that only Africa can produce. The scene at the graveside was unique. I reported for *From Our Own Correspondent*:

> At the final burial scene on Rusinga Island, under a yellow blossoming tree with the strange name of "ayieko", witch doctors and Luo tribal dancers, some on stilts, some covered from head to foot in grass and leaves and looking for all the world like moving bushes, jostled alongside the young-looking African Bishop of Kisii. His Lordship's white and golden robes stood out starkly in the glare of the sun and against a great mass of black faces as he calmly gave Mboya a Christian burial, the service barely heard above the beat of drums and the shouts of thousands.
>
> The bishop at one stage was almost pushed into the grave and had his mitre knocked sideways, but he carried on serenely. Then, after the Christian service, the bishop retired for the Luo tribal elders to take over. The most prominent of these was Tom Mboya's bitter political enemy but co-tribesman, Mr Oginga Odinga.
>
> He was in full tribal regalia: a great cloak and hat of animal skins, legs beaded blue and white and red up to the knees, fly whisk brandished like a pantomime wizard's magic wand. His arrival was a sensation. He danced around 'like a lion', as one African said. A shout went up: "Jaramogi", a sort of title

accorded to him by the Luo. As he talked to press, radio and television, his followers surrounded him and chanted things like "War with the Kikuyu!" and "Dume! Dume!" which means "bull" and is the slogan of Mr Odinga's opposition party, the Kenya People's Union. Ironically, the death of Mboya has had the effect of unleashing one of the major forces in Africa against which he had fought most of his life: the force of tribalism.

It's a sad and anxious thing for Kenya that Kikuyu colleagues with whom Mboya had worked in the ruling Kenya African National Union were not allowed to pay their respects to him at his funeral, or at his house, because they were from the wrong tribe; while his most implacable political opponent could do so because he was from the right tribe.

Another extraordinary figure on view at this most extraordinary of funerals was the man from the *Times*. Sweating under the scorching sun, he was clad in a winter heavyweight city suit, complete with collar and tie. He had been wearing it to work at the office in London whence he had been dispatched, on the instant, to equatorial Africa after the news had broken of Mboya's murder.

I too had flown post-haste from London to Nairobi but had hurriedly packed my usual working safari suit in which I was clad; even so, I was melting in the heat. The *Times* correspondent must have been suffering all kinds of torture.

I assume he survived his sudden foreign assignment, although I never subsequently saw him on another.

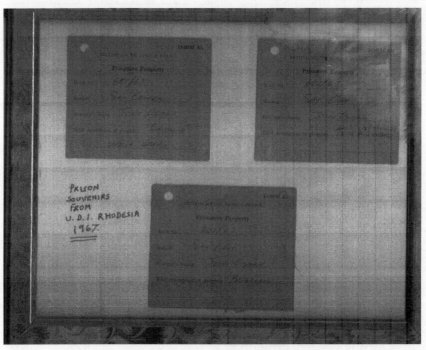

My "Prisoner's property' tags from when I was imprisoned
in the illegal republic of Rhodesia led by Ian Smith.

CHAPTER 21

Age Five: "The Justice"
"Wise Saws and Modern Instances"

After a lifetime of reporting, much of it for the BBC, I propose to offer about the corporation a few unsolicited "saws" and "instances". They are advanced in a constructive spirit and with real concern about "Auntie's" future.

Early in 2005, the culture secretary of the time, Miss Tessa Jowell, announced planned changes that she described, with a touch of understatement, as "radical" to the BBC structure. The Board of Governors was abolished. The then-just-appointed but now-departed BBC director general, Mark Thompson, said that the BBC was in a "fight for survival".

A senior woman administrator with whom I had always worked happily when she was a young producer and later editor, but who was, by the time of these "radical" changes, the director of Radio and Music, Jenny Abramsky (now a dame), declared, "I am not exaggerating when I say that the organisation has been fighting to have a future and that fight is not over yet."

That fight continues, with barely a day passing without criticism of the BBC, sometimes of a virulent nature, being aired by politicians and the media. The BBC was dubbed the "Blatantly Biased Corporation" by the *Daily Telegraph* in a powerfully argued leading article and, apart from political considerations, has come under fire from quite different directions, with BBC or ex-BBC journalists themselves getting into the fray, such as John Humphrys (TV is "vulgar and obsessed with sex"); Martin Bell ("Abuse of public trust was most obvious in the extravagant redundancy payouts to senior managers"); and David Dimbleby (The BBC management needs "to answer questions about whether the BBC has got too big ... whether it is too powerful for its own good ... .whether it's crushing newspapers, local newspapers particularly").

So my sympathies go to the man I remember years ago in the news division as Tony Hall, but who nowadays is Lord Hall of Birkenhead and –poor chap! – the BBC's latest director general. He has mounted a spirited defence of the licence fee in his campaign for renewal of the BBC royal charter, due to expire in 2016. How far he will succeed is anyone's guess.

As a journalist and broadcaster often described as "veteran", I was (and still am) worried about the implications of the disappearance of the Board of Governors and its effect upon the ultimate editorial independence of the BBC. Signs of government pressure had already emerged earlier, when Ms Jowell indicated to a parliamentary select committee that although the government was not considering an end to the system whereby the BBC is authorised by royal charter, that privilege did not exclude the BBC from being "subjection to external regulation".

That assertion had an ominous undertone. It suggested that the BBC might be threatened with the fate of being turned into just another "state broadcaster", like, perhaps, Radio Moscow. The BBC has always been a national broadcaster and for much of its existence an international broadcaster, but it has never has been a "state broadcaster" – despite it being described as that by critics such as competing commercial broadcasters and from newspapers with broadcasting links to commercial broadcasters.

I hope that the BBC never does become a state broadcaster, and I am not alone in my fears. For instance, Andy Smith, former president of another chartered body with which I have long been associated (the world's oldest journalistic association and union, the Chartered Institute of Journalists) has suggested: "The government clearly wants to bring the BBC under closer control to avoid criticism or unwanted scrutiny of its policies by BBC news and current affairs programmes."

He added: "We – that is, the rest of the population, not cabinet ministers or chairmen of quangos – just want a better quality service. We don't really worry about government ministers getting roasted on *Newsnight* or the *Today* programme. In fact, most of us probably enjoy the spectacle. What should concern us, however, is when certain people within the corporation use their positions to pursue a particular political agenda. That's definitely not the job of a public service broadcaster."

As a reputable institution, "Auntie" in recent years has become increasingly vulnerable. The onslaughts come from all directions. Criticisms are not confined to politicians but are expressed, for example, by newspapers and broadcasting interests controlled by Rupert Murdoch, Lord Rothermere, or others who might not be averse to a break-up of the corporation. At the same time, on the political side, both Labour and Conservative governments, while responsible through Parliament for the regular renewal of the royal charter and of the TV and radio licence, have also shown themselves to be wary of the influence of the BBC. Tony Blair's second government was especially hostile after the bitter row over Iraq and the fallout from the Hutton Inquiry. Nor have the conservatives shown any great friendliness towards the BBC, displaying suspicion of its programmes and attitudes.

Few people these days really understand how the new system of BBC governance and management works. Two new boards, the Trust Board and the Executive Board, have replaced the Board of Governors, with the transition representing the greatest shake-up the BBC has experienced in its history.

The state of BBC journalism as reflected in its broadcast output has been closely connected with events leading to the current difficult position. So I should like to draw upon my own long experience as a journalist and broadcaster to advance a few thoughts that I hope might prove helpful to the corporation in its fight for survival. They are directed mainly at those who handle news and current affairs.

Having explained earlier how I myself weathered in mid-career a libel storm that struck myself and the *Daily Telegraph*, I should like to express my pleasure at the way that my fellow journalist Andrew Gilligan seems to have weathered the much greater tempest into which he sailed when he broke his story casting doubt on the Blair government's policy on Iraq, resulting in the Hutton inquiry as well as the death of his principal source, Dr David Kelly. Gilligan seems to be a survivor, having been rescued by various sturdy journalistic vessels, not least the *Daily Telegraph* group.

Journalism in Great Britain is like that, thank God! It usually has been. Reared as I was in the best newspaper tradition of getting things right, I had also been encouraged by strong editors not to be afraid of getting wrong any news that was still unproven, provided that the news itself was something on which it was thought worth taking a chance. This meant that in accepting a known risk, the news had to be of genuine public importance and not just gossip for mere public titillation. It also had to emanate from a source believed to be trustworthy. Such, undoubtedly, was the case with Gilligan's controversial story.

Adventurous, challenging journalism has always entailed risk-taking, with the prospect ever-present of being cross-examined in a court of law over any mistake.

Even the most careful editors or reporters commit errors. It is because of the near certainty of an occasional mistake that newspapers employ lawyers and insure themselves against libel risks. So it was encouraging to old journalists and broadcasters like myself to note that Mark Thompson, early on in his succession to the directorship general after Greg Dyke's departure, acknowledged that despite the adverse Hutton report on the editorial processes of the BBC, "even the most rigorous investigations require journalists and editors to use their judgement and take calculated risks".

He added: "We have to be prepared to go on taking those risks. I'd like to see more, not less, investigative journalism as a result of Hutton." I applaud that: so far, so good!

At the same time, Thompson quite properly took the chance to stress that journalistic accuracy is vital to the reputation of the BBC. Writing in October 2004 a review of his predecessor's book, *Inside Story*, Thompson passed judgement on both Greg Dyke and Andrew Gilligan:

> *Unfortunately, if Gilligan's story wasn't completely wrong, it wasn't exactly right either. Rather than simply reporting what Kelly had told him, Gilligan had also presented one of his own inferences as if it had come out of Kelly's mouth. The allegations had not been put to No 10 – an elementary requirement for fairness and essential if one is to claim any kind of qualified privilege. Later it would emerge that Gilligan had written an*

email to the researcher of one of the MPs on the Foreign Affairs Committee, in which he compromised his own source.

Although Greg today accepts that there were errors, "a couple of which were serious", he argues that Andrew Gilligan's story was "overwhelmingly true" and devotes an important chapter to showing why, based on what we now know. But we have to judge the editorial and management decisions about the Gilligan story on the basis of what we knew then, not now, and above all on the basis of Gilligan's contemporaneous sources and evidence.

If we put on the pitiless spectacles of hindsight and focus solely on the basis on which the story was broadcast at the time, then we have to conclude that there were serious shortcomings in the Gilligan report and that they should have been identified and corrected sooner than they were.

"Broadly right" isn't good enough. All complaints should be taken seriously, even if one suspects the motives of the complainant.

Thompson (who, of course, has long since left the BBC for a big job in the United States) hit the right note. Nobody except unintelligent broadcasters would deny that there is a public desirability for broadcasting organisations, as well as newspapers, to admit mistakes when they are made and to apologise for them. It is a lesson that the BBC learned (and is probably still learning) in the hardest of all possible ways.

When apologies did eventually emerge from the corporation, they entailed the departures of the chairman of the Board of Governors and of the director general. Dyke's book produced reviews that accused him of everything from "self-justification" (Peter Bazalgette) to approaching his role as the BBC's editor-in-chief in a "less than stringent way" (Gerald Kaufman).

In Mark Thompson's review of his predecessor's book, he stressed that the Gilligan story was "exactly the kind of investigative journalism which the BBC should pursue". I agree with that but would place heavy emphasis on the word "pursue". Less haste and more research would have helped the *Today* programme and the BBC to nail down the facts properly in order to have been infallible and more effective.

The trouble is that even when I was with what I now think of as "the old BBC", there were already beginning to appear a few programme producers and editors who gave every indication of ignorance about basic journalistic principles. Most of them, but not all, were in "current affairs" rather than in "news", the difference between the two journalistic streams on the BBC becoming blurred well before I left the staff. That process continued for some years, perhaps beyond the salvation of "news," although I hope not.

I feel, however, just the same about many contemporary newspapers, including those with a more intellectual readership than that of the more sensational tabloids. Many suffer from the same lack of respect for straight news in favour of versions that fit in with their view of the world. The maxim followed broadly by most publishers, broadcasters, and journalists of my generation was the rule laid down in 1921 by C. P. Scott of the *Manchester Guardian* before it transformed itself into the *Guardian*: "Comment is free, but facts are sacred."

If both newspapers and broadcasting stations reminded themselves of the Scott maxim and moved towards its revival, they might recover some of the respect many have lost from their older and more experienced readers, listeners, and viewers. They might even gain more respect from younger readers, listeners, and viewers, even though the younger are more than likely to be gathering what they know about the news of the day from sources other than newspapers or broadcasters, such as the Internet, the Web, and other controversial sources like, say, Wikileaks or Twitter.

The trouble with presenting hard news responsibly is that by its very nature, news itself is immediate, but full facts about it are not always so immediately established. The actual gathering of news is an expensive business, and in this respect, the BBC has an honourable record, employing as it does many good reporters, authoritative specialist correspondents, and a costly worldwide foreign news staff. This contrasts with the way in which many newspapers that used to maintain their own sizeable foreign news staffs have simply dispensed with them.

As for explaining the causes as to *why* precisely events are happening, a whole new can of worms is then opened, with people and organisations (be they political, commercial, religious, moral, homosexual, atheistic, animal loving, or whatever) all grinding their own various axes. Accuracy tends to disappear as excitement grows over interpretation of whatever is claimed as fact.

In handling in my day this complexity known as news and current affairs, one or two BBC producers or editors I knew tended to concentrate on the TV side, on pictures more than words, while others, on the radio side, encouraged broadcasts by heavily opinionated freelances or outside contributors, who had strong views to express but who were not too concerned with accuracy.

Although I myself found I always had more than enough to do for all sorts of programmes both on TV and radio, I could cite a number of examples involving my colleague specialist correspondents who found themselves upstaged by controversialists. Previously reliable journalism was beginning to become slip-shod in different quarters of the BBC.

The undoubted talents of some producers for putting on the air, or onto the screen, lively bulletins or programmes were, I remember, used (in the best journalistic sense) sometimes dubiously. Occasionally I had to spend a good deal of time and effort in dissuading them to kill a story that they were keen to run. The faults usually stemmed from their eagerness to be controversial and provocative, and from their reluctance to examine the facts from more than one viewpoint. This was because they apparently felt this would be too even-handed and so (they thought) dull. Such shortcomings originated from what I always regarded as the showbiz image-making side of broadcasting rather than from its serious news side.

Like actors, journalists ply an unpredictable trade. It is not by coincidence that both scribblers and thespians were long regarded as "rogues and vagabonds". There are probably quite a few people who still think about us along those lines, often justifiably (especially after the phone hacking scandals and the Leveson Inquiry). In many ways comparable to showbiz, journalism has become even more so with the growth of television and Internet self-publicity.

The late Anthony Howard, a respected journalist for fifty years or more, once cited the case of one of our younger colleagues who "used to be a journalist" but "now he's a celebrity too". He was referring to Andrew Marr, who appeared on television screens as the BBC political editor until he succeeded to the slot previously held by David Frost, with his own Sunday morning TV show. Howard suggested that in becoming what he called "the leading celebrity journalist of our day", Marr might find himself in the position in which "the journalist is the story".

This is dangerous exposure for any working journalist. It is not a new phenomenon, as my former colleague John Simpson pointed out in his book, *Strange Places, Questionable People*. Recalling his own rise to fame after his reporting from Baghdad in 1990–91, during the first Gulf War, John commented, "Somehow I passed through a barrier. My identity and my face seem to fit together more in people's minds. I am become a name. There are some of my colleagues to whom this is important. It's not surprising in television; your recognizability is a marketable commodity."

Such recognizability and marketability are not, however, by themselves the qualities required to maintain professional authority. Fame, like money, can all too easily be fatal for anyone temporarily possessing it. It really is what Shakespeare called a "bubble", just as triumph is what Kipling called an "impostor". Celebrity of any kind, television or otherwise, is quite empty unless, behind it, there is something solid.

Anthony Howard's warning about overmuch fame for a working journalist is written with the authority of a former editor of the *New Statesman* and of the *Listener* (that dear old BBC weekly for which I wrote many thousands of words, over many years, before it was so brutally put down). I first met Howard when he was working as a correspondent in Washington, and as a shrewd political observer himself, he rightly praised Andrew Marr for doing "an elegantly stylish job". Marr himself, however, has expressed reservations about some of the devices used by producers and editors in news coverage.

One example that Marr has offered is what he calls the "overuse" of two-way interviews between the programme studio presenter and a correspondent on the spot.

As a viewer and as a former participant in such interviews both on TV and radio, I agree. I was pleased to note after the Hutton fallout that the freshly appointed director of BBC News at that time, Helen Boaden, was reported to be "peeved by the tendency among news anchors to have cosy chats with their correspondents".

It can have the effect of devaluing the seriousness of much news. As one critic put it, the cosiness of two-way chats is "irritating" because it not only "excludes the viewer and looks staged", but "it reeks of insincerity". To such criticisms, I would add one of my own: the sheer idiocy of questions asked by some presenters.

Marr too has attacked this: "'So what's the mood among the Prime Minister's aides now, Andrew?' (Absolutely no idea. It's two in the morning here, and they all went to bed hours ago)." I was cheered also when reading Marr's book (*My Trade: A Short History of British Journalism*) to learn that although thirty years or so younger than I am, he possesses what we used to call "a good note" and that he has reservations about reporters who cannot take a reasonably accurate note.

Worse, to this viewer's mind, are the TV tricks of slowing down or speeding up images in order to stress a point and playing music to highlight a mood that a producer might think appropriate for whatever it is that is happening on screen. I have observed such techniques increasingly applied in TV news bulletins, and they worry me.

The use of so-called "reconstructions" is another device that I find worrying. I found objectionable, too, the artificiality of Marr having been once compelled by his producer or editor to fiddle about with what he described as "plastic chess sets" to explain political manoeuvres. This convoluted gambit on screen, in something supposed to be a news bulletin, which I had the misfortune to watch, was, he suggests, staged "to avoid the problem of most backdrops being drearily familiar". This alleged "problem" exists only in the mind of a film-maker bored with the sight of Westminster. It has nothing to do with news and everything to do with showbiz.

I sympathised with Marr again when, during the 2004 debate on a new bill about gambling, he appeared in a casino while trying to produce a serious political report. Later, when reporting on the problem of rubbish disposal, he was pictured looking at garbage on the banks of the Thames. The sum effect of such contrived pieces on this viewer's mind was that of artificiality.

What was the political editor of BBC TV News doing at a gambling table? Why was he wading in mud at the side of the Thames? Such contrived "atmosphere" is entirely false. It distracts the attention of the viewer from any thoughtful political explanation about the news that the political editor might wish to advance.

Another extraordinary piece I watched recently in a TV news bulletin had the economics correspondent producing a well-measured report on the economy but with the impact of what he was saying much reduced because he had been positioned by traffic lights that appeared to be part of a modern sculpture. They flashed from red to green and then green to red again. The idea, I can only suppose, was to convey some sort of visual aspect to underline points that the correspondent was making about signals in the economy.

It did not work. The lights were distracting. I saw and heard not the news, but I felt the subjection of news to unnecessary visual interference. Such techniques underline the reason why the old BBC worried so much about the unavoidable introduction of television news fifty years ago.

In an amusing booklet published in July 2004 to mark "Fifty Years of BBC Television News", respected newsreader and music buff Richard Baker recalled how it all started. He was the man who uttered the first words of the first news bulletin of the BBC Television Service on 5 July 1954.

Spoken over a picture of Nelson's column (because the presenter himself was not shown!), the words were: "Here is an illustrated summary of the news."

It is easy to laugh at that now. Less easy to laugh at, however, is Baker's rather disapproving recollection: "It was decreed that the journalists of News Division, rather than people who thought in pictures, would be in sole charge."

Inevitably, that evolved, and I am not so sure that all the changes have been for the better. Instances such as those I have cited seem to me to confirm many of the original fears held by the BBC News Division about "people who thought in pictures".

I am inclined to the view that on TV perhaps the pendulum has swung too far away from wordsmiths in favour of people who think in pictures. Debate about this is termed these days as "ongoing", and it looks set to be eternal.

It is the sort of issue that used to be discussed at a country house called Uplands, where I was sent for two or three weeks soon after I joined the BBC to take part in what was styled a "Senior Management Course". I resisted offers made at around that time to become a producer and so to become entangled in the kind of decision-making that results in what eventually goes out over the air and onto our TV screens.

Such decisions are important, and working journalists like me understand that, but I have always preferred, like an old cobbler, to "stick to my last", which is that of reporting. I have found making decisions difficult enough in that field alone, and I have had no desire to seek challenges in production or management.

When I joined the BBC, it was expanding its news operation, especially for television. The BBC job that I obtained had been advertised in the *Times*, and I received a letter from the BBC foreign news editor, inviting me to apply for it. I learned later that he had sent around Fleet Street five other letters issuing similar invitations, and in view of the scrutiny to which BBC journalism has recently become subject, I think it is worth recalling what the recruitment procedures used to be, while adding that I have no idea how the corporation goes about its business these days.

I read with a sense of shock that a review team headed by a former BBC News boss, Ron Neil, had recommended post-Hutton that, among other things, a BBC journalism training college should be established. The idea came under early attack from the commentator, Stephen Glover, who asserted that the BBC "is going to send its journalists back to school". He described it as "a gross insult to the corporation's journalists", of whom there were some seven thousand before cuts were due to start.

Glover rightly argued that journalists should be properly trained, and he urged that the BBC should not take them on unless they had been, something that was, in my day, the case with the majority of BBC journalists. Like most of them, I imagine, Glover also rightly felt this way: "They must observe essential ground rules and, as in any newspaper, if they fail to do so they should be censured and, if they repeat the mistake, be fired."

He feared, though, what he called the "rather sinister" dangers of a new BBC journalism training school, "with its overtones of Soviet-style re-education as journalists are made to conform to guidelines laid down by bureaucrats and apparatchiks who may be hand in glove with the government of the day."

It is a strong point. Argument will continue while the BBC does what it can to regain its previously unchallengeable reputation for quality journalism.

When I was recruited in 1965, a journalist did not just stroll into a BBC staff job, as it appeared was the case when Andrew Marr was appointed BBC political editor in 2000 before going on to present his Sunday morning programme. As the *Daily Telegraph* pointed out in its fierce "blatantly biased corporation" editorial, Marr's main work had been as a columnist on a number of Labour-supporting newspapers; he had been a strong supporter of the New Labour project. "No one would pretend he is un-biased", yet, "it seems that the Beeb was so determined to bring him in that it did not bother, apparently, to approach anyone else."

Well, in my day the top jobs *were* advertised. Many journalists like me were accustomed to strolling into TV or radio studios to broadcast as outside contributors, but for important BBC staff posts, journalistic qualifications for the specific job vacancy were clearly laid down in the advertisement, and if they were lacking, an applicant would simply not be shortlisted.

Once accepted as a candidate, applicants had to undergo a kind of examination. I remember clearly what mine was. I had to write a four-and-a-half-minute script for radio on any topical subject dealing with Commonwealth or Colonial affairs and a one-and-a-half-minute script on the same subject for television. I was to bring the scripts along with me and be prepared to broadcast them. I was to attend a formal interview with a board composed of my potential employers. I also had to be prepared to conduct, at short notice, a television interview with an unspecified Commonwealth leader on an unspecified Commonwealth subject.

I duly wrote the scripts and took them along with me to a house in Portland Place, near Broadcasting House, where applicants were interviewed in a discreetly organised way so that none of us ever bumped embarrassingly into each other. I was handed a piece of paper with the names and positions of my four interviewers on it: the editors of TV News, Radio News, and World Service News, presided over by an official from the BBC appointments board representing the administration.

However, I was not prepared for what happened after my arrival in Portland Place. I was asked to go into a room in the basement of the building, and I opened the door, expecting to be greeted by the board. Instead, I stepped into a windowless and deserted studio, with nothing in it except for an upright reading desk in the middle of the room and a microphone. As I stood hesitantly just inside the door, a disembodied voice, addressing me by name, rather wearily said from a loudspeaker in the corner, "Good afternoon. Please go to the desk and read your radio script."

I walked to the desk and stood at it, searching in my briefcase for the script, trying to remain cool. As I delved, the same voice, even more wearily, said, "Take your time, please." This almost cracked me.

I managed to find the script and read it as well as I could. At the end, the voice, which by now I was beginning to hate, thanked me and asked me to walk upstairs to another room. There, I was at last permitted to meet the tormentors.

The whole point of this exercise was for the board to hear the broadcasting voice before meeting its owner. Judging by the frequently incomprehensible voices heard on the air or from the screen these days, such tests must have long since been dropped, although I do not state that as a fact. Perhaps the tests are still held and are then disregarded.

I felt that the board did not start too well when the chairman, the appointments board representative, began by asking me if I remembered him. I did not. It turned out that he was Patrick Jubb, former head of the Kenya Broadcasting Service, for which I had made a number of broadcasts while working in Africa.

I had never met Jubb himself before, but one Nairobi scoop I had reported for the *Daily Telegraph* was a plan to Africanise the broadcasting operation and to remove Patrick Jubb. My dispatch, he informed me (and his fellow members of the Appointments Board), was the first he had known about his imminent departure from Kenya.

He smiled at me and seemed to be enjoying any discomfiture that I might have displayed. Later I got to know him better as a radio producer; he was a charming and good professional.

One of the questions I remember being asked at the board was this: "How do you go about establishing the truth of any story which you are reporting?" It was, I have always thought, a marvellously BBC type of question.

My reply was something along the lines of this: "I would hesitate to claim that what I was reporting was actually the truth. I would claim, however, to have reported truthfully and accurately what I had seen or what I had been told, if possible with direct quotation and identification.

"I would claim further to have tried to obtain as many versions as possible of whatever it was that happened. With a bit of luck, the truth might be buried away in what I was told; but it would be for the reader, listener, or viewer to decide what the truth might be."

I added that I would, of course, if asked, give my own view of what the truth might be, but I would rarely, if ever, expect that view to be definitive.

To this day, I hold the same views on truth, especially when politicians, priests, lawyers, economists, historians, estate agents, journalists, or criminals claim to be speaking it. I have always had considerable sympathy for St. Thomas, the great doubter. I am wary of people who claim to know absolute truth about anything. Churchill memorably said, "Facts are better than dreams." Less memorably, I would argue that facts are better than truth. Like beauty, truth lies in the eye or the understanding of the beholder; and some beholders dismiss any facts that do not conform to their vision of the truth.

I was not so orotund at my BBC Board. After being questioned for forty-five minutes or so, I was bidden farewell and asked to go to a television studio to read to camera my TV script. Having finished that, the last test remained.

A young correspondent appeared and told me that I had five minutes before going into the TV studio to interview him. He was, he explained, President Jomo Kenyatta of Kenya, and he was in London discussing important and sensitive problems between Britain and Kenya. My job was to extract the news from him. Then he disappeared.

Five minutes later, I duly conducted the interview with President Kenyatta, impressively acted by the correspondent. I had never before met him, but subsequently we worked happily together. Thirty-eight years later, he recalled his performance as "Mzee" (the "Old Man") with a chuckle. He told me that he had repeated it for each of the six applicants for the vacancy. In his mind at the time, he said, I was the likeliest to get the job.

So it turned out, and on I went on with the corporation for the rest of my full-time working career for the next quarter of a century.

Actor-correspondent David Willey worked for the BBC for many years in Rome, where his authority on the Vatican and on Italian affairs was widely acknowledged. The occasion of our reunion was at a party he threw at his club in 2003. He was celebrating his award of the OBE, having been to Buckingham Palace earlier that afternoon for the investiture.

He had much appreciated his presentation to the Queen, but he was even more excited about having met the England footballer David Beckham, who had been another recipient of honours that day. I found myself working beside Willey for a spell after quitting Fleet Street. A group of us with contracts as London-based foreign correspondents, each with his own particular area of the world to look after, worked under the formal control of the foreign news editor, John Crawley, but equally directly under the informal guidance of the BBC's first diplomatic correspondent: the late Thomas Barman.

He was a wonderful chap, white-haired and distinguished with his austere, craggy features; a glint of sardonic humour lurked always in his eyes. He had a withering detestation of "cant" and "humbug", which warmed the hearts of his younger acolytes, such as myself, but which would have upset a lot of people these days (even as it did a few then). He was definitely not in favour of "emoting". He would not have approved of, say, Tony Blair. And as for one BBC correspondent, Barbara Flett, who described in a broadcast in the autumn of 2004 how she had started to cry at the departure from Palestine of somebody she described as a "frail old man", meaning Yasser Arafat, well, I shudder to think what Tom would have had to say about such lachrymose tendencies.

Even in these days, when emotional reporting seems often to be encouraged rather than discouraged, the BBC was mightily embarrassed by Barbara's tears. The corporation said it had been inundated with complaints, receiving more than five hundred.

One of Flett's senior Radio 4 colleagues was reported to have said that most BBC journalists took the view that shedding a tear for someone who had blood on his hands was "not appropriate". The same colleague also pointed out, "It was a daft thing to say but even dafter that no one picked it up prior to broadcast."

In fact, it was reported that senior editors had "remonstrated" with Flett over her words, but it was unclear as to whether or not those remonstrances came before or after the broadcast. Her description of her tears was acknowledged by the corporation to have been a "misjudgement"; and Flett, too, was said to have accepted that her on-air admission had been "misjudged".

I have to add as a personal comment that in my days at the BBC (let alone during Tom Barman's even earlier BBC existence), no producer would have permitted such self-indulgent sentimentality to get onto the air.

During World War II, Tom, who was originally an economist, served in Moscow with Stafford Cripps (later Chancellor of the Exchequer in Attlee's government) when Cripps was the British ambassador to the Soviet Union. I shall never forget Tom's welcoming words to me, as a reasonably well-established mid-career journalist at the age of thirty-five, upon occupation of my BBC office.

"Young man," he said, "I have only three things to say to you. First, I shall be irritated if you are late with the news. Second, I shall be angry if you are wrong with the news. Third, kindly remember that expenses are always a matter of careful diplomatic presentation."

Those three rules of thumb were extremely serviceable. Barman, though, had not yet finished with me: I had a lot more to learn. He asked me what it was that I thought I was going to do. Somewhat puzzled by this because he knew perfectly well what the terms of my job were, I spelled them out. I was, I told him, to report generally for BBC TV and Radio on Commonwealth and Colonial Affairs and to go to Commonwealth countries to cover developments when the BBC wanted me to do so.

In addition, while in London, I was to cover developments at two specific departments of state, both now vanished as independent entities, the Commonwealth Relations Office (now part of the Foreign and Commonwealth Office) and the Colonial Office (later the Department of Dependent Territories within the FCO).

In response to further questions, I replied that I fully expected to write and to broadcast reports for both TV and radio. Tom then explained to me how careless I had been in negotiating my contract and how I could have done much better for myself.

To illustrate this, he explained how his own position had evolved over the years, and I think it is worth recounting because it is not the sort of thing that gets into the volumes of any official history, such as that written about the BBC by Lord Asa Briggs.

Tom said that after the war, he had left the foreign service to join the BBC as diplomatic adviser in the newsroom because no such creature as a BBC diplomatic correspondent existed. His initial job was to advise newsroom editors on how to handle major foreign news developments. Sometimes he would talk to the editor; at other times, he would write a memo. He had a direct private telephone link in his office to the Foreign Office.

That link remained there for some years after he had retired; it was still there in my early years at the BBC; and it was used by his successor, Christopher Serpell, and, later, by myself.

Then one day, while still diplomatic adviser, Tom was asked by the powers that be who had noticed that newspapers possessed diplomatic correspondents, if he would mind doing the same sort of thing for the BBC. All it really meant, they said, was that his memos would be quoted on the air.

He pointed out that he was not a journalist but added that he was prepared to become one if necessary. His contract was renegotiated, to his financial benefit, and so listeners became acquainted in news bulletins with an interpretation of world events by the BBC diplomatic correspondent, as conveyed to them by the bulletin newsreader.

Later Tom was asked if he would mind actually broadcasting his dispatches (formerly his memos) himself. He pointed out this time that he was not a broadcaster, but he would be prepared to become one if necessary.

His contract was renegotiated, once more to his financial benefit, and listeners for the first time could listen to the voice as well as the dispatch of the BBC diplomatic correspondent.

Finally, with the creation of TV news, his contract was yet again changed because, naturally, Tom had never appeared anywhere on screen, but equally naturally, he was prepared to adapt himself to new terms of employment.

The burden of his message was that correspondents of my generation were selling far too cheaply our varied skills as journalists, broadcasters, and TV performers.

Tom Barman's authority as a journalist was such that he himself became an important source for top diplomatic news. Known all over Europe, he occasionally obtained major scoops that, in those days, the BBC was worried about broadcasting simply because they were scoops. (How times change!) Cherishing its reputation for reliability, the corporation did not rush to put on the air its own correspondent's report until the news in it had been confirmed by other news sources.

So, if Tom wanted to get his scoop onto the air, he first had to leak what he had discovered to a fellow correspondent, and he usually did this by talking to one of his foreign chums, almost always a French news agency correspondent.

When Agence France Presse or Reuter had published the news, then the BBC was happy and ran its own correspondent's piece. The fact that the original source for the news agency stories was Tom Barman was usually unknown to the newsroom, where the important thing was that the BBC was in possession of at least two respected sources for the news. It was ironic that in those days, journalists all over Europe trusted Tom Barman more than his employers did, just as it is ironic that those BBC employers who ought to have maintained the scrupulous standards of BBC journalism over the years seem to have allowed them to slip. Now the BBC governors themselves have vanished!

Despite Tom's authority as a journalist, TV News did not like him. Another veteran BBC correspondent, the late Reginald Turnill, for many years the BBC's space expert and a colleague of mine both on the BBC and even earlier (on the Press Association back in the 1950s), recalled in an article marking fifty years of TV News how Tom had been treated. According to Reg, the early days of TV News were "full of tension, even terror!" He described it thus:

"Many a reporter suffered instant execution at the end of the nightly bulletins. 'I don't want that man on *my* screen again!' the duty editor would declare. What was it about TV that created these arrogant monsters? With dismay, I saw it happen to men (and even to one or two women) whose reports I had used as models for my own. I was fortunate in that it never did happen to me.

"An example of TV terror was Tom Barman, veteran diplomatic correspondent. He was so afraid of dropping his script as he faced the all-devouring lens (no recordings then, and the very word 'autocue' had not been invented) that he safety-pinned his script to his thigh. The result was that he appeared to be continually glancing down to assure himself that he was securely zipped up. Senior correspondent or not, he was quickly dropped."

The diplomatic unit over which Tom had presided, and which preceded by many years the comparable TV World Affairs Unit later headed by John Simpson, was a mixed bag of half a dozen well-established and well-known foreign correspondents. Our most junior member was Frederick Forsyth, who went on to make more money and to become better known than any of us by writing excellent thrillers. He was twenty-eight and had joined the BBC from Reuter.

For a spell, he shared my office, a congenial companion. The war over Biafra began in Nigeria, and he was sent to cover the Biafran side of the conflict while the late Angus McDermid reported from the Nigerian federal side. Freddy did what I thought was an admirable job in Biafra, especially since it was his first experience not only of African wars, which I had warned him could be pretty nasty, but of Africa itself, a continent which had its own ways of presenting problems, ranging from malaria and bilharzia to crocodile and elephant.

As part of my duties, it was my task each night, for both TV and radio news, to do a round-up of developments in Nigeria, using material from both sides of the conflict to give as balanced a picture as possible.

One day the foreign news editor, the late Arthur Hutchinson, asked me into his office to read a telexed dispatch from Freddy in Biafra. It was a brilliant eyewitness account of an action between Biafran and federal troops, and I said so. Arthur, however, had qualms about the last paragraph, which I myself had read with some misgiving, because in it Freddy had allowed himself to air a personal opinion in a way that was bound to lead to argument. Something had been reported on the federal side about the area in Biafra, in which Freddy was working, that he knew to be untrue, and he had responded to it with vehemence.

Not content with using a few facts to knock down the federal propaganda, he had gone on to express criticism of Harold Wilson's government for supporting the federal side. This criticism was expressed emotionally and included a sentiment to the effect that Freddy was "ashamed to be British".

This particular phrase was what had upset Arthur. Stabbing with his fingers at the offending sentence, Arthur asked me, "What about this?"

I answered that all the BBC had to do was to lose the last paragraph and to broadcast the rest of the dispatch. No harm would be done, and the BBC would have given to the world a first-class news report.

This is what was done. The foreign news editor was still worried, however, about Freddy's gratuitous and personal feeling of shame, and the next day I was asked to send a service message to him via the Foreign Office.

Communications with Biafra were vestigial, and the BBC had difficulty getting in touch with Freddy directly. For quite a lot of the time he had to go into neighbouring Cameroun to get his dispatches out or to send them by courier, but one link which was relatively reliable (at least for service messages, if not for news dispatches) was via the British Deputy High Commission in Enugu, the capital of Biafra, in the heart of the rebel Ibo region of Nigeria.

This small British diplomatic enclave kept going even when the war was raging, and so did the Enugu link with London via the Diplomatic Wireless Service. The message I was instructed to ask Whitehall to send to the BBC correspondent in Biafra from the BBC foreign news editor was terse.

After congratulating Freddy upon the riveting eyewitness account of the battle he had seen, Arthur Hutchinson added three precise words: "Please eschew editorialisation."

Sometime later, when Freddy returned to London, I congratulated him on the good job he had done in Biafra, while at the same time warning him that he might "get a bit of stick" about his "editorialisation".

He went to see Hutchinson and returned an hour or so later to my office, white and trembling. I asked him what on earth had happened and he answered, "I'm finished!"

"Why?" I asked him. "Have you been sacked?"

His reply was that he had not been fired but that Hutchinson had told him that his reporting was not of the "calibre" required of BBC foreign correspondents. As a result, he was being sent to Westminster as an assistant to one of the predecessors of Nick Robinson and of Andrew Marr – the BBC political correspondent of the time, the late Peter Hardiman Scott.

The plan was that Freddy was to be educated a bit in political impartiality. It was the kind of appointment that hundreds of other journalists aged twenty-eight would have coveted. It was not enough for Freddy, though, and he quit the BBC.

He made the right personal decision. He became devoted to the Biafran cause, lost though it was, and his first book, *The Biafra Story*, was well publicised.

The first I knew about it was when Bill Hardcastle, then presenting the Radio 4 *World at One* programme, called me in to show me the book and to talk about it. Freddy had lambasted the BBC for what he saw as its pro-federal coverage of the war but had singled me out in the book as an experienced and fair interpreter of what had been going on.

In Bill's eyes, Freddy's complimentary words about me were going to be for me "the kiss of death" in the BBC. That didn't happen, of course. Nor was Freddy's departure from the BBC the end for him. His departure from it was, however, distinctly sudden and somewhat mysterious. He had been so upset after his roasting by Hutchinson that the successor to Tom Barman as diplomatic correspondent, the late Christopher Serpell, together with me, had a chat with Arthur to tell him that we thought he had been a bit hard on Freddy.

Arthur began to worry, and things came to a head when one day Peter Hardiman Scott called from Westminster to say that Freddy had not turned up for work, so Parliament and the lobby might be under-covered that day. Fearing that Freddy, in his upset state, might have contemplated harming himself, Arthur arranged for two of the most senior and respected BBC correspondents to go to Freddy's London flat to try to find out "discreetly" what had happened to him.

The two men were the court correspondent and former World War II correspondent, Godfrey Talbot, and the industrial correspondent, Alan Wheatley, both of whom told me about it. Wheatley, a friend of many years since we had worked together on the Press Association, said, "We got to the flat; we could get no reply, and we could not find anyone with a key to let us in."

How, then, did these two elderly pillars of BBC News exercise their

JOHN OSMAN

"discretion" in finding out what had happened to Freddy Forsyth? "We charged the door, and our combined weights broke it open."

Godfrey must have been nearly sixty by then, and Alan was fifty or more, but both were fairly hefty. They found no Freddy with his head in a gas oven. The place was deserted. The Biafra bird had flown.

In Biafra and elsewhere, Freddy had made numerous useful contacts, among them agents of the French intelligence service, from whom it is generally thought that he derived the original idea for his splendid bestseller *Day of the Jackal*. He never looked back, and while continuing to write bestsellers, he remains in fine, robust form as an opinionated letter writer to newspapers and magazines, airing his views without any fear these days of being asked to "eschew" them.

Tom Barman's introductory briefing at the BBC advising me on the need for "careful diplomatic presentation" of my expenses was underlined fairly quickly. I ran into trouble over a bill which I had submitted during a Commonwealth Prime Ministers' Conference, having entertained to lunch a couple of Australian diplomatists when seeking to get an interview with their prime minister.

From Arthur Hutchinson, the man who had reduced Freddy Forsyth to ashen-faced shakes, I received a stern memo:

> After much consideration and with serious doubt, I have finally decided to approve your expense claim. That I do so at all you can regard as a tribute to the very good job you did at the time of the Commonwealth Conference.
>
> This does not mean that you can count again, however, on "results" justifying heavy expenses.
>
> "There are more suitable ways of rewarding results than allowing the correspondent to 'claim' them through his expense accounts.
>
> Moreover, I serve you fair and formal notice that I shall not allow again a claim of anything approaching £11 for a lunch to a press attaché and a colleague. In my view, hospitality of this degree is absolutely unnecessary to maintaining useful contacts.
>
> I am totally unimpressed by the thought that the BBC's Commonwealth Correspondent might not have been received by

– 414 –

the Australian Prime Minister without preparatory hospitality
on this scale.

After this salvo, I was careful to follow meticulously Tom Barman's advice. As many MPs and ex-MPs have discovered in recent years, expenses are of course a subject of proper scrutiny. Just as their expenses were (and are) paid for by the taxpayer, spending BBC money is spending the money of the licence payer.

The subject of BBC expenditure (of all kinds) keeps cropping up, and it is with something of a sympathetic smile that every now and again I read about rows over such problems.

Lord Birt, for example, was reported to have been involved in controversy in 1993 when it was disclosed that he was not on the BBC staff, like previous director generals, but was being paid as a freelance consultant though his company, John Birt Productions. There was, too, unwelcome publicity about an Armani suit being bought on expenses for a director general and for a director general allegedly employing his wife as a secretary when he already had at least one staff secretary.

Then, in 2004, I read of a BBC inquiry into alleged fiddling of expenses by Alan Yentob, BBC creative director, executive, and television presenter. He was cleared of any wrongdoing, with the director general saying that an investigation had found no evidence of dishonesty, although the inquiry was reported to have concluded that Yentob, also head of drama, entertainment, and children's programmes, had taken "insufficient care over some aspects of his affairs".

The man conducting the investigation, the chief operating officer and finance director, John Smith, is reported to have urged the corporation to review the system by which expenses were filed after it had been described as "chaotic".

Expenses are part of the folklore of journalism, and one of the earliest expense stories to have become legendary in Fleet Street involved George Augustus Sala, founder member of both the Savages and of the London Press Club. He is identified in Andrew Marr's book as a dab hand at expenses, with Marr relating how, when Sala presented an invoice, "To expenses in Persia – £3,000", Sala was asked for a few more details. So he wrote, "To arsing and buggering about in Persia – £3,000."

Another legendary reporter who was perfunctory about his expenses was Charles Hands, who at one stage worked for Lord Northcliffe after the founding of the *Daily Mail*. Hands was dispatched to South Africa in the 1880s to cover what later became known as the "First Boer War" and upon his return submitted an expenses claim which, like Sala's original claim, simply said: "To covering war in South Africa, 1881" and put down a sum of money. That was it.

When he was sent off again in 1899 to cover the bigger principal Boer War, he was asked upon his return to provide more detail of his expenditure than he had previously done.

Thus his expense claim showed the cost of sixpence for a hansom cab from Fleet Street to Victoria on his departure in 1899, another sixpence for the cost of the cab from Victoria back to Fleet Street in 1902, and a sum of several thousand pounds for covering the second South African War from 1899 to 1902.

Journalistic folklore on expenses extended to the BBC, where there was a legend about a World War II correspondent who found himself languishing in London for a time and who submitted regular expense claims for lunching a Free Polish Army officer, Colonel Wyzsinski. After a spell, he received a note from BBC accountants, saying that a search of the War Office List and of the Free Polish Army List had failed to find any officer named Colonel Wyzsinski. Would he explain?

He replied with a memo: "Thank you for drawing my attention to Colonel Wyzsinski. For some time, I have had my doubts about this man. I shall no longer entertain him."

I doubt if any correspondent could get away with this now, on the BBC or anywhere else. My own most memorable BBC expenses claim, apart from the one for which I was rebuked, I submitted in 1974. I described it in an article I was asked to write for the BBC house magazine, *Ariel*, about the problems of reporting from Africa.

After describing the effect in Africa of the Lisbon coup that led to the end of the Portuguese empire, I wrote:

> *Peace moves between Portugal and the Frelimo African independence movement recently provided me with the chance to claim some expenses from the Corporation which I think must*

*be unique (I should be interested to hear if any of my colleagues
have had any similar experience).*

*In May, I flew from Lourenco Marques [now Maputo, the
Mozambique capital] via Madagascar, to Tanzania, with the
first Mozambique peace mission of six former prisoners of the
Portuguese Secret Police.*

*In Madagascar, they were unable to use the only money they
had, Mozambique escudos, since nobody outside Mozambique
wants the currency.*

*So, with BBC travellers' cheques, I financed the mission. I
bought them transit visas, hired taxis for them into Tananarive,
stood them lunch and a beer, and got them back to the airport.
In the process, I got exclusive interviews with them and broadcast over the phone to Radio Newsreel from Madagascar.*

*In submitting my expenses later to London, I explained the
circumstances and added the hope that "the Corporation will
regard it as a contribution towards peace in Africa".*

*I am happy to report that the Senior Personnel and
Administrative Assistant in Foreign News has recently informed
me: "I have noted all you say about the peace emissaries; all
is well."*

*I wish we could say the same about peace prospects in
Africa. Anyhow, the BBC has done its bit.*

Another memorable BBC expenses claim that sticks in my mind
impressed itself upon me because I had to sign it. It happened years after
my Mozambique-Madagascar sortie, when I had been transformed into
the BBC Moscow correspondent.

Our Moscow office driver, Vasily Samarsky, submitted the claim after
driving me for a week or so from Moscow to the Hungarian border, a
journey for which it had taken me four months to obtain official permission. Vasily would have been regarded in the West as a smart operator, a
sort of "spiv", but in those Brezhnev-era days, when foreign organisations
represented in the Soviet Union could legally employ Soviet citizens
only through an official department (the UPDK), Vasily's fellow drivers
regarded him with respect.

It was whispered that he held the rank of colonel in the Soviet secret police, the KGB. He possessed some sort of pass that, when he produced it, worked wonders with the Soviet police and militia. He also appeared to have the use of a weekend "dacha" in the countryside, from where he would sometimes return after a weekend's hunting with a haunch of venison that he would offer to us. We would gratefully accept.

Soviet movement control was rigid. Only after having received official permission could foreigners drive more than twenty-five miles (40 kilometres) outside Moscow. The permission had to be applied for at least three days beforehand and was often refused. We could refuel our vehicles only with special foreign exchange vouchers ("D coupons"), for which we had paid in advance with hard currency, not roubles. Our cars had special number plates: *D* for diplomatist; *M* for merchant (a small band of businessmen representing oil companies, British Airways, American Express, and so on); and *K* for "korrespondent" (people like me).

It was hard to avoid being noticed. We could refuel our cars only at designated petrol pumps authorised to refuel us and to accept foreign exchange. Outside Moscow, they were always difficult to locate. We were compelled to stay in hotels previously notified to the authorities (there was usually only one place in town anyway, usually without any bath plug and often without any food). We could travel a maximum of only three hundred kilometres (about 187 miles) a day – restrictions dating back to Tsarist times, when earlier limits were imposed on sledge journeys to ensure the safety of travellers against getting lost or snowbound in forests and blizzards or being attacked by wolves.

Whatever the reason for the travel limits, Vasily coped efficiently with all problems. When our office car, a Volkswagen Golf, broke down at one stage, he deposited my wife and me in a teahouse, where we sat for several hours sipping tea and playing chess, while he disappeared into the back streets of a Ukrainian town to get the exhaust repaired. Eventually, when we crossed into Hungary, taking with us the office car, he returned to Moscow.

He did not hurry to get back, as I discovered later on returning to the Soviet capital from home leave. I had left him with an open return air ticket to Moscow, but when he submitted his expenses claim, I found to my surprise that it included the cost of a couple of weeks in an hotel in Uzhgorod.

Knowing that the official pass he held in his wallet could have got him onto any aircraft he wanted, I expressed surprise at his long sojourn away. He replied that he had visited the airport every day, and every day he was told that the flight was full.

I knew that this was unlikely but also that I was unable to challenge it. Therefore, exhibiting my irritation, I told him that I would have to think about his expenses and reminded him that the cash came from BBC licence payers and that, as a good communist, he should not be misusing public money. He agreed and looked slightly worried when I said that I would have to talk to London about it and that I would let him have the answer in the morning.

Then I told him that I had decided to sign the expenses but that I was extremely displeased. Cheekily he replied: "Gaspodin Osman, so was my wife!" I managed not to laugh.

The earlier warning about my own expenses that I had received from the foreign news editor was softened by an attached, second memo:

> To provide a more welcome accompaniment to my memo on expenses, let me pass on simultaneously the following well-earned praise from Programme Editor, Current Affairs: "I would like to record our warm appreciation of the work of John Osman. I had cause only the other day to comment to Editor, News and Current Affairs himself on the high-quality interview Osman obtained from the Prime Minister at the conclusion of the Commonwealth Conference. We were able to run almost the entire ten-minute recording, and this exceptional length was fully justified by the thoughtful professionalism of Osman's questioning. It seems to us that those two qualities – thoughtfulness and professionalism – characterise all Osman's work."

To those kind words, Arthur Hutchinson added, "Let me say it gives me as much pleasure to pass on these comments as it has caused me regret to have to write to you in the terms I did about your expenses."

The interview mentioned in the memo was one I had conducted with Harold Wilson. I had asked him if he regretted having said, three years before, that the Rhodesian rebellion would be brought to an end "in a matter of months rather than years". In reply, he puffed away at his pipe, scowling at me through the smoke, and admitted that it had been a mistake.

This resulted in newspaper headlines because it was unprecedented in those days for a prime minister ever to admit to a mistake. It is, of course, rare for any politician to admit willingly or unwillingly to a mistake, hence the contortions displayed by Tony Blair as he faced his inquisitors over his policies on Iraq and over his presentation of those policies.

It is often suggested these days that interviewers before Jeremy Paxman, John Humphrys, and Jon Snow displayed too much deference towards those they interviewed. I take issue with this, and would claim that questions from journalists of our generation were every bit as tough as their questions are – and that we were just as tenacious as they are (and I am not suggesting that they are not good professionals, which they clearly are).

They are not actually the first, though, and they themselves would probably agree. I recall other questioners just as impressive: for instance, John Freeman in his *Face to Face* interviews, not to mention the late Robin Day.

My own feeling is that what has mainly altered has nothing to do with undue deference, as it is sometimes suggested, but it has quite a lot to do with courtesy and good manners. We did not so rudely interrupt those we were interviewing as some interviewers do today, and we sought information rather than seeking to prosecute.

We usually allowed somebody to complete a point without interrupting. We questioned or challenged it only when the point had been made. Nor did cabinet ministers display the spurious chumminess so nauseatingly produced in many of today's interviews, with ministers addressing interviewers by their forenames: "Well, John ..." or "Really, Jeremy ..."

Naturally, an interviewer has to try to keep an interviewee to the point and to frustrate attempts to waffle on so that awkward questions can be dodged. This justifies an arbitrary interruption, but it seems to me that such interruptions occur too frequently.

I get the impression often that the interviewer has a view that he or she wants to put over. The interviewer's viewpoint in my day was irrelevant and unwanted, certainly so by bosses such as Arthur Hutchinson. Like many of the characters I mention, Arthur died some time ago. He had a natural air about him of the headmaster; and I suppose that quite a few of us, like myself, were viewed by him as rather unruly acolytes in the disciplines of BBC foreign news. Arthur, like John Crawley and others of our foreign news chiefs, had previously himself been a foreign correspondent, but many of their successors had never actually done the job. Appreciation of the genuine problems faced by men and women in the field seemed to deteriorate as younger men and women, good perhaps as administrators or as technical whiz kids, but lacking any personal knowledge of the problems of covering overseas news developments, were placed in foreign news posts demanding greater background understanding than they could possibly have possessed.

Some of the best editors and news editors I have ever worked with were positively old, but their minds were sharp and they had extraordinary memories and an enormous fund of experience. They were impressive in their depth and breadth of comprehension and in their judgment of what was real news and what was not.

The absence of so many long-serving and *old* editors and news editors shows itself all too clearly in the shallowness of much of today's alleged news coverage, just as it does in the government of the country. Old men do not always forget; young men often do not know very much; and the same goes for old and young women as well.

My last major assignment for the *Daily Telegraph* before joining the BBC was covering the death and the lying-in-state of Winston Churchill. Then off I went to learn about writing TV scripts; putting together a TV News report; working with camera crews; and improving my radio delivery under the supervision of an experienced newsreader.

I also learned, pretty early on, about the dangers of overindulgence in alcohol before broadcasting. After twenty years of written journalism, and being by nature a lover of wine, whisky, and beer, I tried initially to carry on in exactly the same way as I had in my drinking habits, before becoming a broadcaster.

The first sign that all might not be as easy as it used to be arrived when one day I returned to the studio after a merry lunchtime session. After I had recorded a news tape, the studio manager, a woman, warned me: "John, your sibilants are slipping."

She replayed the tape, and she was correct. Fortunately, there was no urgency for it, and I recorded it again later. However, I came unstuck not long afterwards when I was covering a London conference drafting the new constitution for Mauritius, the Indian Ocean island that was about to become an independent state.

One of the principal negotiators on the Mauritian side was Sir Harold Walter, who later became the Mauritian foreign minister and a good friend. He came into Broadcasting House early in the evening to record an interview with me for the Radio 4 *World Tonight* programme (then known as *Ten O'clock*), and at 6.30 or so, we sat down comfortably with a drink. This welcome libation had been supplied from the programme's hospitality cabinet, and we chatted things over, and over, and over, with another little drink, and another little drink, and another little drink.

At 9.50 or so, a rather negligent producer who had not been watching us as closely as he should, came in and asked if we had yet recorded the interview. We had not.

So, rather hurriedly, we did the interview, lasting for five minutes or so, completing it just before the programme went on the air.

Without bothering to stay to listen to the broadcast, the two of us went out on the town and out on the toot. Next morning, feeling somewhat woolly-headed, I got into the office and received a first warning in the shape of a telephone call.

It came from the Mauritius High Commissioner in London. He wanted to know what had happened to the interview with his minister; it had not been broadcast. I said I would find out and call him back.

I joined the morning foreign news meeting, held every day, to discuss coverage of news for the day ahead and to conduct an inquest on the previous day's coverage. The inquest that particular morning was on two corpses: Sir Harold's and mine.

A tape was played of the two of us discussing problems that had to be resolved before Mauritius became independent. My questions were excellent and relevant; his answers were informative and equally relevant. The only problem was that we sounded drunk.

The programme had not broadcast the interview but insisted that Sir Harold and I should do it all again for that night, for the conference was still in progress, and what the minister had to say was still news.

Feeling pretty chastened, and not enjoying the ostentatious laughter at my expense, I returned to my office to call the High Commissioner. He said his minister was with him and wanted to talk to me. Sir Harold and I agreed that we had somewhat overstepped the mark, and he visited the BBC again. We duly rerecorded the interview, with much the same questions and much the same answers. This time, though, we were sober and the interview was broadcast.

This happened early in my BBC days and I am glad that it happened so quickly and relatively so painlessly. The lesson I had learned was this: as a journalist of the written word, I could dictate material while drunk, and provided that the material was up to scratch, it would be published. However, as a journalist of the spoken word or screen appearance, I could not be drunk if the material was going to be broadcasted. Even if the material was acceptable by itself, the voice or appearance would not be.

I am happy to be able to report therefore that I never did broadcast while anything but sober. What is more, I believe that the restraint imposed by broadcasting, especially the need to wait until a broadcast was over before doing any drinking, has probably saved me from greater drunkenness in my life than I have actually experienced. It might even have lengthened my existence!

That existence in the BBC lasted long enough for me to serve under five directors general: Hugh Carleton Greene, Charles Curran, Ian Trethowan, Alasdair Milne, and, briefly, Michael Checkland. After becoming a BBC pensioner, I continued to work as a freelance for the corporation for some years into the reign of John Birt as director general; and as I watched things change, with producers up to all sorts of odd tricks, I was fairly pleased that I had departed when I did. Along with others, I was shocked but essentially unsurprised by later developments culminating in the departures of the chairman of the Board of Governors and the director general as well as the disappearance of the Board of Governors itself. The writing had been on the BBC wall for some time, but nobody had really wanted to read it.

So the BBC has been compelled to start all over again, and her travails have worsened in recent post–Jimmy Savile years. My sympathies remain with "Auntie".

Two pictures of other journalist and me trying to push a broken-down train in the African bush, in an effort to try to report an attempted counter-coup in the capital of the Portuguese colony of Mozambique that had broken out following the 1974 military coup in Lisbon. The train had broken down while we were in it on our way from Johannesburg in South Africa to the Mozambican capital of Lourenco Marques, now Maputo. We were successful in getting to Maputo to report events; but the counter-coup was unsuccessful in its attempt to stop the withdrawal of Portugal from its African empire.

CHAPTER 22

===

"And So He Plays His Part"

While it remains to be seen how the new BBC governing structure will work in practice over the long term, it is a fair bet that BBC journalists will continue to cover the news as best they can. They have endured and survived many "restarts", though none on the scale of the most recent reorganisation.

Few journalists, however, experience restarts more routinely than foreign correspondents. Their individual job changes have never been easy, as I know from long experience. Only the most resilient manage to stick at the job for the larger part of their lives, with many quitting after a few years. The job is more a vocation than mere work.

As far as the foreign correspondent is concerned, his task entails a major commitment that starts over and over again as one tour of duty in a post ends and he or she is moved somewhere else. Like soldiers, sailors, airmen, diplomatists, or business executives of major companies, foreign correspondents (and their families) as a matter of course must uproot themselves regularly from an existence in one country to dig in again elsewhere. Quite apart from any domestic disturbance involved, frequently involving problems of health or of a child's education, it is also necessary to tackle a new language and to learn how to live in a different climate and culture.

The greatest conscious mental effort I have ever made in my adult life involved language learning. It came at the age of fifty-one, when I was dispatched to Moscow, my last foreign posting. Before we went, both my wife and I spent a couple of months immersing ourselves in Russian, in a language laboratory in London, for eight hours a day, plus homework in the evening: "nasha domajznaya zdanya." Then we headed for what was still the Soviet Union.

There, we continued for nearly three years to learn Russian with a tutor who, by the Soviet laws of those days, we were compelled to employ through an official department of the Foreign Ministry, the UPDK. Whatever her associations with the Communist Party might have been, our tutor, Lioubov Romanovna Karphukina, was a cultured woman and a patient teacher. My wife and I became friends with her.

By the time we left Russia three years later, I had acquired a vocabulary of some 4,000 words. Given that the ordinary Russian peasant in Tolstoy's day spent his entire life using a vocabulary of about 150 words of Russian (according to Tolstoy), we did not think that our effort was too bad. It was, though, undoubtedly just that: an effort. This was especially so when our daily lessons of an hour (plus homework) had to be fitted in with a demanding workload.

I remember being irritated during my Moscow stint when the magazine *Private Eye*, in one of its periodic bouts of BBC bashing, twice described me rather disparagingly as the BBC's "non-Russian-speaking Moscow correspondent". I dismissed the snide reference as irrelevant to my broadcasting productivity both for TV and radio and as being possibly motivated by somebody who perhaps wanted to be the BBC Moscow correspondent himself or herself. It was, however, the mean inaccuracy of the reference that most hurt.

I would not claim that I am a great linguist, but I have always made an effort to speak at least something of the language in the countries where I have worked, and *Private Eye* was quite aware of the fact that a tip-top linguist does not necessarily make a tip-top foreign correspondent.

I loved my unpredictable occupation, with all its risks and problems. I regarded it always, however, as being essentially a young man's game; and in my thirties, I had quietly decided to myself that I would get out of foreign correspondence at the age of fifty. This was largely because I had seen one or two correspondents over that age who really were not up to the job anymore. However, I was unable to resist the offer of the Moscow posting as I reached my half century, and I have never had regrets that I did so.

The decision for me to go there was taken after my wife had gone down in Africa with a bad bout of malaria in 1979 and I had suggested to the editor, the late Stan Taylor, that if any chance arose of a reposting for me out of Africa, it would be welcomed by Virginia and me. I had prided myself on never asking for an assignment and for going wherever my employers wanted me to go whenever they wanted it (sometimes, admittedly, after debate). That was my own concept of being a good reporter.

Some months after making my suggestion, I was recalled to London and had a chat with Stan. He told me of changes being made and then said, "You can go anywhere in the world that you like, John." I regard it as the top moment of my professional life: that offer by the world's greatest broadcasting organisation to let me go anywhere in the world I wanted. I chose Moscow.

After I had been there for a year or so, the BBC staff magazine, *Ariel,* asked me to write about the BBC set-up in the Soviet capital, and this is an extract of what I had to say in May 1981:

"The marvellous thing about knocking about the world on the Corporation's behalf is that, every few years, a foreign correspondent finds himself embarking upon a completely new existence. Thus, here in Moscow, I'm rediscovering a freshness to the job and to life itself which is, I think, rather a wonderful thing to be able to say at the age of fifty-two."

Those were sentiments that accurately summed up my feelings then, in 1979, and they remain unchanged today. Seven years earlier, in 1972, at the end of my three years or so in the United States, I had been asked to return to Africa, and I jumped at that chance too, for it was obvious that many of the greatest events in the history of the continent would be coming to a climax. I also possessed quite a bit of useful knowledge about Africa already, and that African posting led to a direct interest in things Russian and equipped me with a good deal of knowledge that proved useful when I ended up in Russia itself.

The occasion of my reposting was a major move by the BBC to divide correspondents into those serving TV and those serving radio. A few exceptions were to continue to serve both media. Until that moment, we had all generally produced news for both broadcasting media. Charles Wheeler and myself, for example, while working happily together in the

United States, would take it in turn to do one month for TV, the next for Radio.

Television, for reasons of its own that I have already touched upon with the case of Tom Barman, found several of the established correspondents unacceptable. Essentially, the TV bosses felt that such correspondents did not look right on the screen, no matter how authoritative or respected the correspondents might have been in their respective fields and among their fellow journalists.

So a TV fashion arose for recruiting and advancing younger men and women, some of whom became widely known and successful. Others disappeared from the screen fairly quickly as their journalistic inadequacies were revealed to be greater than their attractive screen personalities.

Years later, this all changed yet again when the BBC made a great to-do about every correspondent becoming a "bi-media" correspondent. In short, the great "bi-media" restart was more or less a reversion to the original position.

That 1972 division of correspondents between TV and radio news caused a huge reshuffle of foreign correspondents. I was first made aware of my own future being in the melting pot by a telephone call that I received in Washington from Johannesburg. It was from one of the most respected correspondents on the African scene, Angus McDermid. He had been told that he was unacceptable to TV and it was proposed that he should be the new radio man in Washington.

However, the BBC wanted to appoint to succeed him, as its new Southern Africa correspondent, somebody who was acceptable both to TV and radio. That person, he said, was likely to be me. I was taken aback, but Angus was an old friend, and he made it clear that he would love to move to Washington. He said that he himself would also like me to follow him in Africa. If I agreed to do that when asked to do so by my employers, he felt that he would "have Washington clinched". What did I feel about it?

I agreed to the move. At the same time, and participating in the same reshuffling process, Charles Wheeler was extracted from Washington and inserted into Brussels, where he became the first BBC European community correspondent. He and I were two of the exceptions among the BBC journalists of our generation who were regarded by TV as acceptable on screen as well as being known radio voices. Charles was succeeded in Washington as the new TV man by John Humphrys, now principally known as a successful *Today* presenter on Radio 4, while continuing with TV work as well.

My last dispatch from the United States was from the Democratic Party's convention in Miami, at which Senator George McGovern won the 1972 Democratic presidential nomination. My final dispatch was not about McGovern, however, nor was it about the looming election in which Richard Nixon would defeat him. It was about a mysterious burglary at an office of the Democratic Party in a new apartment building in Washington, called Watergate. Angus McDermid moved into an apartment in that building when he got to Washington, and he and John Humphrys reported the Watergate developments that led to the fall of Nixon.

As for me, I went off to Africa again, and there, as I had anticipated, I reported much endemic trouble and bloodshed together with a series of historic changes.

Portuguese rule ended in Africa, resulting swiftly in the death of Rhodesia, the birth of Zimbabwe, and the beginning of the transition from white rule to black rule in South Africa and South-West Africa, now Namibia. The Ethiopian empire ended; the French quit Djibouti; and the Soviets were booted out of Somalia, only for that country to decline into chaos and as a home today for pirates and terrorists.

Elsewhere troubles continued and worsened in the Sudan and the Congo; Uganda collapsed under the brutal Amin regime and is still rebuilding itself; the previously thriving East African Community was wrecked; and there were even coups d'etat in the holiday islands of the Seychelles and in the Comoros. News of the worst kind was always breaking in Africa, as it still seems to do today.

In the process of covering it, and without noticing it, apparently I became "larger than life" in Africa. This is a description applied to me in 2003 by Charles Onyango-Obbo, an African journalist who at that time was a managing editor with the Nation Media Group in Nairobi. He attributed my notoriety to the fact that I was reporting from the continent in the 1970s, "when dictatorships all over the continent clamped down on a free press". Because of this governmental repression of African newspapers and African broadcasting stations, the entire continent seemed to listen to the BBC, a point made by David Lamb of the *Los Angeles Times* in his excellent book about the Africans.

David reported in it how, for instance, "in Somalia, government offices come to a standstill at five o'clock each weekday when the BBC broadcasts its news and commentary in the Somali language". I could add to that how, when covering from the Somali side the "Ogaden War" between Ethiopia and Somalia in the 1970s, a large crowd gathered every time in the main post office in Mogadishu when word got around from the Somali operators that I would be broadcasting at a certain time from there to London. It was just as disconcerting doing my work in front of an intently listening Somali audience in the main hall of the post office as it had been in the incident described earlier, when I stood in front of the door of 10, Downing Street, with a Ministry of Works vehicle reversing rapidly towards me as I talked to the BBC TV camera. That, however, happened only once; the Somali performance was a daily show that went on for weeks.

It must have been a hit because years later, when the Americans made their short-lived and unhappy intervention in Somalia during the Clinton presidency, a BBC correspondent who was there at the time, the late Brian Barron, told me that everywhere he went in Somalia, he was asked if he knew me. He told me that his stock rose when he said that he did.

A similar thing happened much later, when a senior man from the BBC World Service, Mark Brayne, visited Mongolia following the collapse of Soviet Communism. Everywhere he went, he too was asked if he knew me. This was because I had been the first BBC correspondent to have visited Mongolia and to have broadcast, years earlier, from the Mongolian capital, Ulan Bator.

Then, everything was still heavily communist-controlled; the echoes on my satellite connection from Mongolia via Moscow to London were so odd that the presenter in those days of the *Today* programme, John Timpson, remarked that I sounded as if I were talking from "the only bathroom in Mongolia".

Baths were in fact quite rare there, and they were utterly non-existent in the Gobi Desert, where my wife and I were travelling on one of the more distinctive journeys I have experienced in a life full of exciting trips.

We slept on the steppes in what Mongolians call a *ger* and Russians and others call a "yurt". To do now what we did then is sold as an enticing aspect of package tourism today.

A habitation of ancient origin, the *ger* is a circular mobile home of felt, quickly assembled and equally quickly dismantled, for transport upon a horse or on the double-humped back of the Bactrian camel.

It was while seated by a stove in the centre of such a *ger*, sipping strongly fermented camel mare's milk, *khumyss*, that I enjoyed with a grizzled Mongolian nomad herdsman the most extraordinary conversation about English literature that I have ever had in my life. On being told by my Mongolian "minder", escort, and translator that I was English, the old man asked me if I knew an Englishman he had heard of, by the name of William Shakespeare.

I explained that Shakespeare had been dead for some time but that I knew most of his work. Then the old man told me had once been to Ulan Bator, where he had seen a play by "this Englishman, Shakespeare". It had been about a black man who became jealous of his white wife and had murdered her. He had thought it was wonderful. He had in mind, of course, *Othello*.

As the conversation went on, I became aware that my minder was becoming unusually animated. An official of the Mongolian Foreign Ministry, he had served in the West at the United Nations and elsewhere. He was called Choinkhor, and until that moment, he had behaved as most communist officials did with Western correspondents: correct, formal, poker-faced, cold. Suddenly, he became human, smiling and obviously interested in what we were talking about. As we settled down in the ger on the windswept steppe to discuss Shakespeare for a couple of hours or more, the reason emerged for the transformation.

Choinkhor regretted the fact that *Othello* had been translated into Mongolian not from the original Elizabethan English but from a Russian translation of that. It emerged then that most Mongolian versions of foreign literature had been translated not from the original languages but from Russian versions.

As a result, Choinkhor, a keen Shakespearean scholar, had himself embarked upon the translation of the entire works of Shakespeare directly from English into Mongolian, including the sonnets.

I warned him that he was committing himself to the work of a lifetime, especially after he had explained how Mongolian poetry rhymed
at the start of a sentence rather than at the end and how the Mongolian
alphabet is written vertically downward (meaning that in reading and
writing Mongolian, the eye goes up and down, rather than from side to
side). It is far removed from Western scripts and alphabets.

None of my doubts bothered him. His enthusiasm was unbridled,
and I was infected. I returned to Moscow with a list of Shakespearean
Elizabethan words that he wanted defined in modern English. After
consulting what dictionaries and reference books I could, I wrote to
Choinkhor with what I hope was an adequate letter, feeling that perhaps
I should have been working for the British Council rather than the BBC.

Choinkhor's name, like many Mongolian names, was derived from
Tibetan. Incredibly but appropriately, when translated it meant "book
lover". It was very odd sitting in a ger in central Asia, trying to explain
the meanings of words like "fardel" and "bodkin". To this day, I remain in touch with Choinkhor and his wife, and their enthusiasm for
Shakespeare's work is undiminished.

My visit to Mongolia ended with an interview with the Mongolian
leader, President Yuumjaagin Tsedenbal, who at that time was the world's
longest-serving head of any communist state. He had been appointed
general secretary of the Mongolian People's Revolutionary Party at the
age of twenty-three, in 1940. When he talked to me forty years later, he
was still running Mongolia, with Russian "advice". He looked like an
Asian Mr Pickwick and was charm itself.

He dealt deftly with my bluntest questions. He was uncompromisingly pro-Russian, was married to a Russian, and his children were
married to Russians. A statue of Stalin still stood outside the Mongolian
Academy of Sciences in Ulan Bator at a time when statues of Stalin were
being pulled down all over the Soviet Union, except in Stalin's native state
of Georgia. The statue was a reminder to anyone seeing it that Stalin had
saved Mongolia in the 1930s from Japanese invaders when he sent the Red
Army to help defend the country.

By the time I was there, however, Mongolia, like Russia, was more
worried about China than about Japan. Sino-Russian strains were acutely
felt because Mongolia is sandwiched between the two great powers,

possessing a long border with each of them. The degree of Mongolian anxiety about the two could be relied upon as a kind of accurate diplomatic litmus test reflecting the current state of relations between China and Russia.

At one point, my wife and I benefited from this in the most direct way possible: by being offered much-needed food when none was available in our hotel. It happened after a party of forty or so British birdwatchers ran into trouble on a pioneering railway trip from Victoria in London to Victoria in Kowloon, then part of the British Hong Kong territories. When the birdwatchers' train reached Ulan Bator, the Russian crew who had brought it from Moscow handed the train over to a Chinese crew, taking it on to Beijing. Sino-Soviet relations were cool at the time, and some sort of dispute broke out between the Russian and the Chinese railwaymen.

In dudgeon, the Chinese crew set off with the train to China without warning any of the passengers. Most of the birdwatchers were still on the platform and some on the train. A key member of the party was a guide with most of the passports, including the passports of those on the train. He was left on the platform.

Off the stranded birdwatchers trooped to the British Embassy to get things sorted out and to see if the embassy had any food. They foresaw difficulties for their chums arriving at the Mongolian frontier with China without any documentation. To get things repaired, however, was easier said than done.

As a first step, the British ambassador in Mongolia, an old friend of mine from the Sudan, Tom Haining, had to warn his colleagues at the Beijing Embassy that a bunch of British birdwatchers without passports were about to reach the Chinese-Mongolian frontier and to ask the embassy in Beijing to intervene with the Chinese to smooth the party's entry into China. He could not, however, just pick up the telephone and call his fellow diplomatists a mere eight hundred miles or so along the railway track.

For security and communication reasons, he could only get in touch with the embassy in Beijing via the Foreign Office in London. To do that, the wireless operator and cipher clerk of the embassy in Mongolia had to send messages via the Diplomatic Wireless Service to Canberra, the

Australian capital. Thence they were transmitted onward to London, from where they were sent to Beijing. Replies came back over the same route.

Unbelievably, at that time, in 1981, the Diplomatic Wireless Service connection between Mongolia and Australia was operated with the use of Morse. To the best of my knowledge, it was the last Foreign Office Morse code link. Still, it all worked and none of it ever seemed to have been WikiLeaked, as has happened to recent diplomatic messages.

Eventually, the birdwatchers got to where they were supposed to be going.

Their unexpected presence in the Mongolian capital, however, had created a problem for the ambassador and his wife, for those stranded had to be fed while their travel plans were revised, and food was not easy to come by in Ulan Bator. In our enormous empty Stalinesque hotel, for instance, we could get nothing to eat and nothing to drink, except for water. There was not even a cup of tea or coffee.

Fortunately for my wife and me, the problem of the birdwatchers had arisen just as we ourselves reached Ulan Bator. It was in the period just after the Queen's official birthday, an occasion for which Tom and his wife, Patricia, had imported dozens of pizzas to offer to their expected diplomatic and political guests. Pizzas were a great delicacy by the central Asian standards of those days, and although many had been eaten at the embassy party, some of the wonderful "goodies" had been left over for eventual grateful consumption by the birdwatchers, Virginia, and me.

After that, for food in the hotel, we relied mainly upon the charity of the Australian ambassador to Mongolia, David Evans, who was based in Moscow but accredited to Ulan Bator. He had travelled by train from Russia to present his ambassadorial credentials, and he and his wife had brought with them a railway coach-load of food and drink. My wife, who in Moscow was then an active freelance for sixteen news organisations around the world, numbered among her clients the major newspaper, the *Australian*; and she filled several pages of that newspaper with an account of Mongolian-Australian affairs. Meanwhile, David and Pamela Evans helped to fill our stomachs and slake our thirsts with victuals presumably paid for by the Australian taxpayers.

One of the unusual sights in our echoingly vast and unpopulated hotel was the embryo French Embassy. It consisted then of a table in the dining room upon which stood a miniature Tricouleur. The recently appointed ambassador was trying to find a building to rent, in which he could set up diplomatic shop. Meanwhile, he was operating out of the hotel with lonely Gallic dignity and was usually seated at his be-flagged table. As befitted a Frenchman, he had the sole table in the dining room where food was regularly served.

France and Britain were then the only two Western countries with embassies in Ulan Bator, although a few non-aligned countries, such as India, were also represented there. Other embassies were communist, except for Japan, geopolitically western although geographically eastern.

The British ambassador and his Japanese colleague played golf together and were members of a highly unusual golf club. They managed with Mongolian acquiescence to set out some sort of course on the steppe, with the skulls of nomadic horses and camels marking each tee. The club was called, in honour of the Queen and of her fellow head of state, the emperor of Japan, the Royal Imperial Ulan Bator Golf Club, a resounding name for a remote and exclusive group of golfers.

It had taken several months' work in Moscow to obtain visas for my wife and me to obtain entry to Mongolia, the country then being difficult to visit. Now it is an attractive destination for tourists, and I was interested to watch a "docudrama" screened by the BBC on Genghis Khan and to learn that his reputation is being revised. The communists had done their best to obliterate his memory from history, and Russians rarely mentioned him. They thought of him simply as a conqueror who had sacked Kiev and used the Golden Horde to occupy Russia.

Sir John Ure, a former British ambassador who visited Mongolia twenty years or more after I was there produced a highly readable book, *In Search of Nomads*.

He reported in April 2005 that in Mongolia the yak-tail banners of Genghis Khan had replaced the Red Flag and that the Khan's exploits "are once more the subject of song and saga". Sir John encountered a film company shooting a scene depicting the early life of Genghis, with the screen warriors including "Mongolian Army soldiers moonlighting for extras' pay".

After my own Mongolian travels in 1981, the programmes broadcast by the BBC were well received, especially in Mongolia, if only because of their rarity value. It helped to explain why Mark Brayne, as mentioned above, was years later asked in Mongolia if he knew me.

Finding this kind of fame in far-off places is not unusual for a BBC foreign correspondent, and it sometimes helps in newsgathering. If any individual or group of persons has news that they want made known to the world, then that person or group often seeks out the reporter they have listened to on radio or watched on TV.

The other side of the coin, of course, is that if those in power any-where do not like such news being broadcast or published, then the foreign correspondent all too often runs into trouble. The craft is not a soft or glamorous option of the kind that many people, including some journalists, seem to think it is. Trouble and handling it goes with the job.

President Jomo Kenyatta's successor as Kenya's Head of State, President Daniel Arap Moi, gave the BBC and me his first interview as the second leader of independent Kenya when he came to power in 1978.

CHAPTER 23

From Africa to Russia

Despite the collapse of Communism in Russia, heavy-handed Kremlin habits die hard. As recent events have underlined, neighbouring states that were previously part of the Soviet Union, like the Ukraine and Georgia, understand this all too well. As an ex-KGB officer, President Putin knows how to exert pressure against countries, organisations, companies, and people that he feels, for Russia's sake, it is necessary to challenge, control, restrain, or – if necessary – simply eliminate.

My blood (thinning as it probably is at the age of 85) ran even colder than usual as I read in November 2014 that Vladimir Putin had been defending before an audience of young historians in Moscow the notorious 1939 Nazi-Soviet Pact, signed by Germany's foreign minister, Joachim von Ribbentrop, and the Soviet foreign minister, Vyacheslav Molotov. Putin is reported to have suggested that there was nothing bad about that non-aggression treaty between Nazi Germany and the Soviet Union.

He was quoted as saying (in a Kremlin transcript of his speech): "The Soviet Union signed a non-aggression treaty with Germany. People say, 'Ach, that's bad.' But what's bad about that if the Soviet Union didn't want to fight? What's bad about it?"

What, apparently, he did not enlarge upon were the secret protocols attached to the pact. In those, the Nazis and the Communists agreed to divide up Poland, Finland, Estonia, Lithuania, Latvia and Romania into spheres of influence. The secret protocols were officially denied by the Kremlin until 1989 but Putin in his latest explanation of the Russian position implied that the protocols remain a matter of dispute, saying "people still argue about the Molotov-Ribbentrop pact and accuse the Soviet Union of dividing up Poland."

That, of course, is precisely what happened when Hitler invaded Poland: the Soviets simply took over the eastern parts of Poland reserved for them under the secret protocols as their sphere of influence. In the process over 20,000 arrested and captured Poles were executed by the Soviet secret police in the 1940 Katyn massacre.

The truth is that the 1939 Ribbentrop-Molotov Treaty was signed by two foreign ministers acting on behalf of their masters who were perhaps history's two most mass-murdering thugs: Hitler and Stalin. Historians will continue to argue over which of them was worst. Stalin of course became our wartime ally when his fellow-thug turned on him and tried to finish off Soviet Russia. He failed; so learning, like Napoleon before him, that Russia, whether Communist or Tsarist, is no push-over.

The Poles, who have suffered over the centuries unwanted occupation by Swedes, Germans and Russians, even have a bleak joke about Russian toughness. It was told to me in Cracow when I was in that lovely old Polish city a year or two ago and I was talking with a Pole about Russian-Chinese political and economic strains as reflected in Outer Mongolia, squashed between China and Russia. "Ah!" the Pole commented. "At least we don't have to worry like the Mongols about China! The Chinese would have to come through Russia first to get at us!"

Putin's apparent apologia for the Ribbentrop-Molotov treaty follows his earlier condemnation of it in 2009 as "immoral." His latest thesis appears to be that France and Great Britain had in 1938 destroyed any chance for an anti-fascist front with Neville Chamberlain's Munich Agreement.

My shivers over Putin's latest view of the Ribbentrop-Molotov agreement in 1939 were quickened when I read at roughly the same time that the former Russian leader, Mikhail Gorbachev, at the age of 83, had warned us all in a speech near the Brandenburg Gate in Berlin during celebrations to mark the 25th anniversary of the fall of the Berlin Wall, that the world is edging closer to a new Cold War. He said: "Some are even saying that it has already begun."

Apart from endemic difficulties in neighbourly relations (to pick a commercial example from just one of Moscow's many unfinished stories), the Russian government at one stage went along with worrying confrontations involving international oil firms such as BP. Foreign governments condemned what they saw as Russia's increasingly nationalist oil policy, so threatening the rights of energy firms to develop oil and gas possibilities across the country, even when such rights had been negotiated and agreed with the Russian government itself.

An argument advanced later by the Russians was that such rights had been conceded under the previous Yeltsin regime and that many deals done then involved corruption. True or not, it did not prevent suspicion in the rest of the world that Russia was reneging on its agreements. Such suspicions did no good for Putin's international image, and the same went for the Kremlin's murky involvement with the nuclear industry in Iran.

The problem in sorting out such problems is that, as so often is the case, all concerned must agree on what the facts and realities actually are. This process is possibly almost as difficult in today's Russia as it was in my Russia thirty years ago. Historically, under both the tsars and the commissars, Russian affairs had always tended to be opaque, and Winston Churchill's 1939 remark is probably as accurate a summary about Russia over the centuries as it is possible to find: "a riddle wrapped in a mystery inside an enigma."

That was certainly the case when I arrived in Moscow in 1980. If the task of letting people know what was happening in their own countries had been difficult in Africa, the challenge was even greater in the Soviet Union.

What's more, on a purely personal basis, moving from the sun and heat of Africa to the snow and cold of Russia needed adjustment not only to the demands of a different job but also to the requirements of physical existence.

For example, it was not easy to keep fit, as I had done in Africa, by regularly playing squash and tennis. This was because at the time, there was only one squash court in the entire Soviet Union. It was in the grounds of the Indian Embassy in Moscow. According to Muscovite legend, after Indian independence, Stalin was keen to develop Indo-Soviet relations, and when a new Indian ambassador presented his credentials, Stalin asked him if he wanted anything special. India's envoy expressed a wish for a squash court, and Stalin agreed.

When the meeting ended, Stalin asked his staff to find out what a squash court was, for he did not know. Neither did most of his staff. The upshot was that a pavilion in the spacious Indian embassy enclave became a squash court.

In my years in Moscow, that is where anybody who wanted to play squash could go and get a game – provided that the Indians had no objection. In summer, my wife and I also used to play tennis in the grounds of the British Embassy, in those days opposite the Kremlin, across the Moscow River. Since then, Russians have taken up that sport in a professional way and the Russian tennis invasion of "Grand Slam" international events has been notable.

It does not yet seem to have been followed up by any similar outburst of Russian expertise in squash, although some Russians did play the game even when I was there. The desire of one of them, a Soviet Foreign Ministry official, to join the squash set (composed wholly of non-communists) caused animated debate among the regular players.

Because of the suspicious climate of the times, there was hesitation about whether or not we should let him join us. Some felt that he might have motives for joining our circle other than the mere pleasure of the game. It was even suggested that he might try to "bug" the court. He was a pleasant man called Pechernikov, and he told me that he had discovered squash in New Zealand while at the Soviet Embassy there. He was responsible for maintaining contact with the British media, and while we wanted to encourage this, we did not want it at the risk of being spied upon in one of the few places in Moscow where we felt relatively free.

It was agreed that we should talk to our Indian host about the problem, and the ambassador decided that, provided the embassy was always informed in advance when Pechernikov was entering the precincts for a match (thus giving the Indians the chance to carry out any necessary "anti-bugging" or security arrangements), there would be no objection.

I was pleased with the outcome because Pechernikov had been helpful towards me personally even during a period when I had fallen into bad odour with the Soviet authorities. This could have been at some risk to himself. So I brought a new squash racket back from London for him. We even managed a game or two together, once I had been rehabilitated in official Soviet eyes and it seemed safer, for him, to be seen with me again.

The reason for my unpopularity with the Soviets had arisen directly because of my knowledge of things African. It had come at a moment when the Soviet Union was banging its anti-apartheid, anti–South African propaganda drum rather more loudly than usual while entertaining in Moscow several African leaders who, at that time, had a reputation for their close communist links and Soviet backing. They included men like Brigadier Mengistu Haile Mariam from Ethiopia (who, after his role in finishing off Emperor Haile Selassie and the Ethiopian empire, became an exile in Robert Mugabe's unhappy Zimbabwe) and Samora Machel (a Marxist who became president of Mozambique before dying in an air crash).

While orchestrated hostility to South Africa was performed by the Russians in, so to speak, "crescendo", I uncovered discreet Soviet-South African contacts that were being conducted very much in "diminuendo". The discovery started at the Bolshoi Theatre in November 1980. My wife and I were there for a performance of Mussorgsky's opera *Boris Godunov*. During the interval, as I reported later, "I got a real surprise when, going into the bar, I bumped into somebody who was the very last sort of person most people would expect to meet in this country: a senior executive of Harry Oppenheimer's South African mining empire, Anglo-American."

I reported upon the encounter and explained its implications for the world's gold, diamond, and platinum markets. The Soviets were displeased, and the authorities made plain their disapproval of my reporting. They sent me "to Coventry" for several months and struck my name from official invitation lists for foreign correspondents.

It might have been worse: I could, for example, have been expelled from the Soviet Union or even jailed for writing unauthorised material about a sensitive subject such as Soviet gold, a state secret in the eyes of those in power ever since Lenin's time.

The BBC had considered these possibilities when, before broadcasting my dispatch, I held telephone consultations from Moscow with the editor over possible repercussions. A decision was taken by those in authority to go ahead and broadcast the story: "Publish and be damned!"

Some months later, I appeared in April 1981 in a *Panorama* BBC television programme that had followed up my initial report. One of their top reporters had further investigated collusion between the Soviets and the South Africans over gold and diamonds in other countries, such as Switzerland and England, establishing its existence beyond any doubt.

Things began to get a bit hot for me when, at one stage, Moscow Radio asserted that the British Secret Intelligence Service was using the BBC "and its news bureaux abroad" to "harbour agents". This was a most unpropitious moment, and I did not like it at all, implying as it did that I was perhaps a spy.

I explained to Radio 4 in a broadcast in May 1981 why I had been so surprised by the Bolshoi South African encounter and why the Soviets were so annoyed with me for reporting it:

> *The reason I was so astonished, like many others here when I started inquiring about it, is that for years the Soviet Union and South Africa have been expressing nothing but hostility towards each other. The mere suggestion of any links of any kind produces angry denials from the officially controlled mouthpieces of the Soviet Union. As the news agency TASS puts it, "Our country does not support either diplomatic, or political, or economic, or trade, or any other contacts with the South African regime." Tass scornfully dismissed what it described as "talk" of what it called "mythical trade contacts".*
>
> *However, there was nothing mythical about the man in the Bolshoi bar, Mr Gordon Waddell (who was at one time a South African MP and who had been talked of as a potential successor to Harry Oppenheimer as chairman of Anglo-American). Nor was there anything mythical about the other Anglo-American man with Mr Waddell. Neither was there anything insubstantial about the two Soviet officials with the two men from South Africa. It has been noticeable, too, in the fuss which arose after the BBC television programme, Panorama, in April reported possible collusion between this country and South Africa in handling in handling diamond, gold and platinum marketing that, although denials flew thick and fast, there was no denial of Mr Waddell's presence here and no explanation either. When I asked him what he was doing here, his answer was that he was "just passing*

through." I've been unable to find out anything more. The secrecy is not surprising.

The fact was, of course, that the Soviets were furious over the exposure of their political hypocrisy. Their irritation was probably exacerbated by the mere fact that I was daring to trespass upon and into a forbidden field: the subject of what the Russians did with their gold.

South Africa and the Soviet Union were then the world's two biggest producers of gold and diamonds, and although at opposite ends of the political spectrum, they shared a mutual economic interest in maintaining prices and selling their products at the best prices they could get. Important though they were (and still are) to the Soviet economy, everything about the Soviet gold, diamonds and platinum industries was kept as much in the dark as possible. I stressed this in one of my broadcasts:

For instance, the Soviet Encyclopaedia on the subject is typical: it gives figures on foreign gold production, plus details about the proportion of foreign countries' reserves held in gold, but no such information is provided about the Soviet Union. All the Encyclopaedia says, blandly, is that in the USSR and other socialist countries (meaning communist countries), gold reserves "are a part of the national economic reserves saved and used in a planned order according to the interests of building socialism and communism, and to increase the well-being of the people of those countries".

I could not resist adding a personal thought:

Well, perhaps that fits in with one of the main aims of Lenin: "When we are victorious on the world scale," he once said in a famous quotation, "I think we shall use gold for the purpose of building public lavatories."

Now, in 2015, ninety-eight years after the 1917 revolution, the moment for gold-tiled public loos still has not arrived. Gold remains a sought-after commodity, even though in Great Britain a few years ago Gordon Brown, as Chancellor of the Exchequer, appeared, like Lenin, to want to devalue the metal when he sold off quite a chunk of British gold reserves at a price that was thought at the time to be low and turned out indeed to have been so. Perhaps he, as a socialist, was motivated by at least some of the thoughts about gold expressed in the Soviet encyclopaedia, although I do not understand how precisely selling British gold at a low price would have increased "the well-being of the people" of Britain, not to mention taxpayers among those people. As a financial ignoramus, I can presume only that the chancellor needed the money at the time for something or other.

Whatever his reasons, and no matter what financial and political jiggery-pokery is called into play when governments try to talk down the value of the precious ore, the hard reality remains that the metal called gold, like the liquid called oil, has specific and much-needed qualities. To benefit from those, however, a tremendous amount of human knowledge and work has to be applied. As King Midas discovered to his discomfort when his avaricious wish was fulfilled and "everything he touched turned to gold", the metal cannot be eaten, any more than oil can be drunk. The labour and skills required to extract the crude commodities from beneath the earth or its waters, often carried out in appalling geographical and climatic conditions, are well known and much of the gold mining both in Tsarist Russia and in the Soviet Union was for many years carried out with brutality amounting more or less to slave labour.

Few foreigners ever got to see what was going on, in contrast with gold mining in South Africa, where a visit to a gold mine was (and probably remains) on many a tourist itinerary. My disclosures about the Soviet-South African contacts were given a lot of publicity around the world, with major news agencies picking up the story and newspapers and broadcasting stations reporting them.

They resulted in my discovery of yet another unsuspected connection between Moscow and South Africa: a telephone link! An unexpected call from Johannesburg reached me in the BBC Moscow office. It came from an old colleague and friend, Tertius Mybergh, then editor of the Johannesburg *Sunday Times*, who wanted to take the story further for South African consumption. I could not help him much, alas!

After six months or so had passed and I had become accustomed to my status as an official pariah and to exclusion from all Soviet functions, I was eventually restored to the list of the acceptable. Beforehand, though, I was given indirectly to understand that my expulsion was under "active consideration". I was kept in suspense until the actual moment of formal forgiveness arrived. First, however, I had to be rapped over the knuckles.

Thus one day in 1981, I was summoned to meet a senior Soviet Foreign Ministry official, one of the bosses of my squash partner Pechernikov, at a Moscow restaurant. It was more of a command than an invitation: "Osman, you will be there at one p.m.!" I warned my wife to be ready to leave the Soviet Union at short notice.

The moment I arrived at the restaurant, I sensed that I was not going to be kicked out after all. This was because I saw set out for my host and myself on the table two little glass jugs containing "Sto gramma" (one hundred grams) of vodka. I thought it would be unusual that they would offer me a drink if I was about to be deported.

The lunchtime showdown (a kind of diplomatic and journalistic cricket match) began with my host opening the bowling, delivering the first ball with an expression on his face indicating that he was playing more in sorrow than in anger. He put down an opening googly: "Why did you do it?"

I played a straight bat in response: "Do what?"

He then launched an attacking over, bowling a series of fastballs at me, listing my misdeeds. First, why should I find it odd that a prominent South African personality should be in the company of Soviet officials in Moscow? (This at a time when the Soviets were excoriating South Africa hourly for its misdeeds!)

Second, why did I write and broadcast about such a meeting, speculating that it had something to do with gold and diamonds? (Despite the visitor's conspicuous connection with gold and diamonds!)

Third, why did I do all this when African leaders hostile to South Africa were in Moscow as Soviet guests? (Therefore, presumably, making the host look pretty cynical). Fourth, why did *Panorama* make such a song and dance about it all? (The programme began with ethereally beautiful shots of snow falling at night on the Bolshoi, and it continued with my account of the theatre bar encounter, extracted from me by my interviewer, John Humphrys. His cameraman had carefully arranged the BBC Moscow apartment to underline the Russian nature of everything: beside me was a chess set and behind me a samovar).

In short, why had I made such a nuisance of myself to the Soviet authorities?

I opened my innings with caution. I asked if he was challenging any of my facts. Those were scanty but interesting. I put them to him one by one, thus pinching a series of useful singles because he could not deny those facts.

There was the unexpected Moscow meeting itself with a prominent South African in the company of Soviet officials. There was the South African's limp reply to my question as to what he was doing in Moscow. (His impromptu and rather embarrassed phrase, "just passing through", was utterly unbelievable, but it was made in the presence of Soviet officials, so it was perhaps understandable). There was his failure to keep an appointment I had made with him for the following morning at his Moscow hotel (an omission possibly imposed upon him by his hosts). There was my failure to make contact with him over the next three or four days after he had simply disappeared from the hotel. Finally, there was the complete blank I had drawn from all inquiries I had directed at official sources. They included the Foreign Ministry, the Economics Ministry, the Finance Ministry, the Ministry for Mining, the Ministry for Non-Ferrous Metals, and the Soviet Institute for African Affairs. All of those august bodies had replied with "No comment" when I sought information on the South African visit.

Such details I listed to my host, reminding him that I had spelled out these minutiae, illustrating the depth of Soviet official silence, in my very first dispatch on the subject. This had been broadcast only after several days of assiduous but unsuccessful inquiry on my part.

My innings was more or less closed when he said he was not challenging my facts. It was now his turn to face my bowling. I opened with a spinner. I pointed out that the structure I had built upon the undisputed facts was what I hoped had been a thoughtful piece of interpretation and speculation on my part. What was more, I claimed, it was fair speculation on a matter of important international public and financial interest. If he questioned aspects of my interpretation of the facts, what were his questions?

His game began to fall apart, and we more or less abandoned the match. He made a wry face and said in answer to my question about factual interpretation, "That is not the point."

"What is the point?" I asked.

His reply was quintessentially Soviet: "It was unnecessary."

Carelessly, perhaps rudely, but unable to restrain myself, I laughed in his face. I told him that his answer might be correct from the viewpoint of a diplomatist wanting to avoid "unnecessary" disturbance to his country's policies, but that I was a news reporter and had a different viewpoint. I pointed out that I was paid to report anything that I regarded as being newsworthy rather than "necessary".

I restrained myself from saying that I believed his masters were probably more interested in hiding the truth rather than publicising it. Anyhow, that was the end of the lunch match and of my period of existence in official Soviet quarantine. We enjoyed a good meal by the Moscow standards of those days.

I was pleased to receive from London two congratulatory messages from the BBC. One was a letter from the *Panorama* reporter who had assiduously and effectively followed up my Moscow disclosures to produce a brilliantly detailed account of Soviet-South African connections in Zurich, London, and elsewhere. This was from veteran TV journalist Michael Cockerell. He wrote to thank me for the *Panorama* interview, stressing how "effective" it had been and how "nice things" about it had been said by the *Guardian*.

The other message came from the editor of *Panorama* in those days, Roger Bolton. Thanking me for my contribution to the programme, he used a felicitous quotation in telling me that I was its "onlie begetter". As a good professional always on the lookout for more, he added, "Now how about one of Rudyard Kipling's favourite characters?"

I tried, of course, to contact "Kim" (Philby) but got nowhere. Of the infamous trio of British traitors who had fled to Russia and who died there, he was in fact the only one I had ever met (in the Middle East, as already mentioned). Guy Burgess, who had formerly worked for the BBC as well as the Foreign Office, had died much earlier, in 1963; then in 1983 I reported the death in Moscow of Donald Maclean.

Philby lived on until 1988. I note in my edition of the *Cambridge Encyclopaedia* that while Burgess and Maclean are described bluntly as "British traitors", the word is not applied to him. Philby is accurately but perhaps curiously described as a "British double agent". Why, I wonder, does the encyclopaedia not apply the "traitor" description? After all, it was Philby who, according to the encyclopaedia itself, gave the warning to Maclean and Burgess that led to their disappearance to the Soviet Union in 1951.

I do hope that the Cambridge University Press and, more especially, Cambridge University, where all three of the men were recruited as communists while young, do not think of Philby as anything but a traitor. He died laden with Soviet honours as well as Soviet citizenship.

Despite the BBC as an organisation remaining under continual heavy fire from the Soviet authorities, and often being regularly jammed in its broadcasts, I met afterwards with nothing but personal courtesy and correctness from officials and spokespersons.

I duly completed my tour of duty after travelling widely inside the Soviet Union, and I returned there happily many times later, when I became BBC diplomatic correspondent. Throughout that South African episode, displaying clearly difficulties that communists face when the hypocrisy of much of their propaganda is exposed, I had in mind another example from an earlier period, when I had first begun to become more closely acquainted "in the field and on the ground", in Africa itself, with the Russians, the Chinese, and other communists.

I had become chairman of the biggest foreign correspondents' association in Africa, an unusual reporters' club where east met west, with members from all over the world. I got to know several of the communist correspondents as colleagues and fellow members. As spokesperson for the association, I found myself occasionally approached by embassies and foreign ministries who had to deal with us. Every now and again, the position became useful in making delicate contacts.

Such was the case when a new Soviet ambassador, known for his African expertise, was posted to Zambia, then one of the main black-ruled so-called "frontline" African states against white-ruled Southern African states. Many correspondents had been trying to meet him, without success, until one day he agreed to join me for lunch. I booked a table at the best hotel in the Zambian capital, and when we sat down, I asked him if he would like a Stolichnaya, a vodka that in those days was not easily available outside Russia but which I knew was in stock in Lusaka.

To my mild surprise, the ambassador declined the vodka but said he would prefer something else. To my much greater surprise, he went on to say that he would like "some of that excellent South African white wine, the Bellingham Premier Grand Cru." This I did not know was in stock! At the time, sanctions were allegedly in full force against Ian Smith's Rhodesia and apartheid-stricken South Africa, and although I was well aware that sanctions were broken all the time, I had not known that South African wine was still reaching Zambia.

I was impressed by my guest's knowledge. I ordered a bottle promptly, and we enjoyed it. It was a small but not inappropriate illustration of how accustomed communist officials were to ignoring their own policy pretensions while accepting the reality of things as they were and profiting by that reality. It came as no surprise when I got to Moscow to find that this was how most Russians had to live their lives: by paying lip service to Communism while somehow or other evading it, simply to make existence more bearable.

Similar considerations applied for our association members who were correspondents for communist news organisations. One of them became rather drunk one night in my company (not an unusual experience for my companions) and unburdened himself of a few thoughts about his country's leaders, policies, government, and ruling party to a highly fascinated and not totally inebriated listener.

He unloosened to such an extent that he called me next day to ask me to join him in sharing a "hair of the dog". He was ashen-faced with anxiety and swore me to secrecy on his outburst. This I willingly gave to him, but it was a revelation to see that his personal problems were of a much greater nature than the problems of mere news coverage.

With the later collapse of both apartheid South Africa and communist Russia, diplomatic relations between Pretoria and Moscow were soon established. As life in Moscow changed, well after Virginia and I had left, we were pleased eventually to welcome to the west for ten days as our guest, our former tutor of Russian, Liouba. We were staggered when she invited us to a farewell lunch and later opened her handbag to pay the bill, showing us its contents. It was stuffed with United States dollar notes.

She was paid in those dollars, she explained, for teaching Russian to members of the staff of the new South African embassy in Moscow, an establishment that did not exist in the Moscow of our day. We were pleased that Liouba was earning hard currency and was consequently enabled to sample something of the pleasures of capitalism (such as travel abroad).

We were, however, distressed to hear from her of the difficult personal travails she had endured after we had left Moscow and before such freedom was possible. Her experiences illustrated the nastier side of the Soviet system. Even though (we presumed) she herself was a communist, she had somehow or other blotted her communist copybook.

We learned about it for the first time only when she came to stay with us. She had become, she explained, to the annoyance of her communist superiors, too friendly with us. It had happened because two or three months before we left Moscow for London, we had asked her if she would like to visit us. If she did, two initial steps had to be taken. The first was for her to obtain an exit visa from the Soviet Union and the second was to ensure that if the Soviet authorities were to let her out of Russia, then the British authorities would allow her into England. Thus she had to take an important personal decision: whether or not to apply for a Soviet exit visa.

After considering the question for some weeks, she decided that she would do so but that she would not actually begin the formal application process until she was sure that she would face no difficulties from the British side in access to England. I talked to the British ambassador in Moscow about this, and he assured me that there would be no problem. We told Liouba, and she took the great step, for a Russian in those days, of applying for an exit visa to visit England.

We did everything strictly according to the Soviet book. We supported her application formally, explaining how much we had appreciated Liouba's Russian tuition during our three years or so in Moscow; her help in introducing us to Russian culture by escorting us around the great art galleries and museums; and our desire to continue with our learning of Russian.

After a wonderful farewell party with our Russian staff, including our tutor, off we flew to London. Liouba never got out of Moscow, though, until *ten years* or so later.

In a last little spasm all too typical of the old, miserable, suspicious, inhuman communist system, she was refused an exit visa. We were never told this at the time and Liouba herself never mentioned it when, on a number of occasions after our return to London, I visited Moscow as part of my work as diplomatic correspondent. I also "stood in" now and again as Moscow correspondent for a few weeks when one or other of my successors in Russia went on leave. Each time I went, I sent a message to the Soviet authorities requesting a continuation of Russian lessons from Liouba, and usually she was released to continue to teach me for an hour each day. She never mentioned the refusal of her exit visa but left me with the impression that family reasons had prevented her from visiting London.

So it was not until years later, well after my last Moscow assignment, that I learned the truth about the punishment inflicted upon Liouba by her fellow communists for daring to express a wish to visit England. That last assignment was the arrival in power of Mikhail Sergeyevich Gorbachev in 1985 and the subsequent ushering in of "Glaznost" (speaking aloud) and "Perestroika" (reconstructing).

These two internal policies, combined with external Star Wars pressure from Ronald Reagan and Margaret Thatcher on the defence and economic fronts, ultimately led to communist collapse.

Communism simply could not survive with anyone "speaking aloud". Genuine criticism of the totalitarian system had always been impossible inside the Soviet Union, and it had led in the past to great Kremlin upheavals, when any of those in power had tried to express unthinkable thoughts that cast doubt on how the country was ruled.

As for "reconstruction", the reality was that the existing tyranny had to be effectively dismantled before any fundamental changes could begin. Gorbachev did manage to neuter the Communist Party and to survive the attempted coup d'etat against him by a rump of old guard communists, but he was weakened enough for events to get dangerously out of hand, so leading to the memorable assumption of power by Boris Yeltsin. Thus at the end of the twentieth century came the restart of some form of democracy in Russia, following the failure of tsarist attempts at reform almost one hundred years earlier.

Gorbachev undoubtedly earned his place in the history books. For Liouba, and thousands like her, he was a liberator.

During the process of change, like other Russians, Liouba gradually rebuilt her life. In the 1990s, she finally managed to travel from Moscow to stay with us in our home in France, and it was there that at last we heard the details of her story.

After our departure from Moscow, she said, her superiors had refused to permit her to be employed by any westerners to teach them Russian, so she was deprived of her previous access to western-style perks such as gifts of clothes or an opportunity to earn hard currency. Instead, she was compelled to work only for employers from Third World and communist countries, thus going through what was obviously a difficult period for her because she had lost western "goodies" which she had become accustomed to receiving. She said she had also had a lot of trouble in fending off unwanted sexual attention from at least one of her ambassadorial employers and great difficulty in getting paid anything at all, even in unwanted roubles, for her Russian lessons.

Then, to the surprise of my wife and me, she added that I personally had become, after some years and quite by chance, her "saviour". I asked why she thought that. She explained that one of my successors as Moscow correspondent, Jeremy Harris, had put in a request for Russian tuition from her when he had taken up his post, and her superiors once again permitted her to provide a BBC correspondent with such teaching.

She was almost pathetically grateful for my having passed on her name to Jeremy. I was of course glad that Liouba had been able to get back into the BBC Moscow set, but the truth is that it was not I who was her saviour; it was Gorbachev and his reforms. It was just lucky for her that Jeremy Harris requested her services at a moment when she was once again allowed to provide them to westerners.

I had been in Moscow for just a few months when, in 1980, Gorbachev joined the all-powerful Soviet Politburo as its most junior member. Five years later, he was running the country as general secretary of the Communist Party, which he proceeded ultimately and painfully to open up to some extent. Lucky enough to be in Russia when he first emerged,

I was also there when he became the country's leader. In that half decade, I watched and reported upon the activities of no fewer than four of those Soviet leaders, covering a quite extraordinary succession of three changes in the control of the superpower of those days, where such transitions of power had previously been rare.

It fell to my lot to report a series of state funerals to such an extent that I began to think of myself as being not so much a Moscow correspondent but, rather, more of an obituarist. Gorbachev had joined the Politburo when a vacancy arose upon the death of Alexei Nikolayevich Kosygin at the age of seventy-six, so occasioning the first of a series of reports for BBC News that I could describe as "Moscow Funerals of My Time".

Kosygin had been prime minister for sixteen years, working with his boss, Leonid Ilyich Brezhnev, ever since the two of them had taken over in 1964 from the ousted Nikita Khruschev. The world was surprised in 1980 by the sudden emergence of a mere stripling aged fifty who was joining a ruling Politburo gerontocracy of eleven men with an average age of seventy. Who was Mikhail Sergeyevich Gorbachev?

I remember that diplomatists from foreign embassies in Moscow and correspondents like me all scratched around trying to find out something about him that was notable other than his unusual youthfulness for the Soviet controlling body.

We were able to learn only that he had some sort of agricultural background and, in 1979, the previous year, had become a candidate member for the Politburo. This was a clear indication that he was a young man on his way up. Beyond that, we were not able to come up with much.

The dozen or so Politburo members were chosen by the Central Committee and in practice, as distinct from theory, took decisions and imposed them on any personnel or grouping lower down in the party structure. The Politburo boss was the person put forward as Communist Party general secretary by his Politburo colleagues, whom he then inevitably dominated until he died or they turned against him. The choice was rubber-stamped by the Central Committee and the party. A ruthless occupant of the general secretary's post could become an out-and-out dictator, as Stalin had demonstrated.

Stalin did it by disposing of any suspected opponent at the top or even in exile. He went so far as to send an agent to a country as distant as

Mexico to murder Leon Trotsky in 1940. He ordered the killing, imprisonment, exile, outlawing, or ruination of the lives of millions of lesser Soviet civilians and servicemen on a scale that paralleled or possibly overtook the appalling mass crimes of Hitler (historians remain unsure as to whose crimes were the greatest).

He accomplished this with a good deal more secrecy than Hitler ever achieved and with the naive complicity of many in the West who, to this day, seem rather regretful about the collapse of Communism.

The extraordinary thing about Gorbachev is that as a product of this ghastly communist machine, he threw a fatal spanner into its works. When he came to power, I told the BBC from Moscow that if he could not change things in Russia, nobody could. However, I did not envisage the speed of change leading to Soviet collapse. He embarked on his policies of radical reform with the introduction of greater civil liberty, open debate, journalistic and cultural freedom, and a new and more honest look at Soviet history. This had often been officially rewritten earlier, according to the current political requirements of Communism at any given period.

Thus, to cite one example, when Nikita Khruschev denounced Stalinism and the "cult of personality" to the 20th Congress of the Soviet Communist Party in 1956, the communist history books and the Soviet encyclopaedia had to be rewritten. A fresh rewrite was then produced when Khruschev himself fell. I was reminded of this when I found myself covering another state funeral, in 1982, of another senior Politburo member, who had been one of Khruschev's opponents and who had survived at the top until dying at the age of seventy-six: Mikhail Andreyevich Suslov.

He was an unregenerate Stalinist ideologist with a reputation as a doctrinaire and ruthless administrator. He had objected to Khruschev's de-Stalinisation moves as well as to Khruschev's economic and foreign policies. When Khruschev was turfed out in 1964, Suslov was one of those instrumental in getting rid of him.

Eighteen years later, the rulers of Soviet Russia and its communist empire all turned out to offer Suslov the old Stalinist a big ceremonial Kremlin farewell. One of the men who had principally benefited from Khruschev's fall was the principal mourner: Leonid Ilyich Brezhnev, for it was he who had become the Soviet boss on Khruschev's departure.

By the time of Suslov's death, Brezhnev himself was looking pretty old and ill. He possessed, however, enormous power that, like Stalin, he consolidated and clung to until the day he died.

He was the first Soviet leader to have become not only the general secretary of the party, but also, at the same time, head of state as president of the Supreme Soviet. He was in addition appointed field marshal and commander in chief of the Soviet Armed Forces. It was a not unimpressive career for a boy born in the Ukraine in 1906 who became, first, a metallurgist and then a political commissar in the Red Army during World War II. He is remembered now, though, mainly for what became known internationally as the "Brezhnev Doctrine": the justification of military and other forms of intervention in the internal affairs of nearby states such as Czechoslovakia in 1968 and Afghanistan in 1980, not to mention the earlier Soviet intervention in Hungary in 1956. With Russia's acceptance of the 2014 Crimean referendum for the Crimean Peninsula to quit Ukraine and to join Russia, it doesn't look unlikely that President Putin is reactivating the "Brezhnev Doctrine" with different methods.

The last time I saw Brezhnev alive (although he was already moving like a jerky but slow ventriloquist's dummy) was on 7 November 1982. With the other rulers of the Soviet Union, he watched the annual Red Square military parade mark the commemoration of the 1917 Bolshevik Revolution.

It was the sixty-fifth anniversary of the Bolshevik seizure of power, and it was the third successive year in which envoys from Western European and NATO countries had made a point of absenting themselves in order to display their disapproval of Soviet military intervention in Afghanistan.

Brezhnev was put into position and responded to salutes in the manner of a well-controlled automaton. Nevertheless, tough old man and communist that he was, he saw the ceremony through. What's more, he went on at a reception later that day to threaten the West. On BBC TV News that night, I broadcast my last dispatch about him while he was still alive and capable of kicking:

"Mr Brezhnev led the Kremlin line-up on top of Lenin's tomb, standing for two hours on a cold, snowy yet sunny day. He later issued a warning to foreign ambassadors at a Kremlin reception that the Russians would deliver 'a crushing retaliatory strike' against any aggressors. He named no names, but the man standing beside him on the tomb, Defence Minister Marshal Ustinov, did. As Soviet tanks, rockets, and artillery rumbled through Red Square, Marshal Ustinov singled out for critical mention the United States.

The spectacle of Soviet military might fitted in suitably enough with the hard tone of the speeches made by the Soviet leaders, but it contrasted oddly with the massive propaganda slogans on display about peace, and it may well have aroused doubts in the minds of independent observers about Mr Brezhnev's assurances of Soviet peaceful intentions."

Three days later, Brezhnev was dead. The death was not announced, however, until another day had passed. The twenty-six-and-a-half-hour delay between his death at 8.30 a.m. Moscow time on 10 November and the official announcement of it at 11 a.m. Moscow time on 11 November gave me one of the biggest scoops of my life: letting the world – and especially our Russian listeners – know what *might* have happened some twelve hours before the Soviet authorities released the news.

Those twelve hours were fraught, but I had no time to bite my nails in worry, for I was kept far too busy broadcasting or making inquiries.

I reported:

> *Soviet television programmes were unexpectedly rescheduled tonight, and newsreader on the main evening news bulletin wore black. A woman presenter wore a dark dress. An ice hockey match which was to have been broadcast was dropped for classical music, and a variety concert to mark Soviet "Militia Day" was replaced by a film about Lenin and reminiscences of World War II. One source said that instructions had gone out not to show light entertainment for a fortnight, but there was no confirmation of this. The changes caused rumours to sweep through Moscow that a Kremlin leader had died ... perhaps Mr Brezhnev himself. Mr Brezhnev's signature did not appear on a message of congratulation to Angola on that country's national day, although last year he personally signed the message.*

During the following twenty-four hours, I delivered twenty-four dispatches to the BBC by various methods of communication, links to the outside world having been slowed down by a Soviet decision to suspend international direct telephone dialling because of the use made by Russian dissidents to talk to supporters overseas.

Thus in order to communicate in voice or on screen with London, it was necessary not only to book a call at the Russian end but necessary also laboriously to reinforce the chance of establishing communication, in those pre-Internet, pre-mobile telephone days, by telexing the BBC, asking the corporation to get through to me somehow or other so that I could broadcast. The sheer mechanics of communication were time-consuming.

Fortunately, an assistant controller for engineering from the stratospheric heights of the BBC hierarchy happened to be visiting Moscow at that time to discuss BBC long-term programme or engineering projects with Soviet officials. He nobly volunteered to help me out.

This was Norman Taylor, who turned himself into a useful office dogsbody by holding lines open and by keeping London at bay when scores of programmes and news bulletins wanted to talk to me so often that I would never have had time to make inquiries to find out what was going on, let alone write intelligible or reliable reports.

Norman, my wife, and myself kept working for five days and five nights largely fuelled by whisky and vodka, because there was scant time for sleep or for eating. When the whole thing was over, he signed as a souvenir a black-bordered front page of the Soviet Communist Party newspaper, *Pravda*, which reported Brezhnev's death two days after its occurrence. I have kept it as another memento and curiosity from my unpredictable life, and it too hangs on the wall of my study.

The dispatches I got away in the first twenty-four hours included nineteen broadcasts for radio and TV, including two-way interviews with various programmes, all transmitted from the BBC's small Moscow office-cum-studio (where I was very much a one-man band in contrast to the BBC's more impressive set-up today). I also made TV broadcasts direct to camera, an operation that involved driving out through the snow at night to reach the Soviet TV studios at Ostankino. In short, I kept the news flowing one way or the other, using telex when unable to broadcast. My wife, while victualling Norman and myself throughout the period, was herself kept professionally stretched because, as a freelance journalist with Soviet accreditation, she was Moscow correspondent for no fewer than sixteen newspapers and broadcasting organisations.

They included, in England, the *Observer*, the *Yorkshire Post*, BBC *Woman's Hour*, and the *Daily Telegraph* "Woman's Page"; the major Canadian newspaper chain, Southam Newspapers; the Australian newspaper and the Australian ABC broadcasting network; and, in the United States, the RKO Radio and NBC radio networks (as well as writing a regular cookery column for the *Baltimore Sun* on the cuisine of Eastern Europe!)

The demands placed upon her were such that I was compelled to order her out of the BBC office. All sixteen of her employers were putting in calls to her there, to such an extent that lines were liable to become blocked. I asked her to have her calls directed away from the BBC office to our apartment and to work from there. This she did with good grace.

The communication difficulties, however, were nothing compared with the problems of finding out what was actually happening. As seems to have been everlastingly traditional in Russia, communist or tsarist, things tended to be kept dark. This was certainly the case when Brezhnev died.

To begin with, a few days before, one of the Kremlin leaders for the previous twenty years, Andrei Kirilenko, had disappeared from the political scene. His photograph was conspicuously absent from the Politburo portraits erected in Moscow for the Red Square parade. He was seventy-six; he had not been seen in public since August; and there were rumours about his being ill or having been dropped from the Politburo.

Kirilenko had once been thought of as the most likely successor to Brezhnev because of the long association of the two and because they were the only members of the thirteen-man Politburo in 1982 to have served back in the 1960s under Nikita Khruschev. I duly reported on the disappearance of Kirilenko's picture from the line-up of those in power, noting that membership of the ruling group had fallen to twelve.

That figure provoked immediate sardonic humour among Russians. I particularly liked one description I heard that was of a distinctly double-edged nature in an atheistic state: "Lenin's Twelve Disciples". Naturally, I reported the observation as well as a somewhat cruder tag from western diplomatists: "The Dirty Dozen".

Three days later, when the broadcasting schedules were suddenly changed to give a clear indication of an important death in the Soviet leadership, I had to bear in mind that the death might have been that of Kirilenko and not of Brezhnev himself.

There were other possibilities to consider as well. Yet more Politburo members existed whose age and bad health could equally well have caused a not-so-sudden end. The most ancient of them was Arvid Pelshe, aged eighty-three, who claimed to have known Lenin. Pelshe was a faithful Communist Party servant for many years in Latvia, where he was born in 1899. Like Kirilenko, he had been absent from public ceremonies for some time, and he died at about the same time as Brezhnev.

Kirilenko, however, treated Kremlinologists to one last surprise when he suddenly emerged again at Brezhnev's funeral. He appeared, though, as a private mourner and not in the official phalanx of Politburo members. I reported that his fall from grace would be explained if reports circulating in diplomatic circles were true. These were that his son, a scientist in his early fifties, had defected to the west. He was alleged to have finished up in Britain, requesting political asylum.

Given the potentiality for getting things wrong in trying to establish who had actually died, I was compelled for twelve hours or so to hedge my bets.

While weighting my series of reports to suggest that it was indeed Brezhnev who was dead, I could not dare to say so categorically, because the BBC (of those days) would never have forgiven me if I had been wrong. My own reputation as a reporter would have been finished. It was an anxious night for me because even suggesting that Brezhnev might be dead (as I had) would have brought official wrath down on my head the next day and, if he was not, probable expulsion.

I felt in my bones, though, that the changes made to the state broadcasting schedules were so enormous that it must have been Brezhnev himself who had gone. So I stuck to my line that nobody knew for sure who was dead but that Moscow rumours continued to suggest that it was Brezhnev.

At 3 a.m. Moscow time, I was still broadcasting that, with the BBC World Service calling me from Bush House, asking me if I dared to "harden it up a bit" and state flatly that Brezhnev was dead. No, I could not. Thus they continued to broadcast my suggestions that he might be dead, until the official announcement later that day at 11 a.m. Moscow time, 8 a.m. London time, a moment bang in the middle of the *Today* programme.

Soon after the BBC's 3 a.m. call, I received another, from the doyen of the western correspondents in the Soviet capital, the Moscow correspondent of the *Sunday Times*, the late Ed Stevens. Ed, an American who had first gone to Russia as a war correspondent during World War II, had married a Russian ballerina, Nina, and had dug into Moscow life for almost half a century. He was over eighty, but his mind was sharp and his contacts extensive.

He was calling me to tell me that he was 99.99 per cent certain that it was Brezhnev who had died and that he had reported the death as a fact in his dispatch to an Italian morning newspaper that he represented.

I knew Ed well enough to do the unthinkable: I asked him if he could give me any hint of his source. He told me: it was an employee of the Soviet state broadcasting system who had been summoned urgently to work in the middle of the night and had been issued with a special armband. According to the broadcasting employee, the armband was only to be worn in the event of the death of the general secretary of the Soviet Communist Party.

I was grateful to Ed for his call, and I was pretty sure that he was right. In a somewhat defensive way, I told him that the one-tenth of 1 per cent of doubt that he still held in his own mind, despite his 99.9 per cent of certainty, constituted, for me, too much of a risk to take for the BBC. I explained to him that if he were wrong, his reputation would not be ruined by a mistaken report in an Italian newspaper. If the BBC was wrong, my career would be over.

Ed's report was not published. He could have been the first reporter in the world to tell his readers outright that Brezhnev was dead, but it turned out that he was not. This was because his newspaper had spiked his story!

The editor, an old friend of Ed's from wartime days, had contracted cold feet about running Ed's dispatch because the BBC and the news agencies (by that time following the BBC lead) were merely reporting rumours that Brezhnev was dead, rather than saying outright that the

Soviet leader was in fact dead. So the editor had decided to play it safe and do the same.

This produced one of the best stories about the practice of journalism I have ever heard. Ed told me it a few days later. He had felt pleased, he said, when, after Brezhnev's death had been officially announced the next day, he had received a congratulatory message from the editor on his scoop. He was less pleased when the editor apologetically told him that his dispatch had not been published because of editorial doubts.

Ed was angered enough to send his editor an obscene insult, but his good humour was then splendidly restored by the contrite editor. On the following day, the Italian newspaper gave great coverage to the story of how its Moscow correspondent had scooped the world with the news of Brezhnev's death, how the editor had foolishly decided not to run the story, and how Ed had then cursed the editor in unprintable language. In donning its garb of sackcloth and ashes, the Italian newspaper went so far as to print, in large headline type, the actual normally unprintable message which Ed had sent to the editor to express his fury!

Translated from Italian into English, this was the message: "Get f---ed!"

Ed felt that his old chum had generously made amends to him, as did the relatively small Moscow corps in those days of foreign correspondents from western countries.

Veteran communist correspondent Sam Russell related to me a less happy story about what might have been a great Moscow scoop. He had been visiting Moscow in the early 1980s as the diplomatic correspondent of the British communist newspaper, the *Morning Star*, to report upon the proceedings of the 26th Congress of the Soviet Communist Party. Sam, however, was still bitter about how he had been treated by his editor when covering the proceedings of the 20th Congress of the party twenty-five years earlier, in 1956.

It was the occasion when Khruschev had made his denunciation of Stalin behind closed doors to that Congress. Somehow or other, the Soviet leaders wanted the news to be known to the West. However, such was the nervousness about reaction among international communists to the dismantling of Stalin's reputation, they wanted to use a reliable channel to leak the news to the outside world in a way they regarded as suitable. Using a modern idiom, they wanted to "put a spin on it".

So they chose Sam and his newspaper as an appropriate conduit. He possessed all the correct credentials as a communist, working as Moscow correspondent for the British Communist Party newspaper, the *Daily Worker* (the *Morning Star*'s predecessor).

The Soviet authorities, though, had not taken into account the disbelieving Stalinist attitude of the editor of the *Daily Worker* at that time, William Rust, who could not bring himself to accept that the communist leader he had admired all his life had been formally disgraced by his Russian communist "comrades". Like many other communists, Rust could not understand that Stalin had been a mass murderer who had not hesitated to commit crimes akin to genocide against Tartars or any other unfortunate peoples he had happened to suspect.

Even though Sam telephoned his editor in person to guarantee the authority of his party source and the authenticity of his information, Rust spiked the biggest internal political news out of Russia since Stalin had become the country's boss on Lenin's death in 1924. Frustrated, the Soviet authorities leaked it all again to an American news agency which had an experienced Moscow correspondent and whose less ideological employers promptly broke the news to the world of Stalin's posthumous disgrace.

Sam Russell never forgave Rust for killing the biggest story of Sam's life. In 1982, I gained the impression that Sam was just another disillusioned Red. There were quite a lot of such sad, rather grey characters from the West knocking about Moscow in my days there.

I was luckier with my reports from Moscow than either Ed Stevens or Sam Russell had been with theirs. Also lucky, because of my early breaking of the news that Brezhnev might be dead, was the Moscow correspondent of the American CBS TV network, Donald McNeill.

He had quite reasonably chosen to take a few days off to fly to Helsinki for a break. He told me that just as he was checking into his Finnish hotel, he received a call from America to tell him what I was reporting on the BBC World Service. He promptly checked out again and returned from Finland to Russia. He managed to get back into the Soviet Union late that night and before the official announcement the next morning of Brezhnev's death. He arrived just before a clampdown was placed on flights into and out of Soviet airports except for heads of state and government, who quickly arrived from all over the world for the biggest state funeral seen in Russia for years. He said he was most grateful to me.

As for the BBC, I was cheered when I got a message from my editor telling me, "Many thanks, John, for an outstanding day's work. You've got the big one – keep going, plus your big chance to boss an assistant controller around."

From BBC TV came more praise: "Many congratulations on your output; you knocked ITN into a cocked hat."

Perhaps best of all, I received a stunning message from the BBC World Service. For any BBC foreign correspondent, the World Service is always at the forefront of the mind. This is because of the speed with which whatever a reporter might be saying comes back immediately to the part of the world from which he or she happens to be saying it. This sometimes produces an unwelcome effect such as immediate detention and expulsion.

In Bush House (then the home of the World Service), they had of course understood my reservations on their 3am query as to whether or not I could "harden up" the news of Brezhnev's death. They equally understood the Byzantine calculations I had to make in reporting whatever I did. I was pleased later to learn from the World Service editor that the full flavour of all this, reflecting the tortuous and secretive nature of Soviet politics, had come through plainly in my reports, as I had hoped it would.

As for the stunningly expressed appreciation, it consisted of one word: "Superb".

That one-word telexed message is also among the souvenirs in my study. I make no apology for reproducing these "herograms" (as they are known in the trade) because I want to underline how important they can be in removing the sense of isolation that a foreign correspondent has when he or she is producing material at high speed under considerable pressure, often in testing circumstances, without any real understanding of what impact his or her work is producing thousands of miles away. Reaction from editors, whether negative or positive, is always helpful, and in this particular case, my editor's encouragement to "keep going" undoubtedly helped. I managed to do just that.

Goggle-eyed with sleeplessness, my wife and I, with Norman Taylor, had barely a moment to eat or even to wash as events unfolded over the next four or five days.

Our scanty ablutions did not matter too much anyway because, in all too typical Moscow style, the hot water tank had broken down in our apartment at that particular moment, and we were unenthusiastic about using ice-cold November water.

Working for the BBC on a big story in those days was like working for fifty different newspapers at once while being plugged in for voice and vision. News bulletins plus endless TV and radio programmes deluged me with requests for filmed reports, broadcast dispatches, and for two-way interviews on camera and before a microphone. I just about managed to cope with them. The corporation well knew how to extract its pound of flesh from a correspondent.

The final pattern of the story started with the rituals of the lying-in-state and the state funeral, which world leaders flew in to attend. They wanted, if they could, to meet the new Soviet leader, whoever he was to be. That was the biggest story of the lot: the decision as to who was to be the new ruler of what was still the Soviet superpower.

Once again, I was lucky. Appearing by TV satellite from Moscow for Newsnight on the night of the official announcement of Brezhnev's death, Peter Snow in London asked, "Who will the new leader be?" I said I thought it would be Yuri Andropov.

It was a correct guess but not one lightly made. After the virtual elimination of Pelshe (dying at about the same time as Brezhnev) and Kirilenko (ill and anyway in apparent disgrace), the number of the known members of the Politburo after Brezhnev's death had fallen to ten. Conducting a bit of personal Kremlinology, I went through their names and what was known about them.

My thoughts went like this: two of them were unlikely to succeed because they were not Russians (one was from Kazakhstan, Dinmuhamed Kunayev; the other was from the Ukraine, Vladimir Shcherbitsky). Two more were also outsiders: the long-serving foreign minister, Andrei Gromyko (because his personal diplomatic contacts and acknowledged expertise in foreign affairs was needed in the post he already held); and the defence minister, Dmitri Ustinov. He was powerful and had the support of the mighty Soviet "military industrial complex", but he was known to be in ill health.

Of the six others, Gorbachev was at that stage too junior and too young. The next youngest, then aged sixty or so, Grigoriy Romanov, had been in the running before a scandal had tainted him some three years earlier in his Leningrad fiefdom (now once again St. Petersburg). There had been an unfortunate family wedding party during which priceless glassware, some reportedly borrowed for the occasion from the Hermitage Palace and Museum, had been festively smashed, an event that helped to smash also Romanov's pretensions.

Of the remaining four "possibles", the prime minister of the day, Nikolai Tikhonov, was already seventy-six and, like Gorbachev, had been a Politburo member for only sixteen months or so. The Moscow region's man, Viktor Grishin, had to be considered a runner, but while he was strong in the capital, his wider backing and experience was probably not enough.

This process of elimination left only two "probables": Konstantin Chernenko, aged seventy-one, and Yuri Andropov, aged sixty-eight.

I reported that as an associate of and assistant to Brezhnev for many years, Chernenko was thought to be Brezhnev's own favourite.

I reported also that although Andropov was highly regarded in the Party as well educated, able, and experienced, his tenure for many years as chairman of the Committee for State Security might have counted against him rather than for him. They all feared him because he knew too much about all of them! The Committee for State Security was the English translation of its Russian title, the Komitet Gosudarstvennoy Bezopasnosti, the dreaded KGB.

Since 1953, the KGB had been a Soviet secret police organisation with responsibility, among other things, for the surveillance of key members of the Communist Party, the administration and the military. This aspect of Andropov's duties as KGB boss might have proved sensitive to his colleagues, even though they might otherwise have fully approved of his monitoring and regulation of dissidents; his conduct of espionage and subversion abroad; and his general supervision of the internal and external order and security of the Soviet Union.

I summed up this aspect of his chances in a broadcast: "Whether or not that KGB label helps or hinders anyone aspiring to the top job is highly arguable."

Why then, when asked by Newsnight to predict the name of the new Soviet leader, did I bet on Andropov? The clincher in my own mind came just before the official mourning for Brezhnev began, together with the lying-in-state of his body and other rituals, all accompanied by the interminable strains of Chopin's "Funeral March", performed in a hall draped in black and played by musicians on a rota system.

These formal but darkly impressive ceremonies of death were preceded by an announcement that Andropov had been appointed to the chairmanship of the committee organising the funeral. This seemed to me to give him the edge over Chernenko, so I made my Andropov guess.

Newsnight was delighted with the accuracy of the forecast, and subsequently I received a message from the editor, Nick Guthrie. It said: "Now it's all over bar the shouting I just wanted to say one million thanks for your splendid efforts on our behalf over the past week. Thank you so much for putting up with us and our requests with such good grace and executing them so well."

I replied, "Thanks, Nick, for your kind words. Looking back, I think the high spot for me was sticking my neck out on Newsnight with Peter Snow and saying the decision may well have been already taken and my guess would be Andropov. It was rather lucky to have that confirmed about twelve hours later."

My thoughts on the succession, and on when the decision about it had been made, turned out to have been entirely correct, although I did not know it at the time. It emerged that Chernenko himself had proposed Andropov as the new leader. This in itself was a pointer to later Soviet changes, and it turned out to be useful to me in my next BBC incarnation as diplomatic correspondent.

Andropov did not last long. He died fifteen months later, in 1984. It was an inconvenient moment for me because I was away on a skiing holiday. I was summoned back by the BBC to help in covering yet another Soviet funeral and yet another contest for Soviet power.

To the surprise of nobody, Chernenko succeeded Andropov. Soon after he had come to power, the British foreign secretary, Sir Geoffrey

Howe (now Lord Howe) visited Moscow for talks with the Soviet leader. I accompanied him to report the encounter.

Chernenko was obviously ill, and when he too died a year later, it was Gorbachev who took over, a development that led to real change.

I remain pleased that in reporting from Moscow his assumption of power, I declared that if Gorbachev could not change the Soviet Union, nobody could do so; but I certainly did not have in mind the immense scale of the change that ensued, and I imagine that Gorbachev himself was unable then to have foreseen the way in which things would go.

Covering Gorbachev's accession was my last assignment in Russia and the end of my sustained reporting of the Kremlin funerals of old communists. For Russia, Gorbachev's arrival at the top was the beginning of painful national rebirth. For me, it was the beginning of yet another interesting chapter, probably the last, in the book of my journalistic life.

When, in 1983, I moved back from Moscow to London to take up what I knew was going to be my last staff job for the BBC, I left Russia with mixed feelings. I liked the prospect of my new posting, and I had long secretly hoped that I would end my career doing exactly what I did. When the BBC had sent an editor out to talk to me some months earlier about a possible change and offered me the job I had always wanted, I did not hesitate to accept but I put forward a condition.

This was that I should be able to visit both Moscow and Washington at least once a year during my spell as diplomatic correspondent, simply in order to maintain my contacts in the capitals of both superpowers (as they were then both regarded).

The BBC agreed. The corporation was happy, and so was I. Nevertheless, I have sometimes wondered if I should have tried to persuade the BBC to allow to me to stay in Russia. Events had shown that my coverage was not bad, and I felt within myself that I was really beginning to get a deeper understanding of the country. My Russian was more proficient in 1983 than it had been in 1980, and I had developed an enormous affection for Russia and its peoples. On the other hand, I had a downright detestation of its political system, corrupt and brutal.

Despite the wretched politics, though, when I left that extraordinary city, I remained as impressed by Moscow as I had been when I first arrived there. My initial impressions had led to a BBC quip about my surprise when I was becoming acquainted with the place. The joke was recorded in the minutes of the BBC news and current affairs meeting of 22 July 1980:

> It was noted that John Osman, in his first piece for From Our Own Correspondent, had been 'pleasurably stunned by Moscow'. Bob Milne-Tyte [head of "Talks and Features", World Service] offered the suggestion that that was because Osman had gone there after a long spell in Africa.

There was an element of truth in this, especially on the musical front. After years of hearing African drums, originally thrilling but ultimately monotonous, I had managed to put behind me a surfeit of what I can only describe as "bongo-bongo" music, despite the possibility of my use of that description being regarded by any oversensitive reader as an example of racial discrimination. It is not; it is simply an example of my personal musical discrimination. I was able in Moscow to listen quite regularly to some genuinely more varied and harmonious classical music than was ever the case in Africa. I now enjoyed the pleasure of concerts at the Conservatoire, in the Mayakovsky Hall, and in going to the Bolshoi, with its well-established opera and ballet. Such entertainment helped my wife and me survive our first long Russian winter.

However, getting at such delights was far from simple. For example, when buying a season ticket for concerts, it was necessary first to lay hands on the season's programme, something that required a good deal of attention and application. Then the programmes had to be chosen.

They were all listed, not only the music to be played but the performers as well. The only thing missing was the date on which the performances were to be given!

In theory, the tickets were supposed to be posted to the subscriber days before the performance, but in practice the tickets sometimes arrived after the performance. Often the tickets arrived on the same day.

Nevertheless, despite the obstacles put in place by this cumbersome and corrupt system, my wife and I managed to get to most of the concerts for which we had paid. It was never a surprise when we arrived at the concert hall to find our seats already occupied by Russians who knew the system all too well and were hoping to benefit by using the seats in our absence. They never objected when we pointed to our tickets and asked them to move. They simply plonked themselves down in other seats that they hoped would not be needed by yet more people whose tickets had not arrived in time for them to attend. It was a well-established habit among enterprising Muscovite music lovers.

It was even more difficult to get into the Bolshoi. First, as with the concerts, one had to get hold of the season's programme. This meant constant visits to the theatre when the programme was known to be about to be published. This entailed wasting time that neither my wife nor me could afford to lose because of our work, so I ruthlessly employed the office "fixer", Vasily Samarsky, the driver already mentioned.

After he had obtained the programme – and the Bolshoi itself did actually give the dates of performances in advance – we set about applying for a couple of the seats reserved in those days for foreigners who could pay in hard currency.

Even then, it was not easy. It entailed writing two letters to the box office, one in Russian and one in English, applying for seats for the performances we required. Naturally, Vasily had some sort of contact in the box office, a woman, and I always sent a box of chocolates with him to offer to her. So we managed to see most of the productions we wanted to see in the three years or so we were in Moscow.

With one ultra-popular production, however, we always failed: the stunning ballet *Spartacus*. Whenever I applied, there were no seats available. We did get to it in the end, however. The way in which I managed it involved support on the expenses front from the BBC and support on the Soviet front from a man who, rightly or wrongly, I always regarded as my "minder".

This was Mikhail Ilyitch Bruk, a superb linguist who had been the official Soviet translator at the Russian trial of the British spy Greville Wynne and a man who was the Moscow representative of the late Armand Hammer, a multimillionaire who was the boss of Occidental Petroleum and who always carried a letter addressed to him from Lenin himself, a document that eased his way into top Kremlin circles.

In other words, my Moscow minder was no slouch in Russian eyes: a fact that by itself was a compliment not to myself but to the importance of the BBC.

Formally, Mikhail Ilyitch was a Soviet journalist working for the Novosti news agency. As such, various BBC programmes employed him whenever an articulate exposition was required from a Russian whose command of English was superb. On one occasion, I recall that the late Sir Robin Day conducted an interview with him and complimented him upon his English. Mikhail Ilyitch positively purred in pleasure.

Anyhow, at one stage in our delicately balanced relations, at about the time of the Falklands War, he asked me if I could bring back from London for him a recently published new edition of *Captain Cook's Voyages*. He apparently collected fine books, but the unworthy thought crossed my mind that perhaps he wanted Royal Navy charts of the waters around the Falklands which Russian naval vessels and their alleged "spy trawlers" did not yet possess. On the other hand, there would have been nothing to prevent the Soviet naval attaché in London from visiting Hatchards in Piccadilly and buying a copy to send in the diplomatic bag to Moscow.

Therefore, satisfied that I would not be engaging in a mild form of espionage against my own country, I agreed to try to obtain the book for him. Thus when next in London I went along to Hatchards. I found that the price of the book was more than I could afford. I explained the position to the BBC administrative official who kept an eye on my expenses, a civilised chum called Anthony Austin, and I was given permission to buy the book and charge for it on expenses in the interests of maintaining a useful BBC contact in Moscow.

Mikhail Ilyitch was pleased with the gift and reminded me that if I ever wanted anything special from him, I need but ask. As my posting neared its end in Moscow, my wife and I noticed that *Spartacus* was once again due to be performed at the Bolshoi before we left Russia, so I telephoned Mikhail Ilyitch and asked him if he could help us get tickets.

Within a day, they were with us. This was after three years of unsuccessfully trying to get hold of them! What is more, I had not been compelled to write letters in Russian and English to acquire them. Such was the curious way of life in Moscow in those days.

During my Russian posting, I managed to travel widely: from the frozen north, in Murmansk, to the equally frozen Siberian earth and waters of Lake Baikal, near Ulan-Ude and of the River Ob at Novosobirsk. From such icy places, I went to the semi-tropical shores of the Black Sea, at Batumi, complete with groves of bananas and bamboo, not to mention eucalyptus and magnolia trees. I took "the golden road to Samarkand", perhaps not as poetically as James Elroy Flecker but with just as much enthusiasm, as well as travelling on other roads. And alas, I took Aeroflot domestic flights to other Asian cities like Bokhara and Tashkent. I visited the homes of Tolstoy in Yasnaya Polyana and of Tchaikowski in Klin. I went from Estonia to Armenia, from the Ukraine to Uzbekistan, from Tbilisi to Tajikistan.

I acquired some feeling for and knowledge of the extraordinary mixture of peoples that together formed the Soviet empire and that today, as federated or as independent states, still have to live as neighbours with Russia, as well as with their memories of Russian imperialism, whether of the tsarist or communist variety.

With all this, I suppose it was natural that I should have harboured doubts about giving it all up. Who would not have had some hesitation?

In the final weeks of my Moscow existence, after the excitement of reporting events following Brezhnev's death, more messages and newspaper comment reached me. First my wife and I received a message from Norman Taylor, the BBC assistant controller who had so willingly "turned to" while in Moscow to help us out.

We had put him up in our Moscow apartment during the crush of events because it was next door to the office and so saved him much time in getting about in the Moscow snow and through heavy security precautions between his hotel and our workplace. At the end of it all, the three of us were so exhausted from lack of sleep that he nearly missed his plane back to London. However, I had set the alarm clock.

That evening, we received a message from him from London:

"Sorry about hassle this morning. Thank goodness you woke me up in time. Many thanks for taking me in and making me feel so much at home. Last few days a fantastic experience which only the lucky few were privileged to see. Wish I could send you hot water."

This made us laugh. Then, after the welcome words of approval from my BBC masters, came other expressions of appreciation. *Times* critic David Wade drew attention to BBC coverage of "the ascent of Andropov and the burial of Brezhnev", adding, to my satisfaction, that both had been "vividly reported by John Osman".

There arrived from my home town of Worthing a cutting from the local weekly newspaper where I had once worked. Under a three-column headline, "Our Man in Moscow Digs out Facts", my old newspaper reported:

> One man with the unenviable task of finding out just what happened in Moscow last week was former Worthing Herald reporter John Osman.
>
> For as the BBC's man in Moscow it was John's job to find out why Russian TV presenters were wearing dark clothes, funeral music was played on the radio and a film about Lenin had unexpectedly replaced an ice hockey match on the screens. It was, of course, all heralding the news of Leonid Brezhnev's death.
>
> A former Worthing High School pupil, Mr Osman worked as a sports reporter on the Herald, leaving in 1951.

I was especially touched by the fact that thirty-one years after leaving the *Herald*, somebody there still remembered me! This was particularly so since I had no acquaintance with the author of the piece, Eve Richings, who in a brief account of my career commented, accurately enough, that since leaving the *Herald*, "his job has taken him all over the world".

So it had, and so it continued to do for another five years.

I was given on my departure from Moscow a Russian coffee set, presented to me by the Zambian ambassador to Moscow, on behalf of his fellow envoys from African member states of the Commonwealth represented in the Soviet capital. They invited my wife and me to a farewell party at the Zambian Embassy, where one of the ambassadors charmed me by saying it was in gratitude for my broadcasts. Without them, he added, he would never have known what was going on!

I was offered one more leaving memento. It was from Don McNeill, the CBS correspondent who had told me how grateful he was for the early broadcast I had made that had enabled him to dash back to Moscow from Finland before Soviet airports were sealed.

The memento came in the form of his visiting card, with a message scrawled on it. He knew that I would soon be covering Buckingham Palace news as well as major foreign news, and employing a familiar

North American nickname of those days for Queen Elizabeth II, "Betty", he wrote:

> *No other man can ever say that he buried Brezhnev and bounced*
> *to Betty. Regards and Luck.*

Ambassador Popov receives me as the BBC Diplomatic and Court Correspondent, at a Soviet Embassy reception in London in 1984 to mark the 60th anniversary of the establishment in 1924 of diplomatic relations between Great Britain and the Soviet Union. Unusually, the broadcast I made on the BBC 4 Radio "Today" programme about the occasion was warmly received by the Russians, by the British Foreign and Commonwealth Office, and even by Buckingham Palace, where plans were already afoot for a visit by the Queen to Moscow. Also unusually, the ambassador later gave me a Christmas gift of the category that can cause difficulties for the recipient. I enlarge upon the subject in the book. Six years after the picture was taken the Soviet Union had disappeared.

Broadcasting from Moscow in Soviet Russia in the 1980's when for three years I was a one-man band for BBC TV, Radio and the BBC World Service. One hand is bandaged as I had broken a thumb in a ski-ing, accident.

My wife, writer and broadcaster Virginia Waite, and me at the annual Red Suare parade in Moscow that used to mark the anniversary of the Bolshevik revolution.

Our Russian tutor, Liouba (standing, in the pink blouse), who was punished by the Soviets after our departure from Moscow for having become too friendly with us: - she had dared to ask for an exit visa from Russia to holiday with us in England at our invitation. It was only ten years later, after Gorbachev's arrival in power, that she was permitted to leave Russia to visit us at our home in France.

CHAPTER 24

From the Kremlin to Buckingham Palace

Not long after leaving Moscow, where Yuri Andropov had just become the Soviet leader, I was presented to Her Majesty, and I remember vividly her first stark words to me: "Tell me about Mr Andropov, Mr Osman."

Of course, she would have already received information about him through her meetings with her prime minister when he (or she at that period) went to Buckingham Palace for the regular ministerial audience. The foreign secretary could have briefed the Queen, who might also have read reports from the ambassador in Moscow. With all such knowledge, however, she still sought non-governmental assessment.

Aware that I was addressing perhaps the best-informed woman in the world, I did my best to offer an intelligent impression of the new Soviet boss. It was not easy because, like all Russian leaders under Communism, little was known about their personal lives and activities and the communist system went to great lengths to keep it that way. I recall, for example, that when Andropov came into power, it was some time before we correspondents in Moscow were able to confirm beyond doubt that he was married. It was even more difficult to discover anything about his wife.

Russians told me (and I have never confirmed this) that this was because in Andropov's darkish past he had met and married a Jewish woman while he was employed in a formerly Finnish part of the Soviet Union. There he had been engaged, among other duties, in dealing with any problem caused by anti-Soviet Finns who, after World War II, suddenly found themselves turned into Soviet citizens when Finnish Karelia was taken over by Stalin.

A reason for trying to airbrush Andropov's job there out of the official biographies was that he had earned a reputation for ruthlessness in the region. His role later as Soviet ambassador in Hungary during the 1956 uprising against Communism had been equally ambiguous. The mere fact that Nikolai Suslov, the Stalinist ideologue, had approved of Andropov's role in the crushing of the Hungarian revolt illustrated that (1) Andropov had been involved, and (2) that he was tough. Eleven years later, he became head of the KGB, a position he held until the time he came to power.

Throughout his career, Andropov and the Soviet Communist Party had kept Mrs Andropov firmly in the background because, despite official policies, anti-Semitism in Russia was deeply rooted. In any case, the wives and families of top Soviet politicians were always kept out of sight as much as possible, and the first wife of any Russian leader to impinge upon the public consciousness did not exhibit herself until several years later, in the shape of the late Raisa Gorbachev.

Her husband, Mikhail Gorbachev, had been advanced in his progress to the top by Andropov, who was among the first of the communist leaders to realise that Russia simply could not continue under the-then sclerotic system. Thus Andropov searched for a younger man to change things. Eventually, Gorbachev did, although not in the way that Andropov might have envisaged.

How much of this I told the Queen, I cannot honestly recall. The only thing that I do remember stressing, because it seemed to be important for her to have no doubts about it, was that Andropov was plainly not well and that he probably would not last long (he died fourteen months after taking office).

Familiar though I was with the process of being "debriefed" on return from foreign assignments by editors and by BBC directors general, this was the first time I had been asked by my sovereign in person to tell her about anything. Although she was an obviously interested listener, I felt slightly unnerved and remember that I was apologetic about my inability to tell her very much. She smiled at my wary performance, and I began to relax as she displayed her ability to put people at ease.

She really is a working monarch. As an assiduous seeker of information, she asks questions just like an inquiring reporter, without having to write or broadcast about what she has learned! It is not unusual for her to know a good deal about the subject under discussion, sometimes devastatingly so.

A striking example was provided when she visited The *Times* to mark an event in the long history of that newspaper, financially controlled by Rupert Murdoch, who many years ago publicly declared that the monarchy is "irrelevant". Irrelevant or not, the management of his newspaper thought the presence of the monarch to mark the celebratory occasion was attractive enough to invite her; otherwise, the invitation would not have been sent.

The royal visit – alas, for the *Times*! – resulted in coverage not of the type for which the newspaper might have hoped. One of the newspaper's correspondents who had covered the miners' strike advanced arguable views to the Queen, suggesting that the strike was the result of the policies of her government. The Queen replied quietly that she had been told to the contrary: that one man had caused the strike.

She did not actually say who had told her that (presumably her prime minister of the time, Margaret Thatcher), nor did she actually name the "one man". However, everyone assumed inevitably that she was referring to Arthur Scargill, the miners' union leader. Competing media interests to the *Times* were not slow to publicise the difference in views about the strike between the Queen and the man from the *Times*. Shortly afterwards, he was reposted to other duties.

My own less-publicised conversation with the Queen about Andropov took place in Government House in Jamaica, when the Queen gave a party for journalists covering her 1983 six-week tour of Jamaica, the Cayman Islands, and Belize, followed by the west coasts of Mexico, the United States, and Canada. Our talk was widened after some minutes to include one of my colleagues, an American journalist from *Time* magazine. *Time* was preparing a big cover issue on the subject of royalty and had instructed its man to attempt to obtain an interview with the Queen. Royal advisers warned him beforehand that the answer would be no, but nevertheless he insisted upon trying.

He made an excellent and amusing stab at it as he attempted to convince the Queen that, as he put it, "There had to be a first time." The Queen laughed as he developed his arguments, but they were in vain. They ended when I heard Her Majesty employ, unusually in private conversation, the royal "we". She told the *Time* correspondent, "*We* never give interviews, but Philip sometimes does." So *Time* had to content itself with an interview with the prince.

This was the first royal tour I was reporting after my move from the Kremlin to Buckingham Palace, and during the tour, President Ronald Reagan gave a banquet in San Francisco for the Queen. I was pleased to shake his hand as one of his guests, although I am not usually moved to any particular pleasure by routine courtesies after being greeted and welcomed by many heads of state, presidents, prime ministers and so on. However, to me, that handshake was different.

For once, I was genuinely pleased because, in my view, he was one of the most successful post-war American presidents. While in Moscow, I had closely followed the effects there of his alliance with Margaret Thatcher, a double act that was of fundamental importance in bringing down what Reagan described as the Soviet "empire of evil".

Kremlin echoes sounded on the very first day of my new duties at Buckingham Palace after I had returned from Moscow to London. Conducted around the palace corridors to various offices to be introduced to members of the royal staff, I met Sir William Heseltine, then the Queen's assistant private secretary and later to become the private secretary. He greeted me warmly and asked if I thought I was going to enjoy my new job.

No fewer than three of my predecessors, beginning with the late Godfrey Talbot, the first BBC court correspondent, had warned me that the journalistic path for anybody doing the job was strewn with unexpected snares. So I answered somewhat hesitantly. I said it was a bit early to tell. Then I added, "But it should be easier, anyway, than covering the Kremlin."

"Ha!" He gleefully smiled. "I shouldn't be so sure about that if I were you!"

We both laughed, but the laugh from me was perhaps a bit forced. I was aware that inevitably there would be delicate moments ahead, and of course there were.

Bill Heseltine's joking assessment was correct. One of the reasons for any difficulty was not only the nature of the job itself, which entailed reporting as accurately as possible any bad news about the royal family as well as the good but also the BBC's parsimony in those days, displayed by its insistence that one man could do two jobs.

A dreadful example of what could go wrong had been vividly spelled out for me by my immediate predecessor, upon whose watch as diplomatic and court correspondent, an intruder, Michael Fagan, had chosen to find his way into Buckingham Palace and the Queen's bedroom. When that happened, where was my predecessor?

As diplomatic correspondent, he was with the foreign secretary in the Middle East. Since in those days the palace insisted upon talking only to a handful of accredited court correspondents, my colleague swiftly switched from his diplomatic journalistic role to that of court correspondent and flew immediately back to England to cope with reporting the Fagan aftermath. A lapse in security had nearly resulted in the resignation of the home secretary.

People in Buckingham Palace understandably like to know to whom they are talking. Mercifully, nobody penetrated palace security upon my watch. In the five years that followed, I was able to juggle successfully dual coverage of foreign and of royal news, although I had to be careful in deciding when I could commit myself to leaving the country. There was no problem in travelling abroad to cover a royal tour with the Queen because I would be travelling, so to speak, with the ultimate font of royal news; but whenever I left England to accompany the prime minister or the foreign secretary on an overseas assignment, there was always a nagging worry about coverage of Buckingham Palace news in my absence.

The BBC supplied a "stand-in" but his contacts were not as developed as mine. He was younger; and one of the arguments for older correspondents is that if they're any good, then inevitably their field of useful acquaintanceship is more extensive than that of somebody younger.

I was in my mid-fifties at that stage, and there were few capitals in the world into which I could not fly or pick up the telephone and talk to somebody I knew -- and who knew me. Within the hour, I would be broadcasting a reasonably well-informed dispatch back to London.

Both of those early encounters as BBC diplomatic and court

correspondent with the Queen and with the New Zealander Bill Heseltine followed an earlier meeting with Her Majesty in a previous incarnation, as BBC Africa Correspondent, when, in 1979, I was covering the one-month-long royal tour of Africa. That assignment had provided the first occasion upon which I was presented to her, when the British high commissioner in Zambia gave a reception in Lusaka for the Queen.

It also provided the chance for me to observe at close quarters the mechanics of a royal tour. In many ways, it is just like a touring theatrical company. A basic requirement is to be light on one's feet and immaculate in one's appearance. Although we media folk were always permitted sartorial laxness according to operational conditions, we were expected nevertheless to be properly clad at formal functions.

Higher standards of dress were naturally required from the members of the royal household. They had to be properly turned out on all occasions, necessitating quick-change acts worthy of any cabaret behind the scenes. Ladies-in-waiting changed their hats and dresses in mid-air on the royal flight between one engagement and another; and equerries buckled on, or unbuckled, swords and sheaths and changed uniforms, according to the degree of formal ceremony awaiting them at the next function.

These quick offstage wardrobe changes, sometimes conducted in cramped conditions on board one of the smaller aircraft of the Queen's flight, led to badinage of a distinctly green room variety. When on board the royal flight on one occasion, I laughed when I heard one of the ladies-in-waiting, changing her dress behind a curtain, sharply address an equerry on the other side of the curtain, who was also putting on a uniform for the ceremony ahead. She cried out. "Mind where you're sticking that sword!"

Wardrobe manipulation is as much a part of a royal progress as it is of any Paris fashion show, though the garments on display are usually more orthodox than those draped on models. Dress for each event was laid down firmly in a "little blue book" produced for every royal tour.

I came to admire the work of the impressively adaptable ladies-in-waiting and equerries. They did their jobs well in conditions ranging from tropical heat in Africa or Asia to snow or rain in Canada and other northern climes. They had to be resourceful.

What, for instance, does a lady-in-waiting do when, with her arms already full of bouquets and posies that her royal boss has received and handed on to her, the boss is given yet more floral offerings? The lady-in-waiting cannot just dump or discard gracelessly those she is already holding. An amusing solution to the problem that I witnessed in Belize was offered by one of the Queen's regular ladies-in-waiting when, already overburdened with flowers, she simply summoned a nearby British sergeant major to her aid and, with an irresistible smile, handed to him her pile of blossoms and greenery.

Ramrod straight, the sergeant major gallantly accepted them before the delighted grins of the platoon of soldiers ranked behind him. They knew that they were unlikely ever to see him again quite as he appeared at that moment. A sergeant major looking like a Morris dancer colourfully outdid the more familiar spectacle to them of a sergeant major wearing "jungle greens".

Another requirement for long royal tours was physical endurance. Having years ago passed her eightieth birthday, the Queen, who is the most travelled British monarch in history, has understandably reduced the number of such trips.

An important member of the entourage was always the medical officer, who looked after not only the royal Household but, as a matter simply of kindness and medical vocation, any accompanying correspondent or cameraman in need. During my time as court correspondent, he was Surgeon Captain Norman Blacklock, and he helped us with problems ranging from upset stomachs to setting a broken arm for an ITN reporter. On that African tour, we were compelled to charter small aircraft to get down onto bush airstrips in out-of-the-way areas, in variable weather and flying conditions. This sometimes tested people to the limit. For instance, we were cooped up sometimes for several hours in a small plane cabin with no toilet facilities.

Worried about this aspect, a member of the staff of the Buckingham Palace Press Office who was to travel with us at one stage somewhat bashfully asked if I could find a suitable receptacle for her use if the need arose, "such as a jam jar".

The reason that her request was sent in my direction was that she was still in London, while I was already in Nairobi, making prior transport planning arrangements for getting the BBC and other British media representatives, as well as a member of the palace press office, around the continent.

The calls of nature have always been a bit of a problem for royal women and those in their entourage, all compelled by duty to be present for long hours on ceremonial occasions, sometimes without a chance to relieve themselves.

I remembered with amusement the jam jar request when, years later, I visited the chateau of Pau in France. It is the birthplace of Henri IV, known for his political achievements in uniting the divided French as "Henry the Great" and for his numerous amours as "le vert gallant". He is also credited with having wished that every French labourer should have a chicken to eat every Sunday: "la poule au pot". The most unusual thing, however, that sticks in my mind about the Pau chateau is that its name, pronounced "po", was entirely appropriate, for it houses and exhibits with pride a room full of vessels for the urinal use of royal women and their attendants on protracted ceremonial occasions!

Often these chamber pots were concealed beneath long gowns and used "in situ". The royal chamber pots, however, were far removed from any humble jam jar, with many being made of decorated porcelain from Sevres, Limoges, and elsewhere.

It was during a major Commonwealth conference held in Lusaka in Zambia, just before the death of Rhodesia and the birth of Zimbabwe, that my first meeting with the Queen took place. She has always taken seriously her position as Head of the Commonwealth, with its membership of 53 states. Elusive though the political purpose of the organisation might sometimes appear to be, it would be improper for her of all people to suggest such an idea.

The title itself, Head of the Commonwealth, was increasingly employed as the British Empire disappeared and the Commonwealth expanded. As countries received their independence from Britain, they chose either to join the association or to stay outside it. Most joined, and there are even Commonwealth states that were not previously ruled by Britain but have been accepted into the association, such as the former Portuguese African colony of Mozambique and the former Belgian African territory of Rwanda.

Originally called, in the 1931 Statute of Westminster, the "British

Commonwealth of Nations", the word "British" was dropped after the Second World War.

The largely white-populated "Old Commonwealth" of Australia, Canada, and New Zealand, together with white-ruled South Africa and Rhodesia, found itself transformed into the "New Commonwealth" of newly independent states with people of many colours and races. The Queen's father, George VI, was the last of five British emperors formally described as such, although the first of them was in fact an empress, Queen Victoria.

There followed Edward VII, George V, the uncrowned Edward VIII, and then George VI. The Queen's father was also the only British monarch to have been officially known both as emperor and as Head of the Commonwealth, the latter title coming into general use when India approved it after independence in 1947. The title has stuck and has (until the time of this writing in 2014) remained attached to the British monarchy, although efforts to detach it have been made in some Commonwealth quarters. One idea has been to recycle the title among other member states. It has not yet happened, even though a great controversy raged at one stage about the Queen's head possibly disappearing from postage stamps.

The title of emperor or empress, like much of the empire itself, had disappeared by the time the Queen ascended the throne. I find it hard to believe now (although I remember it vividly) that in my childhood we celebrated every year what was known as Empire Day with school holidays and parties. The date was 24 May, Queen Victoria's birthday. I find it equally hard to believe that I have lived in four reigns, starting with George V.

Empire Day continued its existence until as late as 1960, when the name was changed to Commonwealth Day. Then, moving even further away from reminders of Victoria and imperialism, the date was changed in 1967 from Victoria's birthday to the official birthday of the Queen in June. That arrangement in its turn lasted until 1977, when it was decided that Commonwealth Day should be detached from the date of any British royal birthday. The day decided upon was the second Monday in March. That position has remained unchanged until now, thirty-seven years later, with the Commonwealth consisting of fifty-three members only because Robert Mugabe's Zimbabwe remains excluded from being the fifty-fourth. One day, if that country becomes internationally respectable again, it might decide to rejoin and it might be accepted by the association.

A number of Commonwealth countries retain the Queen as head of state; and as such, she has dealt with scores, if not hundreds, of prime ministers. I doubt if anyone has ever tried to count them!

In Great Britain alone, up to the moment at which I write, twelve prime ministers had served as her heads of government: Churchill, Eden, Macmillan, Douglas-Home, Wilson, Callaghan, Heath, Thatcher, Major, Blair, Brown, and Cameron. (Of those dozen people, I interviewed six while each was a prime minister).

Thus it is evident that the Queen has learned about much more than horses, despite allegations suggesting that horses are really all that she is interested in, a charge emanating almost always from disparaging critics, often republicans.

The prime ministers in the remaining realms of the Queen are usually elected politicians, while the governors general of those realms are appointed as her personal representatives. This is a position that on at least one occasion has led to her being somewhat more swiftly informed about events overseas than the British government of the time.

I have in mind, for example, the 1983 upheaval in the Caribbean island of Grenada, when the prime minister was killed in an uprising, and a group of Caribbean countries, alarmed by what was happening, asked the United States to intervene.

The Americans put in troops to restore stable government, but there was bloodshed and confusion. At one stage, everybody worried about the disappearance of the governor general: was he alive, captured, or was he as dead as the prime minister?

He was alive. He had been whisked out of danger and onto an American warship. By courtesy of the US Navy and the Pentagon, Buckingham Palace was quickly assured of the safety of the Queen's representative, and both she and the British government were grateful for that.

However, although Mrs Thatcher welcomed the survival of the governor general, she was said to have been "a bit miffed" that the British government learned about his whereabouts later than Buckingham Palace. It was also suggested at the time that Mrs Thatcher was annoyed that the Americans had acted as they did. This, perhaps, was because it underlined the relative powerlessness of Britain in the Caribbean compared with American capabilities. It was almost as if the Americans were reminding us that the area was their "backyard" and not ours.

The episode underlined also some of the curious official realities that surround the British monarchy and the British government. Constitutional paradox sometimes makes the Queen's position look odd. Once, for example, she found herself endorsing a policy of one of her governments while being obliged to set out a policy quite different from another of her governments.

This happened during the years of Rhodesian UDI, when her British government was implementing a policy of economic sanctions against Ian Smith's rebel regime while, in a speech from the throne in Jamaica, the Queen outlined her Jamaican government's policy, calling for more vigorous military action. The policy difference was noted at the time, but nobody (in Britain anyway) worried about it overmuch. This was because everyone realised that the Queen was simply doing her constitutional duty in both of her realms: reading out words prepared for her by her ministers. The British and Jamaican governments were at loggerheads, while the Queen did her constitutional best to oblige both prime ministers.

She is in danger of getting into hotter water when she delivers the only pronouncement that she makes regularly that is not prepared by her ministers. This is her annual Christmas Day broadcast to the Commonwealth. She makes it as the head of the Commonwealth, not solely as the Queen of Great Britain.

What she has to say in it is a reflection of her personal view of things, compiled of course after careful consultation with her closest advisers, who doubtless include a number of Commonwealth ministers.

The royal Christmas messages still attract millions of listeners and viewers all over the Commonwealth. Audiences may not be as massive as once they were, simply because the novelty of royal messages has worn off, but the numbers of viewers and listeners are still important enough to count. So are the messages themselves.

The media rarely ignore them, and they provoke comment to the extent that the Queen sometimes comes under fire for saying things that people might not like. Such a case arose at Christmas 2004. A woman columnist, Minette Marrin, had some criticism to express.

Admonishing the Queen directly, Marrin wrote:

> *Stay out of politics. Taking a line – any line – on multi-cultur-alism, as you did in your Christmas Day speech, was highly political, especially when a Birmingham theatre had been closed by an ethnic minority riot, and when the government was proposing to give tax breaks to second wives of ethnic minority husbands. For decades you have managed to stay out of politics; don't follow the unwise example of your son, who has not.*

In my view, it was an unfair attack. I had watched that Christmas message and could see nothing remotely political in it unless an expression of royal concern for people of all colours and races is regarded in itself as being a political rather than a moral act. That would seem to me as a mere human being to be a somewhat strange if not actually xenophobic viewpoint. Nevertheless, the criticism illustrated how open to attack the Queen is from those who might not altogether appreciate her dual role as head of state of the United Kingdom and head of the Commonwealth.

Both opponents and supporters of the monarchy and of the Commonwealth have criticised the duality. The double-sided nature of Her Majesty's Commonwealth role renders her potentially vulnerable. The fact that in her Christmas message she is not uttering words provided for her by her ministers but is uttering words of her own leaves her especially exposed. She is speaking in a constitutionally unprotected manner.

Things might become even more difficult should efforts be made to get Britain to commit itself to any plans that go beyond the existing European Union and towards closer, formal political federation (remote though that prospect might appear with the current problems in Europe). As long ago as 2003, it was reported that Buckingham Palace had requested documents for her advisers to study the constitutional implications of any plans by the European Union, and indeed in the eyes of some constitutional students she has already "surrendered the supremacy of the Crown and ended the monarchy". This, it is suggested, was done back in 1972, when Britain decided to join the European Community a year later by accepting the Treaty of Rome and, subsequently, the Maastricht Treaty.

Thus in June 2012, in the week of the Queen's diamond jubilee, Mr Bob Lomas of the Magna Carta Society suggested that "fun" though the Jubilee might have been, "it is the biggest 'con' perpetrated against the British people by the establishment since they were assured that joining what was then called the European Common Market would in no way effect essential national sovereignty when in truth and reality our national sovereignty was surrendered." Lomas argued, "Queen Elizabeth II reigned for just nineteen years [1953 to 1972], not sixty."

Well, doubtless the Lomas views can be challenged, but however correct or incorrect they might be, to judge by the enthusiasm of the allegedly "conned"' British people for the Queen's sixty-two years of un-relenting public duty, such constitutional niceties do not unduly concern them anyway.

Advisers to the Queen do however wonder if the Queen's supreme authority as the guardian of the British constitution, asserted through the sovereignty of Parliament, would be altered or undermined by European constitutional proposals. According to one thoughtful source in 2003, the Labour MP for Birkenhead and former government minister, Mr Frank Field, in most respects, such a European constitution would relegate the Queen to the role of a "glorified head of a county council".

How the European Union will evolve is anybody's guess, especially with the current upheavals, but it is plain that the Queen and her counsel-lors are concerned. Meanwhile, her Commonwealth role continues, with the Queen making no secret of the fact that she is always on the lookout for fresh ideas for her Christmas message.

She takes the task of writing what she has to say, and of deciding how she should appear on television, as seriously as any of her ministers do when they make their own planned speeches. On a couple of occasions during my spell as court correspondent, she told me that if I had any bright thoughts I might have to offer, she would welcome hearing them. I was not of much help, feeling that there were many people infinitely more qualified than I was to offer inspiration.

At the end of Minette Marrin's attack on the Queen's broadcast was a gratuitous throwaway line also attacking the Prince of Wales. It was largely irrelevant because there really is no recognised constitutional obligation upon him (as there is with the monarch) to keep his views to himself. Nor has he deliberately involved himself in politics in the manner insinuated by Marrin. Indeed, many people think (including myself) that one of the most attractive characteristics of Prince Charles is his ability to express unfashionable opinions on questions of taste that have no direct political relevance whatsoever.

He has a talent for saying things with which a lot of us agree but that are either unfashionable or are unwelcome in certain media or political quarters. Those opinions range from his feelings about modern architecture to his feelings about the "Disney language" of a revised Church of England service book. On the latter, he said that the Church had "battered and deformed" Thomas Cranmer's liturgy of 1662, an assertion with which I happen to agree. On the former, his description of an extension of the National Gallery ("a monstrous carbuncle on the face of a much-loved and elegant friend") exhibited such a powerful turn of phrase that it has already become enshrined in the *Dictionaries of Quotations*. His assertion in that case, however, is one with which I happen to disagree. Neither example, like most of the prince's controversial opinions, is actually political. Each is simply an expression of personal taste. Why should he not be allowed to air that?

Of course, things are less clear-cut when he has attempted to define what he thinks about his own role as heir apparent and his future probable role as king. Some of the personal, moral, and religious opinions he has expressed undoubtedly do have constitutional implications and thus inevitably are political. This is because any alteration to existing constitutional arrangements would have to be approved by Parliament and possibly by the parliaments of other Commonwealth countries of which his mother is still the Queen. In the next chapter, I enlarge upon this subject.

CHAPTER 25

Coronation Oaths

Oaths are straws, men's faiths are wafer-cakes.
—Pistol, in Shakespeare's *Henry V*

Not everyone – thank goodness! – is as cynical as Pistol. With the country having affectionately celebrated the diamond jubilee of her coronation in 2013 and the Queen herself now aged eighty-eight, the sensitive subject of inevitable changes to the next coronation service, for King Charles III, is under study. Although Elizabeth II seems happily to be in good health, it is natural that those responsible for coronation ceremonies are planning ahead. The dean of Westminster Abbey was reported as long as eight years ago as saying, in 2006, that the traditional Church of England coronation service must be revised to reflect society's changes since the crowning of the Queen in 1953. He said that the service "needs to find the right way of including people of other faiths." His words carried weight because, as Dean, he was more or less automatically among those responsible for drawing up the service. His remarks were seen as meaning that the coronation of the Prince of Wales might in fact be a "multi-faith" event, with prayers and readings from other religions and denominations, including the Muslim, Sikh, and Jewish faiths.

The Duke of Norfolk, as earl marshal, was also reported to have begun a review of the ceremonies for the accession, probably in consultation with the dean. Preliminary discussions were said also to have started between the duke and Clarence House, while the prince's own office was said to be conducting a parallel review of the accession. The prince's own views are well known because he indicated twenty years ago that he would like his coronation to be more inclusive. "I believe," he said, "that the Catholic subjects of the sovereign are as important [as Protestants], not to mention the Islamic, Hindu, and Zoroastrian."

Canon Hall (who conducted the funerals of the Queen Mother and of Diana, Princess of Wales, as well as conducting the service for the Queen's golden jubilee) praised the prince's success in reaching out to "other communities" within society in today's Britain. As for the Queen, it can be assumed that she too is kept in the picture as discussion continues, for she likes to be kept informed on all sorts of issues, and the manner of her son's coronation is important to her not only constitutionally but is naturally close to her heart.

As the prince ponders upon his future (with the pondering probably sharpening as his mother ages and his succession looms inexorably closer), he has had in mind at least one possible change in the royal titles. Some of the personal, moral, and religious opinions he has expressed as heir apparent undoubtedly have substantial constitutional implications and so can be interpreted as having potential political implications. This is because any alteration to existing constitutional arrangements would have to be approved by Parliament and by the parliaments of other Commonwealth countries of which his mother is still the Queen.

The particular change I have in mind emerged when he was thinking aloud about an ancient title the monarch holds and which is usually only noticed by people when they look at the coins of the realm and see two little letters engraved on them: "FD".

In Latin, this stands for "Fidei Defensor"; in English, "Defender of the Faith". Pope Leo X originally conferred it upon Henry VIII in appreciation of Henry's written opposition to Martin Luther, a fact of the sort that embellishes history with its occasional irony.

I make this comment because it was the behaviour of Henry VIII over the issue of royal divorce and Henry's marriage to Anne Boleyn that led to the breach between Rome and the English monarchy. Despite this, however, the papal title for English monarchs was later confirmed by Parliament, and it has stayed in use to this day by subsequent British kings and queens. Prince Charles, however, aware of the multicultural nature and the mixed religious beliefs of the many peoples living in his mother's realms, has suggested that perhaps it would be a good idea to change the title from "Defender of the Faith" to "Defender of Faith", or even, perhaps, to "Defender of Faiths".

Any alteration on those lines would entail the loss of one word ("the") or the addition of a solitary letter (*s*), changing singular to plural. Tiny though such amendments might be in writing, the change in meaning is important enough to trigger debate among believers of all faiths, even though atheists and agnostics might feel, together with Pistol in Shakespeare's *Henry V*, that "oaths are straws, men's faiths are wafer-cakes".

However, concern among the faithful was provided when a member of the General Synod, the church's "parliament", expressed her views. Reacting to the ideas of the dean of Westminster, Alison Ruoff told the *Sunday Telegraph*, "There is no way that other faiths should be involved in the service. This is a Christian country, and so the coronation service must remain exclusively Christian and we should not apologise for that."

There are many who would challenge Ruoff's assertion that Britain is still a Christian country. If abysmal church attendance figures were to be the sole criterion by which to judge, she would indeed appear to be wrong. Church attendance, though, is not, of course, the sole criterion for judging if Britain remains Christian.

The dean of Westminster at one stage claimed that well over 50 per cent of the population still saw themselves as belonging to the Church of England, and he regarded that as a sign of far greater adherence than is often suggested.

He might well have been right. Thus Alison Ruoff also could claim to be correct. I hope they both are; even though I write as a more or less failed Christian but nevertheless as a confirmed, if rather absentee, member of the Church of England. I am one of those uncountable people brought up as Christian but who usually attend church only for funerals, memorial services, weddings, christenings, and perhaps an occasional Christmas carols service.

One implication of any changes envisaged by the Prince of Wales and by the dean of Westminster would presumably involve new words for the actual Coronation Oaths. As is shown by a glance at the 1953 Coronation Service, the oaths sworn to by the new Sovereign would logically have to be altered.

At the last coronation, the archbishop of Canterbury asked the Queen, among other questions, the following:

> *Will you to the utmost of your power maintain in the United Kingdom the Protestant Reformed Religion established by law?*
>
> *Will you maintain and preserve inviolably the settlement of the Church of England and the doctrine, worship, discipline and government thereof as by law established in England?*
>
> *And will you preserve unto the Bishops and Clergy of England, and to the Churches there committed to their charge, all such rights and privileges as by law do or shall appertain to them or any of them?*

To each of these questions, the Queen replied, "All this I promise to do."

It is therefore obvious that if the new monarch is to swear to become a "Defender of Faith" or "Defender of Faiths", rather than "Defender of *the* Faith", then the 1953 coronation questions might need revising. To avoid any constitutional perturbation it is necessary that any amendment in the Coronation Oaths should be agreed. This agreement must be concluded by the monarch who is swearing the oath; the Church of England, which is administering the oath; and Parliament, which is keeping a sharp eye upon whatever the sovereign and the church might be promising. The agreement would probably involve also the support of the parliaments of other Commonwealth countries that maintain their direct link with the British Crown. All this could well happen.

I am not so sure, however, about the realisation of another possibility frequently discussed: namely the outright disestablishment of the Church of England. This subject hit the headlines in April 2014 when the archbishop of Canterbury joined Prime Minister David Cameron in a firm defence of Christian Britain while the deputy prime minister, Nick Clegg, called for an end to the link between church and state. The *Times* headline: "Coalition Split on Role of Church". The *Times* editorial, wittily headed "Cross Purposes", examined "the British compromise between church and state" as being "peculiar, irrational, and anachronistic" – and as "serving us well".

The former archbishop of Canterbury, Dr Rowan Williams, had made his views plain years ago when, while he was still archbishop of Wales, he suggested that with Tony Blair's government committed to a reform of the Lords, the chance should be taken to review the Queen's religious role. He indicated: "I would be a lot happier not to see the monarch as supreme governor." He went so far as to suggest that disestablishment would take place "by a thousand cuts". The notion of the monarch as supreme governor of the Church of England had, he said, "outlived its usefulness".

The *Times* leader after Nick Clegg's call for disestablishment commented, with justification, that "when secularists and those with faith are singing from the same hymn sheet, some degree of disestablishment is a concept worth thinking about".

The dean of Westminster, on the other hand, while advancing his thoughts on a "multi-faith" coronation, was careful to emphasise that the Church of England must remain at the heart of the coronation because the Prince of Wales would be supreme governor of the Church of England when he becomes king.

Other official voices have been heard in the debate on the coronation, including the voice of the Home Office. A report for that ministry, published in 2000, suggested that the Prince of Wales should be crowned king in a multi-faith inauguration service rather than the thousand-year-old Coronation ceremony.

Tampering with ancient tradition is always controversial, but support has come from several quarters, including (perhaps unexpectedly) those on the right of the political spectrum.

The *Daily Telegraph*, for instance, argued that there was no reason why Britain's religious minorities should not draw upon their past customs to develop rites showing their fealty to the monarch:

> *To incorporate such rites around an unchanged core service would reflect the special identities of British Muslims, British Hindus, and so on. It would also, in our view, make for a splendid ceremony.*

The *Sunday Times* also favoured the idea:

> *Who knows? When Prince Charles is eventually crowned, he may be attended upon by the archbishops of Canterbury and Westminster, the Chief Rabbi, and other religious leaders. The Anglican church will finally have come of age.*

Thus the Prince of Wales appears to have strong allies in seeking any change in the oaths to which he is expected to swear. Bearing in mind the stresses and strains of the years of his life after the death of Princess Diana and up to the time of his second marriage, his ideas about modernising the manner of his coronation do not seem unreasonable.

It would be difficult for him credibly to swear to uphold, say, the "discipline" of the established Church of England when he has already defied that "discipline" and its "doctrine". After his remarriage in a register office, the public repentance both of himself and of his second wife at the Windsor Castle religious ceremony assisted in the recuperation of both his moral reputation and hers, among those of a deeply caring moral or religious nature. It did not mean, however, that the past had been generally or fully forgotten.

Although, like His Royal Highness, there are hundreds of thousands of commoners (such as me) who have also been both adulterers and divorced; unlike him we have not had to conduct our private lives under the merciless and often tendentious surveillance of newspapers, television and radio – not to mention, these days, the Internet and Twitterers. My sympathies – together, I imagine, with the best wishes of millions of others – go to Prince Charles and the Duchess of Cornwall as they contemplate together his remorselessly approaching reign and their virtually unavoidable royal future.

For the most part, the British people appreciate the position in which the couple find themselves, despite any reservations felt by less forgiving critics – including particularly those with republican leanings. It was, I think, heartening to learn soon after the wedding of Prince Charles and the Duchess of Cornwall that their communications secretary of the time, Paddy Harverson, refuted a report that "sackfuls of hate mail" had been sent to the duchess. He wrote:

> Between February 11th and April 20th 2005 more than 25,000 letters were set to Clarence House, of which

just over 900, or less than 4 per cent of the total, were unsupportive of the marriage. The duchess also received several hundred letters personally at her home after the announcement of the marriage. Again the vast majority were supportive. In fact, since the wedding, the proportion of unsupportive letters sent to Clarence House has declined to the extent that 99 per cent have been positive.

I cannot end my thoughts upon the problems of the next Coronation without expressing some relief at the result of last September's referendum in Scotland that rejected the Scottish nationalists' bid for independence. What would have happened if the Scots had endorsed the move for independence and withdrew from the United Kingdom? Would that have meant that Charles III of England would become the first monarch of both countries since his predecessor, Charles II, to be obliged to travel to Scotland to be crowned in a separate coronation ceremony? That, of course, was before the 1707 Act of Union.

Already, the Stone of Scone has been removed from Westminster Abbey to Scotland. The kings of that country traditionally are supposed to have been seated upon it at some time before, during, or after their crowning; and since the Act of Union monarchs of the United Kingdom, including the Queen, were crowned on it while seated upon the Westminster Abbey throne beneath which was lodged the stone. For some years now, there has been an empty space it once occupied – ever since John Major's government let the stone go back to Scotland.

Would a newly independent Scotland have permitted the stone to travel back to Westminster for a combined Coronation ceremony for her successor? Or would it have been necessary for the new sovereign of both countries after the end of the reign of Elizabeth II to be obliged to travel to Edinburgh for a separate ceremony to that at Westminster?

Royal advisers and constitutional experts in both England and Scotland, I suppose, are giving thought to such matters, for as the years go by the Scottish nationalists (as they have already announced) will attempt to pursue their attempt to break the union with England. I would hope that politicians, as well as royal advisers, in both countries are also pondering over the problems that would be involved, although I am doubtful about the politicians.

This is because, with the immediate referendum problem having for the moment passed by, politicians with their propensity not always to think very far ahead, might fail to persuade us all – English, Scots, Welsh, and northern Irish -- about the benefits of belonging to Great Britain and not to little England, little Scotland, little Wales and little Northern Ireland.

In my view they should be thinking constructively about the issue and be doing their utmost to hold the United Kingdom together.

While reflecting upon constitutional matters, perhaps I should mention one other subject that occasionally surfaces. It is the suggestion that the Queen might abdicate. Even the former archbishop of Canterbury, Lord Carey, at one stage reportedly said he thought she might abdicate if she became seriously ill. A Buckingham Palace spokesman, however, emphasised that the position had been made clear that "the Queen will not abdicate".

This is because a constitutional mechanism already exists whereby, even if she did become seriously ill, there would be no need for her to abdicate. She could retire from her duties and Prince Charles could become Prince Regent, just as a previous Prince of Wales did in 1810 when his father, George III, became insane. Ten years later "Prinny" (as the Regent was known) succeeded him on the throne.

The reality today is that, like so many of us, the Queen is gradually retiring from some engagements without actually formalising her withdrawal. This was shown relatively recently when, for the first time in years, she absented herself as Head of the Commonwealth from attending the latest Commonwealth Conference, held in Sri Lanka, and the Prince of Wales represented her at the proceedings.

The position seems to be that the Queen will work on until she can no longer do so. A tradition has existed for many centuries in England by which a Regent can be appointed by, or pursuant to, an Act of Parliament. The tradition was formalised in the 1937 Regency Act.

It provided permanent provision for the selection of a Regent if the sovereign is under eighteen or is found by a commission to be infirm of body or mind. As laid down by the act, such a commission would be composed of the spouse of the monarch, the Lord Chancellor, the Speaker of the House of Commons, the Lord Chief Justice, and the Master of the Rolls.

We still possess such officials, including a new brand of Lord Chancellor despite efforts to abolish the post. The Queen, too, still has a spouse, though he is no youngster either. If those involved at any time feel that she should be given a rest, then presumably they – or at the very least her spouse! – could say so. If she herself feels like putting her feet up, I imagine she would not hesitate to tell him. In short, abdication would be irrelevant.

In the natural course of things, the Prince of Wales would become Prince Regent, although I suppose in theory he could opt out of the succession. This appears to be an unlikely prospect.

If he ever does become Prince Regent, he would be the first since George IV, who encouraged the architect John Nash to such a magnificent extent that the pair bequeathed to us Regent's Park and its terraces, Trafalgar Square, St. James's Park, Marble Arch, Carlton House Terrace, a recreated Buckingham Palace from the former Buckingham House, and (last but not least) that glorious Asian seaside folly, Brighton Pavilion.

What a legacy!

CHAPTER 26

===

Reporting on the Royals

My first acquaintance with reporting on the "royals" came sixty years ago. The occasion was the Badminton Olympic Horse Trials event of 1954 (mentioned in chapter 8). Gracing the event by her attendance was the late Queen Mother, widowed not long before by the death of George VI; her younger daughter, the late Princess Margaret, in young and beautiful full bloom; and other members of the royal family.

For three or four days, I happily filled columns of the *Bristol Evening Post* with my reports from Badminton. One year later, after leaving the West Country for Fleet Street, I found myself rather less happily reporting for Britain's main domestic news agency, the Press Association, upon Princess Margaret's renunciation of a man she loved, Group Captain Peter Townsend.

He was divorced and in those days not acceptable to the Church, to the political establishment, and to many people in the country. How old-fashioned it sounds now!

Five years later, the princess was married to somebody else, Antony Armstrong-Jones, who was soon created Earl of Snowdon. That marriage was dissolved eighteen years after their wedding, and once again, it fell to my lot to deal with the news of Princess Margaret's personal love problems -- this time by not only writing that news but also broadcasting it over the BBC before I had actually had the chance to write anything. The Radio 4 programme *Woman's Hour* was on the air and immediately roped me in to talk about what I had just been told at Buckingham Palace, so predominantly female listeners became the first to know that one of their sex, princess though she was, had run into the kind of marital difficulties experienced by many of them.

It could be regarded as a royal instance of Kipling's military example:

> *For the colonel's lady and Judy O'Grady*
> *Are sisters under their skins!*

I was broadcasting from a mobile BBC studio in a converted London taxicab parked outside Buckingham Palace at Canada Gate, one of the gilded iron gates to the royal parks around the Victoria Memorial. I had hurried to it from inside the palace the moment the briefing had ended to the three other accredited court correspondents of the day and me (then BBC acting court correspondent). My *Woman's Hour* interviewer, I seem to remember, was Sue McGregor.

The moment she had finished questioning me, I wrote a quick news script for the next BBC World Service news bulletin due to go on the air a few moments later, before a subsequent extremely busy evening in larger television and radio studios with which I was more familiar than I was with the taxi studio.

That old London taxi, however, became actually one of my favourite studios and I used it many times. The driver was a BBC broadcasting engineer; the luggage space next to him contained broadcasting technical equipment; and the passenger compartment behind the usual glass screen had a fold-up desk upon which I could quickly write a script and upon which was placed a hand microphone and earphones for my broadcasting use.

Into the middle of the glass screen was built a telescopic radio mast that went up into the air when needed and was lowered when it was not. On the exterior black sides of the taxi were words identifying it as a BBC vehicle. Its mobility, like that of all London taxis, was legendary. This was useful in heavy traffic or when the taxi was called upon to get to a broadcaster quicker than the broadcaster could get to a studio. To cite just one amusing example, involving one of my neighbours and me, a big news story broke in the old Soviet Union in the early hours of the morning, when I was diplomatic correspondent and I was in bed at home. The *Today* programme wanted me on the air at 6 a.m., so it dispatched the taxi to wait outside my house while, still in my pyjamas and dressing gown, I composed my piece indoors and then emerged into Bingham Street, Islington, still clad only in my night gear, to broadcast to the world my interpretation of Russian events.

What I remember most, though, about that particular exercise was the effect the appearance of the taxi had on my neighbour. He was a famous high court judge, and he was just getting up to go to work. He looked out of the window and saw the aerial go aloft and the BBC identification on the taxi. He told me that he immediately thought a check was being made on TV and radio licence holders, and he asked his wife if their licence was up to date! (It was.)

A few minutes later, he heard my voice coming into his home over the air, and he realised what the taxi and me were doing at that early daylight hour in Islington.

The old taxi was not, of course, outside Buckingham Palace by accident on the day that Princess Margaret's forthcoming divorce was announced. A tip to me that something important in royal circles was afoot explained its presence there to provide me with swift communication facilities in the days before mobile phones were in general use.

As acting court correspondent, I was standing in for the full-time diplomatic and court correspondent, the late Donald Milner, who earlier, as a young BBC reporter, had accompanied Antarctic explorer Sir Vivian Fuchs on a major South Pole expedition. He was in hospital for three months, out of action, causing me to be hauled home from my job as Africa correspondent to fill in for him.

As I have explained, the duality of that BBC post sometimes produced difficulties, but on this occasion, I had managed to circumvent them. On the day in question, I had arranged to lunch, on the diplomatic front, with the Greek ambassador, useful probably for me because I had wanted to pick his brains about Cyprus, a large part of which had been taken over by Turkey. However, at midday, I received a call on the court front from the Queen's press secretary of the time, Michael Shea, who asked me if I could visit the palace at 2 p.m. to see him because an announcement was to be made.

I told him that I had an ambassadorial luncheon arranged, and he, as an old Foreign Office man, recognised the possible usefulness of that for me and was not upset when I asked him if the palace announcement was important. His memorable reply: "I think your employers will think so."

I promptly saw my editor; explained the position; asked him to entertain the ambassador in my place; gave him some questions for His Excellency that I wanted answered; and the switch was arranged, with the ambassador probably pleased to find himself talking to the editor rather than a mere correspondent.

Off to Buckingham Palace I went -- and off to Canada Gate went the taxi. Inside the palace, we four accredited court correspondents of those days were handed at 2 p.m. a piece of paper embargo-ed for publication at 2.30 p.m.

It consisted of a brief sentence saying that Princess Margaret and the Earl of Snowdon had agreed to divorce. Fifteen minutes or so ensued on questioning for background details. When and where is the court hearing? Who are the solicitors? What about the children? Then (for me anyway) came a hasty walk across the inner and outer courtyards of Buckingham Palace, a scamper through the London traffic outside the palace railings, and a jump into the taxi-studio to alert news desks with a newsflash. Within a minute, I was switched through to *Woman's Hour*.

A few weeks later, with Donald out of hospital and back at work, I went back to Africa; a few years later to Russia; and finally, to my mild astonishment, I found myself some six years later doing the diplomatic and court correspondent's job full-time.

I liked both sides of the job, entailing as it did travelling the world with the Queen; with her prime minister, the late Mrs Thatcher; and with the foreign secretary, Sir Geoffrey Howe -- now Lord Howe. Quite apart from the extraordinary amount of journeying I did with the politicians – Russia, China, America, Africa, Arabia, Eastern Europe, wherever foreign news was breaking – I travelled also thousands of miles watching the Queen at work, from China to the Caribbean, India to Canada, Africa to Mexico, America to Zanzibar. There was no shortage of news, and the appetite for it seemed insatiable.

So I was a little disconcerted when, some years after my retirement from full-time journalism and broadcasting, I read that one of my successors in reporting upon royalty, Jennie Bond, had been informed when she took the task on that the job had become a "graveyard". It certainly was not that in my day!

By the time Jennie was doing the job, its journalistic description had been altered. She had become not the BBC court correspondent but the BBC royal correspondent. The occupant of that post had also been relieved of the additional task of being diplomatic correspondent and reporting on foreign news (a sensible and long overdue divorce of the two jobs that I had recommended years before to the corporation back while I was still performing both).

I remembered Jennie as a bright young newsroom subeditor who, with efficiency, often handled my dispatches. She wrote a book, *Reporting Royalty: Behind the Scenes with the BBC's Royal Correspondent*, a work that was successful but met with some criticism. One respected reviewer, Hugh Massingberd, commented, "Jennie Bond's attempts to justify her trade with tough talk of 'People in the public eye have to accept the consequence of their actions' and 'The duty of the media to continue their scrutiny' left me feeling uneasy." He added, "What a dreadful circus the 'royal soap opera' has become in our celebrity culture."

I share Massingberd's discomfort. One reason is that, as a journalist who for many years had been covering serious news like wars, revolutions, riots, and political crises, I now had to cope with what Massingberd called "the dreadful circus" and "soap opera" side of royal news events. Another reason was the increasingly intrusive manner of royal reporting with, for example, the development of microphonic monitoring (not to mention illegal telephone hacking). The first case of microphonic monitoring that I recall as being noted as something out of the ordinary occurred as long ago as 1984. It happened in Jordan. The implications of the development were discussed at a BBC news and current affairs meeting after I had reported on a royal visit to that country, including the West Bank.

As Crown Prince Hassan of Jordan explained the West Bank situation to her, the Queen had made a remark about Israeli planes flying overhead and described a map she was shown as "depressing". We reporters standing nearby could not actually hear her remarks, but the usual tools of the broadcasting trade could. The microphones recorded what she said.

At the subsequent BBC news and current affairs meeting, the assistant director general noted that coverage of the visit had been "excellent" but also "slightly unusual" because of the role played by (and this was his phrase) "the reporter as eavesdropper". An editor said that the "small frisson" accompanying the monitored royal comments had been properly reflected and he knew of no criticism of the BBC for reporting them.

The subject cropped up again two years later, after I had covered the Queen's tour of China in 1986.This time, though, the emphasis at the news and current affairs meeting was distinctly different. A BBC editorial executive expressed his surprise that television had been allowed to record so much actuality of royal conversations during the tour and added that it was "a development to be welcomed". The editor of news and current affairs agreed and noted, "The conventions seem to have slipped away." An editor of TV News "confirmed that the palace had no objection to the broadcasting of such actuality".

Thus did microphonic eavesdropping become respectable. It was an important evolution in the history of broadcasting journalism and, I suppose, an inevitable progression towards more openness in reporting events, come what may.

The effects of the journalistic employment of microphones have been sometimes embarrassing for royalty. Prince Charles found this out in 2005, while on a skiing holiday in Klosters with Princes William and Harry. Microphones recorded him muttering about the "bloody people" of the media and as indicating to his sons that he "couldn't bear" the BBC royal correspondent, Nicholas Witchell, who was Jennie Bond's successor. Jennie reportedly commented, "Quite why Prince Charles has taken against Nick Witchell so violently is a mystery." She dismissed the episode as "Charles's little tantrum".

The communications secretary for the prince later said that the royal comments were "regretted", and I imagine that this was indeed the truth. I am glad that in my day, BBC court correspondents were not so directly in the royal line of fire.

Unscripted royal comments can be dangerous, especially cracks containing off-colour humour. This reality has marked the genuinely and generally excellent record of Prince Philip, Prince Charles's father, as a loyal, hard-working, and devoted consort to the Queen.

I've described in an earlier chapter how his spontaneous joke at a tricky moment during Kenya's Independence Day ceremony released the tension and was a great hit.

That was not the case, however, in China in 1986, when he struck a tasteless note while talking to a British student there. The student told a reporter that Prince Philip had said to him, "If you stay here much longer, you'll go back with slitty eyes." I remember the quip well because of the immediately depressing effect it had on the Queen's press secretary, Michael Shea. When, in seeking first official reaction to the prince's careless phrase, I informed him of what the student quoted the prince as saying, Shea replied wryly, "Thank you, John, for ruining my day."

As a good professional, however, Shea did his best to limit any perceived damage. At a news conference when questions were asked about it, the Press Secretary did not attempt in any way to deny what the prince had said, nor did he belittle the student. He stressed instead that it was "grotesque and absurd" to suggest that the prince had insulted the Chinese people in any way. This did little to avoid front-page splash stories next day in the tabloids, denigrating Prince Philip as what the *Daily Mirror*'s headline called "The Great Wally of China". The Times described the princely remark as "crass".

Given that both Prince Philip and Prince Charles are painfully familiar with media treatment of whatever it is they might have to say, it is perhaps surprising that they have nevertheless permitted themselves occasionally to speak somewhat incautiously. On the other hand, such lapses from utterly proper behaviour underline that they are human beings, not just princes. They might have behaved not quite correctly, but that does not make them "a bit bonkers", as a former minister for higher education – of all people! – once reportedly alleged about "all" members of the royal family.

That particular offender was reportedly Kim Howells. When he took up his higher education post in 2004, it was suggested that although he had been continuously in government since 1997, the probable explanation as to why he had not obtained a cabinet seat was because he was "recklessly outspoken". In other words, he was just as much lacking in discretion in what he might have to say as Prince Philip and Prince Charles might occasionally have been.

The Chinese hosts of the Queen and Prince Philip and the Chinese mass media did not seem to notice Prince Philip's conversation with the student until we more implacable British newshounds got on to it. The prince was rueful, and there was no noticeable damage done to relations between Britain and China, although the impact of the incident was such that the protocol adviser to Radio Hong Kong (whence the Queen

JOHN OSMAN

and Prince Philip travelled after their tour of China) recommended that anyone there who talked to the Queen should refuse afterwards to be interviewed by the media. The affair emphasised the care with which royalty must choose its words.

What actually is intrusive reporting? How far can, or should, supposedly private conversations, especially on public occasions, be monitored or reported? There is no simple answer to such questions in these days of determined openness and of advanced monitoring technology. The answer can really only be provided by the people who take part in any conversations that might conceivably be reported. The odds are that whatever they say will be picked up, passed on, and probably published and broadcast.

This broad rule is applicable not only to royalty but to politicians and anybody else in the public eye. It is astonishing – but heart-warming to me as both a human being and a journalist – to observe how often those doing the talking behave carelessly and naturally, rather than carefully and unnaturally!

My other reason for discomfort concerned the difficulty I personally endured in covering what Hugh Massingberd accurately described as the "royal soap opera" side of things in our "celebrity culture". I can best illustrate this by citing two specific examples that involved my own work. First, the difficult bit for me as court correspondent – lightweight news:

Year: 1983
Scene: Buckingham Palace

The Queen is giving a garden party, and among her guests are the court correspondent and his wife.

As requested, correspondent produces a light-hearted piece for the news bulletins. He misses the big story of the day: Princess Diana has broken convention by appearing at the garden party stockingless!

Court correspondent has not noticed. Bows head, with whitening hair, in shame at his own lack of perception of what is news. Clearly a younger man (or, preferably, woman) should do the job.

Second, the easy bit for me as court correspondent (and diplomatic correspondent) – serious news:

Year: 1986
Scene: Aden

Fighting has broken out in the People's Democratic Republic of Yemen; blood is flowing; foreigners want to get out, including British expatriates who have been alerted by Foreign Office messages broadcast on the BBC World Service to gather at a certain point at a certain time. The royal yacht *Britannia*, on her way to New Zealand for yet another royal tour in her career (then) of forty-three years, is diverted to sail around Steamer Point in Aden to the rescue. On the beach, cars are lined up at night with headlights switched on to show Britannia where hundreds of evacuees are gathered and to guide into shore the ship's boats to pick up those fleeing.

Those anxious to get out include Russians who, for years, as Soviet representatives, have been backing some of the tough Yemeni groups whose rivalries have led to this pickle. *Britannia* saves them all from the chaos, including the Soviets; takes them across the Red Sea to Djibouti; lands them; and resumes her voyage to New Zealand.

Story obtained by court correspondent asking Buckingham Palace if BBC can get through to the commander of Britannia; Palace helps; Britannia's captain gives BBC dramatic account; and BBC gets great news scoop.

Well, of course, it is not just reporting royalty in one way or the other that is like that. All journalism can broadly be categorised as "serious" or "pop", and to underline this assertion, I should like to sketch an example of public reaction to some of my own reporting from a remarkable period in 1970–71. In that year, looking back over a variegated career, I spent three of the most extraordinary months of my life.

They began with me covering for TV and radio as the BBC United Nations correspondent the important moment in New York when the UN decided that the Chinese permanent seat on the UN Security Council (where real power resides in the UN) should no longer be occupied by the Nationalist Chinese government in Taiwan but by Communist China. This geopolitical earth tremor occurred on a Monday.

Having reported this seismic UN shift, I flew the next day to Orlando, Florida, to cover the opening of Disney World and spent a day or two filming and interviewing Mickey Mouse, Minnie Mouse, Donald Duck, and Goofy.

Completing the assignment, I was in nearby Miami, about to return to my home in Washington, when news came through that the Soviet prime minister, Alexei Kosygin, who had been visiting Canada, was going to Cuba on his way back to Moscow. Could I get to Cuba?

My response to the BBC was on the lines of "From Miami? You must be joking!"

I explained that (a) being based in Washington was hardly a recommendation in Cuban eyes for access to Cuba; (b) setting out from Miami, with its thousands of anti-Castro refugees and exiles was, in Cuban eyes again, not perhaps the best place to start from; and (c) from where would I obtain a Cuban visa since the only two Cuban embassies in those days in the North and South American continents were in Canada and Mexico?

"That's it!" said my bosses. "Go to Mexico!" Off I flew with my TV crew to Mexico City, and (another argument for correspondents who have knocked around a bit) when I got to the Cuban Embassy there, I bumped into an old contact from the UN who provided us promptly with visas. On we went to Cuba. For three weeks, we followed and filmed Castro and the Soviets everywhere, even onto Soviet warships, which was something of a first for a Western camera crew.

As soon as I was back in Washington, I got a call from London saying that there was going to be a war between India and Pakistan. Could I go to cover the Indian side of the conflict?

I yelped in protest that I was supposed to be a correspondent covering the United States and the United Nations; that I had only just returned from Cuba, well outside the normal American journalistic orbit; that Christmas was on its way and that my parents-in-law were coming to

America to spend the festive season with us; and that I was getting too old for things like wars.

In fact, I was merely forty-two, and I covered quite a few wars after that, but as a point of principle (of physical survival) I never actually volunteered for wars. I went to them when I felt that I could not live with myself if I chickened out, but I was always quite relieved when younger journalists volunteered so that they could make a name for themselves. Essentially, I went to wars only to report upon them, just as a good soldier goes to fight in them: because it was my job.

None of my arguments worked. My bosses laughed at my suggestions that a younger correspondent would be more suitable. They pointed out that I had experience of India from 1959 and the Dalai Lama's flight from Tibet; that I had covered (from the Pakistani side) the last Indo-Pakistani war in 1965; and that – this was their clincher – I was known to the Indian prime minister, Mrs Gandhi, from my previous incarnation as Commonwealth correspondent. Relentlessly the pressure was applied, and after my insistence that I should at least be allowed to fly first class to the war, off I went to report upon it.

I flew out of the United States as my parents-in-law flew in to join us for Christmas. At a stopover in Hawaii, I telephoned them to welcome them to America, and I did not see them until long after Christmas. By then, the war was over; East Pakistan had disappeared; a new country, Bangladesh, had been born; and the map-makers were producing new maps. I had survived another war assignment, and I was pleased to get home to Washington. What did I find in the way of listeners' and viewers' reactions to major international news and a war that reshaped a subcontinent?

There was nothing at all on the UN Security Council's important power shift and nothing on the Soviets in Cuba; but there were letters from India expressing appreciation of BBC war coverage, including one from an Indian listener who had named his son, born during the war, after me.

The real postbag, though, consisted of lots of letters from viewers and listeners about the opening of Disney World. There was praise for what one letter to the BBC described as "John Osman's chats with his lovely friends" (i.e., Donald Duck, Goofy, Mickey, and Minnie Mouse).

Coverage of serious world events that might affect people's lives simply does not seem habitually to spur huge postbags of mail in the same quantities as those spurred by lightweight, gossipy, or scandalous news. Of course, scandals sometimes are important, especially if they have real moral, financial, and political implications understood by even the most obtuse reader, listener, or viewer (parliamentary expenses, for example, or telephone hacking).

Nevertheless, popular journalism, whether tabloid or televisual, seems sometimes to benefit from an apparent public obsession with the trivial rather than the serious. Trivial or serious, though, and whether received by Internet, email, Royal Mail (now dubbed "snail mail"), or plain postcard, the postbags of newspapers and broadcasting stations (like an MP's postbag) all provide for the recipients useful indications of what the public is really thinking about something.

The same applies to royal postbags, as shown by the example mentioned earlier about Clarence House disclosing details of the massive support received in messages from letter writers for the second marriage of the Prince of Wales.

Royal postbags, though, sometimes lead to difficulties in unexpected ways for a broadcaster. I discovered this fairly early on in my stint as BBC court correspondent when I went to Clarence House, then the home of the late Queen Mother, to help prepare beforehand my first broadcast about one of her many birthdays (she died at the age of 101). This annual event was one upon which birthday cards, notes, letters of congratulation, and gifts poured into Clarence House from all over the Commonwealth – and even farther afield – for a much-loved royal figure. I was told that every note or letter was acknowledged, and I mentioned this in my broadcast.

The result was that even more thousands of cards, notes, and letters than usual had been received. While the royal household was delighted at receiving yet more evidence of the affection in which the Queen Mother was held, royal householders were appalled at the extra work entailed for them.

The Queen Mother's press secretary, the late Major John Griffin, wailed that he and his two assistants would need "months" to be able to reply to each well-wisher. He offered himself a stiff pink gin to prepare to begin on the task and, as a sign of pardon for me as the unwitting cause of the extra labour, gave me one as well. Instead of "months", he and his little team managed to complete the job within a week or two by working all round the clock.

Despite such unforeseeable snags in the broadcaster's job of reporting upon royalty, in broad terms I found myself agreeing with Jennie Bond when she wrote, "I have always regarded the royal story as a straightforward job of journalism."

However, I parted company with her when she was quoted as saying, "The main difficulty is that the facts are extremely hard to establish." Things change all the time, of course; and Jennie did her royal correspondent job for fourteen years compared with my mere five years as court correspondent. It surprised me, though, when she reportedly complained that "the royal reporter rarely gets to talk directly to the person about whom he or she is broadcasting, and in my experience, the truth can be dangerously diluted as it is filtered through department after department".

In my day, there was no "department after department" with which to deal. My main sources of information were (to use an old-fashioned but appropriate word) courtiers: people who tried to help me, as an inquiring journalist, in a perfectly proper and helpful way.

Among them were the press secretaries and private secretaries at Buckingham Palace, Clarence House, Kensington Palace, and other royal residences; and court officials ranging from the Lord Chamberlain and the Marshal of the Diplomatic Corps to ladies-in waiting, equerries, and security officers. There were no "departments" in the bureaucratic, governmental sense; and palace sources always seemed to me just as frank when talking to me, whether on or off the record, as any of my governmental sources.

As for it being hard to establish facts, I would compare royal fact gathering to the normal process of newsgathering in any other sphere – whether from the government, the opposition, or from wider political, commercial, and other interests, including those of the BBC. It certainly sometimes took a little time to get at the facts on the court beat, often after a lot of gossip, but it always seemed to me that when Buckingham Palace eventually had something to say, it appeared to be true. I never found any palace statement devious -- unlike some governmental statements with which, at one time or another, I had to deal.

After a long experience of news reporting, my own feeling is that

JOHN OSMAN

any "spin" or "gloss" on any official pronouncement would be more likely to emanate from places like 10 Downing Street or the Foreign and Commonwealth Office than from Buckingham Palace.

As for Jennie's point about the royal reporter "rarely" getting to talk directly to the person about whom she was reporting, all I can say is that I never found overmuch difficulty about that. To begin with, most of the news material flowing from the palace rarely needed personal conversation with the royal personage involved, any more than reporting on Westminster or Whitehall policies needed personal chats with, say, the prime minister, the chancellor of the exchequer, the foreign secretary, the home secretary or the defence secretary; even though, on occasion, cabinet ministers might choose to give interviews or background briefings about their policies.

If the opportunity did occur to talk directly to members of the royal family, whenever they could find a spare moment in their busy schedules (and such moments were not infrequent), I found that they were generally down-to-earth, humorous, sociable, and anxious to help as much as they could. I could scarcely believe Jennie's reported comments from the 2003 Cheltenham Festival of Literature, describing members of the royal family as "distant", "aloof", and "unapproachable".

I was especially stunned to read that she thought it had been "hard for the Queen to make small talk with everyone". What sticks in my own mind is how good the Queen is in conversation when unhooked from her constitutional duties.

Jennie was quoted as saying – rather unkindly, in my view – at the same 2003 Cheltenham event: "The Duke of Edinburgh has perfected the art of saying hello and goodbye in the same handshake." I recall nothing like that. He usually had time for a quick chat, although at one time, because he was suffering from arthritis in his hands, people he was receiving were asked to bear this in mind when he greeted them and not to shake his hand too hard.

Jennie was also reported at Cheltenham as saying, "I think it is very sad that after fourteen years, I have the most distant relationship with them." Why should she feel sad about that? To me, as a working journalist, the existence of a "distant relationship" between the royal family and an objective reporter would appear to be entirely appropriate and correct.

Members of the royal family are not unnaturally wary of reporters and can no more be fairly criticised for that than politicians can be criticised for being wary of political correspondents. Such wariness accompanies any person holding a job or occupying a position to which the exercise of power, or influence, is attached. There is an inbuilt tension between those who possess that power or influence and those whose task it is to report on the use (or worse, the misuse) of that power or influence.

It is no intention of mine to criticise Jennie Bond, for whenever I watched her television reports, they always seemed professional and to the point. At the risk of sounding excessively aged and perhaps pompous, I would surmise that the apparent differences between Jennie and me in our personal perceptions of what our job entailed might possibly originate in our age difference. I am, after all, at the age of eighty-five, much nearer to the ages of the Queen and Prince Philip than Jennie is!

As an illustration of how difficult I find it to accept Jennie's assertion that "small talk" is "hard" for the Queen, I should like to recall how I listened one evening at a party at Buckingham Palace (with the utter fascination of a male bemused by female requirements) to a conversation between the Queen and my wife, Virginia, on the problem of what kind of shoes the Queen should most comfortably wear while doing a lot of standing around and walking about in the course of her royal duties.

The attention of the two women centred on how high the heels of the shoes should be. The Queen made it plain that she had settled for a sensible medium-sized heel rather than a higher heel, even though, as a small woman, she would have appreciated a little extra height.

Does a conversational exchange like that count as "small talk"? I think it does. Even though the subject was plainly important to the Queen and my wife, it was, I imagine, a normal social chat for any two women to have upon a subject interesting to each of them.

The conversation turned then to the love shared by my wife and me for skiing. The Queen did not share our affection for playing about on planks in mountain snows, and she expressed maternal worries about her elder son's enthusiasm for the sport. Her concern was justified (like the concerns of anyone who is not an aficionado) when, not long afterwards, Prince Charles and his skiing companions ran into tragic trouble while skiing.

By mentioning all of this, I am simply trying to explain why my impression of "the royals" differs from impressions apparently formed by one of my successors as a BBC royal news reporter. By virtue of the Queen's constitutional position, not to mention the demands of contemporary security measures, she is more or less compelled to appear in public as "distant", "aloof", or "unapproachable", to employ the three adjectives reportedly used by Jennie. However, I was always impressed by the way in which, on public occasions, she attempted quite deliberately to emphasise her approachability.

For instance, I shall never forget the gesture she made to an assassination-cursed country, the United States of America, when, in the state capital of California, Sacramento, she appeared beside the state governor on a balcony of the state capitol behind a glass bulletproof screen. I watched as she left him standing behind the screen and slowly moved along the balcony on her own to display herself to the people of California and America without any sort of shield between her and them. A great roar of appreciation went up into the blue Californian skies from thousands of appreciative Americans.

By simply exhibiting herself more openly, she demonstrated that, as Queen, she was doing her utmost to reach out to people – even to people who were not her subjects. Such behaviour, in my view, can truly be described as being both royal and majestic (as well as popular), even though others might regard as it as a foolish flouting of the modern shibboleths of security, health, and safety.

It is no light thing to have devoted oneself publicly on one's twenty-first birthday, as the Queen did 67 years ago, to a lifetime of service to the people. Princess Elizabeth did make that promise, and as Queen, she has honoured it. She has in my doubtless unimportant opinion (but one that is nevertheless held by millions of others) become an international symbol of enduring and civilised values. As Head of the Commonwealth, she remains the focus of aspirations by millions of people of many races for a better life. Those millions know that she stands for The Good.

That is precisely why she has been invited to countries all over the world, ranging from giant communist dictatorships like China to struggling and poverty-stricken countries in Africa and elsewhere. Merely by accepting those invitations, she has conferred international respectability on the countries and governments involved; at the same time displaying Great Britain's concern to try to help in often difficult conditions and, in so doing, to improve and develop sometimes difficult diplomatic relations.

She has more than done her bit in the worldwide quest for human advancement. In her ninth decade of life, the Queen deserves wider recognition than the often grudging approval extended to her by a sceptical British media influenced by commercial and political forces, some of them openly republican.

At a ceremony not long ago, when the Queen decorated a young soldier born in Grenada with the Victoria Cross for his bravery in Iraq, she told him, "You are very special." So, I think, is she.

As I write this, I am eighty-five and I am aware that many may regard me as antediluvian and as something of a journalistic dinosaur. However, as one who previously spent several enjoyable years of my life engaged upon reporting for the BBC news about royalty, I think it is worth pointing out that the institution of the court – or "royal" – correspondent is fundamentally a contemporary phenomenon that in historical terms is as nothing compared with the durability of England's thousand-year-old monarchy. Modern media coverage of royal affairs (and I use the phrase in its broadest, not cheapest, sense) is enormously influential in shaping public perceptions.

My old Fleet Street colleagues, including those from tabloid newspapers, could never quite understand why the BBC in my day was so reluctant to exploit more fully the access which the corporation undoubtedly had to the palace and its occupants. The more alarmist among them, puzzled by the BBC's failure then to commit a correspondent to full-time coverage of palace news, were convinced that the corporation had fallen into the hands of republicans. While it is true that those were not lacking inside the BBC, there were also plenty of staunch monarchists.

My own view on the dual arrangement of being both diplomatic and court correspondent is that it really was dictated by news budgetary considerations. In fact, before the dual arrangement itself came into operation, the BBC had a post-war court correspondent in the shape of the late Godfrey Talbot, who was still in action when I joined the staff in 1965. He had been a BBC war correspondent in World War II and was known not only to the Queen but to the late Queen Mother.

He remains the only reporter in my knowledge ever to have extracted from the Queen anything approaching an on-the-record interview. This was recorded during anniversary celebrations of VE Day, when, years after 1945 and the end of the war, she described to him how, as Princess Elizabeth, she had slipped out of the palace in her military uniform of the ATS (the Auxiliary Territorial Service) to join the crowds outside celebrating victory on the great day itself. With her was her younger sister, the late Princess Margaret. I assume that the Queen's interview with Godfrey remains in the BBC archives and will assuredly be broadcast again.

After Godfrey's retirement, the corporation made the decision to cut staff costs, and thus the dual arrangement was established. It lasted for twenty years or so until, after my retirement, things were changed again. My successor, Paul Reynolds, was the last in a line of those who held the dual task of covering both foreign and royal news; and during his tenure of the post, he was appointed as full-time court correspondent. Thus the great wheel of time – and the other great wheel of the bureaucratic machinery of the BBC – slowly turned back towards the original position of having a full-time court correspondent.

I had recommended this overdue separation of journalistic roles during my tenure of the post, and Paul told me later that when my recommendation was eventually acted upon during the 1990s, he had found a copy in the files of my memo from the 1980s that had been "most helpful".

Paul himself has now retired, but his son, James, is following in his father's footsteps as a former foreign correspondent for the BBC. As I write these lines, James is appearing nightly on TV from the Ukraine after stints in Turkey, Iran, and elsewhere in the Middle East.

The perks of the court correspondent's job in my day included, for myself and my wife, annual invitations to Buckingham Palace garden parties as well as access to the royal enclosure at Ascot, plus an occasional invitation to private parties given by the Queen herself or by members of her staff.

I also possessed a pass cleared by security for access to the palace and, a most valuable asset for anybody wanting to find a place to park in central London, permission to park in the grounds of the palace itself. These perquisites I held until my retirement, and I must admit that I felt a mild pang of regret upon relinquishing them. I have no idea as to whether or not the present-day "royal" correspondents are favoured with such useful perquisites, but I hope they are. Somehow I doubt it, though, because one of my successors – Jennie Bond again – wrote in April 2005 that while the BBC did not intrude into royal private lives in the way that many tabloids regarded as routine, the BBC, in return, had "no special privileges, no special access, as is commonly assumed".

Modern BBC royal correspondents such as Jennie Bond and Nicholas Witchell are the most recent in what is now a long line of them. The institution of the court correspondent itself dates from post-war days, when there were simply two of them, representing what were then the two major British domestic news agencies: the Press Association and Exchange Telegraph, or Extel.

As a young reporter working then for PA, I knew both of them. The PA man was "Ronnie" Jones, or, to give him his full resounding byline, R. Gomer Jones. He and his Extel colleague were good professional reporters but were rather unkindly known in the Fleet Street of those days as "Mutt and Geoff", a pair of cartoon characters.

This was because, like the cartoon characters, each of them always wore a dark coat and striped trousers ("court dress") and always carried an umbrella. It was simply a working uniform.

Sartorial appearance on royal occasions is always good for a laugh from colleagues, and I thought sympathetic retrospective thoughts for "Mutt and Geoff" when, years later, I found myself being mildly mocked by the late John Timpson, then the presenter of the BBC Radio 4 *Today* programme, on the opening day of Royal Ascot.

I had been asked to the studio to do a piece with him on what people were requested to wear in the royal enclosure (a hat for a woman, covering the crown of the head, for example); and the producer had specifically asked me the evening before to arrive at the studio in my morning suit (hired at Moss Bros. for the occasion, at BBC expense). The broadcast was live, and John's opening words were, "A vision in grey is drifting into the studio ... Our court correspondent is off to Ascot ..."

There were giggles all round. It was, for me, an amusing change from heavier-weight contributions to the same programme over many years on more serious events.

JOHN OSMAN

BBC News was doubtless influenced in its eventual decision to end the dual diplomatic and court job, thus strengthening Buckingham Palace coverage, by the spate of royal divorces that occurred largely during the palace BBC tours of duty of my successors. The death of Princess Diana further emphasised public interest in anything to do with the royal family. Before the run of scandals and of that accident in an underpass in Paris, it is broadly true to say that, while there was always close public interest in royal news, the news flow itself had not been as strong as it later became.

Despite the specific problem, already mentioned, that was posed for BBC coverage by the Fagan affair, and despite the reservations about the dual nature of the post held by those who actually occupied it, I have to say that it worked well overall. The list of occupants of that extinct BBC double seat is comprised of a roll call of correspondents of what I now think of as the old BBC.

First of them (after Godfrey Talbot's retirement) was the late Daniel Counihan, formerly reporting from far-flung places ranging from Moscow to Cuba, Trieste to Vietnam. Then came the late Donald Milner, who had accompanied to the Antarctic the explorer Vivian Fuchs for the BBC. Next followed the late Angus McDermid, OBE, Freeman of the City of Bangor, whose African coverage was legendary, as well as his Washington reporting of Watergate. After Angus came Australian David McNeil, to whom, as a keen racing man, the possession of the Ascot enclosure pass was crucial. The last of the line of six men to don the double hat of diplomatic correspondent and court correspondent was Paul Reynolds.

Just before Paul's name, I should add my own: not yet "late". It cannot be all that long before I too complete my own version of Shakespeare's "strange eventful history".

CHAPTER 27

Age Six: "With Spectacles on Nose"

When I decided to retire from the BBC staff, I thought on lines similar to those expressed by Prince Philip. I preferred to go while "still capable" rather than wait until people said I was "doddery".

I wanted to avoid, insofar as I could, Shakespeare's "sixth age" of the "lean and slippered pantaloon, with spectacles on nose" … and so on. There was not a great probability of me becoming "lean", because I have always been fairly big and I remain so, but I certainly wear slippers and spectacles.

As for the idea of retirement itself, well, that is obnoxious to some people; but it all depends upon what is meant by retirement. For me, it meant the chance to do many things I wanted to do other than my job, as much as I had enjoyed that.

I was aware also of early personal signs of everyone's inevitable "last scene of all", namely "mere oblivion". Two instances in my last year as a full-time working journalist and broadcaster warned me that I was beginning to slip from the standards of sharpness required from a top reporter.

The first happened after I had flown with the foreign secretary of the day, Sir Geoffrey Howe (now Lord Howe), to cover talks he had held in Lagos with the Nigerian government. On the flight back to England, the head of the Foreign Office News Department, Christopher Meyer, later to be knighted and to serve as British ambassador to Washington, took me aside and told me that the BBC should on no account miss next day the daily routine news conference at noon at the Foreign Office. He could tell me no more than that, but it was a useful tip.

I made a mental note to call the office on my return to London. I intended to ask the editors to ensure that my stand-in was at the Foreign Office the next day to cover whatever it was that was about to happen. We landed in the small hours of the morning; I was exhausted after what had been quite a wearing assignment; and I went home and fell fast asleep.

I forgot to call the office.

It did not matter, for my stand-in, the late Michael Vestey (who for years was the excellent radio critic for the *Spectator* until his death at the early age of sixty-one) had attended the Foreign Office briefing anyway. The news he had to report was big: the disclosure that a couple of dozen or so Soviet diplomatists and officials in England were being expelled for unacceptable activities.

Although the BBC missed no news and nobody (apart from me) knew of my failure to alert the newsroom, I myself felt that I had been slack by omitting to make that telephone call.

The second incident involved the prime minister, Mrs Thatcher. It happened when she had flown to China to sign the agreement on the future of Hong Kong. Everything in Beijing had been wrapped up, and all we correspondents had, as we thought, finished work. Off we went to dine and to get some sleep before heading the next day with her to Washington, where she was due to meet President Reagan.

To my horror, we were suddenly awoken and summoned to a news conference that Mrs Thatcher had decided to hold in the British Embassy in China, at 1 a.m. or thereabouts. She was (as one of her Downing Street entourage put it) "on a high".

There was not much more news to be squeezed out of Hong Kong developments because by then everything about the Sino-British Treaty had been reported and the implications for Hong Kong and for China examined. So I thought that the best thing to do in extracting fresher news was to ask the prime minister about her forthcoming trip to Washington.

What was she going to discuss with Reagan? Would they, for example, be talking about Star Wars? This was a lively issue at the time, and she seized the chance to expound vigorously, and at length, upon what she was intending to say to President Reagan about it. What she had to say provided us with fresh headlines, and my dispatches led the subsequent news bulletins.

Unfortunately, during her long exposition, I fell asleep. A BBC TV cameraman noticed this, kicked my leg, and muttered to me. I pulled myself together and listened with more attention. We had everything that Mrs Thatcher had said on film and on tape, so I missed not a word of her answer.

Fortunately, Mrs Thatcher herself had not noticed my somnolence. However, her able press secretary, Bernard Ingham (later knighted), had spotted me nodding off, and afterwards he politely gave me a deserved rebuke: "I do think, John, that if you've asked the prime minister a question, you might have the courtesy of staying awake to listen to her answer!"

He was quite right, and I apologised for my bad manners. The next day, I interviewed her on the plane flying to America, and in addition to giving us fresh news material, she rather pointedly expressed personal sympathy for me, and general sympathy for my colleagues, for being compelled to work for such long hours and for being forced to travel so many thousands of miles with her.

Needless to say her sympathies, for me in particular, were laughingly picked up and broadcast.

Her appetite for work, as well as for "Realpolitik", really did justify the Russian appellation for her as the "Iron Lady". Although no damage was caused by either of the two incidents, they underlined for me the reality of starting to age (I was nearer sixty than fifty). I was also suffering from back problems, exacerbated by long flights and sometimes by lugging about radio or TV equipment.

In any case, I was approaching the end of my career, and I wanted to do other things, like go off and walk in the mountains.

So I did.

Outside the Foreign and Commonwealth Office in London in November 1986 in my last BBC staff incarnation as BBC Diplomatic and Court Correspondent. Picture ©Anthony Marshall, formerly of *The Daily Telegraph*.

EPILOGUE

In writing this book, I have tried to be as honest about failures in my work as in claiming successes. Upon my BBC departure, to my surprise but pleasure, I received two tempting offers of highly paid contract work for several years to come. I turned both down. One was in broadcasting, and the other was for a respected newspaper.

The money on offer was seductive, and the jobs themselves were attractive, but so were the Pyrenees. Existence in these beautiful mountains has been, and still is, thoroughly enjoyable, with much walking and skiing. I love the French-Catalan life of our little village. We have been members for many years of the French Alpine Club. We are long-standing members of a British-French group of music lovers, "Les Amis de la Musique". We support various French music festivals, including one of the oldest and most respected in the world, the Pablo Casals festival in Prades. My elder daughter and her companions from a delightful English opera group have given four or five concerts in our part of France and this year she conducted the "Voicebox" Choir from Oxfordshire in a couple of successful performances. My family and friends enjoy visiting our primitive but comfortable mountain eyrie. We are exceptionally fortunate in being able to move whenever we like between France; my home county of West Sussex, where we also savour the good things of life; and Cyprus, where my wife maintains a small apartment and, until recently, a small yacht. Despite our ages, we are still able to travel widely, to such an extent that our French village friends refer to us as "les touristes". In a manner of speaking, this is what both my wife and I have been for much of our lives.

Retirement from full-time reporting has not prevented me, however, from working as a journalist and broadcaster when the commissions offered have been appealing. That freedom of choice I find wonderful, especially after having earned a living by going often to places that I did not really want to go to; talking to people I did not really want to meet; and writing and broadcasting about things that often were not of great personal interest (for example, those Oscars!).

I gratefully appreciate the chance life has offered me over the last twenty years or more to do what I have liked with the time left to me. I hope I am not risking a change in my fortunes (especially in good health) when I say that I am indeed a lucky old man!

To possess a choice of doing something or not is often in itself a precious thing, but in the course of life and work, it is all too easy to make a wrong choice.

One of the choices I had to make back in the 1960s was offered to me when the BBC was cautiously moving towards allowing a working journalist to be a television presenter. For a couple of months, while still Commonwealth correspondent, I presented BBC2 news, and at the end of that period, the editor of news and current affairs, the late Desmond Taylor, invited me to dine and offered me the job of a full-time TV presenter and interviewer, a revolutionary idea in the BBC of those days.

I turned it down, saying that I had not become a journalist to sit every night in a studio under TV lights. He replied that he knew I was going to say that but he thought it was worth a try on his part.

Thus it was with amusement that I found myself, many years later, itching to correct something my younger colleague and friend, John Humphrys, had written. I have never got around to it so will now take the chance.

In 1999, John produced an extremely readable book called *Devil's Advocate*, in which he explored a range of his own doubts and fears about changes in Great Britain. My copy has a warm inscription on it from the author. It says: "To John, great old trouper and an old 'uncle' who was an inspiration to me – with fond regards."

I am, of course, glad to be regarded fondly by such a brilliant journalist as Humphrys as an "inspiration", but I am still going to take issue with him. In dealing with changes in broadcasting journalism, he says, accurately enough, that "one of the easiest ways of getting to be famous is to read the news on the box". He goes on to declare, also accurately, that "most of us don't half enjoy" the "bit of fame".

Then he issues a challenge: "Show me a television journalist who says, 'Me become a presenter? I'm a reporter, and that's the really worthwhile job,' and I'll show you a reporter who's never been *asked* to become a presenter."

Well, John's "old trouper" and "old 'uncle'" did exactly that. I have never regretted it. I stayed a foreign correspondent for a long time, and I learned a few years ago, again to my pleasure, that another younger colleague, Martin Bell, actually holds me responsible for his wanting to become a foreign correspondent.

He told me this at a party in November 2005, given by the BBC to celebrate the fiftieth anniversary of the radio programme *From Our Own Correspondent*. I asked him how I was, so to speak, to blame, and he told me the following story.

He had, he said, been a "squaddie" doing his national service in the army in the 1950s in Cyprus, and I had turned up making inquiries about some news development in a part of the island where he was based. He watched me taking notes and talking to people, then getting into my hired car to drive back to Nicosia to write and file my dispatch.

"I was very jealous," said Martin. "I knew that you were driving back to the Ledra Palace Hotel, where you would probably have an iced gin and tonic in an air-conditioned room while I was going back to my hot and sandy tent to clean my rifle and would be lucky if I got hold of a warm beer. So I decided that I would like a job like yours."

I told him that he had not done too badly.

To my mild surprise, I was the oldest guest at that party. I enjoyed meeting many present-day practitioners in foreign newsgathering, some of whom I had not met before. I also enjoyed reading a piece in the *Guardian* that the BBC World Affairs Editor, John Simpson, had written about the fifty years of the programme and about the correspondents who had worked for it during that half century. I naturally and particularly liked the reference he made to me: "the great John Osman".

So, I thought, *somebody in the business actually still remembers me, unlike poor old Cartwright.*

Now, Cartwright, for some reason or other, had impressed himself upon my memory from sixty years ago. He featured in a wonderful book called *The Real Mackay* a collection of essays by Ian Mackay, who for years was a columnist for the old *News Chronicle*.

I feel it should be required reading for all news reporters, especially those with inflated egos, because it sums up the ephemeral nature of journalistic success. It is also beautifully written and evocative of the old Fleet Street. So here it is in full:

Mr Cartwright's scoop:

> *Round about a quarter of a century ago, when mah-jong and hansom cabs were going out and crossword puzzles and double-decker buses were coming in, there was a strange, quiet, shabby man who used to hang about the Fleet Street taverns. His name was Cartwright.*
>
> *He appeared to have no home or relations, and he looked, in his shiny snuff-stained suit and greasy bowler hat, like one of those minor characters in Dickens who dart about for a few pages, between the legs of the great gargoyles and grotesques like Micawber and Mr Guppy, and then vanish forever with a careless flourish of that prodigal pen.*
>
> *Old Cartwright has been dead for some years now, but he became a ghost long before he died – as so many Fleet Street characters do – a sort of seedy leftover from the Grub Street days, with nothing left about them but a sour smell of beer and cigarette ends, in the shabby sunset of their former glory. There was a bleak wintry dignity in his bearing, in spite of his patched shoes and celluloid collar, and though we all knew he had been somebody in his time, none of us had the courage or the cruelty to ask him about it. His favourite haunt was the sawdust bar of the Cheshire Cheese, where he used to meet worthies like T. W. H. Crosland – an even grubbier ghost than himself – and Harold Lake, who wrote "I Hear You Calling Me' on the back of one of the famous steak and lark pie menus.*
>
> *There it was, one autumn night, in the corner by the fire, where old William the waiter used to shout for Mr Labouchere's pudding and Mr Sala's cigar, that Cartwright lifted the veil*

from his mysterious past. He raised just a little of it, it is true, but oh, as Sir Max would say, how revealing! It was the night that Queen Alexandra died, and the talk was all about newspaper scoops and splash stories. We were comparing such epics as de Blowitz's balloon dispatches from beleaguered Paris in 1870, Hugh Martin's "beat" on the death of Edward the Seventh, and Philip Gibbs's exposure of Dr Cook, the Ananias of the Arctic, when Cartwright spoke. He suddenly piped up in a thin, reedy voice: "I had a scoop once, you know!" It was like a bombshell. The old ghost was gratified by the sensation he had caused, and he continued: "Oh, yes, it was quite a big thing at the time, very big indeed."

Then he proceeded to tell us how he was the first newspaperman to find out that Captain O'Shea was to bring divorce proceedings against his wife and to name Mr Parnell as co-respondent. He told us how he tracked the captain down to a poky little villa in Brighton which was filled with aspidistras, horsehair sofas, esparto grass in huge jars, and pictures framed in seashells and bits of broken looking-glass. Captain O'Shea, instead of throwing Cartwright into the street, as he feared, cracked a bottle of port and gave him the whole story, which became the greatest political sensation of the decade. And when his notebook was full, the captain summoned a growler and sent him to the station.

But this was not all! Like a good reporter of the old style, he kept the real surprise to the end, for this was in the days before the dull device of putting everything in the opening paragraph destroyed the drama of the morning paper.

"You see," he said, as he picked up his tankard, 'the reason I remember it so well is that on my way back to London, I shared a compartment with George Meredith and a drunken woman who kept calling the poet 'an old geezer'."

When we got to Victoria, Mr Meredith asked me to have dinner with him at his club, after which I defeated him at chess and then went back to Fleet Street with the Parnell story just in time for the first edition.

Then he emptied his tankard and retired once more behind his veil. He never lifted it again except for one tiny peep, when I asked him, some months later, to tell me more about his meeting with Captain O'Shea.

He looked at me in his wintry way for a long time and said slowly, "There is nothing more to say except that it was very bad port." I may, I hope, be wrong, but I fear I shall not meet anybody like Cartwright in the Cheese tonight.

That old column was published on 15 December 15, 1951, less than a year before Mackay himself died; a few years before the *News Chronicle* died; and thirty years or so before newspaper offices started moving out and old Fleet Street itself died. Of the names mentioned in Mackay's column, only the Cheshire Cheese remains.

It is then not to be wondered at that an old hack like me, reared in the old style and remembering it with doubtless sentimental nostalgia, should tend to empathise with the ghost of Mr Cartwright.

In describing those Fleet Street characters who became ghosts long before they died, Mackay could not have foreseen that similar apparitions are now produced by the broadcasting industry as well as by newspapers. Many of them are celebrities. Mackay would not have been surprised, however. Unlike the Mongolian herdsman who had asked me in his *ger* on the Asian steppes if I happened to know William Shakespeare, Mackay (and doubtless old Cartwright too) would have been familiar with the lines from *Cymbeline*:

> *Golden lads and girls all must,*
> *As chimney-sweepers, come to dust.*

INDEX

D

M

Mackay 530, 532
Maclean 371, 450
Magna Carta Society 491
Mahdi 324–325
Mahdism 324
Makindye 172
Manzur Qadir 271
Mardin 327
Margaret Thatcher 453, 481–482
Margate 141
Mark Brayne 430, 436
Mark Thompson 393, 396–397
Martha's Vineyard, Mass v, 358–359
Martin Bell 202, 229, 393, 529
Martin Luther 216, 358, 494
Martin Luther King 216, 358
Mary Jo Kopechne v, 358
Mary Wilson 129–130
Masaka 167
Matthews 134–135
Maurice Fahmy 275
Mbarara 167
M. Doucoure 306
Michael Berry, Lord Hartwell 302, 304, 342, 351
Michael Checkland 423
Michael Cockerell 449
Michael Cole 229
Michael Fagan 483
Michael Hoare 207
Michael Shea 505, 509
Michael Vestey 524
Midas 446
Mikhail Andreyevich Suslov 456
Mikhail Sergeyevich Gorbachev 453, 455
Milton Friedman 371
Milton Obote 166–167, 174, 199, 203
Modibo Keita 305, 316

Mods 141
Mohammed Hassenein Heikal 227
Moise Tshombe 208
Morse 224, 434
Moses Okello 194
Mosul 328–329
"Mr Cartwright" 530, 532
Mr Koirala 269
Mubende 169–170
Multi-cultural 494
Murmansk xxii, 472
Muscat 222, 231, 288, 290
Mussoorie 258, 263
Mutesa II 166

N

National Association of Head Teachers 47
National Union of Teachers 47
Native 6, 57, 98, 241, 256, 266, 432
NEFA (North-East Frontier Agency) 237, 254
Negro 57, 337–339
Newark 71
Nguvulu 342–343, 354
Nicholas Witchell 508, 521
Nick Clegg 496–497
Nick Guthrie 468
Nick Robinson 377, 413
Nigger 57, 60–62
Nikita Khruschev 125, 455–456, 460
Nikolai Tikhonov 467
Nile 168, 190–193, 196, 322–324, 334–335
Noel Barber 248, 251
Non-Aligned Movement 151
Noraid 38
Norman Blacklock 485
Norman Taylor 459, 465, 473
Novosobirsk 472
Nusaybin 328

V

Vancouver 379
Vasily Samarsky 417, 471
Vessels for the urinal use of royal
    women 486
Virginia Waite xxiii, 98, 112, 477, 546
Vivien Leigh 131
Vladimir Putin 439
Voltaire 75
Vyacheslev Molotov 439

W

"Wabenzi" 343
"Wacky" 379
Wadi Halfa 322, 334
Walter Raleigh (1552-1618) 22
Walter Raleigh (1861-1922) 22
Watergate xxi, 429, 522
Weldon Wallace 347
Wells 120, 299
Weston-super-Mare 121–122
Whateley 282
Wikileaks xvii, 31, 398
William Bartlett 225
William Congreve 82
William Fulbright 369
William Heseltine 482
William Rust 464
William Shakespeare v, xvi, 431, 532
William Wilberforce 304, 311
Women's Auxiliary Air Force
    (WAAF) 148
Women's Land Army (WLA) 71, 148
Women's Royal Naval Service (WRNS)
    148, 177
Women's Voluntary Service
    (WVS) 148
Worthing xix, 3–4, 9, 11, 14–15, 49,
    65, 67, 71, 76, 78–80, 106–108,
115–116, 118, 120–121, 123–124,
149–150, 473–474
"Wren" 148, 177

Y

Yakubu Gowon 184
Yasnaya Polyana 473
Young Conservatives 9
Young Socialist League 9
Yuri Andropov xxii, 466–467, 479
Yuumjaagin Tsedenbal 432

Z

Zain 87–88
Zionists 38–41, 52

ABOUT THE AUTHOR

"The great John Osman" was the description employed about the author of this book by BBC World Affairs Editor John Simpson when singling out Osman for attention while writing in *The Guardian* about foreign correspondents. That was upon the fiftieth anniversary of the BBC Radio 4 programme *From Our Own Correspondent*, in 2005. Then, in December 2010, the BBC director of news at the time, Helen Boaden (now director of radio) informed Osman, in a letter to him about Helen Boaden the problems faced today by broadcasting journalism, that he was "remembered as one of the great BBC correspondents in the pioneering days".

During his career, he pulled off numerous scoops, recalled for what the news itself was: not news as a way of polishing a television, radio, Internet, or journalistic image. Osman belonged to a generation of journalists who, broadly speaking, thought that a reporter's self-effacement, so far as possible, was the best way of seeking truth.

In this book, he breaks with the habit of a lifetime. He expresses personal views upon the famous or infamous people he met and the events that he covered. He comments upon developments flowing from them that constitute what he describes as "unfinished stories". Many people might find his views infuriating; others might agree; and some might be moved to wry laughter, just as the author himself often was. In offering his thoughts for display and doubtless criticism, the author hopes that at least they will not be found boring.

Osman has travelled in one hundred countries over sixty years, and he held several of the world's top journalistic jobs as a foreign correspondent. He thinks he remains to this day the only BBC staffer to have been, for some years in each post, BBC Washington correspondent, BBC Moscow correspondent, and BBC Buckingham Palace correspondent – a rare combination of major assignments. In addition to those posts, he served BBC Radio and TV News and the World Service during a quarter of a century or so in roles as varied as BBC Commonwealth and colonial affairs correspondent, United Nations correspondent, Africa correspondent, and diplomatic correspondent. Earlier, for nearly ten years, he worked for the *Daily Telegraph* and the *Sunday Telegraph* as their special correspondent in the Middle East and Cyprus, Africa, India, Pakistan, Nepal, and Sikkim, his assignments including the flight from Tibet in 1959 of the Dalai Lama. One of his dispatches appeared in the first columns of the *Sunday Telegraph* upon its initial publication in February 1961.

Married twice, he has three children from his first marriage in 1951. That ended in divorce in 1970. In the same year, he remarried. His new bride was Virginia Waite, herself a well-known writer, journalist, and broadcaster. The couple have been wed for forty-four years. Osman is now eighty-five and has ideas for producing three other very different kinds of books to this one before he reaches one hundred or dies. He skied until he was eighty-three; still goes mountain walking (the pair were members of the French Alpine Club for thirty years); sailed until recently in Virginia's little yacht, "Circe", anchored in Paphos Harbour in Cyprus but just sold by his wife; and (camping most of the time) they drive their small Romahome camping-car all over the place – including, in recent years, through twenty countries in West Europe, East Europe, and the Balkans, as far as Capadoccia in Asian Turkey. When not so occupied, they share their time between their cottage in West Sussex, a little house they bought thirty-four years ago in the French Pyrenees, a small apartment in Paphos, and the family in England.